In Contempt of
All Authority

The Defendants in Contempt of all Authority
combined together and resolved to pull down
and destroy all the present
and ancient Inclosures.

John Rushworth, *Historical Collections*,
vol. III, App. 73, St. Ch. decree in A-G vs. Camry et al.,
for riot in Braydon Forest, Trin. 1635.

Proem

The blynde folye of the commons of Englande,
who have folowed as capitaynes in sedition,
rebellion, and treason, smythes, coblers,
tylers, carters, tanners.

HEH, Ellesmere MS 485,
aphorisms, etc., collected
by Lord Chancellor
Ellesmere

BUCHANAN SHARP

In Contempt of All Authority

Rural Artisans and Riot in the
West of England, 1586-1660

University of California Press

BERKELEY LOS ANGELES LONDON

University of California Press
Berkeley and Los Angeles, California
University of California Press, Ltd.
London, England
Copyright © 1980 by
The Regents of the University of California
ISBN 0-520-03681-6
Library of Congress Catalog Card Number: 78-54801
Printed in the United States of America

1 2 3 4 5 6 7 8 9

Contents

Abbreviations

Add.	Additional
A-G	Attorney-General
Ag. H.R.	*Agricultural History Review*
APC	*Acts of the Privy Council*
B.I.H.R.	*Bulletin of the Institute of Historical Research*
BL	British Library
Bod. Lib.	Bodleian Library
CJ	Chief Justice
CJ	*Journal of the House of Commons*
Dep. Lt.	Deputy Lieutenant
DRO	Dorset Record Office, Dorchester
Eas.	Easter Term
Econ. H.R.	*Economic History Review*
E.H.R.	*English Historical Review*
GCL	Gloucester City Library
GRO	Gloucestershire Record Office, Gloucester
HEH	Henry E. Huntington Library
Hil.	Hilary Term
HLS	Harvard Law School Library
HMC	Historical Manuscripts Commission
H. of L. R.O.	House of Lords Record Office
JP	Justice of the Peace

JRL	John Rylands Library, Manchester
KB	King's Bench
LJ	*Journal of the House of Lords*
Ld. Lt.	Lord Lieutenant
Ld. Tr.	Lord Treasurer
Mich.	Michaelmas Term
PC	Privy Council
PRO	Public Record Office
Q.S.	Quarter Sessions
S-G	Solicitor-General
SRO	Somerset Record Office, Taunton
St. Ch.	Star Chamber
T.R.H.S.	*Transactions of the Royal Historical Society*
VCH	*Victoria History of the Counties of England*
W.A.M.	*Wiltshire Natural History and Archaeological Magazine*
WRO	Wiltshire Record Office, Trowbridge

Preface

Shakespeare was no sympathizer with popular disorder, but in his portrait of Jack Cade, albeit rhetorically exaggerated, he captured some of the aspirations that lay behind the kinds of disorderly outbreaks which are the subject of this book:

Be brave then, for your captain is brave and vows reformation. There shall be in England seven half penny loaves sold for a penny; the three hooped pot shall have ten hoops, and I will make it felony to drink small beer. All the realm shall be in common, and in Cheapside shall my palfrey go to grass.[1]

A remarkable but so far little-emphasized tradition in English life is the long history of artisan radicalism. At the end of the eighteenth century the commitment of men in skilled trades to the democratic ideas enshrined in the work of Tom Paine was so obvious as to be beyond dispute. The origins of this tradition are difficult to fix with any assurance. Certainly, the urban craftsmen associated with the Levellers contributed a great deal, as did the close connection between religious dissent and artisans in the late seventeenth century. But so too did that history of popular direct action associated with rural artisans which stretches back to the Rising led by Jack Cade in 1450 and to the Peasants' Revolt of 1381, and whose late sixteenth- to early seventeenth-century manifestations are the concern of this work.

One pleasant task for the author of a first book is thanking those who

1. *Henry VI*, part 2, IV, ii, *ll.* 72-77.

ix

helped him in the beginning of his career as well as through the stages of authorship. I first must thank Professor Robert Ashton who, as a visitor to the University of California at Berkeley in the academic year 1962-1963, introduced me to the detailed study of the economic and social history of Tudor and Stuart England. I also owe a considerable debt of gratitude to Professor Maurice D. Lee, under whose guidance I first explored the topic of artisan radicalism when I was a graduate student at the University of Illinois. My greatest debt of all is to Professor Thomas G. Barnes of the University of California at Berkeley. It was his survey course on Tudor-Stuart England, taught in the fall semester of 1961, that first awakened in me the ambition to become a historian. Since that time I have had countless opportunities to benefit from his unrivaled knowledge of the sixteenth and seventeenth centuries; it was he who posed the questions that were the original stimulus for this work. In my two years as one of Tom Barnes's assistants on the American Bar Foundation Legal History Project I gained an introduction to the records of the court of Star Chamber and the mysteries of English Bill procedure which later proved invaluable to my research in the Public Record Office. At every stage in the production of this book, Tom Barnes, first as thesis director and later as friend and colleague, has provided advice, criticism, and source materials far beyond the call of either duty or friendship. The only repayment I can offer is the book itself, with the hope that its Barnes-inspired archival approach, "largely without benefit of prior conceptualization," will demonstrate that this means of studying the past has relevance for the social historian as well as for the legal and institutional historian.[2]

In an earlier incarnation this work was submitted for the Ph.D. degree at the University of California at Berkeley in 1971. A fellowship from that university enabled me to spend the academic year 1967-1968 in England pursuing my research. I was able to return to England for further research in the fall of 1973, thanks to sabbatical leave and a travel grant from the Faculty Research Committee of my present university, the University of California at Santa Cruz. During those visits the help and courtesy of the staffs of the following archives and libraries were greatly appreciated: the Public Record

2. See T. G. Barnes, "Largely without Benefit of Prior Conceptualization," in *The Historian's Workshop*, ed. L. P. Curtis, 1970, on pp. 123-50 giving a vigorous justification of the archival approach, and on p. 131 posing the problem which was the origin of this work.

Office, the British Library, the Bodleian Library at Oxford, the John Rylands Library in Manchester, the House of Lords Record Office, the Gloucester City Library, and the record offices of Gloucestershire, Dorset, Somerset, and Wiltshire.

The following people read the manuscript and offered helpful criticism and advice: Mr. Christopher Hill, Professor Michael Pullman, Professor Paul Seaver, and Mr. E. P. Thompson. I owe particular thanks to my colleague Professor Forrest Robinson for his efforts in smoothing out many rough passages in the prose.

The maps were prepared by Adrienne Morgan. I am grateful to the editorial staff of the University of California Press for their patience and advice; I am especially indebted to my editor, Jane-Ellen Long, for her constructive efforts to enliven the prose.

Finally, all one can offer to a wife who has lived with and suffered through this project and who has typed many manuscript versions over the past eight years is heartfelt thanks for the love and support which have sustained this effort.

Chapter I

Introduction

The existence of a large number of virtually propertyless wage earners and pieceworkers in certain rural areas of Tudor-Stuart England is a significant, but hitherto unremarked or insufficiently emphasized, social phenomenon. Such people, living in cottages erected on manorial and forest waste or at the sides of highways, are usually described as day laborers who earned a living in agricultural labor supplemented by commoning a few cows, sheep, or pigs. Yet there is much evidence that many of these cottagers were skilled manual workers in the many crafts which existed in pre-industrial rural England, that they were in fact artisans. This is particularly true of the cottagers who crowded some of the main manufacturing areas of the country: forests such as Dean in Gloucestershire, which harbored important mining and ironmaking industries; the forested area running along the borders of eastern Somerset and western Wiltshire, home of much of the export-oriented broadcloth industry; other western and southern centers of clothmaking dependent on overseas markets; and the equally export-dependent new-drapery areas of Essex and Suffolk. To attach the generic name "artisan" to rural craftsmen might seem foolhardy, as it covers an enormous range of skilled trades. But I use the word as an inclusive term, although the contemporary "artificer" might have been better, because it indicates certain social and economic characteristics which skilled men had in common and which differentiated them from other ranks, especially those above them in the social scale.

1

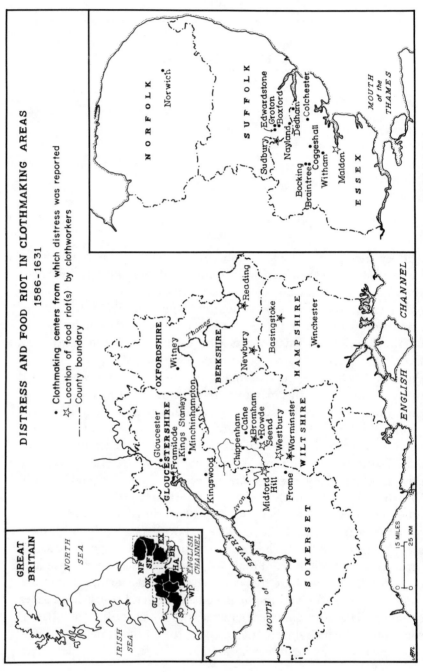

Map. 1. Distress and Food Riot in Clothmaking Areas, 1586-1631

The most notable characteristic of artisans, and the one which provides the thematic thread of this work, was their readiness to engage in riot and insurrection. In surveying the nation-wide incidence of food rioting worthy of report to the Privy Council in London between 1586 and 1631, for example, one is struck by the localization of riot in areas known to produce cloth for overseas markets. Food riots occurred most frequently in the rural broadclothmaking areas of western England (particularly in Gloucestershire and along the Wiltshire-Somerset border), in the new-drapery towns of Essex and Suffolk, and in the clothing areas of Berkshire and Hampshire. Although the social status of participants in these riots was not always recorded, such evidence as is available invariably characterizes the rioters as clothworkers—weavers, spinners, fullers, and the like. While riots also broke out in port towns along the south and east coasts to prevent the movement of foodstuffs during periods of shortage, there can be little doubt that the clothmaking areas were by far the most riotous.[1] The reasons for this are not far to seek.

Reports of local magistrates and petitions for relief received by those in authority during the four main periods of harvest failure or trade depression—1586, 1594-1597, 1622, and 1629-1631—reveal the existence of a large rural industrial proletariat living on wages earned in various clothworking occupations and dependent on the market for food. In the late sixteenth century, harvest failure and the consequent rise in food prices bore heaviest on such workers and were therefore the main cause of food riots, but in the seventeenth century, unemployment resulting from closure or contraction of foreign markets for English cloth was probably a more significant cause of riot. A related phenomenon which appeared in times of food scarcity and depression was attempted insurrection. The few recorded examples, although they were not localized, involved artisans drawn from a wide variety of rural crafts, which suggests that these presumably self-employed artisans producing for local consumption were equally dependent on the market for food.

The best measure of the significance of such riots and attempted insurrections and of the social problems which underlay them is to be found in the response of government. Fear of riot, and of riot's accompanying potential for overturning the established social order, is

---

1. It is impossible to be exact about the number of riots in this period: see below, chap. 2, note 2.

a constant theme in Tudor and Stuart political pronouncements. Lacking adequate means for policing the lower orders or suppressing potentially dangerous outbreaks of disorder when they occurred, Tudor and Stuart governments resorted to a mixture of blustering threats of dire consequences mixed with severe punishments and, more significantly, ameliorative legislative and conciliar acts designed to deal with the short-term consequences of food shortage and depression and, wherever possible, to alleviate the problems associated with chronic poverty. Thus such well-known measures of Tudor paternalism as the Statute of Artificers (1563), the Poor Law, the Vagrancy Statute, and the Enclosure Act of 1598, as well as the less well-known Statute on Cottages (1589), can all be viewed as parts of an attempt to deal with social problems resulting from the existence of a riotous and potentially dangerous rural work force employed in nonagricultural occupations.

These Tudor measures were products of economic crises, mainly harvest failures but including stoppages in the cloth trade. It was not until Charles I's reign that the first concerted attempt was made by the central government to òversee enforcement of Tudor social legislation by local magistrates. This took place in 1629-1631, during a period of cloth-trade depression and food shortage unmatched since the late years of Elizabeth both in its severity and in the extent and intensity of the rioting it produced.

Another common disorder of the period was the anti-enclosure riot in royal forests, most notably those near-insurrections of 1626-1632 known as the Western Rising and led by the eponymous Lady Skimington—the disguise and alias adopted by a number of leaders of separate riots. Again, rural artisans made up most of the leadership, and the rank-and-file consisted largely of artisans and laborers. Many of the significant industrial developments of the period took place in the western forests. One of the main centers of the Western Rising, along the Wiltshire-Somerset border to northern Dorset, coincided with important centers of the western broadcloth industry. Here in particular there was overlap in time and place between the Western Rising and the food riots of 1629-1631; this area had been notable from the late Elizabethan period onward for the frequent occurrence of food riots. Other forests within which the Rising took place either, like Dean Forest in Gloucestershire, sheltered important industries such as mining and ironmaking or, like Braydon Forest in Wiltshire, were inhabited by a large population of poor laborers subsisting on the forest wastes.

The population in such forested and industrial areas consisted largely of cottagers, with no land attached to their dwellings beyond a garden or, at best, an acre or two of pasture. These cottagers supplemented their wages by exploiting the woods and pastures of the royal forests. When the Crown in the early years of Charles I attempted to disafforest in order to raise income, the result was that the cottagers—artisans, laborers, and poor husbandmen holding less than ten acres—rioted to preserve the open and unimproved commons which, in an age of harvest failure and recurrent unemployment in the cloth trade, provided them with essential income supplements: grazing, pannage for pigs, firewood, construction timber, game to be poached, and raw materials for workers in wood, hides, or animal fats.

The disafforestations and enclosures which provoked the Western Rising were a significant fiscal expedient utilized by the government of Charles I as an alterantive to parliamentary taxation. Its study sheds further light upon the by now commonplace assessment of the "Personal Rule" and the policy of "Thorough"—that the King's need for money effectively negated any impulse toward establishing an absolutism which was both solvent and paternalistic. Contrary to accepted opinion on the disafforestations, the enclosures were not arbitrary; the property rights of substantial propertyholders, manorial lords, freeholders, and copyholders claiming rights of common in the forests were scrupulously respected in quite elaborate legal proceedings. Unfortunately, because those most dependent on the forest were those with little or no property, the law did not recognize the validity of their claims to rights of common in the open forests. Government officials appreciated the economic significance of the unenclosed forests for the economic well-being of cottagers, but the fiscal needs of the Crown took first priority. The Rising partially coincided, both in time and in place, with the food scarcity and depression of 1629-1631, but there were limits to Stuart paternalism and ameliorative action.

It has been asserted in the past that men of standing and property were behind the Western Rising. There is in fact no evidence for this, beyond the groundless fears expressed in official correspondence. All the surviving evidence indicates that the riots were genuinely popular disorders generated by the grievances of the marginal poor who lived in and around the forests and who were able to produce their own leaders. The tenacious resistance of such people to the Crown's will made it imperative that all the police and judicial authority of the state be brought to bear for the punishment of the rioters and the prevention of future outbreaks; otherwise, politically dangerous and socially destabilizing consequences were feared. But it will become obvious in the course of this work that in the court of Star Chamber, commissions of oyer and terminer, the *posse*, and the militia, the Stuart state lacked efficient or effectual means of repression.

Emphasis on the important role played by landless rural artisans, and cottagers generally, in popular disorder implies a somewhat different view of pre-industrial English rural society from that which is now virtual orthodoxy. Recent work in agrarian and rural history portrays a rather arcadian view of Tudor-Stuart rural society: the rural population directly involved in agriculture, and rural society structured on the basis of direct relationships to landed property, with substantial landowners and landlords at the top, prosperous yeomen and husbandmen in the middle, and poor husbandmen and landless agricultural laborers at the bottom.[2] This conception of rural society solely in terms of agrarianism, in effect equating rural with agrarian, seems to be based upon an assumption that the divorce of the bulk of the English population from the land or agricultural activity only occurred after the eighteenth century as a result of the Industrial Revolution. Confronted with the evidence that a considerable proportion of the rural population in sixteenth- and seventeenth-century England worked in nonagricultural occupations, most modern historians of rural England argue that such people were engaging in "by-employments," dividing their time between agriculture and a craft. "By-employment" implies a less important source of livelihood than the *real* employment in agriculture.[3] This hybrid peasant/craftsman may have existed in some parts of Tudor-Stuart England, especially in rural areas where production involved independent craftsmen supplying local needs, but he was not present in significant numbers within

2. This is certainly the impression left by such recent works as E. Kerridge, *The Agricultural Revolution*, 1967, and Joan Thirsk, ed., *Agrarian History of England and Wales 1500-1640*, 1967.

3. This assumption concerning by-employments runs throughout the cooperative *Agrarian History*, especially in the contributions of Joan Thirsk and Alan Everitt.

those areas where relatively large-scale capitalists had taken control of production and distribution.

Capitalists had come to dominate the broadcloth industry and the new-drapery—products, aimed at an export market, which demanded considerable investment in raw materials and in the distribution of the finished product. Similarly, in mining and ironmaking demand for increased output resulted in substantial capital investment in large units of production. In these sectors of the economy, the skilled man was a propertyless wage earner or pieceworker, depending for employment upon the clothier or ironmaster, and for his food, upon the market. The locations of such industries were among the most disorderly places in the kingdom, and the connection between landlessness, rural industrialism, and direct action can hardly have been accidental. In a society where political power, social status, and, to a large degree, wealth depended on the possession of landed property, the artisan and the laborer stood literally on the margin, with little hope of alteration in their social and economic circumstances. Such people comprised a rural proletariat divided by the barrier of property from the substantial husbandman, the yeoman, the gentleman. In an age of rapidly rising food prices, those growing for the market or living from economic rents prospered, while those who depended on the market for food and on nonagricultural employment for income were at the mercy of natural calamities and the fluctuations of a mercantile economy.

In this situation, supplements to income provided by the wastes of royal forests were of critical importance. Being royal demesne, however, the forests were subject to the vagaries of royal financial needs. The riots of 1626-1632 against enclosures caused by the Crown's exploitation of its demesne rights were not the response of property-holding peasants, led by or manipulated by their betters, in defense of their immemorial rights; they were, rather, the violent reaction of a rural proletariat to fluctuations in employment, constrictions in the food market, and loss of crucial income supplements. The Dean Forest riots may be the only case of small independent masters resisting developments which were regarded as depriving them of their independence and reducing them in status to mere wage earners.

Concerned with remedying specific grievances, providing work and food, reversing enclosure, and so forth, rather than with altering existing social, political, and economic arrangements, the rural disorders which are the subject of this work were essentially non-ideological and nonrevolutionary in character. Nevertheless, those few rioters' opinions which have survived express intense hatred of their social superiors, especially the gentry. This sentiment, approaching class hatred, was matched in turn by the contempt and fear with which those with power and status regarded the lower orders. Such riots, although nonideological and lacking the emotional excess of the Civil War's extreme radical sects (recently the subject of a new work by Christopher Hill), constituted a significant aspect of the life of rural artisans and laborers.[4] In fact, these riots may provide a more reliable indicator of the realities of rural life and opinion than the irrational excesses of the tiny minority driven to take refuge in antinomian beliefs during the Civil War. This at least provides one way of looking at the eruption of the forest and other riots during the period from 1642 to 1660, which occurred in times of maximum political dislocation and provided the inhabitants of royal forests with an opportunity to settle old scores with impunity.

Continuity of response was also characteristic of successive "revolutionary" governments; faced with identical social problems, they offered the same solutions as the Stuart monarchy. In 1641 the court of Star Chamber, in which the participants in the Western Rising had been punished, was abolished because it was felt to be an instrument of Stuart absolutism. To deal with the riots of 1642-1648 Parliament, in particular the House of Lords, had to assume the functions of the defunct court. In addition, the governments of Commonwealth and Protectorate, in a search for solvency, resorted to policies of disafforestation similar to those of the deposed Stuarts, with familiar results.

The riots of the Civil War period can be regarded as a manifestation of positive political indifference, rather than passive neutrality, a statement that the issues raised by the conflict between King and Parliament were of little or no concern to many ordinary people when weighed in the balance against such pressing local issues as disafforestation and enclosure. It is probably no accident that the most notable form of neutrality, the "Club" movement, was most popular and highly organized in some of those areas in the West of England where the Western Rising took place and which were again the scene

4. *The World Turned Upside Down*, 1972.

of large-scale rioting during the Civil War. The reactions of the common people to the Civil War, with its disruption of traditional social bonds and means of political control, took a variety of forms. The most striking was, of course, the efflorescence of a bewildering array of radical religious and political sects. Nevertheless, indifference to political and religious issues and concentration upon vital, but essentially nonideological, questions was at least as common a response.

Chapter II

Food Riots, 1586-1631

The food riot was a significant indicator of social tension in pre-industrial England, and certainly it was one of the most common forms of popular protest. For example, George Rudé discovered 184 separate outbreaks in the period between 1735 and 1800.[1] While riots were not as numerous as in the eighteenth century, there were between 1586 and 1631 at least forty, as well as two attempted insurrections and a considerable number of other riots and insurrections planned or rumored, all of which were related in some way to the state of the food market.[2] The protests of the Tudor-Stuart period are not as well documented as later food riots, but they have left more than enough recorded remains to permit examination of their causes,

---

1. *The Crowd in History*, chap. 2. Aside from a recent article in *Past and Present* little work has been done on the food riots of the Tudor-Stuart period. Although E. M. Leonard in her pioneering study of the Poor Law, *The Early History of English Poor Relief*, 1900, used some of the evidence related to food riots, and B. E. Supple in *Commercial Crisis and Change in England, 1600-1642*, 1959, has some very important things to say about food riots, it must be admitted that their interests in such popular outbreaks were somewhat tangential to their main concerns. When this work was in an advanced state of preparation an article appeared in *Past and Present* 71 (1976): 22-42, "Dearth and the Social Order in Early Modern England," by J. Walter and K. Wrightson. Although some of their conclusions paralleled mine, I was somewhat surprised at the authors' exclusive focus on dearth and their neglect of unemployment as an element in producing food riots.

2. One cannot be precise on the number of food riots in the Tudor-Stuart period. Quite often what looks at first glance like one riot turns out to be in fact a series of riots in one location over a short period of time. Unless the evidence permits a distinction to be made among all the individual instances, each outbreak has been counted as one riot. Since the JPs brought only the

their temporal and geographical distribution, the social status and behavior of the participants, and the reactions of central and local government.

From this examination certain important points emerge. Although the late Elizabethan-early Stuart evidence confirms to some extent the conclusion drawn from that of the eighteenth century—that food riots occurred in response to a rise in the price of food caused by harvest failure or some other dislocation of the economy—it is quite clear that, especially in 1620-1623 and 1629-1631, slumps in the cloth trade were the principal causes of food riots, with the majority taking place in clothmaking areas or involving clothworkers. This is not to discount the importance of harvest failure as a cause, or to ignore the devastating effect of harvest failure occurring in the middle of a cloth-trade depression. Only once did the latter take place. During the 1629-1631 nationwide slump in the cloth industry the harvest of 1630 failed, producing a period of hunger, rioting, and general social tension as great as any that had been experienced since the late 1540s. The breakdown in public order at this time was further heightened by the outbreak of the riots known as the Western Rising of 1626-1632, which overlapped in time with the depression and food scarcity, and in locality with some of the centers of the depressed western broadcloth industry.

This was the testing time for the measures, evolved by Elizabethan government and handed down to the Stuarts, designed to handle the problems caused by depressions and scarcity. Tudor social and economic policy was largely aimed at decreasing social tensions and maintaining the public peace in economic crises such as harvest failure and depression. The strains imposed on these measures in 1620-1623 and 1629-1631 proved to be so great that in 1631 the government of Charles I had to make a quite fundamental change in its approach to the twin problems of reducing social tensions and preserving order.

The Incidence of Food Riot

Except for three localized instances in 1605, 1608, and 1614, the outbreaks of food riots between 1586 and 1631 were concentrated in the four periods of 1586, 1595-1597, 1622, and 1629-1631, all times of

---

most serious riots to the attention of the PC, further search in local records will no doubt turn up more examples.

harvest failure, depression in the cloth trade, or both in combination. There seems to be no general agreement as to which was the major factor in fostering disorder. No doubt the generally accepted conjunction of these two economic dislocations might be regarded as a sufficient explanation for the occurrence of food riots. Nevertheless, there have been attempts in recent years to assign greater weight to one factor or the other. B. E. Supple, in studying trade and industry, admits an important but subsidiary role for harvest failure. "It has, for instance, been impossible to find any major economic crisis which was solely, or indeed largely, caused by a poor harvest. The more spectacular developments in the English textile industry and the deeper economic crises owed far more to affairs of commerce and currency."[3] More recently an attempt has been made to move away from what some students of rural and agrarian history believe to be too heavy an emphasis on the cloth industry and commerce in the Tudor-Stuart economy, by relating economic crises and consequent distress and social disorder primarily to the state of the harvest. The harvest is described as the heart of the economy, and its fluctuating fortunes as the heartbeat.

The health and well-being of the entire country depended upon the quality of this heartbeat more than upon any other organ and activity. This is not to say that the heart is the only organ of any real significance in the body politic; but its rhythm governed all else. If the corn harvest represented the heart, the textile industry represented perhaps the liver: a major organ whose derangements could cause much unease and misery. But the derangements of the heart could bring the body politic near to a total breakdown; and its healthy beat could stimulate the economy.[4]

The only way to decide between those two views is by close concordance of the chronology of the outbreaks of food riots with the occurrence of depression and food scarcity. Such an examination demonstrates that a major difference between the two emphases lies in the periods of economic crisis chosen for study. A focus upon the Elizabethan period spotlights the four bad harvests in succession

3. Supple, p. 19.
4. W. G. Hoskins, "Harvest Fluctuations and English Economic History, 1480-1619," *Ag. H.R.* XII (1964): 40. In this and a subsequent article Hoskins provides what he calls a cardiogram of the harvest. The authors of "Dearth and the Social Order" seem to be in agreement with Hoskins on the significance of the harvest.

between 1594 and 1597 and their devastating consequences. If the seventeenth century is chosen, then the cloth industry depressions of 1620-1623 and 1629-1631 seem far more significant.

Whatever the immediate cause of food riots and related disturbances, there can be no doubt which group in society engaged most frequently in such protests: it was the artisans, skilled men employed in nonagricultural occupations. The majority of food riots took place in centers of the cloth industry; where the status of the participants can be discovered they are invariably found to have been clothworkers. A good number of the riots took place in the two largest centers of the export cloth industry, those most affected by closure of foreign markets. One of these centers was the broadcloth-producing West: southwestern Gloucestershire in the valleys running from the Cotswolds to the Severn, eastern Somerset, and western Wiltshire. The other was the East Anglican new-drapery area, especially the towns of Colchester, Bocking, Braintree, and Coggeshall in Essex, and Sudbury in Suffolk. Food riots also occurred in other areas which were home to the cloth industry, such as western Somerset, Reading, and Newbury in Berkshire and in the kersey-producing areas of Hampshire.

A related social disturbance which appeared during such times was the insurrection. While most planned insurrections evaporated at the alehouse door or when heads cleared on the morning after, two got as far as the attempt, one in Hampshire in 1586, the other in Oxfordshire in 1596. Almost to a man, the participants in these two attempts were artisans drawn from the wide range of trades to be found in the English countryside.

The other main concentration of food riots was in port towns or distribution centers (like Southampton and the coastal towns of Kent and Norfolk) through which grain was shipped to other areas suffering shortages or to supply urban centers, especially London. These disorders involved people often described only as the poor; where evidence of status is forthcoming we find artisans, laborers, and, on occasion, a large contingent of women. Riots in these locations were responses either to harvest failure or to heavy purchases in the market by grain merchants; the rioters were attempting to prevent grain shipments to distant parts which would intensify local shortages.

The first riots, in the spring and summer of 1586, present the greatest difficulty for deciding upon the relative importance of food scarcity vs. unemployment as a cause. The food riots had come and gone before the 1586 harvest failure. They can be attributed largely to a sharp but short-lived cloth-industry depression, caused by military and diplomatic difficulties which closed the German and Low Country mart towns through which the Merchant Adventurers Company traded;[5] consequently the worst effects were felt in the cloth-producing areas, particularly Gloucestershire, Somerset, and Hampshire. There are indications, however, that by the spring of 1586 food supplies were already inadequate in certain parts of southern and western England. Although this may have been the result of what has been estimated to be a poor harvest in 1585 localized in the West (the harvest nationwide has been rated as average),[6] it could also have been the consequence of an artificial shortage created by hoarding in anticipation of the poor quality of the coming harvest. Whatever the cause, the scarcity of food probably exacerbated conditions created by the depression; this was certainly true in Hampshire, where food shortage played a major role in the disorders.

On March 29, 1586, the government brought into operation one of the traditional remedies for shortage: the commissioners for restraint of the grain trade, basically justices of the peace and borough magistrates, were ordered to prevent exportation of grain and to report their proceedings to the Privy Council by monthly certificates.[7] The first hint of scarcity in the West was contained in a report from Plymouth sent to the Privy Council in April of 1586. According to the mayor of Plymouth, an unseasonable summer the previous year resulting in a poor harvest had caused grain prices to rise sharply over the previous three months, and they were expected to continue to rise. Since it was feared that thousands of poor would perish for lack of food, authority was requested and obtained to seize ships loaded with grain from the Baltic which stopped in Plymouth Harbor en route to other countries, and to sell their cargoes at reasonable prices to the inhabitants of the town.[8]

A similar but even more graphic account of conditions in the city of

5. J. D. Gould, "The Crisis in the Export Trade 1586-7," E.H.R. LXXI (1956): 212-23.
6. Hoskins, p. 46; C. J. Harrison, "Grain Price Analysis and Harvest Qualities, 1465-1634," Ag. H.R. XIX (1971): 150 and 154.
7. APC 1586-87, pp. 45-46.
8. PRO, S.P. 12/188/12, mayor of Plymouth to PC, April 2, 1586; APC 1586-87, pp. 59-60, PC to JPs of Devon, April 10, 1586.

Gloucester was sent at about the same time to Lord Burghley. Despite attempts, by restraints imposed on the activities of badgers (corn dealers) and maltsters, to conserve barley (which along with beans provided much of the diet of the poor), prices in Gloucester markets had continued to rise since early February. In addition, unemployment in the cloth industry was increasing the number of destitute. About one-half of the city's poor who worked in the cloth industry were already out of work and the employment of the rest was threatened.[9]

It was unemployment in the cloth industry which finally drove the poor of Gloucestershire to riot. On April 23, a bark loaded with malt bound down the Severn from Gloucester to Wales was stayed by the tide at Framilode, about ten miles southwest of Gloucester. There she was attacked and her cargo taken by five or six hundred of "the commone sorte of people."[10] At the end of the month another bark, bound this time from Gloucester to Bristol, was rifled by a large group of people at Framilode, who took her cargo of malt worth £120. During the week following this second attack, crowds of up to one hundred or more gathered a few miles below Gloucester on both sides of the Severn, undoubtedly to prevent transportation on the river.[11] Investigating the reason behind the disorders, the justices found that the rioters were in misery, unable to buy food because the clothiers had ceased to give them work: "so great was their necessitye as that dyvers of them justyfie they were dryven to feede their children with oattes dogges [dog-grass] and rootes of nettles with such other like things as they coulde come by."[12] Similar conditions existed among the clothworkers of Bath and eastern Somerset and, although it was feared that the unemployed there would also riot unless some action was taken to revive the cloth trade, no disorders seem to have taken place.[13]

The other location of disorder in 1586 was Hampshire, where food shortage and the stoppage in the cloth trade played equally important roles. Sometime late in April or at the beginning of May, 1586, a group led by a blacksmith, a tailor, and a cooper, complaining of dearth of corn and lack of work in the cloth industry, tried forcibly to

9. PRO, S.P. 12/188/18, Walter Pate, JP, to Burghley, April 13, 1586.

10. PRO, S.P. 12/188/47, JPs of Gloucestershire to PC, April 30, 1586.

11. PRO, S.P. 12/189/7, Thomas Throckmorton, JP, to PC, May 5, 1586; *APC 1586-87*, p. 133, PC to sheriff and JPs of Gloucestershire, May 29, 1586.

12. PRO, S.P. 12/188/47, JPs of Gloucestershire to PC, April 30, 1586.

13. *APC 1586-87*, pp. 93-94, PC to sheriff and JPs of Somerset, May 6, 1586.

prevent a landowner in Romsey from sowing woad. The rioters blamed the high price of food on the planting of woad instead of grain; they were encouraged in their belief by a royal proclamation, in October, 1585, prohibiting the conversion of arable or pasture land to the growing of woad within four miles of a market town or any town in which clothmaking was practiced.[14]

A group of artisans from around Selborne who planned a rising for June 6, 1586, again blamed the scarcity and high price of corn in Hampshire on the sowing of woad. They intended to fire the beacons (designed to give early warning of an invader's approach) to assemble the people to destroy the woad plants, ransack the houses of the gentry responsible for planting the woad, and seize the foodstuffs believed to be hidden in those houses. The plan was disclosed before anything happened; suspects were quickly rounded up and examined by local officials.[15] Twenty-two men were implicated: fifteen artisans, one artisan's son, one gentleman, four husbandmen, and one servant. The artisans, from a cross-section of the trades practiced in the small towns and the countryside of Tudor England, included five tailors, four weavers, a fencemaker, a mason, a tanner, a butcher, a blacksmith, and a carpenter. Although the presence of the weavers may be attributed in part to the depressed state of the cloth industry, the involvement of the other artisans must be explained by the price of grain. As suppliers of goods and services to a local market, they did not suffer the direct effects of the closure of foreign markets as did clothworkers producing for export; like clothworkers, however, they were dependent on the market for their food and suffered in time of high prices, Moreover, during such periods much of the population must have deferred purchase of nonessential goods in order to buy the

---

14. *APC 1586-87*, p. 91, PC to Henry Gifford, JP, of Hants, May 6, 1586; PRO, S.P. 12/189/15, Henry Gifford to PC, May 12, 1586; P. L. Hughes and J. F. Larkin, eds., *Tudor Royal Proclamations*, vol. 2, pp. 516-17, proclamation prohibiting sowing of woad, Oct. 14, 1585.

15. The main sources for the rising are to be found in PRO, S.P. 12/191/15, S-G Egerton to Secretary Walsingham, July, 1586, enclosing nos. 15 I-XV, examinations of suspects at different dates in June, 1586, before various local officials in Hampshire; no. 20, William Doyell and Thomas Carsen to Secretary Walsingham, July 19, 1586; nos. 20 I-IX, interrogatories to be administered to suspects brought to London, examinations on the interrogatories, and a list of suspects. Many of these documents are faded and illegible. A good accurate summary of the contents is to be found in H. T. White, "A Hampshire Plot," *Hants. Field Club & Arch. Soc.* XII (1934): 54-60. One important document missed by White is BL, Cotton MS, Vespasian F. IX, ff. 147-48, examination of Richard Passinger of Selborne, tailor, June 14, 1586.

high-priced food, thereby depressing the domestic market and depriving such artisans of sorely-needed income.

These events in Hampshire were virtually the last of the disorders associated with this period of cloth-trade slump and grain shortage.[16] There is nonetheless one final situation to be considered, that of bad harvest alone. The scarcity caused by the 1586 harvest pushed the price of grain so high that on January 2, 1587, the Book of Orders was issued, instituting a variety of measures (which became the standard remedies) to control grain prices and regulate the market.[17] Except for some talk by five clothworkers of Sandwich in Kent in June, 1587, about a rising to take corn from rich men, however, there is no evidence of any food riots as a result of the bad harvest. This may be explained by the fact that, unless accompanied by a cloth-trade stoppage, more than one bad harvest was required to exhaust supplies of foodstuffs sufficiently to produce serious rioting. By the time the harvest of 1586 did fail the government had taken sufficient stop-gap measures to alleviate the effects of the cloth-trade stoppage, until such time as conditions on the Continent improved, that it has left hardly a trace in the export figures of the London port books.[18] In any case, food supplies in the western clothmaking centers had become sufficiently plentiful during the spring of 1587 to permit the uninterrupted passage of large quantities of grain overland and down the Severn to supply Bristol and Wales.[19]

There can be no doubt at all, however, that harvest failure was responsible for the distress and misery suffered during the period from 1594 to 1597. Unseasonable weather in spring and summer resulted in four bad harvests in a row and produced a period of food shortage unprecedented in the reign of Elizabeth. Although these

16. P. Clark, "Popular Protest and Disturbance in Kent, 1558-1640," *Econ. H.R.* 2nd ser., XXIX (1976): 367.

17. Hughes and Larkin, vol. 2, pp. 532-34, proclamation ordering markets supplied at reasonable prices, Jan. 2, 1586/7; Hoskins, p. 46, and Harrison, pp. 150, 154.

18. These measures included pressure on the clothiers of Gloucestershire, Wiltshire, and Somerset to keep their men in employment, a short-term liberalization of trade which opened up the Merchant Adventurer's monopoly to stranger merchants and put pressure on the company itself to take out a loan to enable it to buy its usual complement of cloth. See *APC 1586-87*, pp. 272-75, PC to Ld. Lts., sheriffs, and JPs of Somerset, Gloucestershire, and Wilts, Dec. 24, 1586; Gould, pp. 215, 220.

19. *APC 1587-88*, pp. 69-70, PC to mayor of Gloucester and JPs of Gloucestershire, April 9, 1587; pp. 110-11, PC to JPs of Wilts, May 2, 1587.

years of scarcity undoubtedly had a depressive effect on the economy in general, as did the war with Spain, there were no major trade stoppages to deprive harvest failure of the dubious honor of being the prime cause of distress and food riots. But, as the evidence of the 1586 harvest failure indicates, unless accompanied by a stoppage in the cloth trade more than one bad harvest was needed to produce a major outbreak of riots. Thus despite the bad harvest of 1594, which resulted in the renewal of the Book of Orders in October, it was not until after the failure of the 1595 harvest that food riots were widespread.[20]

Considerable evidence survives of distress and riots in the western clothmaking areas, all of it the consequence of scarcity. Late in 1595, clothmakers in Warminster, Wiltshire, complained that while they were kept in employment, they did not receive sufficient wages in this time of high prices to enable them to buy their food. At various times in October groups of clothworkers ranging from sixty to one hundred in number seized corn carried by badgers travelling from Warminster to other markets. During this same period fear was expressed that the mounting scarcity of food would drive to riot the Devonshire poor dependent on weaving and spinning. In Somerset during 1596, a group of sixty poor people seized a cartload of cheese bound for market and distributed it among themselves.[21] Distress and severe food shortage continued to be widespread in the western clothmaking areas throughout 1596 and into 1597; much grain had to be brought in from the midlands, Norfolk, and London. There were many reports of "multitudes" of poor, idle people wandering the countryside and engaging in a variety of crimes, mostly theft of food, money, and easily disposable goods.[22]

20. BL, Lans. MS 76, no. 40, draft of PC order renewing Book of Orders, dated 1594; *APC 1595-96*, pp. 25-27, renewal of Book of Orders, Oct. 26, 1595, mentions renewal of the previous year.

21. *APC 1595-96*, pp. 43-44, PC to JPs of Wilts, Nov. 1, 1595; *HMC Salisbury*, vol. VI, pp. 34-35, memorials from the Earl of Bath to PC, Jan. 29, 1595/6; John Strype, *Annals*, vol. IV, p. 407, Edward Hext, JP of Somerset, to Burghley, Sept. 25, 1596.

22. *APC 1595-96*, pp. 312-13, PC to Burghley on lewd wandering persons in Somerset, Mar. 21, 1595/6; p. 314, PC to CJKB on same, Mar. 28, 1596; pp. 316-17, PC to A-G on same, Mar. 28, 1596; p. 344, PC to Edward Hext, JP of Somerset, April 12, 1596; Strype, *Annals*, vol. IV, pp. 405-12, Hext to Burghley, Sept. 25, 1596; *HMC 15th Rep.*, App. VII, "Somerset MSS," pp. 20-31, Thomas Walmesley and Edward Fenner, judges of assize to JPs of Devonshire, Oct. 26, 1596; *APC 1596-97*, pp. 505-6, warrant to allow those appointed by JPs of Somerset to buy 200 quarters of peas and beans in Rutland and Northants and 200 quarters of barley in Norfolk, Feb. 20, 1596/7; *APC 1597*, p. 45, PC to Ld. Mayor of London to allow 200 quarters of wheat to be

Although the clothmaking areas of the West were among the hardest hit by the scarcity, some towns on important road or sea routes as well as supply or transshipment points for grain were little better off. On May 25, 1595, a crowd of about twenty women seized corn in the marketplace at Wye. At Canterbury toward the end of January, 1596, attempts were made by fifteen to twenty poor men to stop the transportation of grain out of the city. Included among the rioters were a number of laborers, a smith, a tailor, and a fletcher. A year later, in the spring of 1597, "lewd disposed" people were said to be stirring the poor on the Kent and Sussex border to riot in the face of continuing food shortage.[23] One of the contributory causes of the shortage in Kent and a particular irritant to the poor was the frequent transportation of large quantities of grain to London.[24]

Transportation of grain was a great grievance for the poor of Norfolk, a county which acted as a granary for many other areas. Between October and December, 1585, grain was shipped through the Norfolk port of King's Lynn to Lincoln, Newcastle, London, and the Low Country ports of Delft, Flushing, and Middleburg.[25] Such transportation was conventionally blamed for creating scarcity and high prices in Norfolk markets; for example, in June, 1586, there were mutterings among the poor "whiche was the rather furthered by the speeches of some lewd disposed persons tending to the practiz of some mutinous misdemeanore."[26] This transportation continued throughout the dear years of the 1590s. So much grain was shipped out of Norfolk that by April, 1597, the market price of grain had risen

bought there for relief of Somerset, April 14, 1597; BL, Add. MS 32092, f. 145, CJKB to JPs of Wilts to see that markets, especially those in clothmaking areas, are well supplied with grain, Jan. 12, 1596/7; *APC 1597*, pp. 84-85, PC to mayor of Southhampton to permit grain for supply of the poor of Salisbury, Wilts, to be trans-shipped without payment of customs, May 5, 1597; pp. 221-22, PC to judges of assize on the Oxford circuit to provide for relief of clothworkers of Kingswood, Wilts, June 19, 1597.

23. *APC 1595-96*, p. 334, PC to JPs of Kent, April 7, 1596; *APC 1597*, p. 74, PC to JPs of Kent and Sussex, April 17, 1597; pp. 92-93, PC to the Lord Admiral, May 5, 1597; Clark, pp. 368, 373-74.

24. *APC 1595-96*, p. 19, PC to Ld. Warden of the Cinque Ports to permit transportation of 900 quarters of grain to London, Oct. 17, 1595; p. 221, PC to officers of Kent ports to permit transportation of 290 quarters of grain to London, Feb. 15, 1595/6; *APC 1596-97*, pp. 534-55, PC to mayor and jurats of Sandwich to permit transportation of 260 quarters of wheat to London, Mar. 4, 1596/7.

25. PRO, S.P. 12/186/17, commissioners for restraint of grain trade in Norfolk to PC, Jan. 15, 1585/6, with no. 17 I, certificate from King's Lynn, enclosed.

26. PRO, S.P. 12/191/12, William Heyden, JP of Norfolk, to Walsingham, June 12, 1586.

to heights never before known, and the justices began to fear that there would not be enough left to feed the county's inhabitants. Inevitably, the poor tried to prevent further movement of grain. At least three food riots occurred, one at King's Lynn where a crowd boarded and unloaded a ship with a cargo of corn bound for a Lincolnshire port.[27]

One other consequence of this time of scarcity was the planning of an insurrection by some artisans who lived in the vicinity of Hampton Gay, Oxfordshire, about seven miles north of the city of Oxford. The ringleaders, Bartholomew Stere, a carpenter, and Richard Bradshawe, a miller, both of Hampton Gay, blamed the scarcity of corn on the enclosure and conversion of arable land to pasture. They decided that the only remedy would be a rising of the poor. It was reported that they intended to cast down enclosures, seize food and arms, and then cut off the enclosers' heads. In addition, the house of the Lord Lieutenant, Lord Norris, who was known to be in London, was to be ransacked for its store of arms and two fieldpieces. Thus armed and provisioned, the rebels would march on London, where they were convinced that the apprentices would join them.[28] After that "yt was but a monethes worke to overrunne the realme."[29] From the middle of October, 1596, onward, Stere and Bradshawe tried to recruit followers, and believing themselves to be more successful in this than the event proved, they set November 22, 1596 (the Monday after St. Hugh's Day) as the date of the rising. On Sunday night, November 21, the two leaders met at the rendezvous on Enslowe Hill, but instead of the anticipated 300 followers only about 10 turned up, armed with a motley collection of weapons including pikestaffs, daggers, and short swords. After a fruitless wait the would-be rebels dispersed to their homes. Meanwhile Sir William Spencer, an Oxfordshire deputy

27. *APC 1596-97*, pp. 269-70, PC to JPs of Norfolk, Oct. 22, 1596, authorizing transport of 1,520 quarters of grain purchased in Norfolk for supply of London; PRO, S.P. 12/262/151, sheriff of Norfolk to Burghley, April 30, 1597.

28. PRO, S.P. 14/28/64, report by A-G Coke to Sir Robert Cecil, Jan., 1596/7. This document is misplaced in State Papers James I. It was printed by E. F. Gay in *TRHS*, 1905, pp. 238-39, who noted that it concerned the Oxfordshire rising, although there is no author, addressee, or date given in this copy. There is another copy calendared in *HMC Salisbury*, vol. VII, pp. 49-50, where this information is given. It conveniently summarizes the main points brought out in the examinations of the suspects.

29. PRO, S.P. 12/262/4, examination of Roger Symondes of Hampton Gay, carpenter, Jan. 8, 1596/7.

lieutenant, had been informed of the business and managed with apparent ease to apprehend the suspects.[30]

Like the participants in the abortive Hampshire rising of 1586, those involved were employed in a cross-section of the trades to be found in the English countryside. Five men were classed as principal offenders by Attorney-General Sir Edward Coke: two millers, one carpenter, one fuller, and one mason. Six other men were identified as being definitely involved, but the occupations of only three are known—a weaver, a carpenter, and a husbandman. Nine others were implicated in the course of the various examinations, the occupations of eight of whom can be discovered: a miller, a carpenter, a bricklayer, a weaver, a servant of a gentleman named Vincent Barry, a carter who was servant to Lord Norris, and a baker and carter, both servants of Sir William Spencer.[31]

It is difficult to estimate to what degree Bartholomew Stere and his companions actually suffered from the consequences of food scarcity. Attorney-General Coke referred to him as a "carpenter and single-man and placed in verie good service."[32] Stere is reported to have said that some of those who would join the rising were as well able to live and had as little need to enter into a rising as he himself. He seems, however, to have been genuinely moved by the plight of the poorer artisans, who suffered in the scarcity, and it was from among them that he tried to recruit his following. One of these followers was Roger Symondes, a poor carpenter with six children, who was drawn in early but then backed out and disclosed the plan to a local magistrate.[33] Stere and Bradshawe had hoped to recruit a hundred "lusty fellowes" from among the large number of poor in the nearby broadclothmaking town of Witney, but only two joined—Stere's brother John, a weaver, and Vincent Rancle, also a weaver.[34]

30. PRO, S.P. 12/261/27, examination of Thomas Horne of Hampton Gay, carpenter, Dec. 17, 1596; no. 32, the declaration of Vincent Barry of Hampton Gay, gent., Dec. 31, 1596; S.P. 12/262/4, examination of Roger Symondes, Jan. 8, 1596/7.

31. The status of the various suspects can be found in PRO, S.P. 14/28/64, A-G Coke's report to Cecil, Jan., 1596/7, and scattered throughout the examinations in S.P. 12/261/10, 15, 27, and 28.

32. PRO, S.P. 14/28/64.

33. PRO, S.P. 12/261/10 II, examination of John Stere, Dec. 5, 1596, and examination of Roger Symondes, Nov. 25 and Dec. 5, 1596.

34. PRO, S.P. 12/261/15 V, examination of John Stere, weaver, of Wittney, Dec. 14, 1596; no. 10 II, examination of Vincent Rancle of Wittney, Dec. 4, 1596.

As in the period 1594-1597, the outbreaks of food rioting in 1605, 1608, and 1614 were the result of scarcity. The shortages in these cases seem to have been localized and the violence limited to three areas, a number of towns in Kent, the port town of Southampton, and the broadclothmaking areas of Wiltshire. During February, 1605, there were five riots in Kent, all at ports along the Medway river. All involved fewer than fifteen people, except for the riot at Chatham on February 20, where the size of the crowd, led by women, was estimated at one hundred. The other riots also involved considerable numbers of women, usually characterized as poor. Since this was not a year of harvest failure, the explanation for these riots must lie in local scarcity created by the shipment of large quantities of grain out of the county; the rioters were clearly trying to stop such transportation through the Medway ports.[35]

While there is some dispute about the quality of the 1608 harvest, the government's behavior indicates that by the middle of 1608 grain scarcity was being experienced in anticipation of a bad harvest. The destruction by fire of the Privy Council registers and most of the State Papers for this part of James I's reign makes it difficult to estimate the geographical extent of the distress or to discover evidence for riot.[36] In December, 1607, Council letters were issued to restrain overseas transportation of grain. These were renewed in May, 1608, and on June 1, 1608, the Book of Orders was reissued.[37] The scattered evidence reveals complaints of distress in Somerset, where there was a steep rise in grain prices "to the intolerable grief of the poor." There was also a report from Northamptonshire in May, 1608, of scarcity and some "stirring" of the poor people over it.[38] The only recorded food riot took place on April 11, when a ship loaded with wheat for London put in at Southampton. Since corn was scarce in the town and the local magistrates feared that the poor were ready to riot, an order was made to stay the ship and to sell its cargo at reasonable prices to those in need. Before the cargo could be discharged, the ship was

---

35. Clark, pp. 368-69.

36. Hoskins, p. 46, on the basis of the price of wheat calls the harvest bad, while Harrison, pp. 150, 154, on the basis of a wider range of grain calls it average.

37. HMC Salisbury, vol. XX, p. 160, PC to Ld. Treasurer Salisbury, May 11, 1608; p. 165, signet to Salisbury, May 13, 1608; PRO, S.P. 14/73 (a book of proclamations of the reign of James I), pp. 174-76, proclamation of June 2, 1608; calendared in Steele, vol. I, p. 124, no. 1058.

38. HMC Salisbury, vol. XX, p. 117, Edward Hext, JP, to Salisbury, Mar. 30, 1608: p. 174, Sir Robert Wingfield to Salisbury, May 29, 1608.

boarded by a group of women—led by the town crier—who began forcibly to unload her.[39]

The effects of the deficient harvest of 1613 seem to have been more localized than those of 1608; certainly they are even more skimpily documented. Only one series of riots seems to have taken place. In May of 1614, clothworkers from three centers of the Wiltshire broadcloth industry, Seend (near Devizes), Westbury, and Warminster, seized a number of horseloads of corn leaving the area.[40]

In the next two occurrences of food riots, in 1622 and 1629-1631, cloth-trade depression began to play a more important, even a paramount, role. The riots of 1622, due almost exclusively to a slump in the sale of English cloth overseas, can be divided into two separate periods and geographical locations. One was concentrated in the western broadclothmaking areas during the spring and summer of 1622, the other in East Anglian new-drapery centers late in 1622.

The sales of English broadcloth on the European continent began to contract in 1620 and continued to shrink through 1622, producing a deep depression in the industry and numerous complaints of unemployment from clothworkers in Somerset, Wiltshire, Gloucestershire, and Oxfordshire.[41] This was one of a number of depressions which racked the undressed-broadcloth industry in the course of its long decline from 1616 onward. A number of explanations have been offered for this depression, including the decline in the competitive position of English cloth in the face of expanding continental production, the Polish and German currency debasements pricing English cloth out of its important central and eastern European markets, and the onset of war disrupting the German market.[42] Whatever the cause, the effects were obvious: unemployment, hunger, and rioting in the West.

In the spring of 1622 the justices of Wiltshire reported to the Privy Council that the unemployed clothworkers of Bromham parish, near Devizes, had grown desperate because they had "now spent all theire

39. J. W. Horrocks, ed., *The Assembly Books of Southampton 1602-16*, vol. I, pp. 61-63.

40. G. D. Ramsay, *The Wiltshire Woollen Industry in the Sixteenth and Seventeenth Centuries*, pp. 72-73; *APC 1613-14*, pp. 457-58, PC to JPs of Wilts, June 7, 1614; pp. 652-53, PC to same, Dec. 6, 1614.

41. For a fuller discussion of this, see below, pp. 58-60

42. Supple, pp. 53-56; J. D. Gould, "The Trade Depression of the Early 1620's," *Econ. H.R.*, 2nd ser., VII (1954-55): 81-90; F. F. Fisher, "London's Export Trade in the Early Seventeenth Century," *Econ. H.R.*, 2nd. ser., III (1950-51): 153.

poore goodes to buy foode for them and their familyes." As a result of this destitution the unemployed "begin to goe in flockes and diverse of them have nowe very lately at severall tymes set upon suche as carryed corne on horses to markettes and have by force taken from them their corne."[43] In Gloucestershire, the unemployed were reduced to wandering, begging, and stealing, and ultimately to riot: plans were laid in June, 1622, for 500 people armed with staves to seize ships loaded with grain sailing from Gloucester down the Severn. During May of 1622, the unemployed in eastern Somerset, in crowds of up to 500, seized corn bound for market. Riots continued to break out in Somerset during July of 1622, including one, west of Bristol at Portbury, involving some laborers who seized a load of wheat.[44]

The claim that these western food riots were caused in part by harvest failure is not substantiated by evidence.[45] The 1621 harvest has been rated as average nationwide and good in the West; harvests since 1618 had been good to abundant. There are no indications at all of scarcity during the spring and early summer of 1622, when the riots took place. Even the harvest of 1622, which has been rated as bad— although recent work indicates that it may in fact have been average— seems to have had little effect in the West.[46] The cloth trade began to revive in the spring of 1623, and while there is evidence of higher than normal grain prices, there is no evidence of much shortage in the markets. On the contrary, the returns on grain supply from the various Somerset divisions in the spring of 1623 report that the markets were well supplied with grain and that although prices were high the poor were not complaining very loudly.[47]

43. PRO, S.P. 14/129/79, JPs of Wilts to PC, April 30, 1622; the riots are noticed in T. Birch, ed., *Court and Times of James I*, vol. 2, pp. 291-92, and G. Roberts, ed., *Diary of Walter Yonge esq, J.P. & M.P. for Honiton co. Devon 1604-1628*, p. 52.

44. PRO, S.P. 14/131/4, JPs of Gloucestershire to PC, June 1, 1622; no. 4 I, information of William Guyse, June 1, 1622; no. 4 II, examination of Richard Webb, weaver, June 1, 1622; *APC 1621-23*, PC to sheriff of Somerset, May 12, 1622; S.P. 14/130/73, sheriff of Somerset to PC, May 14, 1622; no. 99, sheriff of Somerset to PC, May 20, 1622; SRO, Session roll 41 i, ff. 82-83, Sir James Ley, JP, and *custos rotulorum* to his fellow JPs, July 14, 1622; Indictment roll 46, no. 93, indictment of five laborers of Portbury for riot, rout, and unlawful assembly, Aug. 28, 1622.

45. Supple, p. 55.

46. W. G. Hoskins, "Harvest Fluctuations and English Economic History, 1620-1759," *Ag. H.R.* XVI (1968): 28; Harrison, pp. 150, 154.

47. PRO, S.P. 14/144/24, Edward Popham, sheriff of Somerset, to PC, May, 1623, enclosing no. 24 I-XII, twelve certificates received from JPs of different Somerset divisions on the state of corn markets; see also B. H. Cunnington, ed., *Annals of the Borough of Devizes*, p. 71, mayor of Devizes to PC, Feb. 17, 1622/3, which indicates that the markets were well supplied with grain

Late in 1622 a slump also occurred in the East Anglian new-drapery industry. While the long-term trend in this branch of the cloth industry was very favorable, like the broadcloth industry it could not escape the consequences of periodic stoppages. This short-lived slump produced food rioting in December of 1622 along the Essex-Suffolk border, involving unemployed spinners and weavers, mostly from Sudbury in Suffolk.[48] Like the western riots earlier in the year, these were directly caused by unemployment, not food scarcity.

Conditions remained bad in parts of East Anglia throughout the first half of 1623. The hunger and misery here were largely the result of unemployment, but there is no doubt that food scarcity was by now at least a contributing factor. There is some dispute among modern historians over the quality of the 1622 harvest, but the government felt the situation was serious enough to bring the traditional remedies for grain scarcity into operation, including reissue of the Book of Orders in December of 1622.[49]

The returns of the justices of the peace to the Privy Council demonstrate that the scarcity, coming on top of unemployment, hit hardest in certain areas of Norfolk, especially the city of Norwich. In January of 1623 it was reported that the poor of Norwich could only be relieved if "wools combed and spun in other shires may be restrained whereby the exceedinge great multitude of such as are and have allwaies been therein imployed, may be sett on worke." The justices were convinced that otherwise they would be unable to "susteyne and conteyne the poore of this countye within terms of dutye and obedience without the sufferinge of those extreame neces-sityes which weere otherwise likelie out of desperacye to drawe them to disorder."[50] Added to this was food scarcity, which the justices attributed to the grain shipments leaving from the ports of King's Lynn and Yarmouth.[51] By June, 1623, the officials of Norwich did not

---

and the prices were falling, the only problem being lack of work or low wages for the clothworkers.

48. *APC 1621-23*, p. 376, PC to sheriff of Essex, Dec. 26, 1622; BL, Add. MS 39245, f. 70, JPs of Essex to JPs of Suffolk, Jan. 9, 1622/3; J. E. Pilgrim, "The Rise of the New Draperies in Essex," *Univ. of Birm. Hist. Journ.* VII (1959-60): 55-56.

49. *Foedera, Conventiones, Literae*, vol. XVII, p. 429, proclamation renewing the Book of Orders, Dec. 22, 1622; calendared in Steele, vol. I, p. 159, no. 1344.

50. PRO, S.P. 14/137/16, JPs and sheriff of Norfolk to PC, Jan. 15, 1622/3.

51. PRO, S.P. 14/138/35, JPs of Norfolk to PC, Feb. 15, 1622/3; S.P. 14/140/14, mayor and aldermen of Norwich to PC, Mar. 21, 1622/3.

know "what means to finde to keepe the worser sort from mutyne and the more idle and baser sort from begginge and that in such multitudes as the Inhabitants of this City are not able to endure."[52] Neither Norwich nor any other area, however, actually experienced riot in 1623.

Shortages and high food prices during 1623 were localized. There was no nationwide grain scarcity, certainly nothing to match the period 1594-1597. All of the 1622 riots came and went with cloth-trade depressions. Only in 1629-1631 were the effects of the close synchronization of depression with grain scarcity experienced. The bad harvest of 1630 came in the middle of a severe slump in the cloth trade; together they produced an intense period of food rioting. Over one-half of the food riots for the entire period 1586-1631 occurred between 1629 and 1631, including the most violent of the lot. These riots can be divided into two chronological groups: those of 1629 and early 1630, which took place under the influence of cloth-trade stoppages alone; and those of late 1630 and the spring of 1631, which erupted against a background of a bad harvest, continuing cloth-industry stagnation, and what must have been a general economic depression.

A severe slump struck the new draperies in 1629 due to optimistic overproduction following the restoration of stability in the main southern European markets. During the late 1620s trade with these markets had been made difficult by political factors such as wars with Spain and France and domestic constitutional conflicts over the payment of customs duties. Refusal to pay customs came first in the French-wine trade, disrupting not only wine imports but the export of new draperies to France, which was normally handled by the wine importers. The end of the customs dispute and the final peace with France in 1629 resulted in overproduction of bays and says, and, along with the import of more French wine than could be sold, immobilized clothier and merchant capital, thus paralyzing the industry.[53]

Distress appeared immediately in Essex, the leading center of the industry. In January, 1629, grain carriers were attacked a number of times at Wanstead and their loads taken by groups of up to sixty people; two months later, a crowd of women a hundred and forty strong took grain from ships at Maldon bound for the Low Coun-

52. PRO, S.P. 14/147/77, mayor and aldermen of Norwich to PC, June 27, 1623.
53. Supple, pp. 102-8.

tries.[54] By April, unemployment was widespread among the weavers of Braintree and Bocking, who appeared at the Essex quarter sessions to demand that something be done for them. A crowd of about two hundred followed the justices from place to place until they abandoned all other county business and promised to write to the Privy Council about the situation in the new-drapery industry. By this means the justices persuaded the crowd to disperse and forestalled the plans of some of those present to "have gathered together in a Mutinie" and to have marched on London to present their grievances to the King.[55]

The justices could not continue to restrain the unemployed by such shifts. On May 22, 1629, two or three hundred people from Braintree, Bocking, and Witham assembled at Burrow Hill near Maldon. They then proceeded to board a ship loaded with grain bound for Hull. Fifteen quarters of rye were carried off, a number of the sailors were assaulted, and the merchant transporting the cargo was compelled to pay £20 for his own protection. Following this, a number of the rioters broke into a house and seized six quarters of grain.[56] It must be reiterated that unemployment was the sole cause of this riot; there is no evidence at all of scarcity. In fact, when some of the unemployed weavers of Braintree and Bocking had petitioned the King for relief early in May, they had asked him "to consider that they may not starve in tyme of plentie."[57]

In 1629 there was also a stoppage in overseas shipment of broadcloths. The Merchant Adventurers ceased trade from March to May as part of a general refusal to pay customs duties. Although the company resumed cloth purchases in May, this stoppage did produce some ill effects in Somerset. Early in April a large number of poor people assembled at Langport, on the river Parrett, in an attempt to stop grain exports.[58] In May some weavers from North Curry, near Taunton, turned back a ship on the river Tone which was carrying

54. PRO, S.P. 16/133/19, Earl of Totness to PC, Jan. 27, 1628/9, enclosing no. 19 I, JPs of Essex to Earl of Totness, Jan. 27, 1628/9; *APC 1628-29*, pp. 309-10, PC to JPs and Dep. Lts. of Essex, Jan. 30, 1628/9; Walter and Wrightson, p. 36.

55. PRO, S.P. 16/141/1, JPs of Essex to PC, April 17, 1629; Bod. Lib., Firth MS c.4, pp. 494-95, petition of the weavers of Bocking and Braintree to the King, May 8, 1629, which describes the events of April.

56. Bod. Lib., Firth MS c.4, p. 501, JPs of Essex to PC, May 22, 1629; *APC 1629-30*, pp. 24-25, PC to Ld. Lt. of Essex, May 23, 1629; p. 25, PC to Dep. Lts. and JPs of Essex, May 23, 1629.

57. Bod. Lib., Firth MS c.4, pp. 494-95, petition of the weavers of Braintree and Bocking to the King, May 8, 1629.

58. SRO, Phelips MS (DD/PH) 222/92, PC to Sir Robert Phelips, April 30, 1629.

corn to Bridgwater for shipment out of the county. Though the weavers later claimed that they did not touch the cargo, they were indicted for assault and seizure of the corn. There are indications of another riot in south-central Somerset during February, 1630, again to prevent the movement of grain.[59] A proclamation was issued on May 2, 1629, prohibiting the export of grain overseas, but there is no evidence of actual grain scarcity: it seems to have been a purely precautionary move, a result of the Somerset disorders and the distress in Essex.[60]

For the clothmaking areas these Somerset riots were a taste of things to come. In 1630 the long-standing dispute with the Dutch over the amount of the tare (abatements made in the price of substandard cloths sold in the Low Countries) was actively resumed, resulting in severe curtailment in the export of undressed broadcloth. To exert further pressure, the Dutch imposed the tare on English dyed broadcloth and kersies which, for a number of years, had been carried by "interlopers," merchants not members of one of the great chartered companies. The Merchant Adventurers claimed that the interlopers would immediately pay the new tare and thereby defeat the Company's attempt to present a united opposition. To forestall this the Privy Council in October of 1630 informed all merchants that they could trade only in towns designated by the Company, thereby producing a stop in the trade in colored broadcloth and kersies as well as in undressed broadcloth.[61] Widespread unemployment in the clothmaking areas resulted and, since the slump followed almost immediately on the heels of harvest failure in the autumn of 1630, the consequence was a period of six or seven months of intermittent food rioting throughout western, southern, and eastern England.

On November 15, 1630, a merchant from Warminster, Wiltshire, carrying five horseloads of corn up Midford Hill in eastern Somerset on his way to Bristol, was attacked by a crowd of at least one hundred people. They took away seven sacks and insisted that no one would be

59. SRO, session roll 61 i, no. 38, petition of weavers of North Curry to JPs at Taunton Q.S., 1629; no. 78, notes of indictments, includes the three weavers of North Curry indicted for riot and seizure of corn; session roll 63 ii, no. 25, Sir Robert Phelips to all bailiffs, etc., Feb. 24, 1629/30.

60. *Foedera*, vol. XIX, p. 64, proclamation prohibiting the export of grain, May 2, 1629; calendared in Steele, vol. I, p. 186, no. 1581.

61. Supple, pp. 112-15.

allowed to carry corn on that road. On that same day two other merchants were attacked close to Midford Hill by groups of thirty or more people, who also seized a number of sacks of corn. Those participants in the riots who were eventually apprehended came from clothmaking areas along the Somerset-Wiltshire border. An attempt to seize 400 bushels of corn bound for Bristol was also rumored, but nothing seems to have come of that.[62] On January 7, 1631, at Basingstoke, Hampshire, a center of the depressed kersey industry, a group of twenty poor people set upon a cart leaving the town and carried away four quarters of grain.[63] On a number of different occasions during November of 1630 the workers in the Berkshire dyed-broadcloth industry at Newbury, who "want worke and thereby want money to buy corne," seized grain from carts on the way from Newbury to Reading, another Berkshire clothmaking center which was equally depressed and where grain was in short supply.[64] Reading's turn for rioting came in 1631. On a night in March a number of the poor attempted to take corn from the marketplace, but the constables, "charged to keepe a good watche for suppressinge of mutanies or risinges of the poore," apprehended them. Another attempt on the market was made on April 1, led by a shoemaker, but again the constables quickly suppressed it.[65]

In Kent during November, 1630, the "inferior sort of people" made a number of attempts to stop the movement of grain into the port of Faversham in the knowledge that it would be transported to London. During a two-week period in April and May, 1631, there were at least six more food riots in Kent. On April 20, a crowd of twenty to thirty men and women met a cart just outside Cranbrook, a center of the Kent finished-broadcloth industry, and took away five quarters of corn. At about the same time Robert Carr, licensed to buy fodder for the stables of some of the privy councillors, was violently despoiled of fifteen quarters of oats by a large assembly of people at the town of

62. SRO, session roll 64 ii, nos. 200-205, examinations of suspects taken Nov. 17 and 18, 1630: nos. 243-44, informations against suspects, Nov. 1, 1630.

63. *APC 1630-31*, p. 189, PC to JPs of Hants, Jan. 17, 1630/1. For the depressed state of the Hants kersey industry, see below, p. 64.

64. PRO, S.P. 16/176/35, Gabriel Dowse, JP, to PC, Dec. 5, 1630; S.P. 16/177/14, mayor of Newbury to PC, Dec. 15, 1630; no. 52, JPs of Berkshire to PC, Dec. 28, 1630; J. M. Guilding, ed., *Reading Records*, vol. 3, pp. 37-44.

65. *Reading Records*, vol. 3, p. 379, warrant for Thomas Bagley's apprehension, May 11, 1631; p. 68, John Aston's bond for his appearance at the assizes, May 14, 1631.

Herne. Riots also took place at Faversham, Canterbury, Whitstable, and Sittingbourne.[66]

The final disorders in this series took place in East Anglia and were also aimed at stopping grain transportation. From the autumn of 1630 through the first six months of 1631, much of the area (particularly the clothmaking centers in Essex, Suffolk, and Norfolk) endured a deep depression, the combined result of harvest failure and continued difficulties with the French and Spanish markets for new draperies. It was reported from Essex that "although the poore doe suffer much in respect of the high price of corne yet they are in farr greater misery in the most populous partes of the cuntrey whose trades consistes in the makinge of Bayes by reason that the Clothiers doe forbeare to sett the poor weavers on worke."[67] It was also feared that the unemployed new-drapery workers who lived in Sudbury in Suffolk "could noe longer be kept in a peacable and orderly government." Similar conditions of scarcity and unemployment also existed in many parts of Norfolk, including the city of Norwich.[68]

Disorder nearly erupted in East Anglia when Samuel Puckle, a merchant of Norwich, attempted to transport grain overseas. Puckle, who seems to have made a career out of grain profiteering, obtained a license from the Privy Council to export 1100 quarters of buckwheat to Rotterdam through the Norfolk port of Yarmouth. This was achieved by the simple expedient of falsely claiming an abundance of buckwheat in Norfolk and Suffolk. A bread made of barley and buckwheat provided the poor of East Anglia with the staple of their diet during scarcities; they could afford nothing better. By scouring the countryside for buckwheat, Puckle drove up the price of grain in every market he visited and greatly angered the poor. The justices of Suffolk reported that the poor, seeing their bread taken from them to be sent overseas, "turned into all licentious fury and desperation comminge in great troops unto us and telling us they must now needs starve if this corne, which they were only able to buy should be thus taken from

---

66. PRO, S.P. 16/174/20, Vice Admiral Thomas Walsingham to the Ld. Commissioners of the Admiralty, Oct. 10, 1630; no. 22, same to Secretary Nicholas, Oct. 10, 1630; S.P. 16/175/81, sheriff of Kent to PC, Nov. 22, 1630, enclosing no. 81 I, a seditious libel; S.P. 16/191/3, petition of John Carr to PC; no. 4, notes on food riots in Kent; no. 39, John Hales to Sir Edward Hales, May 6, 1631; *APC 1630-31*, PC to JPs of Kent, May 11, 1631; Clark, p. 370.

67. PRO, S.P. 16/188/92, JPs of Essex to PC, April 19, 1631; also see below, pp. 76-79.

68. PRO, S.P. 16/190/54, JPs of Suffolk to PC, May 9, 1631; for Norfolk see below, p. 65.

them."[69] When the buckwheat reached Yarmouth, the justices, in accordance with their instructions, refused to permit it to be exported. The scarcity at Yarmouth was great, there had already been rioting when the poor took grain from boatmen loading ships bound overseas, and the justices feared further riots if Puckle tried to load his grain onto ships.[70]

We have seen the importance of cloth-trade slumps in creating the conditions which produced rioting. A depression by itself created more frequent and more severe disorders than a single bad harvest; as the exceptional case of the years 1594-1597 illustrates, more than one bad harvest was required to deplete food stocks and produce major rioting. The most serious situation was a depression during which a harvest failed: under such conditions, as in 1630, social problems were heightened to critical levels. It would be erroneous to conclude from this that only artisans suffered in times of food scarcity and depression; there is considerable evidence in the returns made by the justices as demanded by the Book of Orders that others, particularly laborers, were laid off by their employers and that they endured hunger and misery. By and large, however, laborers did not engage in riots on their own. Most of the symptoms of social distress are to be found in the words and actions of artisans in general and clothmakers in particular; this distinguished them from other groups in society. In times of scarcity and depression, they made the loudest complaints about food prices and unemployment by means of riot, attempted insurrections, and frequent petitions to local justices and to the Privy Council. Consequently, as will become apparent when the reactions of the Crown are examined, it was to their complaints above all that the authorities listened and responded in the formulation of policy.

Aims and Opinions of Food Rioters

Any examination of the objectives and attitudes of food rioters from 1586 to 1631 is hampered by a lack of evidence, particularly of the kind of circumstantial accounts so valuable for a thorough exploration. For most of the riots of the late sixteenth and early seventeenth

69. PRO, S.P. 16/187/12, JPs of Suffolk to PC, Mar. 21, 1630/1. See W. L. Sasche, ed., *Minutes of the Norwich Court of Mayoralty, 1630-31*, p. 130, for evidence of some of Puckle's other dealings.

70. PRO, S.P. 16/187/13, bailiffs of Yarmouth to PC, Mar. 21, 1630/1.

centuries there survive only brief notices of their occurrence and the objects of the rioters' activities, evidence which, in conjunction with seditious libels, examinations for seditious words, and examinations of suspects in planned insurrections, does permit at least some consideration of this topic.

One is led to agree with E. P. Thompson's conclusions about the eighteenth-century crowd: food riots were not, as some historians have argued, spasmodic outbursts of mindless rage or mere cloaks for criminal behavior, but were, rather, disciplined forms of popular action. The rioters had clearly defined objectives and employed only that minimum amount of force or coercion necessary to achieve those objectives.[71]

On the evidence of surviving accounts, the main aim of rioters in the Elizabethan-early Stuart period was to prevent the transportation of grain out of their home area. Almost every riot involved an attempt to seize grain which was on the move; thus, internal transportation routes and ports were repeatedly the scene of disorders. Among the most frequent locations were the river Severn below Gloucester, down which grain was moved to Bristol and Wales; the roads leading west from Warminster in Wiltshire, along which grain was also transported to Bristol and Wales; and the ports and overland routes in southern and eastern England, which supplied London and the Northeast and through which grain passed on its way overseas.

Except for the unusually violent Essex riot of May, 1629, there is no record of much, if any, physical violence being used against those who transported grain. This conclusion may by itself be misleading: it is quite possible that force was unnecessary. The rioters congregated in great enough numbers—ranging anywhere from 30 to 500 or 600— that the men of a bark stopped on the Severn or corn badgers moving grain on packhorses from Warminster were intimidated into standing by while their loads were carried off. There is in fact evidence that on at least one occasion the crowds were large enough to intimidate even the local authorities. During the riot of April 23, 1586, when five or six hundred people stopped a bark on the Severn, repeated reading of the riot act by the justices failed to disperse them. When two of the ringleaders were arrested by the sheriff of Gloucestershire, they refused to come before one justice, Thomas Throckmorton, and

71. E. P. Thompson, "The Moral Economy of the English Crowd in the Eighteenth Century," *Past and Present* 50 (1971): 76-136.

insisted they would appear before another, Henry Poole. Intimidated by the large crowd which still refused to disperse, the sheriff's officers took the two ringleaders to Poole's house. Since he was not at home and the officers were fearful of the crowd, they released the prisoners on their word that they would appear before Poole on the following morning. When the two came before Poole the intimidation continued. Three or four hundred people "laye in awayte in the woddes and other secreat places" with the intention of rescuing them if they were jailed.[72] On April 30, a second bark was boarded and her cargo of grain taken; for the next week, crowds of up to two hundred people gathered on the banks of the river to prevent further transportation. Nothing was done to disperse them, and Thomas Throckmorton accused his fellow justices of being frightened into inactivity.[73]

In eighteenth-century English food riots there were occasional examples of the *taxation populaire*, setting of food prices by the crowd based on the idea of a just price. Along with the disciplined nature of the food riot, this has been used to demonstrate a moral economy governing the behavior of the crowd in times of scarcity, "grounded upon a consistent traditional view of social norms and obligations, of the proper economic functions of several parties within the community."[74]

Beyond their limited use of force, there is little indication of any moral economy governing the behavior of food rioters in the earlier period. There is only one surviving example of the *taxation populaire*, when during a riot at Southwark in June of 1595 apprentices set market prices of victuals lower than the prevailing rates. This seems to have been a rare occurrence in the sixteenth and early seventeenth centuries.[75] Normally, grain was simply seized and carried away by the rioters and, presumably, divided among them. Too much emphasis on the notion of a moral economy of the crowd can lead to an overly sentimental view of the life and behavior of the poor and can obscure the reality of the pain, desperation, and anger they felt in times of depression and scarcity. In the fragments of surviving evidence on popular attitudes in the Tudor-Stuart period one finds few indications

72. PRO, S.P. 12/188/47, JPs of Gloucestershire to PC, April 30, 1586.

73. PRO, S.P. 12/189/7, Thomas Throckmorton to PC, May 5, 1586; *APC 1586-87*, p. 133, PC to sheriff and JPs of Gloucestershire, May 29, 1586.

74. Thompson, p. 79.

75. Clark, p. 379.

indeed of norms which could be said to make up a moral economy. Instead, a phrase recurs which seems to sum up the actions of the unemployed and hungry in times of depression and scarcity. It is to be found in an anonymous document of 1595, addressed to the mayor and justices of Norwich, in which loud complaints are expressed about the high price of grain and the greed of the rich who have been licensed "to set open shop to sell poor men's skins." It goes on to utter vague threats of rising by the poor and concludes with the justification "necessity hath no lawe."[76] This maxim also occurs in a sixteenth-century observer's account of the consequences of stoppages in the cloth trade. It is worth quoting at length, because it gives a comprehensive summary of the activities of the unemployed:

infinite nombers of Spynners, Carders, Pickers of woll are turned to begging with no smale store of pore children, who driven with necessitie (that hath no lawe) both come idelie abowt to begg to the oppression of the poore husbandmen, And robbe their hedges of lynnen, stele pig, gose, and capon, and leave not a drie hedge within dyvers myles compas of the townes wher they dwell to the great destruction of all mannor of grayen sowen and to the spoile of mens meadowes and pastures, And spoile all springes, steale fruit and corne in the harvest tyme, and robb barnes in the winter tyme, and cawse pore maydes and servantes to purloyne and robbe their masters, which the foresayd spynners etc. receve. Besides many other myscheifes falling owt the Weavers, Walkers, Tukkers, Shermen, Dyers and suche being tall lusty men and extreame pore streyght being forced by povertie stele fish, conies, dere, and such like, and their streight murmur and rayse comocions, as late experience in Suffolke shewed.[77]

There can be little doubt that theft of food was resorted to by the unemployed and hungry and that it can be regarded as an alternative to the food riot. Recent work on Elizabethan Essex indicates that indictments at quarter sessions for thefts, especially of food, rose markedly during the bad harvest years of the 1590s. Repeatedly, simple hunger and necessity were offered as the motives for the crimes.[78] Although the statistical research has not been done, a

76. *HMC Salisbury*, vol. XIII, pp. 168-69, anonymous libel from Norfolk, undated but probably the one referred to in *APC 1595-96*, pp. 88-89, PC to mayor of Norwich, Nov. 26, 1595.

77. Bod. Lib., Rawlinson MS, D. 133 f. 5, quoted in F. J. Fisher, "Commercial Trends and Policy in Sixteenth Century England," *Econ. H.R.*, 1st series, X (1940): 111-12.

78. J. Samaha, *Law and Order in Historical Perspective: The Case of Elizabethan Essex*, pp. 19-20, 35-36, and appendix VI.

preliminary survey of the Wiltshire and Somerset quarter sessions records leaves the impression that during 1621-1623 and 1629-1631 indictments for the stealing of food and of other goods which could be easily sold rose markedly. This not very surprising conclusion receives further confirmation in the frequent complaints of begging and stealing by the unemployed which the Privy Council received in times of depression and scarcity.[79]

One characteristic the eighteenth-century crowd and its sixteenth- and seventeenth-century counterparts shared was a common target. The main objects of eighteenth-century popular animosity were the middlemen—the carrier, the miller, and the baker—upon whose engrossing and profiteering shortages were often blamed. In the earlier period the rioters' attacks were almost all directed at carriers of corn and scarcity was occasionally blamed on the dealings of millers and other middlemen. In 1591 there were numerous complaints in Hertfordshire that bakers, millers, and others were buying up great quantities of corn before it reached market and were making such large purchases in the market itself that little was left for the poor. Threats were made that if the millers continued on this course they would be pulled out of the market by their ears. The scarcity and high price of grain in Hertfordshire and Kent during 1595 were blamed on similar activities engaged in by the bakers and brewers of London. At the Easter quarter sessions of 1607 the poor handicraftsmen of Chelmsford in Essex petitioned the justices, complaining of the abuses of loaders, badgers, and millers in driving up the prices of food in the market. The 1614 grain shortage which produced rioting in Wiltshire was blamed on price rises which were the result of large purchases made by millers, badgers, and others.[80]

This dislike of middlemen—which extended to exporting merchants—accounts for one notable aspect of food riots in market and port towns: the participation of women. Women played important

---

79. A few of many examples are to be found in BL, Lans. MS 54, no. 60, James Ritter to Burghley, Aug. 7, 1587, about conditions in Yorkshire; 76, no. 58, Henry Cooke, JP of Herts, to Burghley, Sept. 31, 1594; Strype, vol. IV, pp. 405-12, Edward Hext, JP of Somerset, to Burghley, Sept. 25, 1596; PRO, S.P. 14/128/50, JPs of Gloucestershire to PC, Mar. 13, 1621/2.

80. BL, Lans. MS 66, no. 20, Henry Cooke, JP of Herts, to Burghley, Jan. 1, 1590/1; Lans. MS 78, no. 61, JPs of Kent to Lord Cobham, the Lord Lt., Oct. 9, 1595; PRO, S.P. 12/254/10, JPs of Herts to PC, Oct. 6, 1595; no. 62, same to Burghley, Nov. 10, 1595; *Calendar of Essex Quarter Sessions Records*, Q.S. roll 183, no. 62, petition to JPs from the poor handicraftsmen of Chelmsford, April 7, 1607; *APC 1613-14*, pp. 457-58, PC to JPs of Wilts, June 7, 1614.

roles, including that of leader, in the riots in Kent at Wye (1595), at the port towns on the Medway (1605), and at several locations in 1631, as well as in food riots at Southampton (1608), at Maldon, Essex (March, 1629), and in Berkshire (1631). It is no doubt true, as Peter Clark noted in his study of Kent popular protests, that "women enjoyed greater immunity from the law than men."[81] In this way women could act as a mouthpiece for their menfolk's grievances. Nonetheless, women no doubt had their own discontents, stemming from their immediate and direct experience, as purchasers, of high prices and the sharp practices of middlemen in the marketplace.

Despite this antipathy to middlemen, popular feeling in the Tudor-Stuart period reserved its most intense outbursts for another target: "the rich." As expressed in anonymous libels, seditious utterances reported from alehouses, and the few surviving examinations of rioters and insurrectionaries, the opinions of common folk reveal a deep hatred of the people possessed of the power, social standing, and landed wealth denied to them. That hatred is the mirror image of the contempt and fear with which their superiors regarded the poor—a justified fear, if the opinions reported were at all typical of their social order. The wrath of the poor was directed at the rich, mainly the gentry but also including prosperous yeomen, in their capacities as large-scale growers and hoarders of corn in times of scarcity and as enclosers blamed for shortages.

At Sandwich in Kent in June, 1587, when five clothworkers planned a rising, one Thomas Bird, a weaver, declared that he "intended to hang up the rich farmers which had corn at their own doors."[82] As a result, no doubt, of the severity of the distress in 1594-1597 and 1629-1631, these two periods were particularly rich in expressions of hatred of the well-to-do. The poor of Somerset who in 1596 seized a load of cheese were reported to be animated by a hatred of all gentlemen because they believed "that the rich men had gotten all into their hands, and will starve the poor."[83]

In the autumn of 1595 in Essex a yeoman and a blacksmith, drinking together at an alehouse, got into a heated argument which resulted in the blacksmith being charged, on the information of the yeoman, with uttering seditious speeches. The smith, Thomas Byndar

81. Clark, pp. 376-77.
82. Ibid., p. 367.
83. Strype, vol. IV, p. 407, Edward Hext, JP of Somerset, to Burghley, Sept. 25, 1596.

of Danbury, had complained of the high price of food, blaming it on the big corn-growers, including among them the yeoman, William Thrustell of Purleigh, with whom he was drinking. Byndar claimed that he and some others would rise and pull corn out of the houses of those who were hoarding it. He vowed that twenty of the hoarders would be hanged at their gates by Christmas day.[84] The following year a weaver in Ardleigh, Essex, was indicted for seditious words. He is reported to have declared that he wished in his heart for a hundred men to join with him in a rising so that he could be their captain and lead them to cut the throats of the "rich churles and the rich cornemongers."[85]

An anonymous libel found in Norwich in 1595 claimed that for seven years the rich had fed on the flesh of the poor and that bribes had made the magistrates content to see the poor famished. Their days were numbered, however, for there were 60,000 craftsmen in London and elsewhere who would no longer bear this ill treatment. The rich would be made to drink to the dregs a draught from the cup of the Lord. Their hedges would be laid open, their fields reaped, their stores of grain taken, and their houses levelled to the ground.[86]

In April, 1597, exaggerated reports of the Oxfordshire rising inspired talk of a rising in Norfolk. John Curtis of Magdalynn met with Thomas Welles, who told Curtis that the poor had risen in the West and would be in Norfolk in a week. Welles said that 4,000 persons would meet with him, go to a justice and ask him "that they might have corne cheape for ther monye and yf they coud not gett anye reasonably for ther money then they wolde aryse and gett it with strength and that yf they did arise they wold knocke downe the best first."[87]

The severe depression and scarcity of 1629-1631 fostered similar incendiary opinions. Toward the end of 1630, after the failure of that year's harvest, the justices were informed of a Somerset stonemason's opinions on the cause of the high price of food: "it would be cheaper

---

84. *Calendar of Essex Quarter Sessions Records*, Q.S. roll 131, no. 34, Arthur Herrys, JP, to Sir Thomas Mildmay et al., JPs of Essex, Sept. 30, 1595; nos. 35 and 36, examinations of witnesses to the seditious words.

85. *Calendar of Essex Quarter Sessions Records*, Q.S. roll 136, no. 111, indictment of Henry Went of Ardleigh, weaver, for seditious words, Nov. 10, 1596.

86. *HMC Salisbury*, vol. XIII, pp. 168-69.

87. PRO, S.P. 12/262/15 II, examination of John Curtys before Humfrey Guybon, sheriff of Norfolk, and Gregorye Pratt, JP, April 25, 1597.

here if it were not for the heard [hard] hearts of unferlie rich men and that if a hundred were of his minde they would kill some of those rich men that the rest might sell corne cheaper."[88] Early in November of 1630, during a time when carts carrying grain to the ports of Faversham in Kent were often attacked, a set of doggerel verses was left on the porch of the minister of Wye, threatening a rising if the rich did nothing to provide relief for the poor.[89]

Finally, in December, 1630, there was talk of a rising in the small midland county of Rutland. William Hull, a shoemaker and alehouse-keeper of Uppingham, tried to rouse the artisans of the surrounding countryside. One he approached was Nicholas Knight, a poor weaver of Liddington, who "hath mainteyned himself all his life time by his said trade havinge nothing else to live upon." Hull told Knight that the poor men of Okeham had proposed to the Uppingham tradesmen a rising to cast down the enclosures on which the food shortage was blamed. Hull was to recruit as many people as possible and to arm them by robbing local militia armories; this plan never got beyond the talking stage.[90]

Two risings which went beyond merely seditious words, those of Hampshire in 1586 and Oxfordshire in 1596, also reveal the participants' deep antagonism toward the gentry. In both instances enclosures made by gentry were blamed for food scarcity; the guilty gentry were to be the main targets of the risings. The Hampshire artisans who planned the rising of June 6, 1586, aimed to destroy the woad which had been planted instead of corn and to seize the grain and other foodstuffs believed to be hoarded in the houses of the gentlemen blamed for the scarcity.[91]

Throughout their examinations, those suspected of involvement in in 1596 Oxfordshire rising blamed the scarcity of food upon local enclosers, both gentlemen and yeomen. In discussions with Bartholomew Stere, the miller Richard Bradshawe was reported to have declared "that he hoped that before yt were long to see some of the

88. SRO, session roll 64 ii, nos. 243-44, information of Florence Peryn and Susan Role and information of Edward Kirton, Nov. 1, 1630.

89. PRO, S.P. 16/175/81, sheriff of Kent to PC, Nov. 22, 1630, enclosing no. 81 I, a seditious libel.

90. PRO, S.P. 16/185/55, JPs of Rutland to PC, Feb. 26, 1630/1, enclosing no. 55 I, information of John Wilbore of Tinwell, clerk, and examinations of Nicholas Knight and William Hull.

91. See above, pp. 16-17.

ditches throwne downe, and that yt wold never be merye till some of the gentlemen were knocked downe," a sentiment which recurred frequently in the examinations of the principal suspects.[92] A number of enclosers were in fact active in the area of Oxfordshire where the rising was planned and two of them, Francis Power and Vincent Barry, were among the gentlemen whose houses were to be despoiled and whose heads Bartholomew Stere planned to cut off.[93] No doubt the others who were to be so despatched were known to be enclosers, including one Rabones, a yeoman. The dislike of gentlemen was so strong that when an attempt was made to recruit followers from among the servants of the gentry, the ringleaders felt sure of success because they believed that servants were kept like dogs and would welcome the opportunity to rise and cut their masters' throats. In recognition of the strength of the sentiment against the gentry revealed in the evidence, Attorney-General Coke considered the aim of destroying enclosures and getting corn to be only an "outward pretence." The real purpose of Bartholomew Stere was "to kill the gentlemen of that countrie and to take the spoile of them, affirming that the commons, long sithens in Spaine did rise and kill all the gentlemen in Spaine and sithens that time have lyved merrily there."[94]

The Hampshire and Oxfordshire risings differed very little in their effects from seditious words and anonymous libels. Seditious words were nothing more than expressions of opinion, and although the artisans of Hampshire and Oxfordshire tried to put their opinions into practice all their planning came to naught. The examination of this evidence leaves the impression that in the artisans of Tudor and Stuart England was a reservoir of social discontent which, filling in times of scarcity and depression, could overflow into seditious words or the planning of a rising—especially on hearing a rumor or report of a similar disorder elsewhere. This overflow would often evaporate, however, under the despairing realization of the impossibility of achievement.

The Hampshire and Oxfordshire risings are examples of rumor or

92. PRO, S.P. 12/261/15 II, examination of James Bradshawe, miller, Dec. 13, 1596; no. 15 V, examination of John Stere, Dec. 14, 1596; S.P. 12/262/4, examinations of Bartholomew Stere, Roger Symondes, and James Bradshawe, Jan. 7 and 8, 1596/7. Except where otherwise noted, the remainder of the paragraph is based on these examinations.

93. VCH: Oxfordshire, vol. VI, pp. 64, 157.

94. PRO, S.P. 14/28/64.

news of a rising in one area stimulating an outbreak elsewhere. The idea for a rising in Hampshire first came to Zachary Mansell, a weaver, when, on the road to deliver kersies to a clothier, he met with a man who told him the poor had risen in the West in protest against the price of corn. In June, 1596, there was a riot of London apprentices sparked by a dispute over the price of butter. The report of this in Oxfordshire created in Bartholomew Stere the hope that if he and his followers marched on London the apprentices would support them.[95] Furthermore, discontent and rumors of risings had been widespread in Oxfordshire for months before this particular insurrection was to take place. Roger Symondes, a carpenter, the first to inform on Stere and his fellows, reported that the poor in the markets he visited had been muttering seditiously about the scarcity, saying that they were almost famished and would soon be compelled to take food out of rich men's houses. Roger Ibill, a miller, also heard similar opinions in a number of marketplaces. Stere first got his idea for a rising when sixty to a hundred poor people from the clothmaking town of Witney assembled at Lord Norris's house to petition for relief. They threatened to cast down enclosures and knock down gentlemen if no remedy was forthcoming. This deluded Stere into believing that there were three hundred ready to rise.[96]

A report in April of 1597 of a rising in the West and the belief that the rebels would be in Norfolk within a week inspired Thomas Welles' wild talk about a rising.[97] Rumors could ignite talk and plans for other risings, but, conversely, action was often prevented by the popular belief that it had been tried before and failed. Richard Passinger, a tailor of Selborne, attempted to dissuade his companions in the Hampshire rising, saying that supplications were a better way of seeking redress for want: "yt was not lyke that smale number of poore men were lyke to doe anye good in this enterprise and that he never herde any lyke attempt to come to good."[98] Enslowe Hill was

---

95. PRO, S.P. 12/191/15 VI, examination of Zachary Mansell before Henry, Earl of Sussex, June 13, 1586; S.P. 12/262/4, examination of Roger Symondes, Jan. 8, 1596/7. For the riot in London, see E. P. Cheyney, *History of England from the Defeat of the Armada to the Death of Elizabeth*, vol. II, pp. 33-34.

96. PRO S.P. 12/261/10 II, examination of Roger Ibill, Nov. 23, 1596; nos. 15 IV and V, examinations of John Horne and John Stere, Dec. 14, 1596; S.P. 12/262/4, examinations of Bartholomew Stere, James Bradshawe, and Roger Symondes, Jan. 7 and 8, 1596/7.

97. See above, p. 37.

98. BL, Cotton MS, Vespasian F. IX, ff. 147-48, examination of Richard Passinger of Selborne, tailor, June 14, 1586.

chosen as the rendezvous for the Oxfordshire rising even though it was believed that the poor commoners who had assembled there once before had been "hanged like dogges."[99] At the same time, this belief in the past failure of insurrections inspired a sort of fatalistic bravery in a few men. One of those involved in the Hampshire rising declared: "Wee shall die for it and therefore if wee can once gett them uppe and rise I will fight for my liffe rather than be hanged."[100] Bartholomew Stere intended to go on to the bitter end, "happ what would for he coulde die but once and that he would not allwaies live like a slave."[101] In this bravado, as in his hatred of gentlemen, Stere is very reminiscent of Shakespeare's fifteenth-century rebel, Jack Cade:

> And you that love the commons, follow me
> Now show yourselves men, tis for liberty.
> We will not leave one lord, one gentleman.
> Spare none, but such as go in clouted shoow,
> For they are thrifty honest men, and such
> As would, but they dare not, take our parts.[102]

It is undoubtedly significant that many of these seditious opinions were probably uttered in alehouses. Alehouses functioned for the common people as media for dissemination of news and rumors and as gathering places where, under the influence of alcohol, opinions could be freely expressed, even to planning risings. The 1586 Hampshire rising, for example, seems to have been devised, and participants recruited, in alehouses in the vicinity of Selborne. It was in an alehouse that Thomas Byndar, the blacksmith of Purleigh, declared that the poor should pull grain out of the houses of the rich, and that "for his parte he woulde be one that would goe with them for he added that he had neither wiffe nor children therfor he cared not." In the opinion of one witness, Byndar was drunk at the time. The information against that Thomas Welles who in April, 1597, talked about a rising in Norfolk reads as if he had just come from an alehouse; at one point he is supposed to have said that the rising was delayed for the moment for want of a drummer. The shoemaker and alehousekeeper of Uppingham in Rutland who late in 1630 tried to

99. PRO, S.P. 12/262/4, examination of Roger Symondes, Jan. 8, 1596/7.
100. PRO, S.P. 12/191/20 II, interrogatories to be administered to Zachery Mansell, July 19, 1586.
101. PRO, S.P. 12/261/10 II, examination of John Stere, Dec. 5, 1596.
102. *Henry VI*, part 2, IV, ii, *ll.* 192-97.

stir up a rising to cast down enclosures was reported to have been drinking hard on the day that he attempted to rouse the poor.[103]

What were on occasion drunken outpourings received most serious attention from the government, who regarded them as a possible first step toward insurrection that gave point to the Crown's insistence on suppression of superfluous alehouses in times of scarcity. At the same time it could be argued that alcohol consumption during hard times was to the benefit of the government and the maintenance of the _status quo_. Drink permitted a relatively harmless outlet for that hatred of the rich which might otherwise have found more socially dangerous forms of expression. Of course, few English artisans were as radical as Bartholomew Stere and Thomas Byndar. Although the opinions of those who uttered seditious words were probably those of most common folk, and while the food riot could on occasion resemble an insurrection (as in the 1629 Essex riot, where talk of a march on London preceded the outbreak), most artisans probably agreed with Richard Passinger, the Selborne tailor, that in times of scarcity the best way to obtain relief was by supplication, not insurrection.

Most food riots can in fact be regarded as extreme forms of petitioning. The unemployed clothworkers of Gloucestershire, who in April of 1586 attacked ships on the Severn, disclaimed any intention of disobedience to the Queen or of harming anyone. Their sole object was to advertise their plight. In times of depression and scarcity, both local and central governments were besieged by petitions pleading for work or increases in wage assessments so that people might buy food. The frequent submission of such petitions, like the repeated outbreak of food riots, can only be understood in the context of governmental policies that responded favorably in the interest of social peace to the demands of the unemployed and hungry.

103. BL, Cotton MS, Vespasian F. IX, ff. 147-48, the examination of Richard Passinger, is a tale of one alehouse meeting after another; _Calendar of Essex Quarter Sessions Records_, Q.S. roll 131, nos. 35 and 36, examinations of witnesses to Thomas Byndar's seditious words, Sept. 20, 1595; PRO, S.P. 12/262/15 II, examinations of John Curtys, April 25, 1597; S.P. 16/185/55, JPs of Rutland to PC, Feb. 26, 1630/1; no. 55 I, information of John Wilbore and examinations of suspects.

Chapter III

The Crown's Response to Food Riots

The government's reaction to food riots went far beyond law enforcement. Determined to maintain social stability and public order, the Crown felt the necessity for meting out punishment, but its concern went much deeper. A series of measures were created which were designed to treat the symptoms of distress due to economic crisis.

Later historians have seen system in this series of emergency measures; they have labeled them as mercantilism or paternalism, either "Christian" or "feudal." They were in fact a series of *ad hoc* statutory and conciliar measures; they were the result of experience gained by enduring short-term but severe economic crises and were designed to be applied in such crises to reduce riot-producing social tensions. They were based upon no systematic working-out of social or religious ideas. Many of these measures, like the Book of Orders, came into force only during times of scarcity and depression. The others—the Poor Law and the Statute of Artificers being good examples—the government enforced actively only in crises; the rest of the time this responsibility was ignored and left to local authorities or, where applicable, to private informers, meaning in practice that systematic application of these laws ceased. The recurrent instabilities of this pre-industrial economy demanded repeated application of the same remedies. It is this repetition that has created the illusion of a policy based on a set of *a priori* philosophical assumptions. Perhaps only in 1631, under pressure of a grave social crisis, was social legislation enforced truly systematically, but that has sufficed to leave the impression of a coherent and thorough social policy.

Although in many instances the actual punishment meted out to rioters or insurrectionaries cannot be discovered, enough evidence survives to indicate the attitudes of those in authority. Toward insurrection, an undeniable attempt to overturn the *status quo*, the Crown was quite merciless. Although the 1596 Oxfordshire rising was abortive, to judge by the severity of the government's reaction it was regarded as fraught with grave danger to the established political and social order. After the suspects had been rounded up and examined by a local magistrate, the examinations were sent to the Privy Council for its instructions on the disposition of the prisoners.[1] The Council ordered the principal suspects brought to London under guard, with their hands pinioned and their legs bound under their horses' bellies; they were not to be allowed to talk to each other on the way.

By December 19 the five men most deeply involved in the plot had reached London and were warded in various prisons. A committee of the Privy Council headed by Attorney-General Coke was authorized to examine the prisoners, if necessary using torture, the usual procedure when the safety of the state was in question.[2] By the beginning of the New Year the Attorney-General had surveyed all the evidence, and he recommended that the leaders be prosecuted.[3] Three were indicted by an Oxfordshire grand jury on February 24, 1597, for levying war against the Queen. In June of 1597 all three were tried in Westminster Hall before a special commission of oyer and terminer headed by Sir John Popham, Chief Justice of the Queen's Bench. The verdicts and judgments in two of the three cases survive; both men were found guilty of high treason and sentenced to the usual barbarous punishment: hanging, then drawing and quartering. The third defendant most probably suffered the same punishment.[4]

1. PRO, S.P. 12/261/10 II, is the first series of examinations taken by William Spencer on Nov. 23, Nov. 25, and Dec. 5; no. 10 1, is Spencer's covering letter to the PC, Dec. 6, 1596.
2. *APC 1596-97*, p. 365, PC to Lord Norris, Dec. 14, 1596; pp. 373-74, PC to the A-G et al., Dec. 19, 1596.
3. PRO, S.P. 14/28/64, and *HMC Salisbury*, vol. VII, pp. 49-50.
4. PRO, K.B. 8/53, mm. 12-15, indictments of Edward Bompas, fuller, Robert Burton, bricklayer, and Richard Bradshawe, miller, Feb. 24, 1596/7; m. 16, commission of oyer and terminer to the Judges of Q.B., June 7, 1597; m. 10, writs of *certiorari* for return of indictments, June 7, 1597; m. 8, writ of *habeas corpus* to bring Bompas, Bradshawe, and Burton before the

The fate of those involved in the 1586 Hampshire rising remains unknown. Twenty-two men were implicated: eighteen of them were attached and questioned by local justices. Ten were jailed and six others sent up to London for further examination by the Privy Council. Beyond that nothing is known. Perhaps they were the men imprisoned in the Marshalsea on a matter concerned with the firing of the beacons whom the Council in April of 1587 ordered to be released on bonds for their good behavior.[5] But analogy with the Oxfordshire rising makes it more likely that at least the principal suspects suffered a much less happy fate. A fairly thorough search in the records of the Queen's Bench has failed, however, to turn up any evidence of a trial.

Tudor and Stuart governments were generally uncompromising toward insurrection, but occasionally punishment less than capital for this offense can be documented. In June, 1587, about five clothworkers from the vicinity of Sandwich in Kent planned a rising to take corn from the houses of rich men. When it came to the attention of the Privy Council, the suspects' trial was turned over to an already sitting commission of oyer and terminer—headed by Roger Manwood, Chief Baron of the Exchequer—which had been authorized to try English soldiers returned from Ostend to Kent without license.[6] At that time the Council expressed the then standard view of the function of punishment in such cases: the commission was "to proceede to their triall and execucion accordingle; or els, if the strictnes of the law did not touch their lives, yet it were expedient for the terror of the like hereafter to inflict some such extraordinarie punishment as to their discrecions should be thought fitt."[7] The upshot was that the commissioners did not find that the offense "touched the lives" of the four suspects who were tried and found guilty; taking a cue from their original charge of punishing deserters from the army, they sentenced the clothworkers to military service in the Netherlands. The ring-

judges, June 7, 1597; mm. 1-3, record of trial and conviction of Bradshawe, June 11, 1597; mm. 4-5, same for Burton, June 11, 1597. There are a number of inaccuracies in the summaries of the documents to be found in Appendix II to the *Fourth Report of the Deputy Keeper of the Public Records*, pp. 289-90. The most striking is the frequent omission of the name of Edward Bompas.

5. PRO, S.P. 12/191/20 VIII, names of those suspected of involvement in the Hampshire rising with notes as to their disposition; *APC 1587-88*, p. 14, order for release of prisoners, April 2, 1587.

6. *APC 1587-88*, p. 110, PC order to issue a commission of oyer and terminer, June 5, 1587; p. 123, PC to JPs of Essex, June 10, 1587.

7. *APC 1587-88*, p. 154, PC to commission of oyer and terminer, July 12, 1587.

leader, a weaver, was additionally sentenced to be flogged and set in the pillory.[8]

In a society without a police force, in which the militia proved inadequate to maintain internal order, the government took seriously all seditious words which might be the first step toward social turmoil. It has proven impossible to discover the usual punishment for uttering seditious words, although in one instance the accused was indicted before the quarter sessions and in another was bound over for trial at the assizes.[9] Perhaps the clearest statement of the government's attitude is to be found in the Council's response to the report of the December, 1630, attempt by William Hull, shoemaker of Uppingham, Rutland, to stir up an anti-enclosure riot. It is an attitude toward the lower orders in which contempt and fear are intermingled:

> this Board is not easily credulous of Light Reports nor apte to take impression from the vaine speeches or ejaculacions of some meane and contemptible persons. Yet because it sorts well with the care and providence of a State to prevent all occacions which ill affected persons may otherwise lay hold of under pretence and collour of the necessitie of the tymes, we have thought good hereby to will and require you forthwith to apprehend and take a more particular examinacion as well of the said Shoemaker as of such others as you shall thinke fitt.[10]

In its dealings with food rioters the Privy Council was considerably more ambivalent. On one side there was an impulse to temper justice with mercy, in the realization of the distress which produced rioting. Thus in December of 1622, after food riots along the Essex-Suffolk border, the Council recommended that proceedings in the quarter sessions be stopped, in the hope that clemency might persuade the rioters to "better conformity and obedience hereafter."[11] In many instances, also, the punishment of food rioters was left in the hands of local officials, which meant relatively lenient sentences, usually only a fine. Fifteen of the participants in the riots on the Severn in April, 1586, were fined at the Gloucestershire quarter sessions. The five

8. Clark, p. 367.

9. *Calendar of Essex Quarter Sessions Records*, Q.S. roll 136, no. 111, indictment of Henry Went of Ardleigh, weaver, for seditious words, Nov. 10, 1596; *APC 1597*, pp. 88-89, PC to sheriff of Norfolk, May 3, 1597, ordering him to bind over Thomas Welles for trial at the next assizes.

10. *APC 1630-31*, pp. 227-28, PC to JPs of Rutland, Feb. 15, 1630/1.

11. *APC 1621-23*, p. 376, PC to sheriff of Essex, Dec. 26, 1622.

Somerset laborers who seized a load of wheat at Portbury in the summer of 1622 were indicted for riot at the quarter sessions, as were the weavers of North Curry who in May of 1629 stopped barley being transported to Bridgwater. In neither of these Somerset cases can the sentence be discovered; however, in another Somerset riot case, in early 1630, twelve suspects were indicted at the quarter sessions, most of whom were fined 3s.4d. each.[12]

Often, however, the Privy Council was far more severe, due in large part to a fear of social upheaval, of which food riots were taken to be an early symptom. Lacking police power to quell rioters, as the justices' intimidation by the Gloucestershire rioters in April, 1586, demonstrated, central and local government had to depend upon punishment as a major deterrent to future violence. Such punishment occasionally occurred in the scarcity years 1594-1597. After the Kentish outbreak of food rioting early in 1596, the Council ordered the justices to fine rioters heavily enough to terrify others similarly disposed into inactivity.[13] The ringleaders of the food riots at King's Lynn, Norfolk, in 1597 were ordered to be imprisoned and then tried before the judges of assize; no doubt the judges could be expected to impose penalties harsher than a fine.[14]

It was in the depression and scarcity years of 1629-1631 that such a deterrent was felt, even by the justices of the peace, to be essential. After the November 1630 Berkshire riots attempting to stop grain transports from Newbury to Reading, twelve suspects were apprehended, "poore ragged woemen whereof manie of them weare verie aged," who had not been directly involved in the riots; they could be accused only of taking corn lying on the ground after the sacks had been cut by others. The justices nevertheless committed seven to the house of correction, and the rest were sentenced to be whipped through the streets "for a further terror and example unto others."[15]

The most severe official reaction was in response to the Essex food

---

12. *APC 1586-87*, p. 133, PC to sheriff and JPs of Gloucestershire, May 29, 1586; PRO, S.P. 12/189/50, JPs of Gloucestershire to PC, May 31, 1586; SRO, indictment roll 46, no. 93, indictment of five laborers of Portbury for riot, Aug. 28, 1622; session roll 61 i, 4 and 5 Chas I, no. 78, indictment of three weavers of North Curry; session roll 63 ii, 25, a certificate from Sir Robert Phelips concerning food riots, Feb. 24, 1629/30.

13. *APC 1595-96*, p. 334, PC to JPs of Kent, April 17, 1596.

14. *APC 1597*, pp. 88-89, PC to sheriff of Norfolk, May 3, 1597.

15. PRO, S.P. 16/176/35, Gabriel Dowse, JP, to PC, Dec. 5, 1630; S.P. 16/177/14, mayor of Newbury to PC, Dec. 15, 1630.

riot of May 22, 1629, in which the discontents of the unemployed clothworkers in the Essex new-drapery industry had come close to pushing them into insurrection. As the government well knew, in the weeks before the actual riot there had been talk of a mutiny and a march on London by the unemployed to bring their distress to the attention of the King. In this talk could be heard echoes of a long tradition in English popular risings stretching back through Ket's Rebellion of 1549 to the Peasants' Revolt of 1381: the King, if he were made aware of them, could solve the problems of the poor; to reach his ear a rising of some sort was required. In that way the poor could bypass the evil or corrupt officials who stood between the people and their King and kept from him accurate knowledge of his subjects' distress. The unemployed in Essex distrusted the promises made by the justices at the quarter sessions that they would inform the King of conditions in the cloth industry, "for they said words would not fill the belly nor cloth the backe." It was this distrust which inspired the talk about a march on London.[16]

When the riot took place, the government regarded it with utmost seriousness. The local magistrates were ordered to have ready for sudden emergencies a number of horse and foot from the trained bands. Severe punishment was ordered for the participants, "the crime being of so high a nature and of so dangerous consequence that it amounteth to a little less than a Rebellion, wee . . . doe expect that an examplarie punishment be inflicted upon the principall offenders for the conservation of the publique peace and the deterring of others to commit the like hereafter."[17] On the day following the riot a special commission of oyer and terminer was issued for the participants' trial, a step usually reserved for the most serious disorders.[18]

In less than two weeks the commission's business had been completed. On June 1, four men were indicted for robbery in taking fifteen quarters of rye from a ship bound for Hull; the self-styled captain, a woman of Maldon, was indicted as an accessory before the fact in helping to assemble the people from Witham, Braintree, and

16. PRO, S.P. 16/141/1, JPs of Essex to PC, April 17, 1629; Bod. Lib., Firth MS c.4, pp. 494-95, petition of the weavers of Bocking and Braintree to the King, May 8, 1629.

17. *APC 1629-30*, pp. 24-25, PC to Ld. Lt. of Essex, May 23, 1629; p. 25, PC to Dep. Lts. and JPs of Essex, May 23, 1629.

18. PRO, C. 231/4, p. 537, commission of oyer and terminer to the Earl of Warwick, Lord Maynard, et al., May 23, 1629; renewed May 26, 1629, with the addition of Sir Arthur Harris.

Bocking for the purpose of the riot. All five were found guilty and sentenced to death. Four of the five were hanged the next day, while the fifth (who was subsequently reprieved) escaped from jail. A second indictment relating to the same series of events charged two tilemakers with breaking into a house in the daytime and stealing six quarters of rye; a baker was charged with being an accessory before the fact. The baker was acquitted; the tilemakers were found guilty of theft, acquitted of the housebreaking, and allowed to sue for mercy. To paraphrase a report of the commission's activities, justice and mercy were mingled, the better sort being pleased and the meaner sort terrified into submission.[19]

Although this Essex case is the only instance so far discovered of the death sentence being imposed for actions relating to a food riot, there are other surviving examples of the government's expressed need to use punishment as a means of keeping the hungry and unemployed in line. On receipt of the first report of the riots on the Newbury-Reading road in November, 1630, the Privy Council considered establishing a commission of oyer and terminer to deal with the rioters, "to the ende they may be speedily proceeded with according to their demerites, for a terror to others." This riot, like that at Essex, was regarded as tantamount to rebellion, and "if a speedy and severe course be not taken for the punishment of the offenders, the consequence may be very dangerous."[20] A commission of oyer and terminer was also proposed to try those involved in the January, 1631, food riots around Basingstoke, Hampshire, in order that they be made an example to others.[21] Finally, the series of riots in Kent during April and May of 1631 was viewed by the Privy Council as "a thing not to be passed over or indured in a well governed state without severe punishment." The justices were instructed to imprison the ringleaders as far as possible from the scenes of the riots, "that so the routes and unlawfull assemblyes of theise tumultuose and mutinouse people may be more remote from the place of their aboade whereby this disorder may be the sooner and easier quieted."[22] Three Herne rioters were

19. Bod. Lib., Firth MS c.4, pp. 503-4, Sir Thomas Fanshaw to Lord Maynard, June 4, 1629.
20. *APC 1630-31*, p. 121, PC to sheriff and JPs of Berks, Nov. 20, 1630.
21. *APC 1630-31*, p. 189, PC to JPs of Hampshire, Jan. 17, 1630/1. It is very doubtful that a commission of oyer and terminer was actually issued in this or the previous case.
22. *APC 1630-31*, pp. 321-22, PC to JPs of Kent, May 11, 1631.

summoned before the Privy Council, but their fate has not been discovered.[23]

These examples further demonstrate the severity of the depression and scarcity of 1629-1631 and the extent of the government's fear of a breakdown in public order. The failure of such attempts to alleviate the economic crisis as regulation of the food market and provision of work or relief for the unemployed contributed a good deal to the Crown's anxiety. These less than successful measures had been designed in large part to prevent food riots from occurring or at least from growing to dangerous proportions. The government now felt compelled to inflict harsher punishments. It accused the poor of ingratitude, as is indicated by directions to the mayor of Newbury on handling those arrested for participation in the November, 1630, Berkshire food riots: "their punishment ought to be the greater because it is done under pretexte of wante and povertie, wherein they are no lesse unthankfull then undutifull to his Majestie, whose Princely care of provision for the poore in this tyme of scarcitie is manifestly knowne to all his loving subjectes."[24]

The provisions made for the poor as they stood at the end of 1630 had been formulated in the reign of Elizabeth and, with only a few minor changes, were the first two Stuarts' main weapons against economic and social crisis. The means of dealing with grain scarcity were enshrined in the Book of Orders first issued on January 2, 1587, and then reissued in October of 1594, on October 26, 1595, August 3, 1596, June 1, 1608, December 22, 1622, and finally on September 28, 1630.[25] Copies of the book were normally sent to the sheriff and justices of each county, along with a royal proclamation and a Privy Council letter commanding strict enforcement.

23. *APC 1630-31*, p. 327, warrant to Anthony Blades to bring three men of Herne before the Council, May 13, 1631.

24. *APC 1630-31*, p. 122, PC to mayor of Newbury, Nov. 20, 1630.

25. Hughes and Larkin, eds., *Tudor Royal Proclamations*, vol. 2, pp. 532-34, proclamation ordering markets supplied at reasonable prices, Jan. 2, 1586/7; *APC 1586-87*, p. 278, PC letter directed to JPs in all counties of England; because of a gap in the Council Register it is impossible to date the next re-issue in 1594 precisely, but it is referred to in the re-issue of 1595 as in October; *APC 1595-96*, pp. 25-27, PC to JPs in all counties of England, Oct. 26, 1595; *APC 1596-97*, pp. 80-83, PC to same, Aug. 3, 1596; PRO, S.P. 14/73 (a book of proclamations of the reign of James I), pp. 174-76, proclamation of June 2, 1608, calendared in Steele, vol. I, p. 124, no. 1058; *Foedera*, vol. XVII, p. 429, proclamation renewing Book of Orders, Dec. 22, 1622, calendared in Steele, vol. I, p. 159, no. 1344; *Foedera*, vol. XIX, p. 95, proclamation for renewal of Book of Orders, Sept. 28, 1630, calendared in Steele, vol. I, p. 192, no. 1624.

In its essentials the Book of Orders introduced nothing particularly novel, consolidating and codifying, rather, the traditional means of dealing with grain shortage. Although Tudor and Stuart governments recognized that harvest failure was often caused by natural phenomena beyond the control of man, there was a persistent belief in government circles, shared with the consuming public, that the profiteering of corn producers and greed of middlemen were a contributory and sometimes a major cause of food scarcity. The main target of the Book of Orders was hoarding, engrossing and regrating, and nonessential use of grain; as much food as possible was to reach market and, once there, was to be sold first to the poor at low prices and in quantities sufficient to satisfy their needs.

To accomplish this, the justices had to know who within their divisions had surplus grain. The sheriff was to summon for each parish a jury of high constables, underconstables, and other honest and substantial inhabitants, including as few as possible of those were were known as major corn farmers or known to have grain to sell. These juries were to discover who had corn stored in house, barn, or elsewhere, how much each had sold and to whom and how much each had bought, from whom and at what price. They were also to ascertain the number of badgers and carriers of corn who lived in the parish, where each bought his corn and who licensed him. The number of maltsters, bakers, brewers, and tipplers in the parish was to be determined along with their names, how much grain they used weekly, and what other occupations they followed.

The justices were then to act on this information, calling before them all people with grain to spare and, after deducting seed corn and the amount necessary to support each individual's family and household until the next harvest, ordering the surplus brought to market every week in assigned quantities. Owners of surplus corn were to be bound in recognizances to observe this procedure and were subject to prosecution for any violation.

All grain was to be sold in open market except that which the justices ordered sold directly to poor artificers and day laborers who could not afford to leave their employment and travel a great distance to market. The sale of grain in the marketplace was governed by stringent regulations: at least one justice was to be present at every market to guarantee that the poor were sold corn at prices as low as the seller could be persuaded to charge; only the poor were allowed to make purchases during the first marketing hour; licensed badgers, bakers, and brewers were to buy their grain only in the open market, and were the only people allowed to buy in lots larger than four bushels; the licenses of these middlemen were to be endorsed with the quantity bought, and every fourteen days justice-appointed market supervisors were to report to the justices. The names of notorious engrossers were to be certified to the Attorney-General for future prosecution, ostensibly in the Star Chamber.

Further provisions were made for the poor. Bakers were to bake rye, barley, peas, and beans. Overseers were appointed to see that bakers and brewers conformed to the assizes of bread and ale, which regulated the quality, price, and weight or measure of these products. The making of malt from barley was restricted as nonessential; where malt could be made from oats the making of barley malt was prohibited entirely. To this end bonds were taken from all brewers, maltsters, and tipplers. Unnecessary alehouses and tippling houses were to be suppressed; those who could make a living in other trades were prohibited from being badgers, bakers, or brewers.[26]

Restrictions were also placed on the overseas trade. Grain export was prohibited and merchants shipping grain coastwise had to enter bonds not to transport it overseas. When the domestic grain scarcity was considered serious enough, foreign grain was to be imported duty-free. Often, in fact, the prohibition on export was the first step taken by the government to regulate the grain supply; this was normally instituted in anticipation of a bad harvest, while the Book of Orders usually appeared only after the actual failure of the harvest.[27]

26. The Book of Orders is printed in Bland et al., eds., *English Economic History: Select Documents*, pp. 374-80.

27. *APC 1586-87*, pp. 45-46, PC to commissioners for restraint of grain trade, Mar. 29, 1586; *HMC Salisbury*, vol. XX, p. 160, PC to Ld. Treasurer Salisbury, May 11, 1608, on the renewal of restraint on the export of grain; p. 165, signet letter to same on import of grain duty-free, May 13, 1608; the operation of the licensing system by which the export of grain was prohibited and the movement of coastal shipments regulated can be followed in documents relating to 1608, PRO, S.P. 14/32/12, Capt. William Winter to the Earl of Nottingham, Ld. Admiral, April 18, 1608; no. 39, same to the Earl of Nottingham, May 6, 1608, enclosing no. 39 I, a petition from a merchant of Southampton to be allowed to transport 80 quarters of barley to Cornwall for the relief of the poor; no. 57, Winter to Nottingham, May 29, 1608, enclosing no. 57 I, a letter from the JPs of Cornwall to permit John Luke to buy and transport grain to Cornwall for relief of the poor, and no. 57 II, a bond by William Foxall to the use of the Ld. Admiral that he will transport 100 quarters of barley into Cornwall; *HMC Salisbury*, vol. XX, p. 244, PC to Salisbury, Sept. 22, 1608, to license John Elliot to buy and transport 500 quarters of corn for supply for the poor of Tenterden with bonds to be taken for his performance of this task; p. 219, Winter to Salisbury, July 18, 1608; *Foedera*, vol. XIX, p. 170, proclamation prohibiting export of grain, June 13, 1630, calendared in Steele, vol. I, p. 190, no. 1610.

Provision of work or relief for the unemployed was also included in the Book of Orders. The justices were first to try to persuade employers "by good and politic means" to keep their poor workmen employed. Able-bodied unemployed were to be set to work upon raw materials provided through the poor rates (locally assessed taxes to provide funds to assist the poor).

A variety of measures supplementary to the Book of Orders were created, largely to deal with severe unemployment in the cloth industry. Whenever a stop in the overseas sales of English cloth threatened, the government's first response was to try to maintain employment by pressure on exporting merchants to continue purchases and on clothiers to continue production although they had no immediate market for the cloth. Such pressures were applied most strenuously in those years when cloth-trade depression was a major cause of distress and food rioting: in 1586 and, with increasing urgency, from 1620 to 1622 and 1629 to 1631. Clothworkers still employed often suffered wage cuts, making it more difficult for them to afford food already more expensive in scarcity years. Government policy toward wage regulation as embodied in the Statute of Artificers of 1563 had subsequently to be clarified.[28]

It is clear from a reading of the statute that its intentions with regard to wages as outlined in the preamble were undercut by the clauses relating to the actual assessment of wages. The preamble states that wages should be rated according to the state of prices in the food market "and yelde unto the hyred persone both in the tyme of scarcitie and in the tyme of plentie a convenyant proporcion of wages," but the statute provided for the rating of a maximum wage, not a minimum, and although wages were to be rated annually the justices were given an out which permitted the automatic renewal of assessments year after year.[29]

The scarcity years 1594-1597 forced the government to eliminate this contradiction. Late in 1595, clothworkers in Warminster in Wiltshire, a center of the broadcloth industry, complaining of low wages and high food prices, on a number of separate occasions seized corn from carriers leaving Warminister. The Privy Council ordered

28. *Statutes of the Realm*, 5 Eliz. c.4; the most readily available text is in R. H. Tawney and E. Power, eds., *Tudor Economic Documents*, vol. 1, pp. 338-50.

29. See S. T. Bindoff, "The Making of the Statute of Artificers," in *Elizabethan Government and Society*, for the best account of many of the contradictions in this statute.

the Wiltshire justices to see that the clothworkers received a reasonable increase in wages.[30] In 1598 Parliament passed a measure
clarifying the Statute of Artificers. The statute of 1598 asserted in no
uncertain terms that wages should be rated to reflect need in times of
plenty or scarcity.[31]

Another such statute was passed in the first year of James I's reign.
Its avowed aim was to remedy abuse in the cloth industry, where
wages had not been rated on a sliding scale according to plenty or
scarcity. Unlike the original statute of 1563, that of 1603 ordered
assessment of minimum wages for clothworkers to reflect the state of
the economy. Penalties were to be imposed on clothiers who paid less
than the assessed minimum. For every offense the clothier was to pay
10s. to the aggrieved party. To insure that the assessment genuinely
met the workers' minimum needs, no justice of the peace who was
also a clothier was to be involved in rating cloth-industry wages.[32]

This legislative activity armed the Privy Council with a wage policy
that could be applied during future cloth-industry depressions. The
scarcity of 1594-1597 also equipped the government with a statutory
means for dealing with unemployment. Although the Poor Law of
1598 was designed largely to relieve the impotent poor, it also
contained a provision that the overseers of the poor in every parish
could by means of the poor rate "rayse wekely or otherwise . . . a
convenyent stocke of flaxe, hempe, wooll, thread, iron and other
necessary ware and stuffe to sett the poore on worke."[33] During future
depressions this would be utilized in an attempt to relieve unemployed clothworkers, as would the authority granted to the justices of
the peace by this statute to rate neighboring parishes to relieve areas
with an extraordinary number of poor.

Although the task of enforcing all these emergency measures was
put squarely on the shoulders of the justices of the peace, the Privy
Council assumed ultimate responsibility for supervising their activities. The judges of assize acted as "the indispensible nexus of

30. *APC 1595-96*, pp. 43-44, PC to JPs of Wilts, Nov. 1, 1595.

31. *Statutes of the Realm*, 39 Eliz. c.12.

32. *Statutes of the Realm*, 1 Jas. I c.6; see also Supple, pp. 26-27, and R. H. Tawney, "The
Assessment of Wages in England by the Justices of the Peace," in *Wage Regulation in Pre-
Industrial England*, pp. 69-78.

33. *Statutes of the Realm*, 39 Eliz. c.3; see Tawney and Power, vol. 2, pp. 346-54; a good
modern introduction to sixteenth-century poor relief is J. Pound, *Poverty and Vagrancy in Tudor
England*.

communication between Privy Council at Westminster and local government."[34] The Book of Orders specified that the justices of the peace in each county were to submit to the Privy Council monthly reports on their activities in enforcing its provisions. In addition, frequent though irregular communication took place between the Council and the justices, particularly with regard to the state of the cloth industry and the living conditions and behavior of clothworkers. In times of distress, when the judges of assize went on their twice-yearly circuits they were charged by the Lord Keeper to insure that the Book of Orders was enforced, and they often assumed responsibility as well for inquiring into the state of the cloth trade.[35]

To describe the frantic activity of Privy Council, judges, and local magistrates in time of harvest failure and unemployment is easier than to measure their success. If by success is meant the actual provision of food for the hungry and work and relief for the unemployed, then to provide a straightforward determination is difficult. For most of the scarcity years between 1586 and 1631, sufficient numbers of certificates produced by the justices survive to justify one incontrovertible conclusion—the justices of the peace consistently and conscientiously enforced those aspects of the Book of Orders intended to insure that stocks of grain in private hands were surveyed and brought to market, the market supervised, and the needs of the poor attended to first.

In many instances, as the Book of Orders had anticipated, it was found more practical to sell food to the poor in their own home parishes than to compel them to come to market. The justices often supplemented the operation of the Council's directions by encouraging those with money or grain to provide low-cost food for the poor. It is impossible to demonstrate that the Book of Orders was enforced by the justices in every particular—doubtless a number of its complex provisions were ignored—but there can be little question that the essential aim of the regulations was agreeable to local officials. The justices were quite willing to modify application of the Book of Orders

---

34. T. G. Barnes, ed., *Somerset Assize Orders, 1629-1640*, p. xx. This introduction provides a good concise account of the activities of the judges.

35. W. P. Baildon, ed., *Les Reportes del Cases in Camera Stellata 1593 to 1609 of John Hawarde*: pp. 19-21, Ld. Keeper's charge to the judges, June 3, 1595; pp. 56-58, charge to judges, July 1, 1596; pp. 367-69, charge to judges, June 16, 1608; *Somerset Assize Orders, 1629-1640*, p. 57, charge to the judges, Hil. 1630/1.

in the light of local experience to obtain greater efficiency in providing food for the poor and thereby maintaining good order.[36]

It is true that on the renewals of the Book of Orders in October of 1595 and August of 1596 the justices themselves were included among the grain hoarders blamed for the continuing high prices and scarcity.[37] Moreover, when after the renewal of 1596 the Council wrote to the Archbishop of Canterbury attributing the scarcity to a lack of Christian charity and an excess of covetousness in hoarders and engrossers of grain, the justices of the peace were cited as among their number. The purpose of the letter was to enlist the aid of the pulpit in urging obedience to the Book of Orders. Preachers throughout the province of Canterbury were to admonish owners of corn about their unChristian dealings; the richer sort were to be encouraged to perform various charitable deeds for the relief of the poor.[38]

Some justices may have deserved such castigation, but there is no evidence that dereliction of duty was widespread; indeed, on only one other occasion—during the desperate months following the 1630 harvest failure—were such charges made. It is much more probable that these accusations and exhortations demonstrate the seriousness of the situation and the government's desperation in the face of an unprecedented string of bad harvests. The justices, like cornbroggers, millers, maltsters, and brewers, became a convenient scapegoat.

36. This conclusion is based upon the study of all surviving certificates received from local magistrates to be found in the State Papers and covering the scarcity years between 1586 and 1631. There are too many to list but they can be tracked down by using the relevant volumes of the *Calendar of State Papers, Domestic.* There are also some other sources which indicate the procedures utilized by the justices to supervise their subordinates: see, for example, SRO, Phelips MS (DD/PH) 212, no. 56, account of proceedings to enforce Book of Orders in the division of Sir Robert Phelips and Sir Edward Hext, JPs of Somerset, Feb. 28, 1622/3; PH 222, no. 91, resolution of the JPs assembled at Wells for the execution of the Book of Orders, Jan. 4, 1622/3. See also A. Fletcher, *A County Community in Peace and War: Sussex 1600-1660,* pp. 147-52, for the activities of the Sussex JPs in time of dearth and for their modifications of conciliar directives in order to meet local needs. I do feel, however, that the author's conclusion, that these modifications involve ignoring Council orders, is too strong, especially since the main one—provision of food at home for the poor—is allowed in the Book of Orders. In addition, the evidence for these modifications is contained in the JPs' reports to the PC in the *State Papers, Domestic.*

37. *APC 1595-96,* pp. 25-27, and *APC 1596-97,* pp. 80-83.

38. *APC 1596-97,* pp. 94-96, PC to the Archbishop of Canterbury, Aug. 8, 1596; Francis Peck, ed., *Desiderata Curiosa,* vol. I, pp. 172-73, John Whitgift, Archbishop of Canterbury, to the Bishop of Lincoln, Aug. 10, 1596; see also pp. 168-69 for a slightly earlier example, May 27, 1595.

Accusations served, moreover, as a spur to greater judicial activity. The available evidence indicates that the Book of Orders was a fairly efficient instrument for redistributing available food supplies; it struck hard at consumption and waste of grain in less than essential products and at those symptoms of food shortage—hoarding and the like—which often exacerbated already serious situations.

The Book of Orders could not produce miracles, the creation of foodstuffs where none existed, but, by and large, miracles were not needed. Sufficient supplies of food seem to have been available so that redistribution according to the Book of Orders and grain transfer from areas with surpluses to those with shortages probably sufficed to meet most emergencies. Grain movement authorized by the Privy Council, particularly into urban areas like London and Bristol and to places enduring scarcity, probably prevented more riots than it provoked. Furthermore, even in the most severe years import of foreign grain no doubt sufficed to stave off real disaster.[39] In all the surviving reports from the justices not one mentions actual starvation. Malnutrition must have been widespread in scarcity years and susceptibility to certain diseases thereby increased, thus pushing up the death rate, and some poor undoubtedly did starve to death, especially in the northern counties of Westmorland and Cumberland where the situation in 1597 and again in 1623 could possibly be described as a *crise de subsistance*.[40] But the rest of England, even in the 1590s, seems to have escaped *crises de subsistance* on the scale experienced in early modern France. The irony of the situation was that those genuinely starving in the remote counties of the Northwest did not riot to bring their plight to the attention of the government in London. It was the hungry and unemployed in the economically more developed South and West who rioted and thereby gained the Crown's undivided attention.

The government's emergency measures to provide work and relief were not fully tested until the depressions of the early seventeenth century. In 1586 pressure was successfully exerted on clothiers to continue producing and on the Merchant Adventurers to continue buying cloth, but the depression was short-lived enough to leave the

39. The evidence for heavy import of foreign grain is surveyed in Cheyney, vol. II, pp. 3-23.
40. A. B. Appleby, "Disease or Famine? Mortality in Cumberland and Westmorland, 1580-1640," *Econ. H.R.*, 2nd ser., XXVI (1973): 403-32.

impression that the success of this move was merely fortuitous.[41] Between 1594 and 1597 the Council occasionally involved itself with questions of employment and wages, but most of the surviving evidence indicates that at that time lack of food was the major problem.[42] Conversely, 1620-1623 and 1629-1631 were years in which questions of employment, wages, and relief for clothworkers took first place. Despite strenuous efforts by Privy Council, judges of assize, and justices of the peace to enforce the existing measures, there are indications that they experienced increasing difficulty in dealing with the large-scale unemployment and destitution resulting from stops in the cloth trade.

In the spring of 1620 the first signs of depression appeared in the West. At the Wiltshire quarter sessions a large number of unemployed weavers, fullers, and spinners complained to the justices that the clothiers had ceased to trade, leaving 132 looms idle. To provide relief the justices put pressure on the clothiers to keep the poor employed, but they expressed skepticism about the success of this expedient. Their main hope was that the Council would take "some spedie course therein" to see that trade was started again.[43] Late in the year the workers in a number of Wiltshire clothmaking centers petitioned the Council: they complained that the clothiers continued to "put off their workmen" despite the efforts of the justices, and they implored that the government would take remedial steps.[44]

In response, the Council established a committee to investigate the state of the industry. The committee took evidence from those Wiltshire clothiers and justices who were in London at the time, as well as from certain London merchants. In the end, the Council ordered the Merchant Adventurers to buy the Wiltshire cloth then stored in Blackwell Hall. At the same time, the Wiltshire justices were instructed to persuade clothiers to rehire their workers. Those clothiers who refused to cooperate were to be certified to the Council. If

41. PRO, S.P. 12/189/50, JPs of Gloucestershire to PC, May 31, 1586; *APC 1586-87*, pp. 93-94, PC to sheriff and JPs of Somerset, May 6, 1586; pp. 272-75, PC to Ld. Lts., sheriffs, and JPs of Somerset, Gloucestershire, and Wilts, Dec. 24, 1586; Gould, "Crisis in the Export Trade," pp. 215, 220.

42. *APC 1595-96*, pp. 43-44, PC to JP of Wilts on the wages of Warminster clothworkers, Nov. 1, 1595; pp. 88-89, PC to mayor of Norwich on putting the poor to work, Nov. 26, 1595.

43. PRO, S.P. 14/115/20, JPs of Wilts to PC, May 11, 1620.

44. PRO, S.P. 14/115/28, petition of the weavers of Bromham, Chippenham, and Calne in Wiltshire to PC [? May], 1620.

there were found to be more unemployed than the clothiers could handle, then the justices were to put into execution the provisions of the Poor Law for raising stocks to put the poor to work.[45]

This Council order was renewed in 1622; this time, because the depression had spread, it was directed to all the principal clothmaking centers.[46] At the 1622 Easter quarter sessions the Wiltshire justices were again petitioned by the unemployed. One petition came from the spinners and weavers of Rowde, who complained that they were on the verge of starvation and begged that the justices might find them work. Another came from the inhabitants of Bromham, who claimed to be in miserable distress and likely to perish if relief were not quickly forthcoming. All forty-four looms in Bromham parish—each, according to the petitioners, employing twenty people in spinning, carding, weaving, and other work—were stopped because of lack of work. The Wiltshire justices informed the Council that despite strong urging the clothiers had refused to rehire their workers. A survey had been taken to ascertain the number of unemployed, and they were found to be "many more than could be relieved by any course within our powers." The Council's response to the evident failure of its policy was to provide more of the same. Diligence was urged, and the justices of Wiltshire were reminded of the measures already announced. The poor of every parish were to be set to work and relieved by the poor rates, toward which abler inhabitants were to contribute larger than normal shares.[47]

Throughout 1622, as the depression spread, similar developments took place in the other broadclothmaking counties. At Oxford on March 6 and at Gloucester on March 13, the judges of assize and justices of the peace were petitioned by unemployed clothworkers seeking relief. The judges attempted to press employers into rehiring their workmen. The clothiers in both counties replied that they were unable to keep their business going; they already had large stocks of unsold cloth that had been accumulating for as long as a year; unless they could sell the cloth it was impossible to maintain production.[48]

45. *APC 1619-21*, pp. 192-93, order setting up a committee to investigate the state of the Wilts cloth industry, May 12, 1620 (see also pp. 200-201); pp. 205-6, PC to JPs of Wilts, May 29, 1620.
46. *APC 1621-23*, pp. 131-33, PC to JPs of clothmaking counties, Feb. 9, 1621/2.
47. WRO, Q.S. Gt. Roll, Eas. 1622, nos. 249 and 250; PRO, S.P. 14/129/79, JPs of Wilts to PC, April 30, 1622; *APC 1621-23*, pp. 214-15, PC to sheriff and JPs of Wilts, May 8, 1622.
48. PRO, S.P. 14/128/49, Humphrey Wynche and William Jones, judges of assize, to PC,

The justices of Gloucestershire were no more able than those of Wiltshire to deal with the consequences of massive unemployment. It was reported that the unemployed poor "through want doe already steale and are like to starve or doe worse." Their number was so great that it was impossible to relieve them "by raisinge of publique stockes for their imployment in worke." The only way to help them was to maintain their normal employment, to which end the justices requested that the Council provide vent for the clothiers' product, "otherwise the miserye of our Countye wilbe very greate."[49] This sentiment was echoed by the judges of assize, who, finding it impossible to compel the clothiers to take back their workers when they had no sale for their cloth, referred the whole matter back to the Privy Council: "Craveinge pardon for our bouldnes, wee humbly leave this greate and weighty cause to your grave and juditious consideration."[50]

Three months later the justices of Gloucestershire were still reporting the same bleak conditions. The clothiers were finding it increasingly difficult to sell their cloth and, as a consequence, "the complaintes of the weavers and other poore workefolkes dependinge uppon the trade of clothinge . . . doe daylie increase in that their worke and meanes of reliefe doe more and more decay." It was concluded that the county was "unable to releeve the infynite nomber of poore people residing within the same drawne hither by meanes of clothing."[51]

Suffolk was another county where the justices, despite all their efforts, had great difficulty in providing relief for the unemployed. On receipt of the Privy Council letter of February 9, 1622, instructing the local officials in a number of clothmaking counties to pressure the clothiers to keep their businesses going and to raise stocks to provide work for those who could not be reemployed, the justices of Suffolk called before them the constables of Babergh hundred (where the county's broadcloth industry was located) to hear the letter and to receive further instructions. The constables were to determine how many clothiers had given over trade altogether and how many unsold

Mar. 13, 1621/2; no. 20, JPs of Oxfordshire to PC, Mar. 6, 1621/2; no. 51, statement of Oxfordshire clothiers on the state of the cloth industry; no. 50, JPs of Gloucestershire to PC, Mar. 13, 1621/2; no. 49 I, statement of clothiers of Gloucestershire and the city of Gloucester concerning their trade, Mar. 12, 1621/2.

49. PRO, S.P. 14/128/50, JPs of Gloucestershire to PC, Mar. 13, 1621/2.
50. PRO, S.P. 14/128/49, Humphrey Wynche and William Jones to PC, Mar. 13, 1621/2.
51. PRO, S.P. 14/131/4, JPs of Gloucestershire to the PC, June 1, 1622.

cloths were on hand. In addition, the churchwardens and overseers of the poor in the three clothing towns of Babergh hundred were ordered to relieve the impotent and aged poor, "but also to have speciall care that the other which are of able bodies to be provided of meanes to maynteyne themselves by their labor."[52]

After meeting with the clothiers and receiving the findings of the constables, the justices made a report to the Council which was almost identical to those received from the western clothing counties. Many clothiers who normally set "multitudes of poore people on work" were unable to keep their trade going because they had during the last two years accumulated 4,453 unsold broadcloths. The Council was therefore requested to find a market for the cloth at reasonable prices; in the meantime, the justices would do all in their power to employ the "industrious poore in laboure."[53]

Despite such good intentions, little was done for the unemployed. About nine months later, in November of 1622, the justices again wrote to the churchwardens and overseers of the poor of the parishes in Babergh hundred. Nothing had been accomplished since the previous order to raise stocks to set the unemployed to work. The poor were still complaining of lack of work and were wandering about the countryside begging. The justices threatened that churchwardens and overseers who failed to provide employment for able-bodied poor would be punished for dereliction of duty.

One innovation in the enforcement of the Poor Law in Suffolk provides a good example of the desperate lengths to which the problem of unemployment drove the justices. The unemployed complained that the wives, children, and servants of yeomen and wealthy husbandmen were virtually monopolizing the spinning of yarn usually done by the poor. Consequently, the churchwardens and overseers in Babergh hundred were given orders that from time to time, while the depression continued, they were to persuade the clothiers to give out their spinning to the poor, and to discourage the wives of yeomen and husbandmen from taking spinning work. If that failed and the unemployed became a charge upon their parish, then all able persons

52. BL, Add. MS 39245, f. 54, JPs of Suffolk to the constables of Babergh hundred, Feb. 19, 1621/2; f. 55, JPs of Suffolk to the churchwardens and overseers of the poor of Boxford, Groton, and Edwardston, Feb. 19, 1621/2.
53. PRO, S.P. 14/128/67, JPs of Suffolk to the PC, Mar. 23, 1621/2.

whose wives, children, or servants took in such work were to be rated weekly to supply the basic necessities of the poor inhabitants.[54]

While all this was taking place, the central government had tried without success to get the Merchant Adventurers to buy their usual amounts of cloth at Blackwell Hall. This kind of pressure had met with some success in 1620 in response to complaints from Wiltshire, but when it was tried again in 1622 in the face of deepening depression, the company refused and threatened to stop trading altogether. Persuading clothiers or Merchant Adventurers to keep on at their business was ineffective beyond the very short term. As soon as their available liquid capital had been absorbed in stocks of unsold cloth, nothing could be done to keep them active in trade.

In April, 1622, a commission of investigation was established to discover the cause of the crisis and to find ways to increase overseas sales. For two months it took evidence from the Merchant Adventurers and from clothiers representing twenty-five counties. The commission's findings provided a catalogue of the various conventional explanations for trade depression. It proved unable to offer practical proposals which the government could implement to increase trade. Aside from a recommendation for the temporary loosening of the Merchant Adventurers monopoly on broadcloth exports—in the hope that more merchants in the trade would mean the export of the cloth lying unsold in Blackwell Hall and in the clothiers' storerooms—nothing could be done.[55] The heart of the matter was the collapse of continental markets; until they improved the effects of the depression had to be endured.

As this depression revealed, the government's means for dealing with unemployment were taxed to the utmost in trying to fulfill their task. The Poor Law, the only existing institution which could offer direct relief to the destitute, was particularly strained. Designed largely to relieve those in chronic need, it was put under severe pressure by a stoppage in the cloth trade, which meant that hundreds, perhaps thousands, of men were thrown out of work simultaneously

54. BL, Add. MS 39245, ff. 64-65, JPs of Suffolk to churchwardens and overseers of the poor in Babergh hundred, Nov. 16, 1622.
55. *APC 1621-23*, pp. 190-91, PC to JPs and sheriffs of twenty-five named counties, April 10, 1622; pp. 201-2, PC to certain gentlemen to be of the commission, April 23, 1622; p. 203, PC to merchant adventurers to send representatives to the commission, April 29, 1622; Supple, pp. 65-67.

within limited geographical areas. Some means of relief had to be found for them and their families.

If any thoughts had been given to alterations in policy they were quickly dismissed when harvests improved and overseas shipments of cloth resumed at something like normal levels. Given the chronic instability demonstrated by this mercantile economy, however, it was inevitable that trade stoppage would recur. The difficulties faced by government, central and local, in attempting to provide work and relief for the unemployed during the 1629-1631 depression were in all essentials a continuation of those already discussed for 1620-1623. While these problems were compounded by the harvest failure in 1630, it is quite clear from the reports sent to the Privy Council that the prime difficulty was unemployment.

From Berkshire it was reported in December, 1630, that the makers of dyed cloth had no vent for their cloth and "in that respect the poore want worke and thereby want money to buy corne."[56] Petitions were presented to the Council by the mayors of Reading and Newbury, claiming that the manufacture of colored cloth was in decay because of restrictions placed on the export trade, a result of the dispute with the Dutch about the tare; many poor people were "left destitute of worke and ymployment to their utter ruine." The Privy Council then relented somewhat, by permitting merchants who were not members of the Merchant Adventurers to trade colored cloths to ports other than the Company's mart towns.[57] It was many months before any improvement occurred; in February, 1631, the clothiers of Reading were complaining that trade was as bad as it had been in 1622. At Newbury the cloth industry remained depressed into May of 1631, with production half of normal and the poor rates overburdened with unemployed.[58]

The problems in Berkshire were aggravated by the harvest failure of 1630. The magistrates did what they could to supply the needs of the unemployed; some grain was sold at a shilling a bushel lower than market price to those poor who could only afford to buy such small quantitites as pecks and half-pecks. The burgesses of Reading made

56. PRO, S.P. 16/177/52, JPs of Berks to PC, Dec. 28, 1630.
57. *Reading Records*, vol. 3, p. 44, Dec. 20, 1630; *APC 1630-31*, p. 174, council order on the export of dyed broadcloth, Dec. 31, 1630.
58. *Reading Records*, vol. 3, p. 47, Feb. 15, 1630/1; PRO, S.P. 16/192/14 II, JPs of Newbury to sheriff of Berks, May 16, 1631.

voluntary contributions to buy grain to sell to the poor below market price. It was claimed in the spring of 1631, however, that only private charity kept the unemployed clothworkers of Reading from starvation.[59]

Similar conditions existed in the kerseymaking areas of Hampshire. In December, 1630, it was reported by a justice that "the dayly complaintes of the poore about me so fill my eares with their miserable wants who at this present are like to perishe with their families for want of worke to maintaine their charge." Corn was being brought to market, as provided by the Book of Orders, but "the poore wantinge worke they had no money to buy and so lack bread." Unemployment resulted from the merchants' refusal to buy cloth from the clothiers.[60] Early in 1631 the justices of Hampshire submitted a further report indicating that it was impossible to provide work for the poor: "we are streightly required to see that clothiers keepe their workmen and people in imploiment which in this case we cannot tell how to helpe."[61] At Basingstoke the decay of trade had reduced to dependence on "the almes of the parish" 60 households—totaling 300 people—who normally earned livings in weaving, spinning, and other clothing trades.[62]

These conditions persisted throughout the spring of 1631. Despite pressure from the justices, the Hampshire clothiers refused to rehire their workers until they had a market for their cloth. Unemployment remained so widespread that the justices, who had already increased the rates for poor relief, did not know how to remedy the situation unless the Council took steps to revive the cloth trade. In July, 1631, 500 unemployed were reported in desperate need of relief at Winchester. The judges of assize ordered an increase in the poor rates to raise stocks to set them to work but as late as February of 1632 no effective relief had been provided.[63]

59. PRO, S.P. 16/182/18, JPs of Berks to PC, Jan. 20, 1630/1; Reading Records, vol. 3, p. 45, Jan. 18, 1630/1; S.P. 16/191/40 I, JPs of Reading division to sheriff of Berks, April 30, 1631.

60. S.P. 16/176/36, Thomas Jenoise, JP, to Viscount Conway, Lord President of the Council, Dec. 6, 1630.

61 PRO, S.P. 16/182/45, JPs of Hants to PC, Jan. 12, 1630/1.

62. PRO, S.P. 16/182/45 I, petition of clothiers of Basingstoke to JPs of Hants.

63. PRO, S.P. 16/185/23, JPs of Hants to sheriff, Mar. 3, 1630/1; S.P. 16/188/55, JPs of Hants to sheriff, April 12, 1631; S.P. 16/189/43, bailiffs of Basingstoke to sheriff of Hants, April 27, 1631; Assizes 24/20, f. 31, order of judges of assize, July 24, 1631; f. 44, order of judges of assize, Feb. 23, 1631/2.

On the other side of the country, in East Anglia, conditions were equally bad from late 1630 through the first half of 1631. In December, 1630, the mayor of Norwich informed the Privy Council of conditions in the city.

The scarcety and dearth of corne and other victualls lyeth so heavy upon the poore amongest us, whose number by reason thereof and of the want of trade and consequently of meanes to sett them on worke doth so increase as wee [the magistrates] . . . though formerly rated for their relief at an exceedinge height are now enforced to sett our selves at a treble weekely rate, and to tax all other the citizens and Inhabitants of this City to pay weekely twyce so much as they formerly paid.[64]

The situation at Norwich remained critical for months. By March of 1631 the misery of the unemployed was so great that the poor rates paid by all able inhabitants had to be trebled to supply them with food; £300 had already been spent to buy corn which was sold weekly to the poor at well below prevailing market price. A further £300 was borrowed to continue this practice, and a collection was organized among the wealthier citizens to buy even more corn. In other areas of the country, between November of 1630 and April of 1631 the price of grain was so high that "the poor laboring men" were unable to buy food. The justices therefore caused rates to be levied in order to buy grain which could be sold to the "poor artificers" at a price they could afford.[65]

In the new-drapery area of Essex and Suffolk between late 1630 and the middle of 1631 a difficult situation also existed—the result of grain scarcity coming on top of continuing cloth-trade depression. After the harvest failure the justices of Essex made strenuous efforts to see that corn was transported from those areas within the county which had a surplus in order to supply the markets of the main clothing areas. The justices were also successful in compelling the principal inhabitants of various parishes to buy corn and sell it to the

64. PRO, S.P. 16/177/55, mayor and aldermen of Norwich to PC, Dec. 30, 1630.
65. PRO, S.P. 16/186/26, mayor and aldermen of Norwich to PC, Mar. 4, 1630/1; the *Minutes of the Norwich Court of Mayoralty, 1630-31*, ed. W. L. Sasche, provide a remarkably detailed picture of the strenuous efforts by the Norwich magistrates to provide low-cost food for the poor. For conditions elsewhere in Norfolk, see: PRO, S.P. 16/186/16, sheriff of Norfolk to PC, Mar. 3, 1630/1; S.P. 16/190/20, JPs of Norfolk to the sheriff, May 3, 1631; S.P. 16/191/44, sheriff of Norfolk to Chief Justice Hide, May 16, 1631. Certificates of Norfolk JPs to the sheriff are: S.P. 16/191/78, May 20, 1631; no. 79, May 20, 1631; S.P. 16/192/79, May 31, 1631; S.P. 16/193/40, June 7, 1631; no. 74, June 12, 1631; no. 88, June 14, 1631; S.P. 16/195/46, June, 1631; no. 47, June, 1631.

poor at one to two shillings a bushel below the market price.[66] Nonetheless, it was soon apparent that the supply of grain in the county was very limited. At Colchester in February, 1631, the poor clothworkers were ready "to famish and to commit outrage" because of a lack of corn.[67] The justices of the division within which Colchester was located were able to aid the town bailiffs in supplying their market with grain and in pressuring corn owners to supply the market on a regular basis, but they feared that the supply would be insufficient.

By April the poor of Essex and Suffolk were still suffering greatly as a result of the high price of corn; those in greatest difficulty were the new-drapery clothworkers, whom the clothiers could not put on work. In the spring of 1631 so many were unemployed in the new-drapery town of Sudbury that the justices were at a loss to provide relief unless the Council could pressure merchants to buy the large stock of unsold cloth on the clothiers' hands.[68]

This quite representative sample of the available evidence demonstrates the difficulty in stating categorically the degree of success enjoyed by the Crown's policy in providing food, work, and relief. It is, for example, difficult to uncover the reality behind that oft-repeated refrain in the reports of the justices that the number of the unemployed in an area was so great that little relief could be provided for them. How much of this was accurate reporting of conditions, and how much hyperbole designed to shift responsibility for action onto the Council and to exert pressure to get something done to revive trade? It is probable, moreover, that organized private charity and unsystematic alms-giving, subjects beyond the scope of this work, were of vital importance in sustaining the unemployed.

It is certain that by late 1630 the Crown viewed its own measures as having failed. The situation was regarded as serious enough to demand a search for scapegoats, the usual resort of the government when frustrated in the exercise of its will. The Elizabethan Book of Orders, with some revisions, had been renewed in September of 1630 on news of the harvest failure. In November the Privy Council began

66. Certificates of Essex JPs to the PC are: PRO, S.P. 16/177/32, Dec. 21, 1630; no. 43, Dec. 29, 1630; S.P. 16/182/20, Jan. 7, 1630/1; no. 67, Jan. 18, 1630/1; no. 68, Jan. 18, 1630/1.
67. PRO, S.P. 16/184/30, bailiffs of Colchester to PC, Feb. 7, 1630/1.
68. PRO, S.P. 16/187/39, JPs of Essex to PC, Mar. 26, 1631; S.P. 16/188/92, JPs of Essex to PC, April 19, 1631; S.P. 16/190/54, JPs of Suffolk to PC, May 9, 1631.

to lash out at the justices of the peace for their lack of activity in applying these measures and for their failure to submit the required reports to Westminster. Before the end of the year the justices were being accused of total negligence in failing to enforce the Book of Orders.[69]

Surviving certificates produced by the justices of the peace indicate that these accusations had no basis in fact. The justices were merely serving as whipping-boys for the Council. In the eyes of the Crown, the success of its emergency policy was not measured by the number of people fed at prices they could afford, reemployed in their trades, or provided with some sort of relief; rather, success was gauged by the degree to which social tensions were reduced and riot or insurrection thereby prevented. It is of course obvious that provision of basic necessities and reduction of social tensions were closely connected, but to the English government of the period it was the latter which really mattered. Thus in January, 1631, when the Crown introduced a new Book of Orders as a solution to the chronic social problems which plagued English society, the failure of the Elizabethan Book of Orders was expressed as its inability to prevent disorder.[70]

Prevention or neutralization of disorder, especially in the cloth-making areas, had always been the central aim of the remedies applied in times of economic dislocation, as can be demonstrated by an examination of the actions and statements of Elizabethan and early Stuart governments. Contemporary wisdom in the Tudor period was summed up in the well-known opinion of William Cecil that cloth-making in the kingdom ought to be decreased, because "the people that depend upon makying of cloth ar worss condition to be quyetly governed than the husband men."[71] It can be argued that the actions of the government were intended to combine Christian charity and a desire for good order; or, as the Privy Council stated in a letter to the justices of Somerset in 1586 ordering them to provide work for unemployed clothworkers, it was "a matter not onlie full of pittie in respect of the people but of dangerous consequence to the State if

---

69. *APC 1630-31*, p. 116, PC to sheriffs of all counties of England, Nov. 11, 1630; pp. 131-32, PC to JPs of six counties, Nov. 30, 1630; pp. 172-73, PC to JPs of ten counties, Dec. 31, 1630.

70. *APC 1630-31*, pp. 213-15, PC to all sheriffs and the mayors of all cities and corporations in England, Jan. 31, 1630/1.

71. PRO, S.P. 12/35/33, undated memorandum by Cecil on the export trade in cloth and wool (prob. 1564) printed in Tawney and Power, vol. 2, pp. 45-47.

speedie order be not taken theirin."[72] Most of the actions and
statements of Elizabethan and early Stuart governments indicate that
Cecil's fear about the consequence of stoppages in the cloth trade—"by
lack of vent tumults will follow in clothying countreys"—weighed
much more heavily than charitable motives.[73]

The Crown was driven by fear of riot and possible insurrection. Its
response to riot or the threat of riot was not simply a call for the
restoration of good order or for the punishment of the rioters;
remedial measures were offered both to prevent riots altogether and
to reduce the likelihood of future outbreaks. This ambivalence, which
persisted throughout the late Elizabethan-early Stuart period, was
written into the Book of Orders from the outset. It is reflected in the
attempt to make a distinction between what might be called the
deserving poor and the undeserving, unemployed on the one side,
rogues and vagabonds on the other. While the Book of Orders made
positive provision for the relief of the unemployed, vagrants were to be
committed to Houses of Correction. In hard times the unemployed
workman and the vagrant were identical; life on the road was the
inevitable resort of the unemployed who went out to look for work, or
fell in desperation into begging and stealing.[74]

The Crown nonetheless continued to insist upon the distinction
between the able-bodied unemployed who stayed in their parish of
residence, and those who wandered: the Poor Law of 1598 was
matched by the vagrancy statute of that same year.[75] The greatest
significance of that statute was the circumstances of its issue. From
almost every country for which evidence survives concerning the
scarcity and depression of the 1590s came complaints that the hungry
and unemployed were wandering about the countryside raising trouble. In Norfolk, Somerset, and Kent, such "loose wandering" persons
were accused of inciting the food riots; they thereby provided the

72. *APC 1586-87*, pp. 93-94, May 6, 1586.
73. *HMC Salisbury*, vol. II, p. 251, memorandum by Cecil, April 23, 1578.
74. May own quite unsystematic survey of the printed *Reading Records*, vols. 2 and 3
(covering the years 1622 to 1631), revealed that the vast majority of strangers picked up under
the vagrancy statute or arrested for more serious crimes were artisans, including a good number
of clothworkers; the rest were mainly laborers, with a sprinkling of servants. Many of those
examined claimed to be unemployed and looking for work. For recent work which confirms and
expands on this view of vagrants, see A. L. Beier, "Vagrants and the Social Order in Elizabethan
England," *Past and Present* 64 (1974): 3-29.
75. 39 Eliz. c.4 in Tawney and Power, vol. 2, pp. 354-62.

occasion for the vagrancy statute. Edward Hext, a Somerset justice who reported graphically to Burghley on the wandering poor in his own county in 1596, introduced into Parliament (with the support of Robert Cecil in the Commons and Burghley in the Lords) some of the provisions of what ultimately became the Act for the punishment of rogues, vagabonds, and sturdy beggars.[76]

This measure reflected an unshakable association in the official mind between vagrancy and food riots. The deserving unemployed should be relieved; the vagrants who wandered about the countryside stirring up riots deserved only punishment. Whenever a food riot took place or was threatened, the call went out to punish vagrants.[77] This attitude is perhaps best summed up in the proclamation of December, 1622, which renewed the Book of Orders:

> his Majestie having thus carefully provided for Relief of his poor sort of Subjects doth declaire and strictly chardge and command that if any under pretence of Povertie and Want shall leave their ordinarie Labor or assemble together in unfit manner, or otherwise insolently behave themselves that they be corrected and punished according to their Demerits.[78]

So strong was the belief in the threat posed by the vagrant that in December of 1623, at the end of one period of depression and riot, a proclamation issued with the purpose of preventing further outbreaks of riot emphasized the need to punish vagabonds and to supply the Houses of Correction with sufficient stocks on which they could labor.[79] The disorders which brought about the issue of the new Book of Orders in 1631 were similarly attributed at least in part to failure to execute the vagrancy laws properly.[80]

Coexisting with this reaction were attempts to deal with the grievances of the rioters. In 1586, when informed of the riot against the sowing of woad in Romsey, Hampshire, the Privy Council was remarkably even-handed in its response. The landowner was to be

---

76. *HMC Salisbury*, vol. XX, p. 117, Edward Hext to the Earl of Salisbury, Mar. 30, 1608, recounting these events.

77. Two of the numerous examples of this are: *APC 1621-23*, pp. 214-15, PC to sheriff and JPs of Wilts, May 8, 1622; pp. 224-25, PC to sheriffs and JPs of nine clothing counties, May 17, 1622.

78. *Foedera*, vol. XVII, p. 429.

79. *Foedera*, vol. XVII, pp. 527-28, proclamation of Dec. 27, 1623, calendared in Steele, vol. I, p. 161, no. 1365.

80. *APC 1630-31*, pp. 213-15, PC to sheriffs of all counties in England and Wales and to all cities and corporations, Jan. 31, 1630/1.

imprisoned for disobeying the proclamation; the ringleaders of the unlawful assembly were also to be committed to prison; to remove any further sources of complaint, the justices were to see that the markets were well supplied with grain and that the clothiers gave their people work. On receiving knowledge of the anonymous libel threatening drastic action by the poor of Norwich in 1595, the Council instructed the mayor that such mutinous people were not to be tolerated and he was to confer with the other magistrates on how best to apprehend the authors of the libel; but to insure the future peace of the city he was to take steps to provide work for the poor. When the clothmakers of Warminster, Wiltshire, complaining of low wages, began to attack carts loaded with corn, the Privy Council ordered the justices to see to it that the clothiers gave the artificers a reasonable increase in wages. In the Council's opinion the workmen would then have no just cause to think themselves uncharitably dealt with, and no new "inconvenience" would occur.[81]

The government's response even to the 1596 Oxford Rising represented more than an intention to punish treason. To his first report to the Privy Council Lord Norris added a postscript in his own hand requesting that "souch good order may be takin for inclosure on the fair parte of the shere where thise styrr and commossion dyd begin as the pore may be able to lyve."[82] As a consequence one Francis Power and William Frere, Sheriff of Oxfordshire, were summoned before the Council to answer complaints against them concerning enclosure. It is unclear what, if any, action was taken against the Oxfordshire enclosers, but it has been maintained that it was as a result of this rising that Oxfordshire was included in the Enclosure Act of 1598.[83]

Positive action to provide relief was also taken after outbreaks of rioting during the depression of 1620-1622. When the judges of assize visited Oxford and Gloucester in March, 1622, the clothiers were

---

81. *APC 1586-87*, p. 91, PC to Henry Gifford, JP of Hants, May 6, 1586; PRO, S.P. 12/189/15, Gifford to PC, May 12, 1586; *APC 1595-96*, pp. 88-89, PC to mayor of Norwich, Nov. 26, 1595; pp. 43-44, PC to JPs of Wilts, Nov. 1, 1595.

82. PRO, S.P. 12/261/10, Dec. 6, 1596.

83. *APC 1596-97*, p. 449, notice of appearance of William Frere, Jan. 27, 1596/7; pp. 450-51, notice of appearance of Francis Power, Jan. 30, 1596/7; p. 455, PC to A-G on appearance of a number of gentlemen on question of enclosure, Jan. 31, 1596/7; *APC 1597*, p. 39, notice of appearance of William Frere on first Star Chamber day as provided by his bond, April 14, 1597; *VCH: Oxfordshire*, vol. VI, p. 157.

urged to continue their workers' employment, "for the stay of the present mutinous assemblies."[84] In February of that year the Council had already written to the justices in the main clothmaking counties that every effort was being made to pressure the exporting merchants into buying the cloth still on the hands of the clothiers; the justices in turn were to put pressure on the clothiers to keep their workmen employed. The reason for these steps was quite frankly stated: unless they were employed, the clothworkers would disturb the quiet and good government of the areas in which they lived.[85] After food rioting had broken out in the western broadclothmaking areas in the spring and summer of 1622, the Privy Council wrote to the justices in several counties to forestall future outbreaks. In addition to ordering strict watch and ward to be kept for the apprehension of rioters and vagrants, relief was promised. The King had directed a course for the revival of the cloth trade, but until that happy event occurred every parish was to provide stocks on which to set the poor to work, and the able inhabitants were to increase their contributions to poor relief.[86]

By this time actual riot was really not necessary in order to bring distress to the Council's attention; rumor or threat of riot, or a well-drafted petition illustrating deep distress of the kind the Council knew from experience could produce disorders, was sufficient. During periods of depression both central and local government responded positively to many such petitions. One example was the petition of the unemployed Wiltshire weavers to the Privy Council in the late spring of 1620. The authors rejected a number of alternatives open to them in their great need: "to starve is woeful, to steale ungodly and to beg unlawfull whereunto we may well add that to endure our present estate anywhere, is almost impossible." They took the only other step available: "wee most humbly even upon our knees, begge and intreat of your Lordships throughly to weigh and consider this our most lamentable condicion that if it be possible a remedy may be found that wee as forlorne wretches perrish not in the same."[87] The Council invariably took action on this kind of petition.

84. PRO, S.P. 14/128/49, Henry Wynche and William Jones, judges of KB, to PC, Mar. 13, 1621/2.

85. *APC 1621-23*, pp. 131-33, PC letter, Feb. 9, 1621/2.

86. *APC 1621-23*, pp. 224-25, PC to the JPs and sheriffs of nine clothing counties, May 17, 1622.

87. PRO, S.P. 14/115/58, petition of the weavers of Bromham, Chippenham, and Calne in Wiltshire to PC, [? May], 1620.

Two Essex examples, one from the depression in the new-draperies trade late in 1622 and the other from the depression which began in 1629, most fully illustrate the close connection of petitions, the possibility of riot, and the outbreak of riot with positive action to provide relief. Anticipating riots by the unemployed, the Council wrote to the Essex justices in December of 1622 instructing them to suppress all tumults. To forestall the clothworkers, they were to be informed that the Crown had taken steps for their relief and reemployment. On the heels of this action, riots broke out along the Essex-Suffolk border, prompting the Council to recommend leniency and a stay of prosecution in an attempt to maintain the peace. Meanwhile, the Essex justices found in a survey of the new-drapery trade that many of the workers in the main centers of the industry (Coggeshall, Braintree, and Bocking) were unemployed and in great distress. The justices were able to preserve good order for the moment by promising speedy redress for grievances, but rioting was feared unless action was taken quickly to aid the unemployed. On receiving this report, the Council summoned the clothiers to give information on the cause of depression so that a remedy for their distress could be proposed.[88]

Events between 1629 and 1631 in the new-drapery areas of Essex and Suffolk demonstrate very clearly both the close relationship between riot and the government's tension-reducing measures, and the complexity of the economic problems confronting local officials during periods of depression. In April of 1629 the justices of Essex, meeting at the quarter sessions in Chelmsford, were petitioned by Braintree and Bocking weavers, who were in great distress because of unemployment and wage-cutting. The petition asserted that the unsold cloth must be bought from the clothiers so that they could start up production again, for the weavers and their families were "not able to subsist the day." A few days later a second petition, this time from Bocking clothiers, confirmed the weavers' claims.[89]

---

88. *APC 1621-23*, pp. 371-72, PC to sheriff and Dep. Lts. of Essex, Dec. 20, 1622; p. 376, PC to sheriff of Essex, Dec. 26, 1622; PRO, S.P. 14/137/13, JPs of Essex to PC, Jan. 10, 1622/3; *APC 1621-23*, p. 392, PC to JPs of Essex, Jan. 14, 1622/3.

89. *Calendar of Essex Quarter Session Records*, Q.S. roll 266, Eas. 1629, no. 121, petition of the weavers of Braintree and Bocking (also printed in A. C. Edwards, ed., *English History from Essex Sources 1550-1750*, p. 44); no. 120, petition of the inhabitants of Bocking that mentions the previous petition of the weavers.

The weavers' petition was presented by a crowd of two hundred, among whom there was much talk of a march on London to present complaints to the King. The weavers were appeased and violence averted only when local officials, including the Earl of Warwick, the lord lieutenant, and Lord Maynard, promised that the King would be informed of the plight of the unemployed and relief would immediately be forthcoming. When the justices wrote to the Council about this business they expressed their belief that unless some remedial actions were taken quickly the clothworkers would not long remain pacified and riot would be inevitable.[90]

In reply the Council informed the justices of Essex that the King and his councillors were negotiating with the exporting merchants to purchase the unsold cloth. In the meantime, peace and order were to be maintained in the county. All disorder was to be speedily suppressed; the unemployed were not to be allowed to gather together in large and tumultuous assemblies or to wander up and down the countryside. They were to be employed either in their own trades or in any other labor available; if no work could be provided, then relief of some sort was to be given. If necessary, neighboring parishes were to be rated toward the relief of the poor in the clothmaking areas. To insure that these remedies would be effective in preserving order, the Council wrote to the ministers and churchwardens of Braintree and Bocking, requiring them to acquaint their parishioners of the steps the government had taken to provide relief.[91]

Despite this urging, little in a practical way was done to reduce tensions around Braintree and Bocking. The justices of the peace in the division informed the Council that the clothmaking parishes were incapable of employing their own poor and that they alone did not have the authority to assess neighboring parishes for the relief of the poor of Bocking and Braintree; only the justices meeting in a general quarter sessions could do that.[92] When the justices met again in the

90. PRO, S.P. 16/141/1, JPs of Essex to PC, April 17, 1629; Bod. Lib., Firth MS, c.4, pp. 494-95, petition of weavers of Bocking and Braintree to the King, May 8, 1629, which refers to the earlier events.

91. *APC 1628-29*, p. 416, PC to JP of Essex, April 29, 1629; *APC 1629-30*, pp. 4-5, PC to JPs and Dep. Lts. of Essex and Suffolk, May 5, 1629; p. 9, PC to Earl of Warwick, Ld. Lt. of Essex, May 10, 1629; Bod. Lib., Firth MS, c.4, pp. 485-86, PC to the ministers and churchwardens of Braintree and Bocking, April 18, 1629.

92. Bod. Lib., Firth MS, c.4, pp. 493-94, JPs from Braintree to PC, undated, but early in May, 1629.

middle of May little was accomplished. In their opinion, the poor rates could not support so many unemployed. In addition, they found that the people of parishes near the clothmaking areas were reluctant to pay rates for the relief of the clothworkers; many argued that they were not bound by the provisions of the Poor Law to pay for the relief of the unemployed but only for those who were "lame, impotent, old, blinde and such others as beinge poore are not able to worke." The justices had stayed proceedings until they received a legal ruling from the Crown on these difficulties, but they stated that the only possible solution would be the revival of the trade, which was in the hands of the Council.[93]

The discontent of the unemployed at the government's inaction continued to mount. Early in May, 1629, the weavers of Braintree and Bocking petitioned the King. They had hoped that the King would have been told of their plight after their petition had been submitted to the justices in April, as the magistrates had promised. In expectation of aid, the unemployed had been content to maintain themselves and their families on extremely small portions of bread. Now, finding no action taken, "they thinke theire miseries are not creditted which they beseech your Majestye to consider that they may not starve in tyme of plentie."[94]

In response the Crown continued to apply its standard measures for the reduction of social tensions. Periodically throughout May, the English and foreign merchants who traded to France were summoned before the Council and requested to double their purchases of new draperies; the merchants each time refused to buy more cloth, citing lack of sale for their imported French wine and harassment in French ports.[95] To provide temporary relief until trade was restored, a proclamation was issued on May 17, 1629, ordering the execution of the laws for relieving the impotent poor and employing the able-bodied, because "the neglecting whereof is the Occasion of much disorder, whereby the poorer sorte growe to idleness and consequently run into many inconveniences."[96]

Particular attention was focused on Essex. In reply to the last letter

93. Bod. Lib., Firth MS, c. 4, pp. 496-97, JPs of Essex to PC, May 15, 1629.
94. Bod. Lib., Firth MS, c.4., pp. 494-95, petition of the weavers of Bocking and Braintree to the King, May 8, 1629.
95. *APC 1629-30*, p. 15, May 12, 1629; pp. 21-22, May 15, 1629.
96. *Foedera*, vol. XIX, p. 70; calendared in Steele, vol. I, p. 186, no. 1584.

from the justices, the Council on May 22 advised them that it was the opinion of the judges that justices had sufficient power under the law to raise money from better-off parishes in order to aid parishes overburdened with poor and unemployed. The justices were urged to put the proclamation for enforcement of the Poor Laws into effect "because wee understand that in your country there is more than ordinarie occation to use all diligence and industrie at this tyme." They were also reminded that the King was doing all in his power to find an outlet for the new draperies.[97]

All this activity was to no avail, for on the very day that this letter was sent to the Essex justices two or three hundred people of Bocking, Braintree, and Witham assembled at Burrow Hill and committed the "divers outrages" which resulted in the authorization of a commission of oyer and terminer to try the participants. Of course, savage punishments inflicted on some of the rioters did not end the matter; many weavers still remained unemployed. Consequently, throughout June and July of 1629 the Privy Council continued to apply pressure on the merchants to buy new draperies, a measure still being urged as late as December.[98]

The combination of punishment and pressure finally did have some effect. In a July petition to the justices of Essex the weavers of Bocking and Braintree admitted to some improvement in their condition because of increased sales of cloth. Now their complaints were of an effective reduction in their wages by the clothiers, who demanded the weaving of larger cloths but paid the old rates, and of the practice of some journeymen weavers and clothiers in taking on too many apprentices and thereby depriving the petitioners of work. In requesting the justices to forward these complaints to the King and Privy Council, the petitioners disassociated themselves from the rioters and promised to engage only in peaceful petitioning in the future: "many of our poor brethren have runn beyond compasse by violatinge his Majesties Lawes and have suffered therefore . . . we allwayes persuaded the contrary and that they would take a legall course in all humble and obedient manner, the which wee are persuaded that they will, for they are very sorrowfull for that which is done."[99]

97. *APC 1629-30*, pp. 23-24, PC to JPs and Dep. Lts. of Essex and Suffolk, May 22, 1629.
98. *APC 1629-30*, p. 44, June 5, 1629; p. 70, July 3, 1629; p. 216, Dec. 23, 1629.
99. Bod. Lib., Firth MS, c.4, pp. 504-5, petition of the weavers of Bocking and Braintree to the justices at quarter sessions [midsummer], 1629.

This petition marked a turning point in the activities of both justices and weavers. During the rest of the year the justices, on instructions from the Council, tried to devise an equitable method for rating wages and reducing the number of apprentices in the trade. The weavers remained peaceful, as they promised, but there can be little doubt that it was the violent riot of May 22 which kept Privy Council and justices attentive to the business of wages and apprentices. All signs of remissness in the justices of the peace, as had been exhibited in the question of enforcing the Poor Law in the weeks before the riot, vanished.

Wage-cutting was a standard practice by clothiers in time of depression. The clothiers reduced prices to dispose of surplus production, and then compensated by reducing the wages of the workmen.[100] Referring to the statute of James I's reign which provided for the rating of minimum wages for clothworkers according to the price of food, the Council ordered the Essex justices to determine if the clothiers were in fact demanding the weaving of larger cloths at the old rates. The justices found clear evidence that the earnings of the weavers were much reduced; but the payment structure for piecework was so complex, due to the infinite variety of the cloths, that they found it beyond their capacity to make new wage assessments. The justices did discover that one main cause for the low wages was a matter of which the weavers had complained, the excessive number of apprentices in the trade. This was encouraged by the clothiers "for by that meanes they can have theire worke done better cheape."[101]

A superfluity of apprentices and the fact that many of them did not serve a full seven-year term had long been a grievance in the new-draperies but, as some complaints of 1622 noted, the industry was not covered by the apprenticeship provisions of the 1563 Statute of Artificers.[102] Such complaints were standard responses to declining employment opportunities and normally appeared in times of depres-

100. One example from Wiltshire took place early in 1623: PRO, S.P. 14/138/54, mayor of Devizes to PC, Feb. 20, 1622/3; WRO, Q.S. Gt. Roll, Eas. 1623, no. 243; see also *HMC Various*, vol. I, p. 94.

101. PRO, S.P. 16/147/43, Earl of Warwick to PC, July 27, 1629; *APC 1629-30*, pp. 114-15, PC to Ld. Lt. and JPs of Essex, July 30, 1629; Bod. Lib., Firth MS, c.4, pp. 509-11, JPs of Essex to the judges of assize, Dec. 2, 1629.

102. PRO, S.P. 14/130/65, JPs of Essex to PC, May 13, 1622; no. 78, JPs of Suffolk and Norfolk to PC, May 15, 1622.

sion. In the broadclothmaking areas it took the form of calls for enforcement of the Statute of Artificers, since˙ it was only in trade depressions that the government took full responsibility for its enforcement:

The tendency of so many of the presentments by public agencies to fall within periods of at least local economic stress shows that their main concern was not with the enforcement of apprenticeship for its own sake, but was part of their recurrent struggle with the problems of vagrancy and poor relief.[103]

Weavers in the Essex new-drapery industry, suffering from the same situation, could not ask for enforcement of the statute, but they did request that steps be taken to limit the number of apprentices until a new parliament sat, at which time—they hoped—a statutory remedy would be forthcoming.[104] When the justices did instruct the clothiers to rid themselves of their excess apprentices, further complications ensued. A good number of apprentices were children of the poor, who under the Elizabethan Poor Laws could be bound out to masters at the direction of at least two justices of the peace. To protect the interests of such apprentices, the judges of assize prohibited their removal. This unforeseen conflict was resolved at the end of 1629 when, with the agreement of the judges, the justices resolved that poor apprentices who had been bound out as the law provided were to remain with their masters and those who had been bound out without knowledge of the justices were to be dismissed by the clothiers. The justices also guaranteed a new master—in another trade—for each dismissed apprentice.[105]

After the harvest failure of 1630 drove up the price of food in Essex and Suffolk, there were renewed complaints of wage-cutting in the new-drapery industry. At the end of September, 1630, the Privy Council instructed the justices to raise the wage assessments during "these tymes of scarcitie and dearth," as provided by the Statute of Artificers and the clothworkers' wage statute of James I's reign.[106]

---

103. M. G. Davies, *The Enforcement of English Apprenticeship 1563-1642*, p. 203.

104. Bod. Lib., Firth MS, c.4, pp. 504-5, petition of the weavers of Bocking and Braintree to the JPS at quarter sessions [midsummer], 1629.

105. This business can be followed in Bod. Lib., Firth MS, c.4, p. 508, order of the Essex quarter sessions that a clothier must put away an apprentice, Oct. 1, 1629; pp. 508-9, judges of assize to JPs of Essex, Nov. 20, 1629; pp. 509-11, JPs of Essex to judges of assize, Dec. 2, 1629; p. 512, judges of assize to JPs, Dec. 18, 1629.

106. *APC 1630-31*, p. 89, PC to JPs of Cambridge, Norfolk, Suffolk, and Essex, Sept. 29, 1630.

Whatever action the justices took at this time had little effect, for in February of 1631 a petition complaining of wage cuts was submitted to the Privy Council by Sylva Herbert, a spinner, on behalf of the combers, spinners, and weavers in the Essex and Suffolk new-drapery industry. According to this petition, the clothiers had cut the wages of the "poor artizans": one penny in every ninepence for spinners, four shillings in every twenty for weavers, and an unspecified amount for combers. The clothworkers, who had for many years supported their wives and children by their "painful labours," now found themselves compelled to sell their beds, spinning wheels, looms, and other tools to buy bread for themselves and their families.[107]

The Council sent the petition to the Sudbury aldermen and a group of Suffolk and Essex justices, who were to investigate the allegations and settle on a just assessment of wages. Evidence from the clothiers substantiated the petition; accordingly, in an assessment order the justices markedly increased the clothworkers' wages and prohibited any further reductions. In May, petitioned by three hundred poor people of Colchester, Essex, who were in distress because the clothiers had cut their wages, the Council ordered the justices to apply the new wage rates agreed to by the clothiers who employed the Sudbury clothworkers.[108] There can be little doubt that it was the memory of the great riot of 1629 which galvanized the Council and the Essex and Suffolk justices into action on receipt of the news of wage-cutting in September of 1630. The fear, frequently expressed in reports to the Council, that unemployment, low wages, and the high price of food would spark new riots among the clothworkers of Essex and Suffolk kept them active in this business throughout the early part of 1631.[109]

This series of events in Essex demonstrates a quite extraordinary commitment on the part of the government to the maintenance of good order and social peace. The riot of May 22, 1629, must have been regarded as a sign of failure; efforts were redoubled, to prevent it from happening again. Similarly, the disorders which broke out in Somerset, Berkshire, Hampshire, and Kent late in 1630 and early in 1631

107. BL, Add. MS 39245, f. 152, petition of Sylva Herbert, appended to f. 151, a copy of PC letter of Feb. 16, 1630/1.
108. *APC 1630-31*, pp. 230-31, PC to JPs of Essex and Suffolk, Feb. 16, 1630/1; PRO, S.P. 16/189/40, JPs of Essex and Suffolk to PC, April 27, 1631; no. 40 I, order made by JPs regulating wages, April 8, 1631; *APC 1630-31*, pp. 358-59, PC to JPs of Essex, May 31, 1631.
109. See above, p. 30 and pp. 65-66.

despite the government's best attempts to forestall them were regarded as signs of failure, as was the general difficulty encountered in enforcing emergency measures. All this resulted in the proclamation of the new Book of Orders on January 31, 1631, a means of maximizing future efforts to preserve social peace.

This measure was in itself insufficient to ameliorate conditions created by continuing depression and harvest failure. Hunger, unemployment, downward pressure on wages, and food riots continued into 1631. The emergency measures of the past remained in full force and the Council continued to berate the justices for their laxity and to urge them, especially in clothmaking areas, to provide work and relief to keep the poor from rioting.[110] In truth, the roots of social tension in the instability of a pre-industrial economy and the propertylessness of wage-earning artisans were beyond the reach of any government. England had to ride out these bad times, like all the previous ones, until good harvests and the resolution of the international difficulties that had disrupted cloth exports combined to restore stability.

The new Book of Orders however, was not intended to deal directly with this 1631 crisis; instead, it was designed to treat and thereby to moderate the symptoms of poverty before future economic crises occurred. To achieve this, it proposed regular enforcement, under the close supervision of the judges of assize, of the numerous duties laid upon local magistrates. There was nothing new in the details of the program. All had been subjects of statutes and Council orders since the reign of Elizabeth. The novelty lay in putting all of the justices' duties into one book, and in the aim of sustained application. This was intended to supplement the series of crisis-oriented measures with a policy applied continuously beyond the occasion of any particular depression.

Until this time the social policy of the Crown had been designed only to meet crises. As F. J. Fisher has convincingly demonstrated, all the landmark items of Elizabethan social and economic legislation were responses to economic crisis—depression, food scarcity, and rioting.[111] While this legislation was no doubt intended to be enforced

---

110. See, for example, *APC 1630-31*, pp. 262-63, PC to JPs of Essex, Mar. 18, 1630/1; p. 277, PC to sheriffs and JPs of all counties in England, Mar. 31, 1631; pp. 303-4, PC to JPs of Berks and mayor of Reading, April 23, 1631; PRO, S.P. 16/188/55, JPs of Hants to sheriff, April 12, 1631; S.P. 16/190/54, JPs of Suffolk to PC, May 9, 1631.

111. Fisher, "Commerical Trends and Policy."

regularly, practice until 1631 indicates that the government assumed responsibility for enforcement only sporadically, in times of economic crisis, in order to supplement the Book of Orders.[112]

Beginning with the Caroline Book of Orders, most of the statutes were to be enforced regularly. Since the occasion for the introduction of this new measure was a period of unemployment and scarcity, heavy emphasis was laid upon enforcement of the Poor Law and the vagrancy statutes.[113] The method of supervision was modeled on the earlier Book of Orders: the justices of each division within a county were to hold monthly petty sessions in which their subordinate officers (constables, churchwardens, overseers of the poor) reported on their proceedings. Then a quarterly report from each division was given to the sheriff, who sent them on to the judges of assize. It was the judges' responsibility to supervise the justices and to forward to the Privy Council their certificates and the quarterly reports. This machinery operated continuously during the next nine years, a remarkable commitment to the preservation of good order and social peace for that or any other time. If the evidence from Somerset is at all typical, this effort did result in more effective enforcement of the Poor Law; the poor rates were doubled or even tripled, providing increased means for relieving both the impotent and the able-bodied poor. There was also a marked rise in the number of poor children bound out as apprentices. Of course, the more repressive side of such legislation, especially the vagrancy statute, was also more efficiently enforced.[114]

Such long-term commitment by both Crown and local government to a social program—until virtually the eve of Civil War—argues a common attitude toward certain basic problems. Poverty, unemploy-

---

112. This is certainly the conclusion toward which the works of B. E. Supple and M. G. Davies point.

113. *APC 1630-31*, pp. 213-15, PC to sheriffs of all counties of England and Wales and to all cities and corporate towns, Jan. 31, 1630/1, a covering letter for the Book of Orders which strongly emphasizes these points. The Crown also remained concerned with continuing the policy of minimum wages for clothworkers: see PRO, P.C. 2/42, p. 443, PC to judges of assize, March 5, 1631/2, ordering that the wages of poor spinners were to be increased in accord with the Statute of Artificers and the Statute of the first year of James I's reign.

114. T. G. Barnes, *Somerset 1625-1640: A County's Government during the "Personal Rule,"* pp. 174-202. This book contains the best and most recent discussion of the Caroline Book of Orders.

ment, hunger, and their consequent social tensions were as immediate to the men of the 1630s—Privy Councillors and justices of the peace, future Royalists and future Parliamentarians—as they had been to their Elizabethan predecessors. Attention was focused on them by food riots and by the great riots of 1626-1632 known collectively as the Western Rising. Maintenance of a "paternalistic" social policy was a small enough price to pay for insurance against uncontrolled social tensions producing ungovernable violence. Thus, most propertied members of society were willing to accept that policy in order to keep the propertyless quiescent.

In retrospect, perhaps, the traditional responses of the government inherited from Elizabethan times seem more successful than they did in 1631. Given the extent of unemployment and distress during the various crises between 1586 and 1631, food rioting was less frequent than might have been expected. By being seen to respond to the needs of the hungry and unemployed, and by shifting the blame for the scarcity onto those who were already objects of popular animosity, the Crown and its agents may have gained a sufficient psychological advantage to reduce social tension. This conclusion gains considerable credence in the light of E. P. Thompson's observation that the memory of the Elizabethan Book of Orders survived into the eighteenth century and provided a good deal of the content of the moral economy directing the behavior of the crowd over one hundred years after its last official reissue.

Chapter IV

The Western Rising, 1626-1632

In the period 1626-1632, the royal forests of western England were the scene of a series of massive anti-enclosure riots. Close to insurrections in intensity, duration, and the numbers of people involved, these outbreaks have been aptly named "The Western Rising." The disorders of the Western Rising took place in Gillingham Forest on the Wiltshire-Dorset border, Braydon Forest in Wiltshire, and Dean Forest in Gloucestershire. Although not strictly in the West, the concurrent riots in Feckenham Forest in Worcestershire and in Leicester Forest should also be considered in any account of the Rising.

The Western Rising has attracted very little scholarly attention, a surprising omission considering the general interest shown by historians in the period of Charles I's "personal rule." This neglect is particularly striking since the Rising provides an excellent means for measuring Stuart paternalism and concern for the poor, and for assessing government effectiveness in enforcing policy decisions in the face of popular opposition. No reliable secondary authority discusses the events that occurred, their immediate cause, and the response of the government to them.[1] The nature of the sources

---

1. The only other general account of the rising is to be found in D. G. C. Allan, "The Rising in the West, 1628-1631," *Econ. H.R.*, 2nd ser., V (1952): 76-85. Unfortunately, this pioneering article is marred by errors of fact and misleading interpretations, most of which result from a misplaced trust in the reliability of the *Calendar of State Papers, Domestic* as providing a sufficient and accurate source, eliminating the need to consult the original State Papers. Other

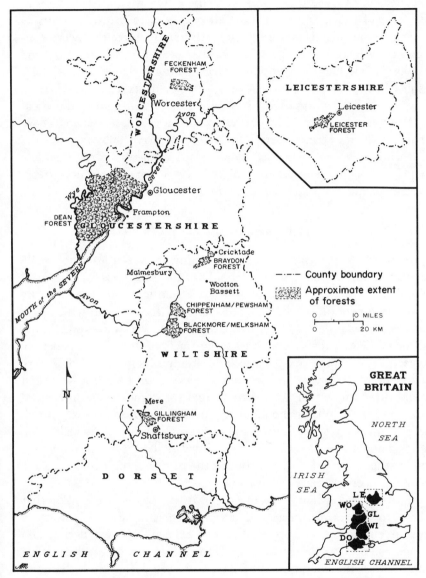

Map. 2. Location of the Western Rising, 1626-1632

accounts of the riots in particular counties, such as those to be found in E. Kerridge, "The Revolts in Wiltshire against Charles I," *W.A.M.* LVII (1958): 64-75, and in C. E. Hart, *The Free Miners of the Royal Forest of Dean* and *The Commoners of Dean Forest*, reproduce a good number of Allan's errors and add a few of their own.

dictates that we see the events from the point of view of the Crown, its local officials, and the courts, all of whom regarded the riots as rebellions against lawful authority. Although the rioters were concerned solely with the pressing local issues of disafforestation and enclosure and had no intention of overturning the government, there is justification for the Crown's view, since the riots were provoked by, and were directly opposed to, royal policy. Furthermore, the great difficulties connected with suppression of the riots and the apprehension, trial, and punishment of the rioters gave substance to the government's fear that this growing snowball of disorders, unless deprived of its momentum, might sweep away deference to established authority and social distinctions.

Disafforestation and Riot

By the seventeenth century, the royal forests were the economically underdeveloped remnants of the hunting preserves of medieval English kings. The medieval forest law, designed to preserve the game, the vert on which they browsed, and the cover in which they sheltered, had lost its terrors and was at best only sporadically enforced. The forests, or at least large tracts of them, were generally regarded as undeveloped waste, potentially of substantial monetary value to the Crown. "In ascending order of profitability woodland could offer timber for construction, fuel for domestic and industrial use and virgin soil for the plough."[2] Except for Dean Forest, with its important stands of timber and substantial mineral deposits, the forests under consideration were regarded as likely sources of revenue under the last rubric, "virgin soil for the plough"; their timber seems to have been of marginal importance.

With the exception of Dean Forest, it was by disafforestation that the Crown, its financial difficulties increasing during the early seventeenth century, tapped this resource. Each forest was declared no longer subject to the forest law. Once the extent of royal demesne land within the bounds of the forest had been determined, that land was leased to Crown farmers, mainly courtiers, who were authorized to kill off the game, cut down and sell the trees, and divide the land into

2. G. Hammersley, "The Revival of the Forest Laws under Charles I," *History* XLV (1960): 88.

enclosed parcels. These parcels were then leased for crop cultivation or cattle-grazing.

Robert Cecil, Earl of Salisbury, Lord Treasurer from 1608 to 1612, was the first to consider disafforestation seriously. In his search for means to increase the Crown's revenues, he proposed disafforestation for a number of forests which were distant enough from royal residences to prevent their use for the chase and which provided little salable timber.[3] This plan was not, however, energetically pursued. Only Knaresborough Forest in Yorkshire seems to have been disafforested as a result of Salisbury's efforts.[4] His direct influence on the exploitation of forest resources is more clearly seen in a number of other money-making schemes: For example, at Dean, beginning in 1611, both the amount of wood sold to the farmers of the royal ironworks and the price charged increased sharply, and early in 1612 enclosures were made in Chippenham and Blackmore forests in Wiltshire to enhance the value of the grazing rights leased to the farmer of the herbage and pannage.[5]

Effective implementation of the policy of disafforestation was left to Lionel Cranfield, a member of the Treasury Commission in 1619 and Lord Treasurer from 1621 until his fall by impeachment in the Parliament of 1624. He brought commitment and a sense of urgency to the problems of royal finance. From this time until the eve of the Civil War, disafforestation played a constant and relatively important role in the Crown's search for alternatives to Parliamentary taxation. During Cranfield's ascendancy the first commissions were issued to survey a number of forests and wastes, including Feckenham Forest in Worcestershire, marshy Sedgemoor in Somerset, and Selwood Forest in Somerset and Wiltshire, all ultimately disafforested in the reign of

3. Unfortunately, exploitation of forest resources as part of royal financial policy is a neglected subject. A comprehensive treatment is not within the scope of this work; what is said here about the general policy of disafforestation and those responsible for it is subject to correction and amplification. There are numerous sources for this period indicating increased appreciation of forests as sources of revenue to be exploited either for their woods or through disafforestation. See PRO, L.R. 2/194, f. 19, survey of Feckenham Forest; f. 31, survey of Braydon Forest; f. 3, considerations to be had in selling the King's woods, Dec. 19, 1608; f. 5, observations on the same, Dec. 21, 1608; similar are to be found in ff. 173-74 and ff. 276-77; S.P. 14/53/50, Robert Johnson to Ld. Tr. Salisbury, Mar. 30, 1610; J. Thirsk and J. P. Cooper, eds., *Seventeenth Century Economic Documents*, pp. 116-20, "The King's Surveyor on the Improvement of the Forests, 1612."

4. *APC 1615-16*, pp. 532-35, PC order on Knaresborough Forest, May 7, 1616.

5. See below, pp. 91-92 and pp. 190-91.

Charles I.[6] Although only the twin forests of Chippenham and Blackmore in Wiltshire and Gillingham Forest in Dorset were disafforested as a result of Cranfield's direct influence, he did establish a precedent faithfully followed during the reign of Charles I.[7] Braydon and Leicester, for example, were disafforested following the recommendations of the commission appointed in 1626 for retrenchment of royal expenditure and expansion of royal revenues.[8]

The proceedings in each disafforestation were almost identical, an Exchequer special commission being appointed to survey the forest, to obtain the commoners' consent to the disafforestation, and to negotiate the compensation granted them on the extinction of their rights to common. The Attorney-General then brought an action of intrusion, and the agreement was confirmed by Exchequer decree. The response of the inhabitants of each forest was to riot almost as soon as the post-disafforestation enclosure had begun. These riots were broadly similar in aim and character, directed toward the restoration of the open forest and involving destruction of the enclosing hedges, ditches, and fences and, in a few cases, pulling down houses inhabited by the agents of the enclosers, and assaults on their workmen.

Gillingham in Dorset, the scene of the first outbreaks, had been granted (along with the manor of Gillingham) to Queen Anne as her jointure in 1603. After her death in 1619, it was granted to Charles, Prince of Wales.[9] In February and again in May of 1625, commissions headed by Sir James Fullerton were authorized to disafforest Gillingham, to compound with the freeholders and copyholders of the forest manors of Gillingham and Mere for their claims of common in the forest, and to obtain their consent to improvements. Late in 1625, Charles I ordered the commission's work to be confirmed by a court of Exchequer decree making disafforestation legally binding on the

6. PRO, S.P. 14/141 (Grant Book of reign of Jas. I), p. 339, commission to Lionel Cranfield et al. for disafforestation of Pewsham and Blackmore, Jan. 18, 1620/1; p. 359, commission to Cranfield et al. to disafforest Barnwood in Bucks, Feckenham in Worcs, Sedgemoor in Somerset, and Frome Selwood in Wilts and Somerset, April 12, 1622; C. 231/4, p. 276, same, April 12, 1622.

7. PRO, S.P. 14/141, p. 235, commission to the Archbishop of Canterbury et al. to disafforest Chippenham and Blackmore, Sept. 21, 1618; R. H. Tawney, *Business and Politics under James I*, pp. 207-8.

8. *HMC, 11th Report*, App. I, "Skrine MSS," p. 80, despatch of Tuscan Resident to Grand Duke of Florence, July 24, 1626; *HMC, 12th Report*, App. I, "Cowper MSS," pp. 291-95, proceedings of commission for retrenchment of royal revenue.

9. Hutchins, *History of Dorset*, 3rd ed., vol. III, p. 616.

parties involved.[10] The Attorney-General then brought an action in the court against the tenants of the two royal manors of Gillingham and Mere. The final decree was issued on May 28, 1627, and the work of a commission authorized by the decree to make minor adjustments in allotments was confirmed on October 27 of that year.[11]

In 1625, the demesne waste of the former forest—2,408 acres free and clear of all claims of common—had, along with the herbage and pannage of Gillingham Park, been granted to the Socttish courtier Sir James Fullerton, Groom of the Stole, for a term of forty-one years at the annual rent of £131.8s. The terms of the lease were soon renegotiated. In 1628 Fullerton obtained a new forty-one-year lease with an annual rent of £416.1s.3d. As a sweetener Gillingham Park, 753 acres in extent, was included, with authority to dispark it. This lease in turn was speedily renegotiated, no doubt because Fullerton, heavily in debt, was incapable of paying this annual sum, in part because the litigation connected with the property and replacement of the destroyed enclosures must have cost him dearly. In 1630 Fullerton was granted the forest and park at the annual rent of £96.1s.3d. In December of 1630, shortly before his death, he settled two-thirds of his interest on his stepson Thomas, Lord Bruce, with the provision that his widow, Lady Magdalen Bruce, should receive all the profits until she had paid off Fullerton's debts. The other third, about 900 acres, was settled on his colleague George Kirke, a Groom of the Bedchamber, to whom Fullerton was heavily in debt. In 1631 the King let the manor of Gillingham and the two-thirds interest settled on Lord Bruce to him for a fine of £3,000 and an annual rent of £108.6s.8d.[12]

Gillingham riots erupted in 1626 and continued intermittently through 1628. Lack of evidence makes it difficult to date the beginning of the outbreak precisely. In June, 1626, the inhabitants threatened to

10. PRO, C. 231/4, p. 373, commission to Sir James Fullerton et al. to disafforest Gillingham, May 9, 1625; Hutchins, vol. III, p. 649, which gives the substance of the now lost proceedings of the commission: E. 178/3732, privy-seal letter to Ld. Tr. et al., Dec. 7, 1625.

11. PRO, E. 125/3, ff. 250-51, decree in A-G vs. tenants of Gillingham, May 28, 1627; f. 316, decree confirming work of commission, Oct. 27, 1627; f. 328, affidavit as to the truth of the commission's findings, Nov. 14, 1627. The commission and its findings are in E. 178/3732.

12. PRO, S.P. 39/19/59, warrant for grant to Fullerton, July 27, 1625; C. 66/2348, no. 18, July 27, 1625; S.P. 39/23/419, warrant, Mar. 13, 1627/8; C. 66/2439, no. 13, Mar. 13, 1627/8; DRO, Deed 4780, assignment by Fullerton to Lord Bruce of his interest in Gillingham, Dec. 28, 1630 (this source mentions £1,400 in legal costs); PRO, C. 66/2570, no. 10, grant to Bruce, June 29, 1631; Hutchins, vol. III, p. 650; G. Aylmer, *The King's Servants*, pp. 164, 317-18.

destroy the enclosures being erected in the forest. By the end of the year of the court of Star Chamber had ordered the attachment of twenty-six inhabitants of Gillingham Forest and its environs, fourteen men and the wives of twelve of them.[13] Six of the men and one woman were tried in Star Chamber for participation in the riots; four of the men were fined, and the other two and the woman were found not guilty.[14]

Early in 1628, after the enclosure commissions had done their work and Fullerton's workmen were in the process of dividing the forest into enclosed parcels, a series of better-documented riots took place in Gillingham. Soldiers billeted in nearby Shaftesbury entered the forest and destroyed some of the enclosures.[15] There can be little doubt that they were incited to this course, and probably led, by some of the local people. Within a month, four inhabitants of Gillingham were summoned before the Privy Council; three of them were tried and fined in Star Chamber.[16] Throughout the course of 1628 the people of Gillingham continued to riot, burning the plants intended for the enclosed grounds and killing many of the deer left in the forest. At the same time threats were made against the lives and property of Fullerton's laborers in an attempt to force them to stop the work of enclosure. At least two messengers of the Chamber, sent to serve process on the rioters, were assaulted (according to one account, they were tied to a post and whipped) and their prisoners rescued.[17]

---

13. PRO, E. 125/1, ff. 270-71, order in the case of A-G vs. inhabitants of Gillingham, June 26, 1626; P.R.O. 30/38/22, f. 68, process of attachment, Dec. 15, 1626; f. 69, same, Jan. 5, 1626/7.

14. PRO, E. 159/472, Trin. 8 Chas. I, rot. 38, estreat of St. Ch. fines, Gillingham Forest rioters, Hil. 1629/30; E. 159/473 Trin. 9 Chas. I, rot. 59, letters patent under the Great Seal, April 10, 1630, giving judgment of court and including names of those found not guilty and those who forfeited recognizances for nonappearance. I am grateful to Prof. T. G. Barnes for drawing my attention to these sources and for providing me with transcripts.

15. *APC 1627-28*, p. 248, PC to commissioners for billeted soldiers in Dorset, Jan. 24, 1627/8; pp. 272-73, PC to Dep. Lts. and JPs of Dorset, Feb. 6, 1627/8.

16. *APC 1627-28*, p. 359, warrants to bring the constable of Mere, John Crowch, William Frith, and John Wolridge before the PC, Mar. 23, 1627/8; p. 371, Wolridge and William Rodgers (probably to be identified with constable of Mere) appeared and were committed to custody until further orders from PC, April 3, 1628; PRO, E. 159/472, Trin. 8 Chas. I, rot. 38, John Crouch, William Frith, and John Wolridge all fined.

17. PRO, S.P. 16/105/6 I, copy of letter of Viscount Conway to Capt. Storie, May 29, 1628; *APC 1627-28*, p. 495, PC to mayor and magistrates of Shaftesbury, June 16, 1628; T. Birch, ed., *Court and Times of Charles I*, vol. 1, pp. 453-54, Mr. John Pory to Rev. Joseph Mead, Dec. 19, 1628; J. Rushworth, *Historical Collections*, vol. III, App. 28, St. Ch. decree in A-G vs. Gillingham rioters, Hil. 1629/30.

The last of the Gillingham disorders seems to have taken place late in 1628, when the sheriffs of Dorset, Wiltshire, and Somerset were instructed to raise the power of their counties to execute process issued by the court of Star Chamber and apprehend over 100 suspected rioters.[18] Consequently, the sheriff of Dorset raised the *posse*, but when he went to attach the rioters he found them numerous, well-armed, and resolute. They were reported to have declared, "Here were we born and here we will die."[19] The sheriff beat a hasty retreat, rather than press on in a situation where blood would probably have been shed and, more to the point, his outnumbered forces might easily have suffered a humiliating defeat.

Meanwhile, in December of 1626 and again in March of 1627 Sir Miles Fleetwood, Receiver General of the court of Wards, headed a commission to survey and disafforest Leicester, to compensate commoners with a valid claim, and to enclose the rest for the King's own use. In Easter term of 1627 the Attorney-General began a suit in the court of Exchequer against the commoners in the forest, to seek confirmation of the agreements made with Fleetwood. The final decree disafforesting Leicester and confirming Fleetwood's arrangements with the commoners—which included setting aside part of the forest for the King, free and clear of claims of common—was issued by the court in February, 1628. The King's share, 1,598 acres, was let to neighboring landowners for fines totaling £7,760 and nominal annual rents totaling £80.[20] There is little surviving documentation of the Leicester Forest riots. Sometime in the spring of 1627, when the Exchequer suit had begun, a number of people opposed to the disafforestation destroyed some enclosures which had already been

---

18. JRL, Nicholas MS 72/11, Sir James Fullerton to ?, Oct. 3, 1628, reporting the progress of the St. Ch. suit; PRO, P.R.O. 30/38/23, f. 127, commission of rebellion to sheriffs of Dorset, Somerset, and Wilts to apprehend named suspects, Dec. 1, 1628; *APC 1628-29*, p. 238, PC to same sheriffs to execute all St. Ch. process directed to them, Nov. 20, 1628.

19. Birch, vol. 1, pp. 453-54, Mr. John Pory to Rev. Joseph Mead, Dec. 19, 1628.

20. PRO, C. 231/4, p. 430, commission to Fleetwood et al. to survey Leicester Forest, Dec. 30, 1626; p. 444, commission to Fleetwood et al. to disafforest Leicester, Mar. 30, 1627; E. 112/195/10, information and answers in A-G vs. inhabitants of Leicester Forest, Eas. and Trin. 1627; E. 126/3, ff. 209-21, decree in the same case, Feb. 7, 1627/8. The disafforestation proceedings for Leicester, E. 178/5403, proved to be missing at the PRO when I went to consult them in 1973. The loss of these records makes it difficult to estimate, from the Exchequer decree alone, the size of the Crown's share of the forest. This estimate is based on the one in L. Fox and P. Russell, *Leicester Forest*, pp. 136-38, which draws on the decree and a document printed in J. Nichols, *History and Antiquities of the County of Leicester*, vol. IV, p. 782.

erected.[21] Following on the decree of the court of Exchequer in 1628 and the final division of the forest, "a certain number of ignorant women" unlawfully assembled and again pulled down the enclosures.[22]

Proceedings for the disafforestation of Braydon in Wiltshire began on July 26, 1626, with the issue of a commission to Sir John Bridgman, Chief Justice of Chester, John Essington, keeper of the King's woods in Wiltshire, and a number of others to survey the forest and compound with the freeholders and copyholders. Their report, filed the following year, set out the extent of the forest and the amount of land which ought to be provided as compensation to the commoners.[23] Landholding patterns in and around the forest proved so complex that a further commission was empowered in 1629 to compensate landowners overlooked by its predecessor.[24] Meanwhile, on November 3, 1627, the forest and the demesne woods outside its bounds— about 4,000 acres in all—were demised for forty-one years to the Crown Jeweller, Phillip Jacobsen, and to Edward Sewster, a London merchant. They were to pay the Crown £21,000 immediately, £11,000 as an entry fine and £10,000 for all the game and timber in the forest and for a license to erect an ironworks; about £10,000 of this cancelled debts the King owed Jacobsen for jewels. The lessees were authorized to divide the forest into enclosed parcels suitable for agricultural leasing. An annual rent of £450 was also to be paid, beginning only when Jacobsen and Sewster got quiet possession, which the King guaranteed to obtain through decrees in the courts of Exchequer and the Duchy Chamber of Lancaster.[25]

21. PRO, E. 112/195/10, information in the case of A-G vs. the inhabitants of Leicester Forest, Eas. 1627, mentions the destruction of enclosures.

22. H. of L.R.O., Main Papers, petition of the inhabitants of the borough of Leicester to the H. of L., received June 23, 1628; *APC 1627-28*, pp. 475-77, PC order on Leicester Forest, May 31, 1628.

23. PRO, E. 178/2470.

24. PRO, E. 178/2470, commission to Thomas Earl of Berks, Sir John Bridgman, et al., June 25, 1629, returned with proceedings, Aug. 24, 1629.

25. F. H. Manley, "The Disafforesting of Braden," *W.A.M.* XLV (1930-32): 559-60; PRO, S.P. 16/288/80, notes on the state of Jacobsen's lease, May 13, 1635; S.P. 16/299/73, further notes, undated. Before this grant to Jacobsen and Sewster some consideration had been given to the Crown itself taking on the job of dividing the forest into enclosed parcels, leasing them to neighboring landowners, and selling off the trees. A special commission to this effect was drafted: see PRO, S.P. 39/19/184, warrant for commission to Edward Lord Gorges et al. with instructions annexed, Mar. 8, 1626/7; C. 231/4, p. 440, same, Mar. 17, 1626/7. This idea was

To obtain quiet possession required a suit in Exchequer against the leading manorial lords and their principal tenants within and around the boundaries of the forest. The aim of the suit was on the one hand to establish the King's title to the royal demesne in the forest free of claims to common, and on the other to determine which manors had rights of common and the specific nature of the compensation to which the tenants were entitled. The court's decisions confirming the disafforestation and the details of the compensation for those who proved right of common are embodied in Exchequer decrees of 1628 and 1630.[26]

In May and June of 1631 the enclosures made by Phillip Jacobsen's agents were destroyed by the inhabitants of Braydon Forest in a series of massive riots. Assembled in groups estimated to have been as large as 1,000 in number, the rioters also threatened to kill Simon Keble, Jacobsen's agent in the forest, and to pull down the houses of his workmen. The house of one who was a servant to Sir John Hungerford and who had revealed the names of seventeen rioters to the authorities was in fact destroyed. On one occasion, when the sheriff and his *posse* arrived to suppress the riots and aid a messenger of the Chamber to execute Star Chamber process, it was reported that the undersheriff and the messenger were fired upon.[27]

Sometime in either June or July of 1631 the Braydon rioters went to nearby Chippenham Forest, also in Wiltshire, and tried to create disorders there. Disafforestation of Chippenham *alias* Pewsham, and its neighbor, Blackmore *alias* Melksham, was begun in 1619, but the government's interest in their financial possibilities had quickened earlier. During the Lord Treasurership of Robert Cecil, Earl of Salisbury, one-third of Blackmore Forest and about one-half of Chippenham were enclosed so that the royal farmer of the herbage and pannage of both forests might use them as grazing for cattle. Although the beasts of those claiming rights to common were to be

---

soon dropped, however, no doubt because it was a slow and cumbersome way in which to obtain money, the main object of disafforestation. A grant to a farmer for a large fine was a much more efficient way of realizing assets and had the added advantage of making the farmer responsible for dealing with troublesome details.

26. PRO, E. 126/3, ff. 264-70, decree in A-G vs. Earls of Herts, Berks, Danby, et al., Oct. 23, 1628; ff. 378-85, decree in A-G vs. added defendants in case, June 10, 1630.

27. *APC 1630-31*, pp. 352-53, PC to sheriff, Dep. Lts., and JPs of Wilts, May 27, 1631; PRO, S.P. 16/193/11, Simon Keble to Phillip Jacobsen, June 2, 1631; Rushworth, vol. III, App. 73, St. Ch. decree in A-G vs. Braydon rioters, Trin. 1635.

excluded from the enclosed grounds, they were allowed to graze as usual in the remainder of the forest. Such enclosures, as long as they were no higher than a doe with a one-month-old fawn could leap, were allowed by the forest law and thus did not amount to disafforestation.[28] This nevertheless provoked persistent, if low-key, opposition over the next few years from some of the inhabitants of Chippenham and Blackmore, who continued to drive their beasts into the enclosed grounds.[29] On a few occasions this resulted in destruction of the fences erected at the King's expense.[30]

In 1619 the process of disafforestation began, with the establishment of a special commission to award compensation to those with valid claims to common and to negotiate for disposal of the royal demesne in the forests, surveyed at 2,512 acres. By the time the commission completed its work 2,419 acres in Blackmore and Chippenham had been leased to the lords and tenants of surrounding manors for fines totaling £899.1s.6d. and annual rents of £913.4s.6d.[31] In 1623 the arrears of rents and fines owed to the King and the reversion of all the lands demised by the commissioners, along with the remaining timber trees and the judicial profits from all spoils of woods and timber, were granted in fee farm to Christopher Villiers,

---

28. PRO, E. 112/131/226, information and answer in A-G vs. Sir Francis Fane et al., commoners in Blackmore Forest, Hil. 1611/12; E. 124/13, ff. 279-83, decree in the same case, Feb. 3, 1611/12; E. 112/131/232, bill and answer in Otto Nicholson, farmer of the agistment, pasturage, and pannage of the forests of Chippenham and Blackmore, vs. Sir Henry Baynton et al., who claimed common in Chippenham, 1612 (no term visible). There are a number of special commissions and returns connected with this business to be found in E. 178/4577. The reference to the doe with a one-month-old fawn comes from E. 134/16 Eliz/Eas. 6, depositions by commission in Dyrdo et al. vs. Sir John Zouche, warden of Gillingham Forest.

29. PRO, E. 112/131/237, information in A-G vs. Francis, Earl of Rutland, and the tenants of his manor of Rowde for taking common in the part of Blackmore Forest reserved for the King, 1612 (no term visible); no. 235, bill and answer in Blake vs. Nicholson, Eas. 1613; no. 236, information in A-G vs. Blake, 1613 (no term visible, a cross-suit); E 134/11 Jas. I/Mich. 4, and E. 134/11 Jas. I/Mich. 10, depositions by commission in the latter suit; E. 112/131/262, information in A-G vs. Bruncker, et al., Hil. 1618/19.

30. PRO, E. 112/131/254, information and answers in A-G vs. Mondaye et al., Mich. 1616, mentions destruction of fence rails to the value of £100 over the previous four years; E. 124/22, f. 311, an order in the same case, Oct. 16, 1616.

31. PRO, E. 178/4577, mm. 33-61, special commission for survey of Chippenham and Blackmore forests, Mar. 23, 1618/19, with articles of instruction and bargains made with inhabitants for compensation and for disposal of the King's demesne. Other copies are to be found in Bod. Lib., Rawlinson MS, B 443, and in PRO, E. 101/536/40, accounts of John Pym, Receiver-General of Crown revenues in Hampshire, Wiltshire, and Gloucestershire for the issues of the disafforested forests of Pewsham and Blackmore, 1619-1624.

Earl of Anglesey and brother of the Duke of Buckingham.[32]

For the years immediately following the' disafforestation, there survive indications of discontent on the part of some of the inhabitants of both forests, including on occasion destruction of the enclosures.[33] The first report of serious trouble appeared in 1631 when a postscript was added to Privy Council letters of June 13 commanding local officials in Wiltshire and Dorset to suppress all forest riots, that "the lyke disorders and outrages are threatened to be attempted in the Forrests of Pusam and Blackmore by throwing down of the inclosures."[34] Then on July 21 a commission of rebellion was issued by Star Chamber for the attachment of those who had destroyed the enclosures in Chippenham Forest. All seven men named were suspected of involvement in the Braydon Forest riots.[35] Clearly, the rioters had marched over from Braydon in the hope of rousing the inhabitants of Chippenham to riot. The only other surviving evidence is a singularly bad poem by Sir William Davenant entitled "The Countess of Anglesey led captive by the Rebells at the Disafforesting of Pewsham."[36] Only the title is of any value; it confirms that there actually was a riot, nothing else.

The Feckenham disafforestation began in November of 1627 with the issue of a commission to Sir Miles Fleetwood and others to survey the forest and compound with the tenants. Before the end of the year the forest had been let to William Ashton and William Turnor for a fine of £4,000 and an annual rent of £20, but it was not until June of 1629 that the agreement made between Fleetwood and the inhabitants claiming common was confirmed by Exchequer decree.[37] On March 28, 1631, the first riot broke out at Feckenham; an estimated 300 people destroyed the enclosures. When the sheriff and his men

32. PRO, S.P. 38/12, warrant for grant to Christopher Villiers, Mar. 14, 1622/3; E. 112/254/7, bill in Earl of Anglesey vs. Burglye et al., for arrears of rent, 1626.

33. PRO, E. 112/131/291, information in A-G vs. Snell et al., for intruding cattle into enclosed grounds in Blackmore, Eas. 1624; E. 112/254/22, information in A-G vs. Woodland et al., for destruction of the enclosure of a four-acre close in Chippenham Forest, Trin. 1628; no. 38, bill in Countess Dowager of Anglesey vs. Edward Haketts, for threatening to cast down enclosures in Melksham, Eas. 1630.

34. APC 1630-31, pp. 382-83.

35. WRO, 130/486/5, commission of rebellion, July 21, 1631.

36. Works (1673), p. 288.

37. PRO, E. 178/4781, commission to Sir Miles Fleetwood et al., Nov. 28, 1627, with articles of instruction and depositions taken Jan. 21, 1627/8; S.P. 16/339/30, undated statement of the Crown's legal rights in forests; E. 125/7, ff. 75-84, June 23, 1629.

arrived to restore order they were assaulted by the rioters and forced to withdraw. To protect the enclosures, the court of Exchequer, on the motion of the Attorney-General, issued an injunction to permit the King, his farmers, and the compensated lords, freeholders, and tenants of the forest manors to enjoy quiet possession of their enclosed parcels. The inhabitants were enjoined from future destruction of the enclosures and ordered to allow the repair of those already destroyed.[38]

This injunction had no effect in quieting the forest; the following March there was another riot. Learning that 300 people were destroying the enclosures, the sheriff, a deputy lieutenant, and a justice of the peace, accompanied by forty well-armed men, entered the forest. There they met the rioters, "who in a most dareinge and presumptious manner presented themselves unto us with warlike weapons (vizt.) pikes, forrest bills, pichforkes, swordes and the like." The magistrates demanded their surrender. In reply, the rioters "did nott onely slight our power, but assailed our persons and protested they would fight itt out to the last before they would yeld." This time the sheriff and his men did not retreat, for this was "flatt rebellion." To preserve the King's peace they moved to arrest the rioters, with the result that "there were diverse of them hurte (yett none as wee hope mortally) in their apprenhension." The action was felt to be justified as a means of preventing future riots, "fearinge if wee should have suffered them to escape they would speedily have growne to soe great a head, that much blood would have beene spilte in the suppressinge of them."[39] After this decisive action, no further disorders occurred in Feckenham.

The events in Dean Forest in Gloucestershire in the late 1620s and early 1630s were akin to those in other western forests, even though only partial disafforestation took place because the forest possessed unique resources, in the form of timber and iron ore, which could be managed in the financial interest of the Crown without wholesale

38. PRO, E. 125/9, ff. 248-49, Exchequer injunction, April 27, 1631, including the substance of an affidavit made on April 20 by John Hide, gent., of St. Andrews, Holborn, Middlesex; *APC 1630-31*, p. 295, PC to sheriff and JPs of Worcestershire, April 18, 1631; Rushworth, vol. III, App. 48, St. Ch. decree in A-G vs. Feckenham rioters, Mich. 1632.

39. PRO, S.P. 16/214/46, sheriff and JPs of Worcestershire to PC, Mar. 17, 1631/2; see also no. 47, warrant for arrest of two suspects escaped from custody, Mar. 17, 1631/2; P.C. 2/41, pp. 486-87, PC to sheriff and JPs of Worcestershire, Mar. 22, 1631/2; pp. 509-10, PC order concerning Feckenham, April 11, 1632.

alienation of the soil. The early years of Charles I's reign increased exploitation of the forest beyond even that of James I's reign. Sales of wood to fuel the royal and other ironworks in the forest increased, and certain parcels of ground within the forest were enclosed so that they could be more efficiently worked to supply ore for the ironworks. A number of separate grants of lands in the forest, totaling about 3,000 acres, were made to courtiers and government officials. The grantees received power to enclose, to cut wood for charcoal, and to open iron and coal mines.[40] To enable such enclosures—in effect a partial disafforestation—to take place peacefully, the Attorney-General in 1627 pursued an action of intrusion against those freeholders and copyholders who claimed common in the forest. The resultant decree in 1628 recognized the Crown's right to make enclosures in specified areas of the forest and extinguished all rights to common claimed within the grounds to be enclosed. In return, the freeholders and copyholders claiming common in the forest had their rights allowed in the remaining 17,000 acres of royal demesne in Dean.[41]

During the spring of 1631, the enclosures of the disafforested grounds were systematically destroyed by the forest's inhabitants. On March 25, 1631, an estimated 500 men "did with two drummes, two coulers and one fife in a warlike and outragious manner assemble themselves together armed with gunnes, pykes, halberdes and other weapons." They first cast down the enclosures of an area in the forest known as the Snead, which in March of 1626 had been demised by the Crown for three lives to Tristam Flower. Then the rioters marched to Mailescott Woods, granted in 1625 to Sir Edward Villiers, half-brother of the Duke of Buckingham. There Sir Giles Mompesson, the "odious projector," acting as the agent of Lady Barbara Villiers, Sir Edward's widow, had set men to enclose the ground and sink ore pits. When they marched past the house of Robert Bridges, an agent of Lady Villiers, the rioters fired on it and threatened to pull it down if he informed against them. Then they entered the enclosed ground, destroyed hedges and ditches, assaulted the miners employed by Mompesson to dig the ore, filled in three ore pits, and cast cut oak timber into the river Wye. As the pits were being filled, the rioters

40. See below, chapters 7 and 8, for a detailed discussion of the policies of James I and Charles I with respect to Dean.
41. PRO, E. 125/4, ff. 50-54, decree in Winter et al. vs. A-G, Feb. 11, 1627/8; the bill and answer are in E. 112/179/28.

threw in an effigy of Sir Giles Mompesson.[42] Then the crowd assembled in front of Bridges' house, "made an Oyes and commaunding silence said that if this deponent [Bridges] would make the like worke against May Day next they would bee ready to doe him the like service and dared him to come out of his house which he feared to doe."[43]

On April 5 the rioters, this time estimated at 3,000 in number, again assembled with drums and banners, broke down the enclosures in most of the other improved parts of the forest, and burned some houses. They threatened to return to finish their work on Easter Eve, April 9. By April 28 the enclosures of all the improvements specified in the Exchequer decree of 1628 as excluded from claims of common had been destroyed.[44] A few riots on a smaller scale continued to occur. The enclosures of Cannop Chase, held by John Gibbons, secretary to Lord Treasurer Weston, which had been destroyed in April of 1631, were again cast down in January of 1632. Further disorders followed; in July, 1633, the restored enclosures in Mailescott Woods were destroyed "by loose and disorderly persons in the night tyme."[45]

Defense of the King's Peace

Despite their relative lack of physical violence—no one was killed— and their focus upon purely local issues, the government regarded the disorders which compose the Western Rising as insurrections threatening the good order and stability of the state. The King and the Privy Council were especially fearful that unless the riots were quickly suppressed and the rioters effectively punished, the disturbances might grow to unmanageable proportions. They repeatedly expressed

42. PRO, S.P. 16/188/20, copy of affidavit by Robert Bridges submitted to the court of Exchequer, April 5, 1631; GRO, D. 421/19/22, abstract of records concerning the claims of the miners of Dean; PRO, S.P. 38/13, docquet of a grant to Villiers, May 23, 1625; S.P. 16/257/94, *Cartae de Forresta de Deane*; *APC 1630-31*, pp. 284-85, three PC letters—to Ld. Lt. of Gloucestershire, to John Bridgman, C.J., of Chester, and to the sheriff and JPs of Gloucestershire, April 5, 1631: *HMC, 12th Report*, App. I, pp. 429-30, Sir John Kyrle to Sec. Coke, April 6, 1631.

43. PRO, S.P. 16/188/20, Bridges's affidavit, April 5, 1631.

44. *HMC, 12th Report*, App. I, pp. 429-30, Kyrle to Coke, April 6, 1631; *APC 1630-31*, p. 290, PC to Ld. Lt. of Gloucestershire, April 8, 1631; PRO, E. 125/9, ff. 240-41, injunction in favor of Lady Barbara Villiers against Mouselt et al., April 28, 1631.

45. PRO, K.B. 9/797/5, Latin information in K.B. by A-G Noye, naming seven rioters at Cannop, Jan. 23, 1631/2, endorsed with directions to make a *distringas*; S.O. 1/2, p. 301, signet letter to the judges of assize on the Oxford circuit, July 24, 1633.

these views in the orders sent to local officials. A letter from the Council to the Earl of Bridgewater, Lord President of the Council in the Marches of Wales, commanding him to supervise the work of the deputy lieutenants of Worcestershire, called the riots at Feckenham "rebellious attempts" that had to be suppressed by all possible means because they "carry with them so dangerous a consequence."[46] The riots at Gillingham were described as "such like rude actions not to be tolerated in a well governed State." The local officials of Wiltshire were urged to take special care in preserving the King's peace in Braydon lest disorder "grow to a great head and inconvenience if it not be spedily prevented and sharply punished in the beginning." Finally, to suppress the Dean riots, the magistrates of Gloucestershire were urged to "use all possible diligence to resist and suppresse these exorbitaunt outrages rather in the nature of a Rebellion than a Ryott."[47]

One special concern of the government was that most of the riots were being fomented and coordinated by a single group of ringleaders. This led to extraordinary efforts being taken to apprehend three men: Henry Hoskins, yeoman, and John Phillips, tanner, both of Gillingham in Dorset, and John Williams *alias* "Skimington," of English Bicknor in the forest of Dean. Although these men were important as leaders of riots in their own homes areas, the government's fears were grounded upon little more than unsubstantiated rumors. Accompanied by misinterpretations of the evidence, these rumors have misled modern historians into ascribing to Hoskins, Phillips, and Williams larger roles in the Western Rising than they actually played.

Two historians who have studied the Western Rising have asserted that Hoskins and Phillips, leaders of the Gillingham riots of 1626-1628, helped to incite the Braydon Forest riots of mid-1631 and undocumented riots in Gillingham which are supposed to have followed in their wake.[48] This interpretation puts too much weight on the vague fears expressed in Privy Council orders. Except for some possible contact between Hoskins and the Braydon rioters, there is no evidence of any relationship between the riots in the two forests.

46. PRO, P.C. 2/41, pp. 487-88, Mar. 27, 1632.

47. *APC 1627-28*, p. 248, PC to commissioners for billeted soldiers in Dorset, Jan. 24, 1627/8; *APC 1630-31*, pp. 352-53, PC to sheriff, Dep. Lts., and JPs of Wilts, May 27, 1631; pp. 284-85, PC to sheriff and JPs of Gloucestershire, April 5, 1631.

48. Allan, pp. 76-83; Kerridge, p 69.

Furthermore, there is no evidence at all of riots in Gillingham during 1631.

Those involved in the Gillingham riots of 1626-1628 were fined in Star Chamber early in 1630. After the sentencing, peace seems to have settled on the forest and the enclosure went on apace. The first evidence of a new threat to the tranquillity of Gillingham is a curious document dated June 10, 1631, a few days after the outbreak of riots in Braydon.[49] It is a one-folio sheet headed "The Examinacion of Henry Hoskins of Gillingham in the Countie of Dorsett taken by William Whitakers esq. one of his Majesties Justices of Peace in the said Countie." Despite the title, the document does not follow the normal diplomatic form of an examination taken before a justice of the peace. It is, rather, a report made by Whitaker on the activities of Henry Hoskins and John Phillips; the document is not a letter, for it lacks not only a signature but also any address or close. Council letters issued on June 13, framed partially on the basis of this document, preclude the possibility that it was enclosed within a letter sent from Dorset. The most likely explanation is that it is a report made in person to the Privy Council by Whitaker, taken down verbatim or in substance by a clerk; although there is no confirming evidence of Whitaker's presence before the Privy Council at this time, on at least one other occasion, in October of 1631, he appeared in person at the Council's request before Attorney-General Heath to report on Phillips's behavior.[50]

Whitaker claimed that Henry Hoskins, who had not been apprehended and had therefore escaped the fine and imprisonment imposed on him by Star Chamber for his part in the Gillingham riots, had lately returned to the forest and was again urging the inhabitants to destroy the enclosures. He had recently gone into Braydon Forest, where he and some others urged "Lady Skimington," the *alias* of the Braydon riot leaders, and "her" followers to come to Gillingham to destroy the enclosures, promising to aid them with men, money, and food. The activities of John Phillips, who had been fined in Star Chamber, were also discussed in the report. According to Whitaker, Phillips had recently pulled down some enclosures and threatened to

---

49. PRO, S.P. 16/193/66.
50. PRO, S.P. 16/200/42 I, PC request that A-G Heath meet with Whitaker to obtain a report on Phillips's activities, Sept. 29, 1631; no. 42 II, Heath's report to PC of his findings, Oct. 13, 1631.

destroy all the rest. On being called before the justice he confessed, saying he did it to try his right and title to common. When Phillips refused to bound over to the assizes, Whitaker committed him to jail. Upon being bailed by another justice, it was reported in "The Examinacion" that he "is come againe to Gillingham which doth much more animate him and others of his adherents."

Other than Phillips's activities, no anti-enclosure violence at Gillingham was reported; there were certainly no riots. The Council, however, fearful that Hoskins and Phillips might stir up new disorders, acted swiftly on Whitaker's information, and on June 13 a warrant was issued for their arrest.[51] Letters directed at the same time to the local governors of Wiltshire and Dorset reveal the government's fear that Phillips and Hoskins were coordinating riots in the two counties. Authorizing the use of the trained bands and the *posse comitatus* to suppress future disorders at Braydon and Gillingham, the Council letters also refer to Hoskins's and Phillips's roles in fomenting past riots: "And whereas Henry Hoskins and John Phillipps of Gillingham are informed to be cheefe actors in theise disorders we have sent downe a Serjant at Armes with warrant for the apprehending of them."[52] These words have been taken to mean that the two were the ringleaders of the June, 1631, riots in Braydon and of contemporaneous riots in Gillingham, but the letters will not bear this interpretation. Their phraseology is a measure of the Council's nervousness about future riots and the activities of Hoskins and Phillips rather than an accurate reflection of the report by Whitaker on which they were based.

John Phillips's fate is an indication that there were no riots in Gillingham in 1631. Although Hoskins was never apprehended, Phillips was. In September and again in October of 1631 he was petitioning for his release from the Fleet prison in London. It is clear from the petitions and related documents that he was not in prison for participation in any riot. His crime was the single-handed destruction of the enclosures in contempt both of the decree of the court of Exchequer disafforesting Gillingham and of the sentence of the court of Star Chamber, which had included binding him for two years to his

---

51. *APC 1630-31*, p. 382, warrant to Randall Church, sgt.-at-arms, June 13, 1631.

52. *APC 1630-31*, pp. 382-83, PC to Ld. Lts. of Wiltshire and Dorset, June 13, 1631; p. 383, PC to sheriff and JPs of Wiltshire and Dorset, June 13, 1631—the quotation comes from this latter source.

good behavior not to interfere with the enclosure. In October of 1631, when quiet had returned to most of the western forests, plans were afoot to release Phillips from the Fleet, bound anew to his good behavior.[53]

Probably more can be discovered about John Williams, the leading figure in the Dean Forest riots, than about any other individual involved in the Western Rising. The frequency of references to him in the records of the day can be explained largely by the importance the government attached to his capture and punishment. Although on one occasion called a laborer, Williams was probably a miner; the words *laborer* and *miner* seem to have been used almost interchangeably in Dean to describe those who worked the coal and iron pits.[54]

Williams first appears as one of the leaders of the great riots in March and April of 1631. Later in the same year the sheriff of Gloucestershire made an attempt to capture him:[55] the undersheriff, with 120 men, was sent "before the breake of the day towards the howse of one John Williams called by the name of Skymington thinking to have caught him in his bedd." But the *posse* was discovered and Williams escaped. After this failure the sheriff tried to bribe inhabitants of the forest to betray Williams.[56] This was no more successful than force had been. The report of the attempted capture is the first occasion on which Williams is referred to as Skimington; ever after he is John Williams *alias* Skimington, an *alias* also used by the three leaders of the Braydon riots.

In January, 1632, Williams was involved in another riot, this time at Cannop Chase in Dean. The only clear evidence of this which survives is an Attorney-General's Latin information in King's Bench against

---

53. PRO, S.P. 16/205/43, petition from John Phillips to PC, undated, but can be placed by internal evidence to the period between June 13 and September 29, 1631; S.P. 16/200/42 and 42 I, petition from Phillips to PC, heard by the Privy Council on September 29, 1631; no. 42 II, report to PC by A-G Heath, Oct. 13, 1631; no. 42 III, petition from Phillips to PC, undated, but it follows Heath's report. Search in the Privy Council Register has failed to reveal the actual date of his release.

54. PRO, K.B. 9/797/5, A-G information of Jan. 23, 1631/2, calls Williams and five of his six companions laborers—all were probably miners; E. 112/83/41, 1613, John Williams, miner, is defendant in a suit by the Earl of Pembroke. Williams is called yeoman in Bod. Lib., Bankes MS 45/72, a £2,000 bond for his good behavior, Aug. 12, 1637. He had spent five years in prison; this was possibly an attempt to portray him as a man of standing worthy of release, or was simply a mistake by the drafter of the bond.

55. PRO, S.P. 16/188/20, a copy of John Bridges's affidavit in Exchequer, April 5, 1631; *APC 1630-31*, p. 285, warrant for attachment of John Williams and others, April 5, 1631.

56. PRO, S.P. 16/203/36, sheriff of Gloucestershire to PC, Nov. 14, 1631.

him and six others,[57] but there is one additional piece of evidence which probably belongs in this context; it points to the government's anxieties about Williams's activities. On January 25, 1632, two days after the information was exhibited in King's Bench, the Attorney-General moved successfully in Star Chamber for a sergeant-at-arms to be sent with a commission to attach the ranger and others in a certain, unnamed, chase. The ranger had entertained one "Skimington," permitting him to hunt and kill deer in the chase, which was to be disafforested by an Exchequer-confirmed agreement with the inhabitants. Angered at this, Skimington "threatened and used some violence to the agents for the king, that he would serve them as he did others that intrenched upon his liberties in the forest of Deane."[58] Coincidence of time, place, and name lead one to believe that the unnamed chase was Cannop in Dean Forest, leased to John Gibbons and included in the Exchequer decree of 1628 as one of the areas which could be enclosed.[59] No doubt the violence referred to was the riot which occasioned Attorney-General Noy's information in King's Bench on January 23, 1632. The final inference is that Skimington of the Star Chamber report was "John Williams *alias* Skymerton" of the information.

Williams was finally captured sometime in March of 1632 by William Cowse, one of the King's forest officers. Four years later the £379.7s.8d Cowse owed to the Exchequer for the sale of woods in Dean were remitted because of his efforts in apprehending Williams.[60] John Williams was warded in Gloucester Castle and then transferred to Newgate Prison, London, in April of 1632.[61] Steps taken immediately to protect Cowse from the revenge of the forest inhabitants proved ineffectual.[62]

57. PRO, K.B. 9/797/5, Jan. 23, 1631/2.
58. S. R. Gardiner, ed., *Reports of Cases in the Courts of Star Chamber and High Commission*, p. 95.
59. PRO, E. 125/4, ff. 50-54, Feb. 11, 1627/8.
60. PRO, P.C. 2/41, pp. 498-99, PC to commissioners of oyer and terminer, April 4, 1632; S.P. 38/16, warrant for a pardon and release to William Cowse, Jan. 11, 1635/6; E. 159/475, Hil. 11 Chas. I, rot. 158, Letters Patent under the Great Seal granting remission to Cowse, Jan. 13, 1635/6. I am grateful to Prof. T. G. Barnes for providing me with a transcript of this last source.
61. PRO, P.C. 2/41, pp. 499-500, PC to sheriff of Gloucestershire, April 4, 1632; p. 530, warrant to keeper of Newgate to bring John Williams, alias Skimington, before the A-G, April 26, 1632.
62. PRO, P.C. 2/41, pp. 498-99, PC to Sir John Bridgman and other commissioners of oyer and terminer, April 4, 1632.

On Sunday, April 8, 1632, Cowse and William Rolles, his fellow commissioner for the sale of log wood, accompanied by two husband-men and armed, "yt seems for their defence," with two pistols, a pettronel, and swords, arrived at Newland parish church to hear divine service. The presence of the man who had captured Skimington provoked "the under sort of people." A confused affray took place, two pistols were discharged, and Cowse and his companions were assaulted, although the justices were never able to determine exactly what happened or how it began. The result was that Henry and Christopher Hawkins, stonemasons, along with persons unknown, were accused of assault and riotous disturbance of the King's peace, but a jury summoned to hear the evidence failed to indict them.[63] In response, the Council ordered the justices of Gloucestershire to provide guards for Cowse and Rolles whenever they entered the forest on the King's business. Additionally, a number of those suspected of being involved in the assault on Cowse, including Williams's wife, were summoned before the Council. When the suspects appeared, no evidence could be produced against them and they were ordered discharged.[64]

John Williams remained imprisoned in Newgate for five years. It is probable that he was never tried but simply left to rot in prison.[65] In 1637 he twice petitioned for his release, once to the Council and once to the King, claiming that he was in poverty and misery, unable to support himself and his family and incapable of putting up bond. His release was finally authorized on August 7, 1637.[66] The importance

63. PRO, S.P. 16/215/57, JPs of Gloucestershire to PC, April 18, 1632, enclosing no. 57 II, bill of indictment found *ignoramus*.

64. PRO, P.C. 2/41, pp. 521-22, PC to JPs of Gloucestershire, April 20, 1632; p. 523, warrants directed to messengers of the Chamber to bring in nine named individuals, April 20, 1632; p. 529, a warrant to bring in five others, April 25, 1632; P.C. 2/42, p. 13, appearance of suspects recorded May 4, 1632; p. 17, A-G ordered to examine suspects and the truth of the complaint made against them, May 4, 1632; p. 24, discharge ordered, May 9, 1632.

65. Search in the records of K.B. has failed to turn up any account of Williams's trial. At the same time, the proceedings against the six men named with him in the A-G's information of 1632 are well documented. See, e.g., K.B. 29/280, Hil. 7 Chas I, rot. 131; K.B. 29/281, Eas. 8 Chas I, rot. 32, and Mich. 8 Chas I, rot. 136; K.B. 29/282, Eas. 9 Chas I, rot. 33 and rot. 60; K.B. 29/287, Trin. 14 Chas. I; K.B. 27/1591, Eas. 8 Chas I, rot. 71; K.B. 27/1595, Mich. 8 Chas I, rot. 31; K.B. 27/1599, Eas. 9 Chas I, rot. 95; K.B. 27/1602, Trin. 9 Chas I; K.B. 27/1643, Trin. 14 Chas I, rot. 34.

66. PRO, S.P. 16/375/35, undated petition of John Williams to PC; Bod. Lib., Bankes MS 56/6, petition of John Williams to the King, received May 6, 1637, endorsed by the Earl of Holland as sent to A-G Bankes, Aug. 7, 1637.

the government attached to Williams as leader of the Dean riots is indicated by the fact that after five years in prison he was released only after being bound to his good behavior with sureties in the amount of £2,000.[67]

Much has been written about John Williams's role as leader of the riots in the other western forests. Because it is known from a commission of rebellion that a John Williams was involved in the Braydon riots and from the decree in the case that the leaders assumed the *alias* of Skimington, it could be concluded that this man was the John Williams *alias* Skimington of Dean Forest;[68] since Henry Hoskins went to Braydon to try to get "Lady Skimington" to come to Gillingham Forest, it has been assumed that John Williams of Dean Forest had a hand in riots in Gillingham.[69]

These identifications of John Williams *alias* Skimington of Dean Forest with the John Williams found guilty for his part in the Braydon Forest riots, and of John Williams with every mention of Skimington, will not stand up in the face of close scrutiny and fresh evidence. In the Star Chamber fines estreated into Exchequer, John Williams, senior, of Leigh, a carpenter, was fined £20 for his participation in the Braydon riots, but the three Skimingtons were sentenced in the decree to the largest fines; from the evidence of the estreat, John Williams was not one of the Skimingtons.[70] It becomes clear that John Williams of Braydon and John Williams of Dean were two different persons, and only the latter used the *alias* Skimington.

It is equally clear that John Williams *alias* Skimington played no role in the Gillingham riots. The Gillingham Forest riots had been over for three years before disorder broke out at Dean, and the possibility of a direct connection between the Gillingham and the Braydon riots, beyond Hoskins's abortive mission to Braydon in 1631, has already been dismissed. It might be noted that at Gillingham, too,

---

67. Bod. Lib., Bankes MS 45/72, John Williams alias Skimington bond of £2,000 for his good behavior, Aug. 12, 1637. The sureties were Robert Wood, gent. of Clerkenwell, Middlesex, William King, fishmonger of St. Sepulchre, London, and Thomas Slape, fishmonger of Fetter Lane, London. It would be interesting to know their motives in standing surety for Williams.

68. BL, Add. Ch. 40105, commission of rebellion to sheriff, JPs, and Dep. Lts. of Wilts, July 7, 1631.

69. PRO, S.P. 16/193/66, report of William Whitaker, June 10, 1631; Allan, pp. 76-83. Here, as elsewhere, Allan has been misled by overdependence on the inadequate *Calendar of State Papers, Domestic.*

70. PRO, E. 159/475, Hil. 11 Chas. I, rot. 65, estreat of St. Ch. fines, Braydon Forest riots, Trin. 1635; Rushworth, vol. III, App. 73, decree in A-G vs. Braydon rioters, Trin. 1635.

there was a John Williams the younger suspected of participation in the riots and named in Star Chamber process but not included among those fined.[71] His father, John Williams, senior, was a poor carpenter in Mere who successfully petitioned the Wiltshire quarter sessions in 1628 for permission to erect a new cottage on waste ground because the lease on the cottage which he had held for thirty-five years had expired.[72]

Although it is tempting to merge the three John Williamses into one, there is no evidence to support this; one must conclude that John Williams *alias* Skimington was not the organizer and leader of most of the western forest riots. Each forest community produced its own riot leaders, and although they may have been spurred on by events in other forests, there were no "outside agitators." If there was any relationship among the various forest riots, it was that a riot in one forest could stimulate a riot in another where similar conditions already existed. Thus Simon Keble, in his report to Phillip Jacobsen about the Braydon riots, claimed that the rioters were inspired by the reported success of the Dean Forest rioters and the slow and weak response of those in authority.[73] The close chronological proximity of the Dean riots, breaking out in April, 1631, with the Braydon riots, dating from May and June of 1631, argues strongly that this kind of knowledge and influence existed, especially since the leaders of the riots in both places adopted the *alias* of Skimington.

This *alias* came from the custom of "Skimington riding," a demonstration of community disapproval for conduct considered scandalous or immoral. Often the object of the community's reproach was a woman who had gained notoriety as a scold or as one who had cuckolded her husband. In a "Skimington," the community assembled in a loud and raucous procession carrying fowling-pieces and beating drums or suitable domestic substitutes such as pots and pans, and then marched on the house of the offender. In the procession would be included some symbolic representation of the offender—either an effigy, or a person appropriately garbed, such as a man in women's clothes. There would also be a representation of the innocent victim—

71. PRO, P.R.O. 30/38/23, f. 230, subpoena, Sept. 11, 1629; E. 159/472, Trin. 8 Chas. I, rot. 38, estreat of St. Ch. fines, Gillingham Forest riots, Hil. 1629/30.
72. WRO, Q.S. Gt. Roll, Trin. 1628, no. 138, petition of John Williams, endorsed, licensed; Q.S. minute book (order book) Mich. 2 Chas. I to Hil. 6 Chas. I, so ordered midsummer sessions, 1628.
73. PRO, S.P. 16/193/11, June 2, 1631.

for example, a man wearing horns, or one tied to the tail of a horse and symbolically beaten by the person representing his shrewish wife. Outside the house of the offender a loud demonstration would take place. If the offender could be captured, an appropriate punishment such as ducking or being cast in the mud and beaten would be administered; otherwise the effigy was either buried or burned.[74]

At both Dean and Braydon the riots seem to have partaken of some of the quality of a "Skimington," as the community demonstrated its disapproval of enclosure. In the Braydon riots the three leaders wore women's clothes; the first Dean riot of April 5, 1631, with its loud demonstrative procession involving threats to Robert Bridges and concluding with the burial of an effigy of Sir Giles Mompesson, followed almost exactly the pattern of the "Skimington." Skimington was not the *alias* of any one individual: it was common property and was only utilized in those areas—Braydon and Dean—where it represented a genuine expression of the community's outrage. The government, however, feared that Skimington was everywhere, and its fears have misled modern historians into belief in the existence of a single agitator called Skimington. A case in point is that John Williams *alias* Skimington has been erroneously credited with stirring up an anti-enclosure riot at Frampton-on-Severn in Gloucestershire in June, 1631.

In 1609 Robert, Viscount Lisle, later Earl of Leicester, had leased to two gentlemen approximately 350 acres of land new-gained from the river Severn lying between Slymbridge and Frampton in Gloucestershire. Early in 1610, after the ground had been enclosed for use as a sheep pasture, the local inhaitants who claimed common of pasture in the new-gained ground responded by destroying the enclosures.[75] The enclosures were subsequently restored, and for about twenty years the area seems to have remained quiet, although the existence of the enclosure no doubt continued to aggrieve some of the local people. Then in June, 1631, a rumor circulated that "Skymingtones leiuetenaunte and some fyve more of his company were come to

---

74. Two accounts of Skimingtons drawn from the Wiltshire Quarter Sessions Records for 1618 and 1626 are to be found in B. H. Cunnington, ed., *Records of the County of Wiltshire*, pp. 66-67, 79-80. On pp. 64-66 Cunnington also provides other information on Skimingtons, derived from a variety of sources.

75. PRO, STAC. 8/226/28, bill and answer in Oldisworth vs. Hardwick et al., inhabitants of Frampton, Feb. 11, 1609/10, and May 10, 1610; E 178/3836, mm. 1-4, special commission to survey new-gained ground at Slymbridge, June 15, 1608.

Frampton-upon-Seaverne in the County of Gloucester with an intent to throwe in the inclosures of the new groundes."[76] Four of the six men were apprehended and examined before the justices, who discovered that Skimington was not involved in the business at all; nonetheless, the simple fact that some Gloucestershire justices thought it necessary to report in detail to the Privy Council on what turned out to be a very minor matter reveals something of the apprehensiveness of local and central government officials at the time.

The examinations of the suspects suggest a tense atmosphere, full of rumors and false alarms occasioned by the Western Rising. William Gough, a former inhabitant of Frampton, had gone to Bristol in search of work as a laborer and while there, "hearinge the drum strike upp for souldiers to goe to the Kinge of Sweden he, this examinate, did receave impresse money . . . to goe into that service." In conversation with some soldiers in his company Gough told of Skimington's success in Dean Forest and of the riots in Braydon. Then he mentioned the enclosures at Frampton, which the inhabitants hoped Skimington would come and cast down; in return they were willing to provide money and victuals.[77] Gough persuaded five or six of his fellow recruits to go with him on a scouting expedition to discover if the people of Frampton would pay the soldiers to destroy the enclosures in place of Skimington. In the words of one of the recruits, "being a souldier and wantinge money hee hearkened to the mocion but would not undertake it untill he had talked withe some gentlemen that shoulde beare him out in it and provide money and victualls."[78] The expedition proved to be a failure; four of the six would-be rioters were apprehended before they could accomplish anything. Since there was in fact no riot but only "an intention of a Riott," which was not punishable by the justices, the pretext for imprisonment of those involved was that they could not find sureties for their good behavior.[79] No direct connection could be discovered between this and

76. PRO, S.P. 16/194/60, JPs of Gloucestershire to PC, June 23, 1631.

77. PRO, S.P. 16/194/60 I, examination of William Gough taken before Sir William Guise and Nathaniel Stephens, esq., June 21, 1631.

78. PRO, S.P. 16/194/60 II, examination of Francis Nicholls taken before Guise and Stephens, June 21, 1631; see also no. 60 III and IV, examinations of John Joliffe and John Marker, June 21, 1631.

79. PRO, S.P. 16/194/60, JPs of Gloucestershire to PC, June 23, 1631; no. 60 V, examination of William Maverly, constable, June 23, 1631.

the Western Rising, as the following words taken from one of the examinations made clear: "hee denyed that ever hee was in the Forest of Deane or that he was ever in the Forest of Braydon, neither dothe hee knowe what Scimington means."[80]

The Western Rising was not, then, in any real sense a single movement involving coordinated planning and common leadership. However, the riots did spread and intensify as news of events in one western forest reached the next, acting as a catalyst for violence within forests where similar social conditions and tensions existed. This wildfire spread of riot helped to create the impression in the minds of government officials (and, later, historians) that a single group of ringleaders were behind the Western Rising. Of even greater concern to the government were the grave problems of law enforcement created by the rapid diffusion of rioting. Every piece of the cumbersome machinery available to the Crown and its officials was mobilized for the suppression of riot, the arrest and punishment of rioters, and the prevention of future outbreaks.

The prosecution of most of the rioters was handled in the court of Star Chamber, where suits were begun almost as soon as the riots broke out—as soon after reports of the riots reached the lessees of the royal forests as they could get the ear of the Attorney-General. The loss of almost all the records of the court makes it very difficult to date the beginning of the suits. In the Gillingham case, when the first outbreak was reported the Attorney-General must have been prompt in submitting an information in Star Chamber against named suspects, for by the end of 1626 process of attachment had already been issued for the arrest of a number of them.[81] As riots continued and more individuals were identified, new names were added to the information and further process of attachment issued. Speed was also shown in beginning suits against the Braydon and Feckenham rioters. The riots broke out in Braydon in May, 1631, and on the 27th of that month the Attorney-General entered an information in Star Chamber against the rioters.[82] It is impossible to date precisely the beginning of the Star Chamber suit against the Feckenham rioters, but the

80. PRO, S.P. 16/194/60 II, examination of Francis Nicholls, June 21, 1631.

81. PRO, P.R.O. 30/38/22, f. 68, process of attachment, Dec. 25, 1626; f. 69, same, Jan. 5, 1626/7.

82. *APC 1630-31*, pp. 352-53, PC to sheriff, Dep. Lts., and JPs of Wilts, May 27, 1631.

Attorney-General commenced the suit as soon as the first reports about the riots were received by the Council.[83]

Use of Star Chamber rather than commissions of oyer and terminer, the other institution normally employed to deal with riots of a serious nature, was due in part to the types of punishments normally imposed: heavy fines, imprisonment, and humiliating public confession. In the Gillingham case, which had its final hearing on February 23, 1630, seventy-four men were found guilty for their part in the riots. All were committed to the Fleet prison until they found sureties for their good behavior. Twenty-nine were fined £200 each, thirty-six fined £100 each, and the other nine fined £40 each. Those fined £200 and £100 were to be bound in recognizances for their good behavior for two years. Sir James Fullerton was to receive £200 in damages, while the two messengers beaten by the rioters were to be paid £30 each by the rescued prisoners and their rescuers. The decree of the court was to be read in public at the next assizes on the Western circuit; on the same occasion the four ringleaders were to be set in the pillory with papers on their heads describing their offenses.[84]

The Braydon Forest rioters were sentenced on June 12, 1635. All were committed to the Fleet until bound in recognizances for their good behavior. The three ringleaders were fined £500 each and ordered set in the pillory at the Western assizes dressed in women's clothes—their disguise in the riots—with papers on their heads describing the offense. Three others were fined £300 each; the other twenty-eight were each fined £200. Phillip Jacobsen, the lessee of the forest, was to receive £2,000 in damages. One other defendant, John Parker the elder, was sentenced to pay a fine of £500 and to be bound in a recognizance to his good behavior, for threatening and contemptuous speeches to a messenger of the Chamber sent to apprehend the rioters. These fines were later much mitigated: £500 fines were reduced to £50, £300 to £30, and £200 to £20.[85]

The decree in the Feckenham case was issued in Michaelmas term

83. *APC 1630-31*, p. 295, PC to sheriff and JPs of Worcestershire, April 18, 1631.

84. Rushworth, vol. III, App. 28, St. Ch. decree in A-G vs. Hoskins et al., Hil. 1629/30; PRO, E. 159/473, Trin. 9 Chas. I, rot. 59, Letters Patent under the Great Seal giving the judgment of the court, April 10, 1630; Birch, vol. 2, pp. 60-61, Rev. Joseph Mead to Sir Martin Stuteville, Feb. 27, 1629/30; Lincoln's Inn Library, C.4 MS 3, f. 94, report of the case.

85. Rushworth, vol. III, App. 73, St. Ch. decree in A-G vs. Camry et al., Trin. 1635; HLS, MS 1128, no. 299, report of the decision in the case, June 12, 1635; PRO, E. 159/475, Hil. 11 Chas. I, rot. 65, estreat of St. Ch. fines, Trin. 1635.

of 1632. The rioters were committed to the Fleet prison, fined £500 each, and bound in recognizances to their good behavior. Damages were assessed for repair of the enclosures. Finally, at the next Worcestershire quarter sessions they were to acknowledge their offenses in public and show themselves repentant. Only eight people were found guilty and fined, and even their fines were ultimately respited.[86]

Little is known about the legal proceedings connected with the Leicester Forest riots. A Star Chamber suit was begun by the Attorney-General when news of the outbreak of the riots was received but the suit seems to have been dropped, for reasons that remain obscure. It is known that petitions were submitted to the King and Privy Council by inhabitants of the forest and by the corporation and inhabitants of the nearby borough of Leicester complaining of the injustice of the enclosure. As a consequence, a Privy Council committee was set up to investigate the disafforestation but, finding no evidence of unjust dealing on the part of Sir Miles Fleetwood and the other commissioners, it recommended that the disafforestation as it stood should be reconfirmed by Exchequer.[87]

Thwarted in this attempt, the inhabitants of the forest and the borough petitioned the House of Lords in June, 1628, again complaining of the injustice of the disafforestation.[88] The Lords committee for petitions, after examining witnesses and hearing counsel for both sides, found that the proceedings of Fleetwood and the commission had been warranted by "Justice and Judgment." The committee's findings were confirmed by an order of the House of Lords that also praised Fleetwood for adding £8,000 to the King's revenue by the disafforestation.[89] The order contained a provision that the Attorney-

86. Rushworth, vol. III, App. 48, St. Ch. decree in A-G vs. Steward et al., Mich. 1632; PRO, S.P. 16/244/22, undated St. Ch. cause list; S.P. 16/232/43 and 103, two undated St. Ch. mitigation agendas.

87. H. Stocks, ed., *Records of the Borough of Leicester, 1603-1688*, pp. 239-40, undated petition of the inhabitants of Leicester to the King; p. 241, undated list of grievances resulting from disafforestation which probably accompanied the petition; *APC 1627-28*, pp. 475-77, May 31, 1628.

88. *LJ*, III, p. 872, petition of the inhabitants of Leicester Forest, received June 23, 1628; H. of L.R.O., Main Papers, petition of the inhabitants, borderers, and commoners of Leicester Forest to the H. of L., received June 23, 1628, and petition of the inhabitants of the borough of Leicester to the H. of L., received June 23, 1628.

89. *LJ*, III, p. 875, list of witnesses to be examined by the committee for petitions, June 25, 1628; p. 878, order of the H. of L., June 26, 1628.

General should move the King on behalf of the Lords to halt proceedings in the Star Chamber suit against the rioters, which could always be resumed if the riots continued. No doubt this was successful, for the suit seems to have been dropped. It may be surmised that a *quid pro quo* had been worked out: if the forest's inhabitants stopped rioting and petitioning, the government would drop all legal proceedings.

Punishments imposed in Star Chamber, such as commitment to prison with release dependent on finding sureties for good behavior, and exposure to public humiliation, were advantageous to the Crown because they could be used as a deterrent to further riots. Even more important in this regard were the fines. The heavy fines imposed on the Gillingham rioters, for example, were not designed to be collected; they were intended to preserve public order in the future. The rioters were poor men, quite unable to pay such large amounts. The fines and the recognizances forfeited by those who did not appear were granted in April, 1630, to Sir James Fullerton, the victim of the riots, with full power to make whatever arrangements he wished for their collection.[90] Fullerton's agreement with the rioters was that they would be released from prison on promise of their future good behavior, and he, in return, would not collect the fines so long as they refrained from exhibiting further opposition to the enclosure.[91] On Fullerton's death the right to the fines passed to his widow, Lady Magdalen Bruce, and the threat of collection hung over the heads of the convicted rioters throughout the 1630s. This was no doubt salutary in preserving good order in the forest, as the case of John Wolridge demonstrates.

Wolridge, a yeoman, bailiff of the manor of Gillingham at the time of the disafforestation, had been fined £200 for his part in the riots. He was one of the diehards who refused to acquiesce in the enclosure because it deprived him of a number of lucrative perquisites in the forest which pertained to the office of bailiff. After the suppression of the riots and punishment of the rioters he carried on a campaign of his own against the disafforestation. Sometime in the early 1630s Wolridge sent a petition protesting the enclosure to Arthur Pyne, a

90. PRO, E. 159/473, Trin. 9 Chas. I, Letters Patent under the Great Seal granting the fines and forfeited recognisances to Sir James Fullerton, April 10, 1630.

91. PRO, E. 133/139/1, Barons' depositions in Wolridge vs. Earl of Elgin, Feb. 15, 1637/8 and May 23, 1638; E. 134/14 Chas. I/Eas. 24, depositions by commission in the same case.

Somerset justice of the peace. Arthur Pyne was the son of Hugh Pyne, a vociferous opponent of royal financial expedients in the 1620s who came very close to trial for treason in 1626. Arthur himself was thought to be well disposed to "popular causes." He delivered Wolridge's petition to his sister, Prince Charles's nurse, to give to the King.[92] As a consequence, four influential gentlemen met at Gillingham, as referees commissioned by the judges of assize, to redress wrongs done at the time of disafforestation. Little can be discovered about their proceedings except that they recommended an allotment to the poor of the parish of Mere who had received no compensation on disafforestation.[93]

Wolridge's continued opposition to the enclosure in violation of the agreement with Fullerton resulted in his recommittal to the Fleet prison at the behest of Thomas, Lord Bruce, Earl of Elgin, Fullerton's stepson and executor.[94] Wolridge was released on a promise, soon broken, to be on his best behavior. He returned to the forest and tried to persuade the tenants of Gillingham Manor to refuse to pay the rents to the lord of the manor, the Earl of Elgin.[95] The Earl, driven to the limits of his patience, used the ultimate weapon at his disposal: he moved to levy the Star Chamber fine. To compel payment, Wolridge's goods and the six acres of land he received as compensation at the enclosure of Gillingham were extended by the Exchequer at Elgin's suit. Wolridge in turn sued Elgin, his mother, and his bailiff Thomas Brunker, claiming that the extent was illegal since Sir James Fullerton had unconditionally released him from payment of the fine.[96]

The evidence in the case is as convincing to the modern reader as it was to the Barons of the Exchequer, namely, that Wolridge and the other rioters were not completely absolved of payment by Fullerton: he

92. PRO, E. 134/14 Chas. I/Eas. 24, deposition of Phillip Marsh, linenweaver, who carried the petition to Pyne. For Hugh Pyne's career see T. G. Barnes, *Somerset 1625-1640*, p. 34.

93. PRO, E. 134/14 Chas. I/Eas. 24, deposition of Branden Shepherd, tanner. A report of the commissioners recommending an allotment for the poor of Mere is in JRL, Nicholas MS 71/2, a document containing the claims of the inhabitants of Mere to common in Gillingham Forest, Feb., 1645/6. The four commissioners were Sir Ralph Hopton, Sir Henry Ludlow, Robert Hopton, esq., and Robert Hide, esq.

94. PRO, E. 133/139/1, depositions of Robert Bennet, gent., and John Leightborne, servant to the Warden of the Fleet.

95. This is clearly implied in the defendant's interrogatories in PRO, E. 134/14 Chas. I/Eas. 24.

96. PRO, E. 112/174/63, bill and answer in Wolridge vs. the Earl of Elgin et al., bill undated, answer dated Mich., 1637; E. 125/22, ff. 133-34, an order in the same case, Oct. 28, 1637, which neatly summarizes the points at issue.

had only promised to refrain from levying the fines so long as the convicted rioters refrained from interference with the enclosures. He and his heirs were still at liberty to levy the fines if that agreement was broken. Thus, the judgment of the court found "that the fine of £200 was not discharged or released by the said Sir James Fullerton in his lifetime nor since." Wolridge's bill was "absolutely dismissed out of this Court without costs."[97]

Given Wolridge's experience, it is little wonder that aside from his own activities and those of John Phillips, the rioters lapsed into quiescence after the Star Chamber case had been decided. Yet the quiet was deceptive. The disorders of 1643 and beyond prove that the only thing needed to spark new riots was the removal of the threat of punishment at the hands of the Earl of Elgin, as was to come with the dislocation caused by the Civil War.

Perhaps the most important reason for the use of Star Chamber as the main instrument for punishing rioters was that it enabled the Attorney-General and the Privy Council, both as Privy Council and as Star Chamber, to keep abreast of the main problem connected with the riots, that of apprehending the rioters and compelling their appearance for trial. Council warrants were used to stiffen Star Chamber process.[98] Council letters were sent to justices, sheriffs, and deputy lieutenants urging them to carry out the duties laid on them by commissions of rebellion out of Star Chamber.[99] Local magistrates were commanded to aid messengers of the Chamber and sergeants-at-arms in the work of attachment.[100]

Great difficulties existed for the government in preventing new outbreaks of riots and in effecting the arrest of suspected rioters, as

97. PRO, E. 125/25, f. 334, order of dismissal, Oct. 28, 1639.

98. A good example comes from the process dealing with the Braydon rioters: PRO, S.P. 16/203/96, copy of St. Ch. order, Nov. 29, 1631, with no. 96 I, a list of rioters to be apprehended, strengthened by P.C. 2/41, pp. 302-4, warrant with clause of assistance for apprehension of the same suspects, Dec. 12, 1631.

99. An example of this is to be found in the Gillingham case: PRO, P.R.O. 30/38/23, f. 127, a commission of rebellion to the sheriffs of Dorset, Somerset, and Wilts, Dec. 1, 1628; *APC 1628-29*, p. 238, PC to same sheriffs to execute all process to be sent to them from St. Ch., Nov. 20, 1628. Another example concerns the Braydon riots: BL, Add. Ch. 40105, a commission of rebellion to the sheriff, JPs, and Dep. Lts. of Wilts, July 7, 1631, supported by PRO, P.C. 2/41, pp. 122-23, warrant with clause of assistance for apprehension of the same suspects, July 24, 1631.

100. Warrants noted above in PRO, P.C. 2/41, pp. 122-23 and 302-4, contain clauses of assistance directed to local officials to give all possible aid to the Crown's officers in the apprehension of suspects.

can be seen in the attempts made to execute Star Chamber process. At Gillingham, messengers of the Chamber trying to apprehend suspects were on occasion beaten and their prisoners rescued. It was also reported that the Gillingham rioters burned forty warrants from the Privy Council and forty processes out of Star Chamber.[101] Although this number ought not to be taken literally, a glance at surviving Star Chamber process books indicates that much process had to be issued for the arrest of rioters. There were six stages through which such procedures went: first, a subpoena to appear; failing response to that, attachment, which brought the sheriff into the proceedings to aid the execution; next, alias attachment; attachment with proclamation; alias attachment with proclamation; and, finally, commission of rebellion.[102] To attach most of the Gillingham rioters this round of process had to be renewed at least once and sometimes twice. Many suspects in fact never appeared to answer the Attorney-General's information in Star Chamber. Over 300 Gillingham riot suspects were named in Star Chamber process, but only 97 seem to have appeared or been brought in, and of these, 13 were ultimately found not guilty. After this first appearance many were bound in recognizances of £100 each to appear in person at the final hearing; they were not to become involved in any other riot in the meantime and were to aid and assist in the suppression of new riots. Thirty-two of the seventy-four ultimately fined forfeited their recognizances for non-appearance at the final hearing.[103]

There survives one other indication of the difficulty faced by the Crown's officers in executing process against the Gillingham rioters. In Michaelmas term of 1628 the court of Star Chamber issued a writ to the sheriff of Dorset grounded on the Statute of Northampton cap. 3 (1328) for the apprehension of the riotous inhabitants of Gillingham and Mere. This statute enacted that any armed person who attempted to intimidate an officer of the Crown during the execution of his office was liable to imprisonment at the King's pleasure.[104]

101. Birch, vol. 1, pp. 453-54, Mr. John Pory to Rev. Joseph Mead, Dec. 19, 1628.

102. PRO, P.R.O., 30/38/22-23, Star Chamber process books *passim*.

103. PRO, E. 159/472, Trin. 9 Chas I, rot. 38, estreat of St. Ch. fines, Gillingham rioters, Hil. 1629/30; E. 159/473, Trin. 9 Chas. I, rot. 59, Letters Patent under the Great Seal giving judgment of the court, April 10, 1630.

104. JRL, Nicholas MS 72/11, Fullerton to ?, Oct. 3, 1628; BL, Lans. MS 639, f. 16, writ grounded on the Statute of Northampton issued by order of the court of Star Chamber, Mich., 1628.

Although the Star Chamber process books covering the period of the Braydon and Feckenham riots are no longer extant, we know that in both cases process went as far as commission of rebellion.[105] Furthermore, in one Star Chamber order relating to the Braydon riots it was admitted that some of the individuals named had already been served a number of times but had neither appeared to answer the Attorney-General's information nor given bonds for their future appearance. In the same case, 142 people were named in process but only 34 were actually fined in Star Chamber.[106] Although it is not known how many suspects actually appeared and how many were found not guilty, it is probably safe to conclude from the Gillingham example that a large number of those named never appeared, a conclusion that no doubt applies equally to the Feckenham case, in which only 8 individuals were found guilty.[107]

It is not entirely clear why a commission of oyer and terminer was the judicial instrument chosen to deal with the Dean Forest rioters. One may surmise, however, that it was recommended by the possibility of obtaining indictments and convictions for felony and, hence, some salutary hangings. In such a commission neither the Privy Council nor the Attorney-General was directly involved in the apprehension and prosecution of suspects. Instead, their place was taken by commissioners of oyer and terminer, headed in the Dean cases by Sir John Bridgman, Chief Justice of Chester, who sat periodically with his fellow commissioners at Painswick in Gloucestershire from August of 1631 through the first six months of 1632.[108]

In the Star Chamber prosecutions, difficulty was experienced in compelling every rioter to appear, and no doubt a considerable number escaped punishment, but all the leading rioters and many of the rank-and-file were brought to justice. The commission of oyer and terminer in the Dean case proved to be an almost total failure as an instrument for imposing punishment on rioters. What little is known

105. BL, Add. Ch. 40105, commission of rebellion for apprehension of Braydon rioters, July 7, 1631; PRO, S.P. 16/214/46, sheriff and JPs of Worcestershire to PC, Mar. 17, 1631/2, which notes that they arrested rioters while executing a St. Ch. commission of rebellion.

106. PRO, S.P. 16/203/96, copy of St. Ch. order, Nov. 29, 1631, with no. 96 I, a list of suspects to be apprehended; E. 159/475, Hil. 11 Chas I, rot. 65, estreat of St. Ch. fines, Braydon rioters, Trin. 1635.

107. PRO, S.P. 16/232/43, list of fines taxed and forfeited in St. Ch.

108. PRO, C. 231/5, p. 53, commission of oyer and terminer to the Earl of Northampton, Sir John Bridgman, et al., June 21, 1631; p. 79, renewed April 19, 1632.

of the commission's proceedings indicates that although a large number of people were indicted for riot, very few were ever arrested, brought to trial, and convicted. By the fourth sitting—late in October of 1631—only two rioters had been convicted. One had been fined £100, the other £66.13s.4d; this last fine was later remitted. Both were sentenced to prison for a year and were to find sureties for their good behavior before they could be released. A number of suspects indicted at the third session had not been apprehended, and at this fourth session eighty-four more were indicted.[109] Despite urging from the Privy Council, neither the commissioners nor the sheriff of Gloucestershire was able to increase the numbers apprehended.

In 1632 the commission was renewed and the commissioners proceeded on the indictments of the previous year. By May, 1632, one more rioter had been tried, convicted, and sentenced to a fine of £6.13s.4d. and imprisonment for six months. Two others had been acquitted. One hundred and forty indicted rioters were yet to be tried, "and every sessions process have byn made and delivered to the Sheriff for the arrestinge of them with strict charge to perform his duety therein, yett we have not had above one or two at a Session brought in whereby we could not performe that service wee desire."[110] This is the last surviving notice of the commission.

The Statute of Westminster II cap. 46 of 1285 was a measure designed to deal with serious rural unrest. The Statute of Merton cap. 4 of 1236, recognizing that the soil of wastes and commons belonged to the lord, gave to each manorial lord the power of approvement— the right to take excess waste lands into his own demesne and extinguish the rights to common on it claimed by his tenants, if he left enough to meet their needs. It dealt only with the lord's rights against his own tenants; neighbors who had rights to common could still protect them against approvement by an action of novel disseisin. Westminster II cap. 46 altered this situation by giving the lord the same rights of approvement against neighbors as he had against his own tenants. In anticipation of violent reaction, the statute also dealt

109. PRO, S.P. 16/203/7, commissioners of oyer and terminer to PC, Nov. 3, 1631; K.B. 29/281, Trin. 8 Chas I, rot. 87, writ of *habeas corpus* to bring John Knight, fined 100 marks, out of the custody of sheriff of Gloucestershire, with marginal note *"remittet."*
110. PRO, P.C. 2/41, p. 277, PC to sheriff of Gloucestershire, Nov. 30, 1631; pp. 277-78, PC to Sir John Bridgman et al., Nov. 30, 1631; S.P. 16/216/77, commissioners of oyer and terminer to PC, May 25, 1632; see also *HMC 12th Report*, App. I, p. 452, Bridgman to Sec. Coke, Mar. 17, 1631/2.

with anti-enclosure riots by persons unknown. Previously, unless the lord whose enclosures had been destroyed could name the defendants he had no remedy at common law, but this statute made neighboring townships, through process of distraint, liable for repair of enclosures and for damages to the injured party in cases of riot by persons unknown. The first notable reenactment came in the reign of Edward VI; on the heels of Ket's rebellion in Norfolk the Statutes 3 and 4 of Edward VI cap. 3 (1549) renewed Merton cap. 4 and Westminster II cap. 46.[111]

During the Western Rising in May of 1631, the Privy Council ordered the magistrates of Wiltshire to inform the inhabitants of the townships in and around Braydon Forest that if the identities of the rioters were not revealed, the Statute of Westminster II cap. 46 would be enforced.[112] There is no evidence that the statute was applied in this case, or in any other disorder ultimately punished in Star Chamber, no doubt because many of the rioters were eventually identified and fined and therefore damages could be, and were, assessed on them. The Crown's reference to the statute does, however, testify to the difficulties it was encountering in apprehending rioters.

In the case of Dean the statute was actually enforced, undoubtedly because so few rioters could be identified and held responsible for their depredations. In Trinity term of 1631 John Gibbons obtained a writ returnable in King's Bench, grounded on the statute, to discover who was responsible for the destruction of his enclosures in Cannop Chase. The sheriff of Gloucestershire summoned a jury which found that the enclosures had been destroyed in the night by persons unknown. In Michaelmas of 1632 the neighboring townships were distrained for damages and the repair of the Cannop Chase enclosures.[113]

It was on the backs of local officials—sheriffs, justices of the peace, and deputy lieutenants—that the burden of identifying and apprehending the rioters and preventing future riots was laid; their difficulties in the Western Rising generally and their almost total

---

111. T. F. T. Plucknett, *The Legislation of Edward I*, pp. 83-86; W. S. Holdsworth, *A History of English Law*, vol. III, pp. 123-25; W. K. Jordan, *Edward VI*, vol. II, p. 40.

112. *APC 1630-31*, pp. 352-53, PC to sheriff, Dep. Lts., and JPs of Wilts, May 27, 1631.

113. PRO, K.B. 27/1591, Eas. 8 Chas I; K.B. 29/281, Eas. 8 Chas. I, rot. 22 and rot. 33; Mich. 8 Chas I, rot. 124; Hil. 8 Chas. I, rot. 185; William Jones, *Les Reportes*, p. 306; GCL, MS L. F.1. 1, ff. 12-15, lamentable state of Dean Forest.

failure in the forest of Dean must be explained. The problems faced by the individual messenger of the Chamber or sergeant-at-arms sent by the government to apprehend rioters seem self-evident. He carried little authority or weight of force with which to overawe the rioters.[114] Local officials, who were expected to provide force through the *posse* or the trained bands, faced difficulties compounded of three elements. The scale of the riots and obvious intransigence of the rioters is reflected in the frequent recurrence of disorders in the same areas despite repeated attempts to suppress them; at times the over-whelming magnitude of the riots, particularly in Dean Forest, terrified local authorities into inactivity. The second element is the unreliability of the forces on which local officials had to depend. Finally, there is the geographical problem, the difficulty of operating in forest terrain which offered opportunities for dispersal, concealment, and advance notice of the approach of the *posse* or militia. This last problem was most severe in Dean, a forest of 30,000 acres with a particularly close-knit community hostile to outside interference.

Despite much encouragement from King and Privy Council to use the *posse* or the militia to suppress riots, armed clashes with the rioters were generally avoided. On only two occasions, at Gillingham and at Feckenham, did such encounters take place. Faced with near-insurrections, local officials were often powerless and reduced to inactivity. Simon Keble accused the neighboring justices of being unwilling to act against the Braydon rioters, while in Gloucestershire the sheriff and other officials seem to have been paralyzed in the face of the Dean riots.[115] The central government's explanation of this situation was simple—negligence on the part of local governors. Before the summer assizes of 1631, the Lord Keeper charged the judges on the Western and Oxford circuits to discover the names of the rioters and their abettors and to identify the negligent authorities.

As reinforcement for the Lord Keeper's charge the King wrote to the judges on both circuits deploring the laxness of local officials in

---

114. See, for example, the incredible harassment suffered by John Wragg, Messenger of the Chamber, sent to Gloucestershire to aid the commissioners of oyer and terminer in the work of apprehending suspects: PRO, P.C. 2/41, p. 156, warrant to John Wragg, Aug. 31, 1631; S.P. 16/203/104, undated petition by Wragg to PC; P.C. 2/41, p. 174, PC to sheriff of Gloucestershire, Sept. 23, 1631.

115. PRO, S.P. 16/193/11, Simon Keble to Phillip Jacobsen, June 2, 1631; for Gloucestershire, see below, p. 119.

Wiltshire, Worcestershire, and Gloucestershire in allowing riots to continue in Braydon, Feckenham, and Dean forests. Such riots, the King complained, tended "to the disturbance of our settled peace and government whereof we are very tender." The judges were urged to proceed against the rioters "with all the severity which in Justice yee may" and to inform all local magistrates "that wee look for better performance hereafter." If the rioters were not quickly identified and punished, "we shall impute the fault thereof to none but them who have powre to doe itt."[116]

This exhortation had only two recorded results. One was an order made at the Salisbury assizes, July 18, 1631, for the suppression of the riots still continuing in Braydon Forest. The constables of the hundreds were commanded to set a sufficient watch and ward night and day to arrest all "lewde and rebellious persons" who were to be jailed or bound over with sufficient sureties to the next assizes. The other was at the Trinity quarter sessions of 1631, when the justices of Wiltshire replaced the constable of the hundred of Highworth Cricklade. The former constable, being unlearned and having no land or living, was felt to be unfit for the duties of his office, especially that of suppressing the riots in Braydon.[117] One might reasonably infer that the deprived constable was sympathetic to the rioters.

Exhortations to duty and accusations of negligence, common form in Privy Council letters to local officials in the counties of the Western Rising, were issued most frequently and insistently to the authorities in Gloucestershire, who seemed reduced to complete ineffectualness in the face of the Dean riots.[118] As soon as Giles Bridges' affidavit had been submitted to the Exchequer, giving the Crown its first information about the Dean Forest riots, the lord lieutenant of Gloucestershire was ordered to have the trained bands ready to suppress any new riots. Sir John Bridgman, Chief Justice of Chester, was requested to

116. PRO, S.P. 16/196/56, draft of signet letter sent to the judges of assize on the Western circuit, July 13, 1631, and to the judges on the Oxford circuit, July 14, 1631.

117. PRO, Assizes 24/20, f. 33, order made at Salisbury, Wilts, July 18, 1631; WRO, Q.S. Great Roll, Trin. 1631, no. 98.

118. For Gillingham, *APC 1627-28*, pp. 272-73, PC to Dep. lts. and JPs of Dorset, June 16, 1628; for Braydon, *APC 1630-31*, pp. 382-83, PC to Dep. Lts. of Wilts and Dorset, June 13, 1631; pp. 382-83, PC to sheriffs and JPs of Wilts and Dorset, June 13, 1631; for Feckenham, PRO, P.C. 2/41, pp. 486-87, PC to sheriff, JPs, and Dep. Lts. of Worcestershire, Mar. 27, 1632; pp. 487-88, PC to Earl of Bridgewater, Ld. Pres. of the Council in the Marches of Wales, Mar. 27, 1632.

keep a close watch on the business and to urge local magistrates to perform their duties.[119]

At the same time, an angry letter was written to the sheriff and justices of Gloucestershire, expressing the government's displeasure at their inactivity. The Council marvelled that riots of such magnitude could occur without the justices attempting to suppress them. "We hold this for an extreame neglect of your duetyes, whereof yee must looke to give a severe account, if upon this admonicion yee shall not take better care for the peace of the country." If necessary they were to raise the power of the county to apprehend the leading rioters. All proceedings were to be certified to the Council. "Hereof yee must not faile as yee tender his Majesties heavy displeasure."[120]

This paralysis of local government continued. On April 5, 1631, "a greater ryott or rather rebellious assembly" occurred. The Council ordered the lord lieutenant to have the deputy lieutenants ready the trained bands to suppress further riots and arrest the rioters, but ten days later, the Council was complaining of the deputy lieutenants' failure to act.[121] As late as June, the Council was still castigating the local governors of Gloucestershire for their failure to deal with the riots, especially "when we consider what expresse and carefull directions have been from tyme to tyme given by this board as well for the suppressing and preventing of the outragious assemblies within the Forrest of Deane as for the discoverie and apprehending of the offenders and proceeding with them in an exemplarie way." Concerning the negligence of the local magistrates, "his Majestie intends to take a strict enquirie and examinacion, and not to passe by such disobedience with an ordenarie reprehencion." The sheriff and justices were again ordered to use the trained bands.[122] The lord lieutenant was also to see that the deputy lieutenants did their job, while John Bridgman, Chief Justice of Chester, the only official whom the Council could trust, was to supervise and direct the work of sheriff, justices, and deputy lieutenants.[123]

119. *APC 1630-31*, p. 284, PC to Earl of Northampton and PC to Justice Bridgman, April 5, 1631.

120. *APC 1630-31*, pp. 284-85, PC to sheriff and JPs of Gloucestershire, April 5, 1631.

121. *APC 1630-31*, p. 290, PC to Earl of Northampton, April 8, 1631; p. 294, PC to same, April 15, 1631.

122. *APC 1630-31*, pp. 390-91, PC to sheriff, Dep. Lts., and JPs of Gloucestershire, June 22, 1631.

123. *APC 1630-31*, p. 391, PC to Earl of Northampton and PC to Sir John Bridgman, June 22, 1631.

This reluctance to act can be explained at least in part by the large number of rioters involved. Although the estimates of size—ranging in magnitude from 100 or more at Gillingham and 300 at some Feckenham riots, to 1,000 at Braydon and 3,000 in the Dean riots—are probably not to be taken literally, they convey a sense that groups too large to be confidently handled in a head-on clash were involved. The usual procedure was to wait until matters had cooled down before the sheriff and his men moved in to arrest as many known suspects as they could lay their hands on. The kind of intimidation which paralyzed local magistrates also affected potential witnesses who could identify and give evidence against the rioters. Witnesses to the Braydon riots, fearing destruction of their houses, were reluctant to depose before Wiltshire justices or to give evidence in London. Similarly, witnesses to the Dean Forest riots, in fear for their lives, fled into the Marches of Wales to avoid giving evidence before the commission of oyer and terminer.[124]

One other reason for local officials' hesitancy to act against the rioters lay in the weakness of the police powers available to them. In spite of frequent urging from the Council there is no evidence that the trained bands were used during the Western Rising, except for one unusual instance at Dean. When disorders broke out there must have been real aversion to calling out a militia that might prove unreliable in suppressing riots involving, if not neighbors, at least fellow countrymen. In any case, the county militia was a poorly trained and inadequate military force.

The deputy lieutenants of Wiltshire, unwilling to use the militia for the suppression of the Braydon riots, explained their reluctance as a result of lack of authorization from the Council, but even when authority was conveyed they still did not raise the militia.[125] The real explanation for this is revealed in a series of events worthy of the pen of W. S. Gilbert.

Toward the end of 1631 the sheriff of Wiltshire, John Topp, was directed by a writ from Chancery to execute the court's judgment and deliver Clayhill Farm in Selwood Forest to the possession of Hopton

124. PRO, S.P. 16/193/11, Simon Keble to Phillip Jacobsen, June 2, 1631; P.C. 2/41, pp. 158-60, PC to Earl of Bridgewater, Ld. Pres. of the Council in the Marches of Wales, Aug. 31, 1631; pp. 157-58, PC to Sir John Bridgman et al., Aug. 31, 1631.
125. PRO, S.P. 16/193/11, Simon Keble to Phillip Jacobsen, June 2, 1631; *APC 1630-31*, pp. 382-83, PC to Ld. Lts. of Wilts and Dorset, June 13, 1631.

Haynes, plaintiff in a suit. Topp, however, found it impossible to execute the writ. The defendant, Thomas Carr, refused to surrender possession and the farm was "strongly deteyned by the seyd Carr with force of armes and musketts and a multitude of base and desperate persons."[126] On being informed "of the aforesaid insolencies nott to be suffered in a civill state under any pretence or colour whatsoever," the Council authorized raising enough companies of the trained bands to aid the sheriff in his execution of the Chancery decree.[127] A company of militia foot, composed of fifty musketeers and fifty pikemen, was raised and marched to the property in question, accompanied by ordnance brought from Bristol. When proclamation was made demanding possession, the rioters refused to surrender and seven men came out of the farmhouse, muskets at the ready. Only at this point was the state of the militia company's arms examined. It turned out that some of the men had neither powder nor shot; others had only powder; still others had only shot. "Only foure were furnished for service, none could be gotten to light their matches." The pikemen had corselets in their packs but refused to put them on. To end the farce the sheriff of Wiltshire "thought fitt to excuse my departure by reason of the foulnes of the weather and the neereness of the night, then to goe on upon the service with much hazard."[128]

On receipt of this information the Council commanded the officials concerned to try again with enough men and ammunition to insure success.[129] The sheriff was unable to get an expedition organized. Gunners for the ordnance were needed, to overawe and, if necessary, to blast out the armed men barricaded in the farmhouse. Since, by the sheriff's account, there was no ordnance in Wiltshire, the requisite weapons and a gunner had to be fetched from Bristol. For the first expedition the plaintiff Haynes went to Bristol and brought back a cannon and a gunner. For the second, the sheriff decided to replace the Bristol gunner with one from Warham, Dorset, since the one from Bristol was suspected of unspecified treacherous dealings.

126. PRO, S.P. 16/201/5, John Topp to PC, Oct. 2, 1631.
127. PRO, P.C. 2/41, pp. 199-200, PC to Earl of Pembroke and Montgomery, Ld. Lt. of Wilts, Oct. 21, 1631; pp. 200-201, PC to sheriff of Wilts, Oct. 21, 1631.
128. PRO, S.P. 16/203/106, sheriff of Wilts to PC, Nov. 8, 1631; see also no. 106 I, copy of letter of sheriff of Wilts to Sir Edward Baynton and Sir Walter Vaughan, Nov. 6, 1631, and no. 106 II, warrant from sheriff to Baynton to raise the trained bands.
129. PRO, P.C. 2/41, p. 236, PC to Ld. Lt. of Wilts; pp. 237-38, PC to Dep. Lts. of Wilts; pp. 238-39, PC to sheriff of Wilts, Nov. 16, 1631.

The new gunner turned out to be even more unreliable. On looking at the ordnance, he decided it was not of large enough caliber. When the sheriff ordered him to go to Bristol and get another cannon, he refused unless promised a pension for his wife and children in the event of his death on the expedition. The gunner admitted that when he had gone to look at the farmhouse to judge what would be needed for a successful bombardment, the defenders had told him that he and all those who tried to attack the farm would be killed. The sheriff charged the gunner in the King's name to aid in the capture of the farm. He replied that he would appear on the appointed day, but would not touch the ordnance.[130] Thereupon Topp wrote to the mayor of Bristol requesting another cannon, ammunition, and two new gunners. These new gunners refused to touch the guns unless a proclamation was made at the King's command that it would be considered murder if they were killed but that it would not be murder if they killed any of the defenders of the farm. The sheriff in turn appealed to the Council to order the gunners to undertake the business.[131]

Losing patience, the Privy Council ordered the various gunners to put in appearances to answer for their behavior. At the same time, convinced of Topp's negligence, the Council turned its wrath on the unfortunate sheriff. He was discharged from any further concern with the Clayhill Farm business and a warrant was issued for his appearance in London. He was also ordered to turn over all written orders and process to his successor. Topp soon cleared himself of all suspicion, satisfying the Council that he had done what he could to carry out its instructions. Meanwhile, the deputy lieutenants of Wiltshire were ordered to raise the trained bands to aid the new sheriff in the work of obtaining possession of the farm, and the sheriff was instructed to get new ordnance from Bristol.[132] Unfortunately, at this point the matter disappears from view, and the fate of all concerned remains unknown. The moral of this tale, however, is crystal clear: if the Wiltshire trained bands had such difficulty in

130. PRO, S.P. 16/204/2, sheriff of Wilts to PC, Dec. 5, 1631.
131. PRO, S.P. 16/210/20, copy of letter from sheriff of Wilts to mayor of Bristol, Dec. 1, 1631; S.P. 16/204/2, sheriff of Wilts to PC, Dec. 5, 1631.
132. PRO, P.C. 2/41, p. 299, warrants to bring the gunners and John Topp before the PC, Dec. 12, 1631; pp. 325-26, order setting Topp at liberty, Dec. 12, 1631; pp. 299-300, PC to Ld. Lt. of Wilts and PC to sheriff of Wilts, Dec. 12, 1631.

taking a farmhouse defended by a handful of desperadoes, little imagination is needed to conceive of what they would have done in the face of hundreds of determined rioters.

The other aspect of the ineffectiveness of the militia is indicated by the behavior of the two gunners from Bristol. The friends or relatives of a slain rioter could move a prosecution for murder in King's Bench against the individuals responsible; this possibility must have greatly increased reluctance to fire in an armed clash with rioters. During the Braydon riots a proclamation like that demanded by the Bristol gunners had to be made by order of the court of Star Chamber: it would be murder if rioters killed any of the sheriff's men, while it would not be murder for the sheriff's men to kill any of the rioters.[133]

Although we do not know the exact state of the Dorset, Gloucestershire, and Worcestershire militias at this time, it is doubtful that the Wiltshire militia was unique in its lack of equipment and training; certainly this view of the militia fits well with a recent study made of the subject by Professor Thomas G. Barnes.[134] There can be little doubt, then, why the trained bands were never used in the Western Rising. Rioters were normally apprehended by a sheriff leading a substantial group of well-armed men on whom he could depend, such as his officers and servants and those of the other local governors.

The problem of geography—the extensive and inhospitable terrain of the forests—compounded the difficulties of local officials in dealing with the rioters. Simon Keble, the agent of Philip Jacobsen, was faced with the obstacle of distance in his attempts to suppress the Braydon Forest riots. He was forced to ride thirty-four miles for the sheriff, who alone had the authority to raise the *posse comitatus.* When he returned with the sheriff, the rioters—who had already pulled down most of the fences—fled. Only twelve were taken prisoner "accidentally" and imprisoned. Once the sheriff had left the rioters reappeared, and on the very day on which Keble was writing his report they had killed twenty-two of his sheep and had "gathered together to pull downe that which is left and how to prevent it or to save the lodge or my family from their fury I cannott imagine."[135]

It was in Dean Forest that the terrain presented an insurmountable problem. Many of those who had been indicted for their participation

133. PRO, S.P. 16/204/2, sheriff of Wilts to PC, Dec. 5, 1631.
134. T. G. Barnes, *Somerset 1625-1640*, pp. 244-80.
135. PRO, S.P. 16/193/11, Keble to Jacobsen, June 2, 1631.

in the riots fled into the Marches of Wales, Herefordshire and Monmouthshire, to escape prosecution.[136] Even those who remained in Dean were difficult to arrest. During August of 1631 Sir Ralph Dutton, the sheriff of Gloucestershire, entered the forest to execute warrants issued by the commission of oyer and terminer for the attachment of a number of suspects. The Council was informed that after arresting two men, Dutton was met by a number of armed men who forced him to flee for his life with his prisoners. He was rebuked severely by the Council, which expressed amazement that the sheriff could be so quickly and easily repulsed "by such base disorderly persons" and then fail to raise the *posse comitatus* for the proper execution of the warrants. Dutton had been expressly charged by the Council to execute all warrants of the commission with the aid of the *posse* and, if necessary, to call on the deputy lieutenants to help him with the trained bands.[137]

In his reply Dutton denied the report that he and his servants had been repulsed by armed men, although he did admit that he and 120 men went into the forest secretly in the night, captured only two suspects, and then withdrew when discovered by the inhabitants. Dutton laid the main blame for his failures upon the terrain, "in regard of the Seaverne on the one side and the River of Wye, the other two shires on the other side, and the hills, woods, myne pitts and colepitts where they dwell, the apprehending of them becomes very difficult and must be effected only by policy never by strength."[138]

Dutton resorted to a number of "policies." On receipt of a second writ from the commission of oyer and terminer to arrest suspects, he issued warrants for their attachment to the constables of the hundreds and parishes where they lived. Also, his undersheriff and bailiffs "laid waite for them at the faires and marketts of those partes." As a result of this activity, only two suspects were taken, so Dutton tried a second scheme. Since many of the rioters were reputed to be members of the militia, he had the deputy lieutenants call out the trained bands of the forest division. At the same time, the militia of two other divisions were summoned to meet at the rendezvous in order to arrest all

136. PRO, P.C. 2/41, pp. 158-60, PC to Earl of Bridgewater, Aug. 31, 1631; pp. 157-58, PC to Sir John Bridgman et al., Aug. 31, 1631.

137. PRO, P.C. 2/41, pp. 160-61, PC to sheriff of Gloucestershire, Aug. 31, 1631; p. 157, PC to Earl of Northampton, Aug. 31, 1631.

138. PRO, S.P. 16/203/36, Ralph Dutton, sheriff of Gloucestershire, to PC, Nov. 14, 1631.

suspected rioters found in the ranks of the forest division. When only one rioter was found in this way, the sheriff and the trained bands—in their only recorded action during the Western Rising—spent two days conducting a fruitless house-to-house search for the rioters, only to discover that they had fled into the neighboring counties of Hereford and Monmouth. His final "policy" was bribery. Dutton entered into secret negotiations with some forest dwellers, to whom he gave "some ready money" and to whom he promised large rewards for the capture of John Williams, leader of the rioters.[139] None of Dutton's "policies" worked, and the problem of bringing the Dean rioters to justice remained insoluble.

Ironically, the most lasting impression left by a survey of the Western Rising from the Crown's point of view is that of the dogged determination of the rioters. Despite the central government's opinion of the riots as insurrections against established authority, and the consequent use of every means of suppression available to the Stuart monarchy, the weakness of such methods in the face of popular opposition is apparent. To understand this deep-rooted opposition to the Crown requires an examination of the social and economic organization of the forests to determine the groups most directly threatened by enclosure.

139. PRO, S.P. 16/203/36, Dutton to PC, Nov. 14, 1631.

Chapter V

The Participants in the Western Rising

The standard view of the causes of the Western Rising and the related question of the social status of the rioters suffers, as does much of the study of English rural history in the Tudor-Stuart period, from the remnants of the Whig Interpretation, combined with a sentimental Arcadianism. The disafforestations are regarded as notorious examples of arbitrary enclosure, in which the financially desperate Stuart monarchy ruthlessly deprived the commoners in the forests of their legal rights. In response, yeomen and husbandmen, aided and abetted by their social betters, rose in righteous wrath to defend their immemorial rights against the despotic monarch.[1]

This view is based upon a set of premises lacking evidential support. The assumption that the social makeup of the rioters consisted of yeomen and husbandmen backed by gentry is based upon the further assumption that the enclosures were arbitrary violations of the rights of property owners; it offers as evidence only the unsubstantiated fears expressed by Stuart officialdom that men of standing were behind the riots. These suppositions quickly break down when confronted by evidence, recently discovered, of the names and social status of those fined in Star Chamber for their parts in the Gillingham and Braydon riots. With what can be gleaned from the

1. The arguments that the enclosures were arbitrary in nature and that the gentry aided and abetted the rioters are developed by both Allan, "The Rising in the West," and E. Kerridge, "The Revolts in Wiltshire."

records relating to the Dean Forest riots, this evidence suggests that people of lower status, particularly artisans, predominated among the known rioters. Only one gentleman was fined for participation in the Western Rising, and he was not one of the leaders.

There is no corroboration whatever for the contention that the riots involved mass participation of yeomen and husbandmen with gentry in the background urging them on. The disafforestations, rather than being arbitrary enclosures, were excellent examples of enclosure by agreement: substantial freeholders and copyholders were asked to grant their consent to the enclosure and the consequent extinction of their rights to common, in return for compensatory allotments of land. Although this segment of society did express some dissatisfaction with the arrangements, only in exceptional cases did that dissatisfaction lead to participation in the riots. Such discontent as there was usually took the form of calculated attempts to employ the processes of the law in order to obtain greater compensation.

It is more probable that most of the rioters were the marginally poor and landless, including artisans. The existence of a large population of poor in the forests is well documented, particularly by the charitable provision made for them by the Crown at disafforestation. Since they lacked landed property, such poor were not entitled to compensatory land allotments, and those lands that the Crown set aside for them were an inadequate substitute for their enjoyment of common without stint in the unenclosed forest. In the particularly well-documented case of Gillingham Forest, those artisans convicted of riot who can be identified as tenants named in manorial records are invariably found to be cottagers, that is, individuals who held little or no land.

The social or occupational status of the seventy-four convicted Gillingham rioters was as follows.[2]

Woollen weaver	1	Flaxdresser	1
Linen weaver	3	Tailor	5
Weaver	8	Glover	3
Fuller	1	Tanner	3
Slaymaker	1	Shoemaker	3
Feltmaker	1	Chandler	1

2. PRO, E. 159/472, Trin. 8 Chas. I, rot. 38, estreat of St. Ch. fines for Gillingham riots, Hil. 1629/30.

Carpenter	4	Husbandman	16
Joiner	1	Yeoman	5
Mason	1		—
Blacksmith	1	Total Farmers	21
Baker	2		
Miller	1	Laborer	2
Butcher	2	Groom	1
Thatcher	1	Mercer	1
Barber	1	No status given	4
	—		—
Total Artisans	45	Total Others	8

Two points should be noted here which will be discussed later at length. The first is the number of men engaged in the cloth industry. Probably most if not all of the weavers mentioned were weavers of woollen cloth. The rather substantial total of nine weavers along with one fuller, one feltmaker, and one slaymaker indicates that Gillingham was an outlying district of the Wiltshire cloth industry, a fact confirmed by the existence of at least three fulling mills in the area, two in the manor of Mere and one in the manor of Gillingham.[3] The second point to be noted is the presence of a number of artisans who depended on the products of the forest's woods and pastures for raw materials—three glovers, three tanners, three shoemakers, four carpenters, one joiner, and one chandler. (Aside from these two obvious industrial concentrations, the trades identified are those typical of both the market town and the manor.) The preponderance of artisans is even more marked with regard to the status of the twenty-nine rioters fined £200 as the most notorious offenders: twenty were artisans, six were yeomen or husbandmen, one was a laborer, and two were of unknown status. Three of the four named ringleaders were artisans: a tailor, a carpenter, and a baker. The other was a yeoman.

The names and statuses of the thirty-four Braydon rioters fined in Star Chamber also survive:[4]

Blacksmith	1	Baker	2
Shoemaker	1	Butcher	2
Sievemaker	1	Gardener	2
Carpenter	1		—
Tailor	1	Total Artisans	11

3. See below, pp. 159–60.
4. PRO, E. 159/475, Hil. 11 Chas. I, rot. 65, estreat of St. Ch. fines for Braydon riots, Trin. 1635.

Yeoman	6	Laborer	3
Husbandman	12	Gentleman	1
		No status given	1
Total Farmers	18		
		Total Others	5

This evidence is not so obviously in favor of artisan predominance in the riots, and there is no evidence of an important industrial concentration. The leaders of the riots, however, the three "Lady Skimingtons," were artisans: a tailor, a sievemaker, and a gardener.

Since the commission of oyer and terminer was unable to bring the Dean Forest rioters to justice, no list of names comparable to those for the Gillingham and Braydon riots was made. Council warrants, examinations, and depositions yield the names of thirty-six actual or suspected participants in the riots of 1631, but only occasionally do they provide the status of the person named. Exchequer records and the records of the forest eyre of 1634 offer clues to the status of a few, although this evidence is not entirely satisfactory: the frequent occurrence of individuals with the same name but different status makes identification of known suspects with persons named in other records uncertain.

The riots of 1631 were definitely led by artisans. We already know John Williams *alias* Skimington, a miner or laborer. William Awbrey, a limeburner, before the riot of March 25, 1631 "had proclaymed the buryeing of Skimmyngton in Malescott and had invited all sortes of people to come with their tooles therto."[5] A witness confirmed that Awbrey "made proclamacion of the said meeting and gave notice at all the townes thereabouts." One of the drummers in the riot was identified as a cobbler named Stephen.[6] Almost all the other thirty-three individuals named in the records were only suspected of involvement in the riots, a far cry from being convicted, and therefore they cannot be taken as a representative sample. In any case, the status of only fourteen of the thirty-three can be discovered with any certainty: four were yeomen, nine were artisans—four miners, one collier, one blacksmith, one trenchermaker, one shoemaker, and one carpenter—and one was a laborer. Two others could with equal

5. PRO, S.P. 16/130/45, examination of Peter Simon, May 7, 1631; as a deponent in 1641, then aged 52, Awbrey was called a limeburner, E. 134/16-17 Chas. I/Hil. 1.

6. PRO, S.P. 16/195/5, examination of Thomas Yarwood (Yerworth), yeoman, by A-G Heath, June 24, 1631.

probability be either yeomen or laborers. The best evidence for the status of rioters concerns the riot of January, 1632. Seven suspects were prosecuted in King's Bench, an indication of strong evidence against them. One of the seven was a yeoman, and the other six, called laborers, were probably miners.[7] Finally, in the Newland Church riot in 1632, the two suspects whom the jury failed to indict were masons.[8] Of the fourteen others summoned before the Council for suspected involvement, the status of two is known: both were miners.[9]

This evidence of artisans' involvement in the riots carries even more weight when it is realized that the lists of known rioters and suspects would tend to exclude those of low status. Not all who participated in the riots could have been punished. The numbers fined are small compared to eyewitness reports of the numbers involved and to the number of known suspects: in Gillingham, 74 fined to over 300 rioters; at Braydon, 34 fined out of over 140; at Dean, the names of only 55 actual or suspected participants survive for riots which according to contemporary opinion involved up to 3,000 people. Estimates of size cannot be taken literally, but the implication is clear: far more people must have engaged in the riots than the lists of suspects would lead one to believe.

Most of those escaping punishment were persons of the lower orders. The Crown's object was to capture and punish the ringleaders in order to set an example to others and to break the spirit of the rank-and-file. Since Stuart government took for granted that a ringleader was a person of quality, gentlemen were prime suspects, while artisans and laborers would more easily have escaped notice.

A recurring theme in official opinions on the Western Rising is the belief that the lower orders were incapable of organizing and directing themselves and, consequently, that persons of quality were behind the riots. This was, of course, only one manifestation of an opinion universally held in the seventeenth century. It is expressed, for example, in that near-limitless storehouse of the period's aphorisms and commonplaces, the essays of Francis Bacon. In "On Sedition" Bacon ascribes the root of sedition to poverty in the common people and discontent among their betters: "If poverty and broken estate in the better sort be joined with a want and necessity in the mean people,

---

7. PRO, K.B. 9/797/5.
8. PRO, S.P. 16/215/57 II, indictment at Gloucestershire Q.S., endorsed *"ignoramus."*
9. PRO, P.C. 2/41, pp. 523, 529.

the danger is imminent and great: for the rebellions of the belly are the worst." Sedition required the better sort to provide leadership, "for common people are of slow motion, if they be not excited by the greater sort."

To ferret out and punish persons of quality was vitally important. They were cankers at the heart of society; renegades of power, position, and wealth were much more dangerous than the desperate poor. It was also more financially rewarding to prosecute the well-to-do. Large fines could be imposed on them, and their lands and tenements, goods and chattels levied upon for payment. In 1628 the court of Star Chamber resolved that the campaign for the apprehension of the Gillingham Forest rioters should concentrate on the leaders.[10]

Much fruitless energy was expended in trying to discover persons of quality behind the Dean Forest riots. Two influential and important landowners in the forest, Sir Baynham Throckmorton and Benedict Hall, Esq., were suspected of having some hand in the riots. When the Council examined Robert Bridges, Lady Villiers's agent, after he had submitted his affidavit to the court of Exchequer on the riots in Mailescott Woods, Bridges disclosed that a number of the men employed by Throckmorton and Hall were involved in the riots and, on that basis alone, implicated their employers.[11] In April of 1631 both men appeared before the Privy Council, but the suspicions turned out to be groundless.[12] The Council then turned its wrath on the unfortunate Bridges, who was summoned to London to wait its pleasure as to his fate.[13] Attorney-General Heath interceded on his behalf, arguing that since in such cases the main problem was getting anyone to give information against rioters, punishing Bridges would merely discourage other informants from coming forward.

I assure you the great fault in thes cases is, that none will appear to complain, be the fault never so foule and apparent and soe the offenders escape unpunished and if he should be further punished I feare it would bring

---

10. JRL, Nicholas MS 72/11, Fullerton to ?, Oct. 3, 1628.

11. PRO, S.P. 16/195/9, A-G Heath to Thomas Meautys, Clerk of the Council, June 26, 1631; S.P. 16/192/82, undated petition of Robert Bridges to PC.

12. *APC 1630-31*, p. 285, warrant for Hall to appear before the PC, April 5, 1631; p. 290, warrant for Throckmorton's appearance, April 8, 1631; p. 305, note that both appeared and were to attend the PC until further notice, April 26, 1631.

13. *APC 1630-31*, p. 319, warrant to bring Bridges before PC, May 9, 1631.

some inconvenience to the service, for others would be afraid to tell what they knowe.[14]

As a result, Bridges was allowed to return home.[15]

The other person of quality suspected of participation in the Dean riots was Peter Simon, curate of Newland Parish in the forest. On May 7, 1631, he was examined, no doubt at the Privy Council's behest, before the Bishop of Winchester (a member of the Council) to explain certain words and actions attributed to him. This examination has been misinterpreted by modern historians to mean that Simon was one of the rioters and a holder of advanced egalitarian views, an error resulting from dependence on the inaccurate summary in the *Calendar of State Papers Domestic* instead of on the original document.[16] Simon did have contact with the rioters, but he insisted that it was in the exercise of his pastoral duty. He exhorted them and prayed with them "to bring them to patience and the acknowledgment of their offence so farre forth as their owne conscience did accuse them to be either actors or abettors in the late rebellious tumult." He denied any involvement in the riots, appealing "to all that hath heard him in the catechising upon the fifte commandement wherein he hath directly instructed the people of the honour and obedience that they owe to the King and his government."

Simon admitted having said "that setting the Kings place and qualitie aside, we were all equal in respect of Manhood unto him." This was, however, the purely theological position that all men shared in a common humanity in the sight of God. For him it carried no political or social implications:

He doth with his soule detest all Anabaptisticall and Jesuiticall opinions and positions that oppose the authority power dignity preheminency and safety of princes; and that he doth acknowledge that there is upon Kinges and Princes, Gods charecter which maketh their persons sacred as Gods annointed and to be distinguished from others and that he ever hath mayntained this doctrine.[17]

14. PRO, S.P. 16/195/9, A-G Heath to Thomas Meautys, Clerk of the Council, June 26, 1631.

15. PRO, P.C. 2/41, p. 76, PC order concerning Bridges, July 1, 1631.

16. Allan, p. 83; C. Hill, *Century of Revolution*, p. 28, repeated in his essays "Propagating the Gospel," in *Historical Essays 1600-1750 Presented to David Ogg*, pp. 35-36, and "The Many-Headed Monster in Late Tudor and Early Stuart Political Thinking," in *From the Renaissance to the Counter-Reformation: Essays in Honor of Garrett Mattingly*, p. 316.

17. PRO. S.P. 16/190/45, examination of Peter Simon before Richard, Bishop of Winchester, May 7, 1631.

The Council, convinced of Simon's sincerity, ordered him set at liberty.[18] All that is left is a tantalizing and at present unanswerable question. Simon had been curate at Newland for three years. Did his belief that all men were equal in manhood strike a responsive chord in his parishioners, and did they accept the notion literally, without Simon's own qualifications?

The returns obtained from the government's search for persons of quality behind the riots were meager indeed. Not one gentleman was found among the Dean rioters. No gentlemen were convicted of participation in the Gillingham riots, although among the thirteen suspects found not guilty two were gentlemen and one was a lady. Furthermore, at least one esquire and twelve gentlemen, as well as the wife of one of them, were named in Star Chamber process as suspects.[19]

In the Braydon case one gentleman was fined £20 (the smallest monetary punishment), while three others were named as suspects in Star Chamber process.[20] No doubt these suspected gentlemen appeared before the court and were discharged for want of evidence; this is confirmed by a 1632 Exchequer case in which a sergeant-at-arms sued twenty-four Braydon suspects whom he had brought before the Council for payment of the fees due him. Two of the defendants were gentlemen who had been named in Council warrants and Star Chamber process as suspects but not convicted by the court. Three others, probably yeomen, were also named in process as suspects. Six of the defendants were later convicted as rioters, while the other thirteen, including one knight, are nowhere else implicated in the riots.[21]

If there had been any real evidence against persons of quality there is little doubt they would have been punished, and that severely. Since both local and central government were on the watch for gentlemen suspects, it is difficult to believe that those named escaped prosecution because of inherent difficulties of apprehension. They had too many

18. *APC 1630-31*, p. 321, warrant to Sgt. Denby to release Peter Simon, May 11, 1631.

19. The names of those found not guilty are included in PRO, E. 159/473 Trin 9 Chas. I, rot. 59, Letters Patent under the Great Seal recording the judgment of the court, April 10, 1630. The status of the suspects can be found occasionally in the St. Ch. process books P.R.O. 30/38/21-23 or in manorial records which can then be compared with the process books.

20. BL, Add. Ch. 40105, commission of rebellion directed to the sheriff, Dep. Lts., and JPs of Wilts, July 7, 1631.

21. PRO, E. 112/254/41, bill and answers in Denby vs. Masklyn et al., Hil. 1631/2.

social and political obligations and too much visibility to be able to melt into the mass of the "mean people" with the rank-and-file who did avoid punishment. This argument makes the large proportion of artisans among the known rioters, especially in positions of leadership, all the more impressive. Almost the only men of any standing the government could discover as involved in the riots were yeomen, four at Gillingham and six at Braydon.

The nature of the disafforestation proceedings explains why relatively few yeomen and only one gentleman definitely took part in the riots either as participants or as manipulators. Rather than acting in a high-handed and arbitrary manner, the Crown was flexible in dealing both with its own tenants in Gillingham and with manorial lords and their important tenants in other forests. The rights to common claimed by freeholders and copyholders was recognized in law, as was their right to compensation on enclosure. They did not need to resort to riot in defense of property rights: they had sufficient education or experience to know that the law, the courts, and the instinctive responses of the Crown's legal officers would guarantee their protection, and they could afford competent legal advice.

The best-documented disafforestations bear all the marks, not of arbitrary enclosure, but of the enclosures by agreement with which some modern historians have contrasted them.[22] Characteristically, enclosure by agreement considered the rights and interest both of the lord of the soil and of the tenants. The lord sought the consent of the tenants with interests in the matter; where the Crown was a party this was normally accomplished through special commissions out of the court of Exchequer or the court of the Duchy of Lancaster. In return for the extinction of their rights to common, tenants obtained compensation in an amount specified and approved in the agreement. The agreement was then confirmed by an action in court, either Chancery or Exchequer, making the enclosure valid at law and in equity. Even in enclosures by agreement there was often a dissenting minority, who refused to agree either because of complete opposition to the proceedings or in the hope of greater compensation.[23]

When the disafforestations in the West are examined it is clear that

22. E. Kerridge in *VCH: Wiltshire*, vol. IV, pp. 47-49, and in his "The Revolts in Wiltshire," pp. 64-65.

23. This is basically Kerridge's view of enclosure by agreement in *VCH: Wiltshire*, vol. IV, pp. 47-49.

they fit this pattern exactly. All were carried out by Exechequer special commissions, supplemented in a few cases by Duchy of Lancaster special commissions, that surveyed the forest to determine the extent of the royal demesne. Then the commissioners met with the freeholders and copyholders of the surrounding manors to determine the validity of their claims to common. Those with validated claims then signed an agreement to the disafforestation that extinguished their rights to common in return for compensation the commissioners were empowered to grant out of the royal demesne. The agreements were confirmed by actions in the court of Exchequer and, where necessary, the Duchy Chamber of Lancaster. Finally, commissions distributed the allotments and established roads and ways through the forest to enable the tenants to get to their lands.[24]

Since the central concerns of the freeholders and copyholders were the recognition of their rights to common and the amount of their compensation, it is impossible to argue that the disafforestations were examples of arbitrary enclosure. Although the precise nature of legal rights of common varied from manor to manor and forest to forest, tenants in all of them shared a clear tendency to push their rights beyond the legal definition. Two of the most important rights in the forest were pasturage for cattle and pannage for swine normally "levant and couchant" on the tenants' manorial holdings. Both freeholders and copyholders went far beyond the legal limits by keeping cattle permanently in the forest.[25] The same was true of sheep. By law sheep were not commonable, yet the tenants of Gillingham pastured their sheep in the forest, as did the manorial lords and their tenants about Braydon and Feckenham.[26]

24. Although the records of the commission which disafforested Gillingham have perished, its proceedings can be determined from depositions in PRO, E. 134/3 Chas. I/Eas. 17, and a document printed in John Hutchins's *History of Dorset*, vol. III, p. 649, an abstract of proceedings relating to the disafforestation of Gillingham. For Braydon there is E. 178/2470, special commission to Sir John Bridgman et al., July 26, 1626, special commission to the Earl of Berks, Sir John Bridgman, et al., June 25, 1629, executed Aug. 24, 1629; D.L. 44/1099, Duchy of Lancaster special commission to same, June 1, 1629, executed Aug. 24, 1629. For Feckenham there is E. 178/4781, commission to Sir Miles Fleetwood et al., Nov. 28, 1627, with instructions and proceedings, Jan. 21, 1627/8. E. 125/7, ff. 75-84, disafforestation decree, June 23, 1629, gives a good circumstantial account of the commission's proceedings and the Crown's intentions. The records of the Leicester disafforestation, E. 178/5403, are missing at the PRO but the proceedings are summarized in the decree E. 126/3, ff. 209-21, Feb. 7, 1627/8.

25. PRO, L.R. 2/194, ff. 276-77, abuses in royal forests, April 27, 1609.

26. JRL, Nicholas MS 65, ff. 10-12, customs of Gillingham Forest, undated, *temp*. Eliz. I; PRO,

Another aspect of commoning was the right to take deadwood for fires and timber to erect and repair buildings, fences, and farming implements on ancient tenements. A distinction was made between royal demesne manors, which enjoyed such rights in the forest, and the rest, which did not. The tenants of Gillingham and Mere, both demesne manors of the Crown, exercised these rights in Gillingham Forest by allowance of the steward of the manor, while the manorial lords around Braydon, Feckenham, and Leicester did not claim them.[27] Again, whatever the legal distinctions, it is clear from general complaints of despoliation of wood and from records of swanimote courts, special commissions, and estreated fines that the people living around the forests took what wood they wanted.[28] Even if they were caught, it was simpler to pay a fine than to buy wood in the first place. "Casual purchase of wood and timber from a forest would have required a warrant from the chief justice of the forests. Taking the wood or timber and paying a fine to the swanimote was easier and probably also a great deal cheaper than a warrant."[29]

The Crown was interested not in defining rights of common but in extinguishing them so that the demesne waste of the forest could be enclosed and improved. In return for their agreement, freeholders and copyholders were offered considerable compensation, the exact extent of which can be determined from Exchequer decrees and the records of the special commissions in all but one case.

The exception is Gillingham, where the decree is uninformative and the records of the commission lost. It is possible to determine from other sources that the tenants of Mere and Gillingham manors

---

E. 178/2408, special commission to Sir Roger Taverner et al., Feb. 12, 1572/3, with articles of instruction and depositions on rights of common in Braydon; E. 126/3, ff. 264-70, decree in A-G vs. tenants of Braydon, Oct. 23, 1628, and depositions in E. 134/6 Chas. I/Trin. 5 and E. 134/6 Chas. I/Trin. 9; E. 178/4781, commission to Sir Miles Fleetwood et al., Nov. 28, 1627, with depositions taken Jan. 21, 1627/8; L.R. 2/194, f. 19, survey of Feckenham, undated, *temp.* Jas. I.

27. PRO, E. 134/16 Eliz./Eas. 6, depositions by commission dated Feb. 11, 1573/4, in Dirdo et al., tenants of Gillingham, vs. Sir John Zouche, warden of Gillingham Forest; E. 123/5, ff. 124/25, decree in same case, May 13, 1574; E. 134/3 Chas. I/Eas. 17, depositions in A-G vs. tenants of Gillingham.

28. For Braydon there is a series of estreated fines for destruction of woods and timber 1602-1608 in PRO, E. 101/138/26-27 and a series of swanimote court rolls 1610-1623 in D.L. 39/4/23, 25-27, 29-32, D.L. 39/5/1-5. For Feckenham there are E. 178/4781, commission for survey of spoils, Feb. 12, 1623/4, with depositions taken April 13, 1624; E. 178/4781, commission to Sir Miles Fleetwood et al., Nov. 28, 1627, with depositions taken Jan. 21, 1627/8.

29. G. Hammersley, "The Crown Woods and Their Exploitation in the Sixteenth and Seventeenth Centuries," *B.I.H.R.* XXX (1957): 146.

received one acre for every ten acres of land, whether copyhold or freehold, held within the bounds of the forest.[30] The allotments were to be enclosed at the King's expense and held either by free and common socage of the manor of Gillingham, if claimed for freehold, or by copy of court roll, if claimed for copyhold.[31] This compensation to the tenants of Gillingham Manor totaled 400 acres.[32] A further 100 acres went to the tenants of Mere although, contrary to the original provision, this was held in common, not in severalty.[33] An unspecified amount was set out for access roads to the allotments and for the King's highway through the forest. Subtracting a further 250 acres allotted to cottagers and to the poor of Gillingham Manor, this left the Crown with some 2,408 acres free of claims of common and capable of improvement.

The settlement made in Leicester Forest, while of considerable complexity, leaves the impression of generous provision for manorial lords and their tenants. Five manorial lords claimed a total of about 2,755 acres as common waste appurtenant to their manors. They agreed to divide with the King, who obtained approximately 1,030 acres, leaving the rest to the lords free and clear of all claims to common and able to be enclosed. Out of their parcels the lords also agreed to compensate their own tenants for loss of common rights in the forest. A total of 554 acres was distributed out of the lords' shares, apportioned according to the size of each tenant's holdings at 4, 4½, or 6 acres to the yardland and 1½ or 2 acres for every ancient cottage. The Crown allowed another 993 acres to compensate freeholders in other forest townships at a rate of 6 acres to every yardland and 2 acres to every cottage. The borough of Leicester was allotted 40 acres to help maintain its poor. All the lands granted by the Crown were to be held in free and common socage either of the manor of Greenwich or the manor of Enfield.[34]

Generous provision was also made at Braydon for lords of manors

30. PRO, E. 134/3 Chas. I/Eas. 17, depositions in A-G vs. Hide et al., tenants of Gillingham.

31. PRO, E. 178/3732, privy-seal letter to the Ld. Treasurer et al., Dec. 7, 1625; E. 134/3 Chas. I/Eas. 17, depositions in A-G vs. Hide.

32. PRO, E. 112/173/3, information in A-G vs. Hide, Trin. 1626.

33. T. H. Barker, "Notes on the History of Mere," *W.A.M.* XXIX (1897): 308-9, Richard Greene to Richard Major, esq., Mar. 23, 1651/2.

34. PRO, E. 112/195/10, information in A-G vs. Sir Henry Hastings et al., commoners in Leicester, Eas. 1627, answers, Trin. 1627; E. 126/3, ff. 209-21, decree in same case, Feb. 7, 1627/8; E. 126/4, ff. 20-21, additional order, May 12, 1631.

within the inner bounds of the forest. Two large wastes—Pouchers Ragg, 224 acres, and Keynes Ragg, 350 acres—were separated from the forest and allowed to Sir John Hungerford and Sir Giles Bridges, respectively, who claimed them as part of their manorial wastes. Two parcels of land totaling 296 acres were allowed to the inhabitants of the township of Chelworth; 100 acres, later increased to 150, were apportioned among those tenants of Chelworth whose holdings in the part of the township within the inner bounds of the forest permitted them to claim rights to common. A further 150 acres were allotted for highways. Finally, other inhabitants of the forest who established claims to common for lands held within the inner bounds of the forest were given unspecified allotments in recompense, which seem to have amounted to another 240 acres.[35] Excluding the 150 acres provided for the poor, this left free and clear to the Crown 2,541 acres within the inner bounds and 1,498 acres (the Duchy woods) outside the forest.

The Feckenham disafforestation made by far the most ample provision for freeholders and copyholders of the forest manors. The forest totaled 2,100 acres, extending through three parishes. In Feckenham Parish were 900 acres, of which 700 were allotted to the tenants in compensation for the extinction of their rights, to be held either in severalty or in common and to be divided or stinted in proportion to the tenements for which they claimed common. The poor were granted 60 acres, leaving the King with 140 acres. Of the 900 acres in Hanbury Parish, 360 went to the copyholders and freeholders, 100 to the poor cottagers, and 440 to the Crown. In Bradley Parish, which contained 300 acres, 140 went to the free-holders and cottagers, 60 to the lord of the manor of Bradley, and 100 to the Crown.[36]

As in other enclosures by agreement, the legal proceedings connected with disafforestations were not entirely smooth or without opposition. Few substantial propertyholders, however, offered the sort of opposition that would ultimately lead to participation in the riots. Most confined themselves to the tactical maneuvers available to the litigant, with the aim of getting more compensation from the

35. PRO, E. 126/3, ff. 378-83, decree in A-G vs. inhabitants of Braydon, June 10, 1630; E. 178/2470, order in same case, Mich. 1630; E. 125/9, ff. 106-9, decree in same case, Nov. 19, 1630; F. H. Manley, "The Disafforesting of Braden," *W.A.M.* XLV (1930-32): 559.

36. PRO, E. 125/7, ff. 75-84, decree in A-G vs. inhabitants of Feckenham, June 23, 1629; E. 125/8, ff. 296-99, confirmation of the decree, June 16, 1630.

Crown. At Gillingham this took the form of refusal either to agree to allotments proposed by the commissioners or to be satisfied with allotments already made. Predictably, the Attorney-General began an action in Exchequer against the tenants to give the Crown quiet possession of the disafforested lands. This in turn gave the tenants the opportunity to convince a court that they deserved considerably more compensation.[37]

The tenants of Gillingham hoped to prove that the Bailiff's Walk of about 1,000 acres, in which most of the allotments were set out, was not part of the forest but a part of the waste of Gillingham Manor, in which the tenants enjoyed common of pasture for all their beasts, including sheep. They claimed that at disafforestation the Bailiff's Walk should have remained to the manor and the allotments should have been carved out of the land they considered to be the forest proper. Although the tenants were able to show that they had exploited the Bailiff's Walk to the hilt, their evidence that it was part of the manor was unconvincing.[38]

The Attorney-General satisfied the court that the Bailiff's Walk had always been considered an integral part of the forest. The most recent proof of this was the presentment of a jury at Gillingham in 1625 when a special commission met to survey the forest. At that time the jurors, including many of the defendants, had subscribed to a plot of the forest that included the Walk. Finally, the Attorney-General produced a book of survey recording the agreements to the compensatory allotments which proved that a majority of the tenants, among whom were many of the defendants, had signed in full knowledge that most of the allotments would be laid out in the Bailiff's Walk. The court confirmed the Bailiff's Walk to be part of the forest and ratified all the proceedings of the commission. That minority of the tenants who refused any allotment were given the choice of either accepting the compensation set out for them or obtaining nothing.[39]

Given the clear evidence that the tenants were aware of the extent of the forest and where their allotments were to be located, the Gillingham ploy does not seem to indicate any deep-seated opposition to enclosure; it was merely a try-on with an eye to squeezing more

37. PRO, E. 112/173/3, information in A-G vs. tenants of Gillingham, Trin. 1626.
38. PRO, E. 134/3 Chas. I/Eas. 17, depositions in A-G vs. tenants of Gillingham.
39. PRO, E. 126/3, ff. 111-12, order for injunction to quiet possession in A-G vs. tenants of Gillingham; E. 125/3, ff. 250-51, decree in same case, May 28, 1627.

compensation from the Crown before an Exchequer decree confirmed the agreements. This may in fact have been only an elaborate attempt to obtain the issue of a new special commission, authorized in the final Exchequer decree, to take care of a number of rather small but no doubt important complaints concerning the size of the allotments. The commission visited Gillingham, resurveyed the allotments to insure they were the proper size, and made additions and adjustments where necessary. As a result of its proceedings seventy additional acres were alloted to the tenants.[40]

Enclosures by agreement were not new to the freeholders and copyholders of Gillingham. In 1611 an agreement was made between the farmer of the manor and the tenants to allow enclosure of certain common meadows, with part to go to the farmer's use and the rest to the tenants'. In a session of the manorial court held in 1616 it was agreed that the freeholders and copyholders could enclose their arable and meadow lands in the common fields; the freeholders were to give twenty shillings for each acre enclosed as compensation to the poor who thereby lost their use of the common. In the following year eight men were appointed as trustees to handle the money received for the use of the poor. A penalty of £5 and the laying open of the enclosures was to be imposed on those who did not pay. One freeholder who enclosed thirty acres but failed to pay compensation or to live up to other conditions of the agreement—such as abating four sheep in the common grazing for every acre of meadow enclosed and two sheep for every acre of arable land, and leaving ways for the other tenants to get to their lands—had his enclosures destroyed.[41]

The propertied forest inhabitants at Braydon offered even less open hostility to enclosure. The major problem here was rooted in the fact that there were at least fifteen separate manors bordering on the forest, none of them royal demesne manors, and each had its complement of tenants claiming common. This meant an enormous increase over a forest like Gillingham in the work of special commissions, and prolonged proceedings in the courts of Exchequer and the Duchy Chamber of Lancaster to determine which holdings

40. PRO, E. 178/3732, commission dated June 13, 1627, with articles of instruction and proceedings, Aug. 20-25, 1627; JRL, Nicholas MS 71/1, state of the forest of Gillingham, undated, ca. 1640.

41. JRL, Nicholas MS 69, ff. 2-11, orders in Gillingham Manor court, 1611-1637; PRO, STAC. 8/175/10, bill and answer in Robert Harbin, gent., vs. Hugh Sweet and other tenants of Gillingham Manor, bill, Jan. 12, 1620/1, answer, Feb. 11, 1620/1.

could rightfully claim common appurtenant within the inner bounds of the forest. The periodic appearance of numbers of new claimants to common resulted in three separate informations being exhibited in Exchequer by the Attorney-General and two final decrees being issued by the court.[42]

Doubtless some of the delay was due to dissatisfaction with the amount of compensation. For example, the inhabitants of Chelworth held out for more than the hundred acres offered to them, obtaining in the end an extra fifty acres.[43] In the few modern accounts of the disafforestation of Braydon, however, the intransigence of the substantial propertyholders has been overemphasized. Based on the belief that persons of substance were behind the riots, it has been erroneously implied that the rioters forced the Crown to make concessions in 1631, when it was ruled that Poucher's Ragg, Keynes Ragg, and two parcels of land totaling 296 acres claimed by the tenants of Chelworth were outside the royal demesne.[44] Yet as early as 1626, five years before the riots, these points had already been conceded on the Crown's behalf by the special commissioners appointed to disafforest Braydon.[45]

There was considerably greater opposition to the enclosure of the Duchy woods, 1,500 acres of royal demesne lands lying outside the inner bounds of the forest and parcel of the lands of the Duchy of Lancaster. Like that at Gillingham, this opposition took the peaceful form of resort to legal process. In 1635 the tenants of the manor of Okesey sued the Attorney-General of the Duchy of Lancaster and the royal farmers of Braydon for the compensation they felt ought to have been theirs at the disafforestation. In the end the court decreed that they had no valid legal title to common or to compensation as a result of the enclosures.[46]

42. PRO, E. 112/254/6, information in A-G vs. Earl of Herts et al., Mich. 1626, answers, Hil. 1626/7; E. 112/254/21, information in A-G *ex rel.* Jacobsen vs. Sir Henry Poole et al., Hil. 1628/9, answers, Eas. 1629; E. 112/254/24, information and answers in A-G *ex rel.* Jacobsen vs. Earl of Danby et al., Eas. 1629; E. 126/3, ff. 264-69, decree, Oct. 23, 1628, and ff. 378-85, decree, June 10, 1630.

43. PRO, E. 178/2470, order in A-G vs. inhabitants of Braydon, Mich. 1630.

44. Manley, "Disafforesting of Braden," p. 558; *VCH: Wiltshire*, vol. IV, pp. 405-7.

45. This is made clear by the decree PRO, E. 126/3, ff. 378-85, June 10, 1630; see also the decree concerning Pouchers Ragg, E. 126/3, f. 294, Feb. 5, 1628/9.

46. PRO, D.L. 4/89/29, interrogatories and depositions in Allis et al., tenants of Okesey, vs. the A-G of the Duchy of Lancaster et al., commission dated May 11, 1635; D.L. 5/32, ff. 181-85, decree in same case, Feb. 9, 1635/6.

The Leicester and Feckenham disafforestations proceeded with remarkable smoothness; they provide classic examples of collusive actions. In each case an action brought by the Attorney-General was the medium by which a division of the forest agreeable to the Crown, lords of manors, and their substantial tenants was confirmed and made legally binding on all parties concerned.[47] The generous compensation allowed by the Crown explains the ease with which both proceeded. After the decree was issued in the Feckenham case, a number of inhabitants of the forest submitted an answer in Exchequer, not warranted by any bill or information, in which they opposed the disafforestation and stated that they had received no allotments of common. In turn the Attorney-General filed a new information against all those who claimed not to have been parties to the previous suit. It was discovered that none of the defendants had any right to compensation, most of them being propertyless poor; the outcome of the case was simply confirmation of the previous decree.[48]

The Crown's proceedings in the late 1620s for enclosures in Dean Forest, although they did not result in complete disafforestation, followed this same pattern. The agreement of all manorial lords and other substantial propertyholders with valid claims to common was actively sought before the enclosure.[49] Other well-documented disafforestations, such as those at Chippenham and Blackmore in Wiltshire and Neroche and Frome Selwood in Somerset, followed a similar pattern.[50]

The conclusion to which this survey points is inescapable: the disafforestations, far from being arbitrary, were in essence enclosures by agreement in which the approval of the tenants with valid rights of common was sought, their interests recognized by compensatory allotments, and agreements on both sides given legal validity through actions brought in Exchequer. Finally, the opposition of freeholders

---

47. PRO, E. 112/195/10, information in A-G vs. Sir Henry Hastings et al., commoners in Leicester Forest, Eas. 1627, answers, Trin. 1627; E. 126/3, ff. 209-21, decree in same case; E. 125/7, ff. 75-84, decree in A-G vs. inhabitants of Feckenham, June 23, 1629.

48. PRO, E. 125/7, f. 98, order in A-G vs. inhabitants of Feckenham, Oct. 23, 1629; E. 125/8, ff. 296-99, June 16, 1630.

49. See below, pp. 204-5.

50. For Chippenham and Blackmore see PRO, E. 178/4577, mm. 33-61, special commission, Mar. 23, 1618/19, with survey of forests, bargains made with the tenants, and compensation allowed on extinguishing of rights to common. For Neroche and Frome Selwood see T. G. Barnes, *Somerset 1625-1640*, pp. 156-57.

and substantial copyholders was not of a kind to lead to riot; it was designed to improve their chances of obtaining more compensation through actions in the courts. This can be confirmed by comparing the defendants in the Exchequer suits with the known rioters.

Only two of the twenty-five defendants in the Exchequer proceedings connected with the Gillingham disafforestation are to be found among the seventy-four fined Gillingham rioters: a butcher fined £200, and a yeoman fined £100. Almost all of the twenty-five defendants were men of substantial property. Ten were gentlemen, two were yeomen, five were either yeomen or husbandmen, and one was a butcher. Only four were cottagers (one of whom was a shoemaker); the status of the other three cannot be determined.[51] Similarly, of the one hundred and twenty defendants in the three Exchequer informations on the Braydon disafforestation, only four were fined in Star Chamber for riot—a gentleman, two yeomen, and a husbandman. The status of the defendants in Exchequer again implies that they were substantial propertyholders—three earls, a dozen knights and baronets, and at least thirty esquires and gentlemen, with the rest probably yeomen and substantial husbandmen.[52]

The names of so few rioters at Dean and Feckenham survive—none survive for Leicester—that it is difficult to provide a convincing comparison in these instances. The eighty-one defendants in the Feckenham disafforestation case were all men of substance, including one knight and at least thirty gentlemen and esquires. Eight people were convicted for participation in the Feckenham riots; among them was only one of the eighty-one defendants in Exchequer.[53] The Exchequer case that led to the legal confirmation of enclosures in Dean Forest preceded the riots; there were forty-one plaintiffs—one knight, thirty esquires and gentlemen, and ten yeomen. Only one of them, a yeoman, is to be found among the fifty-eight known or

51. The status of the gentlemen is given in PRO, E. 112/173/3; the status of the rest can be determined by comparing them with names and status of known rioters in E. 159/472, Trin. 8 Chas. I, rot. 38, estreat of St. Ch. fines for Gillingham riots, Hil. 1629/30, and of tenants named in manorial records.

52. This is based on a comparison of the names in the three Exchequer informations, PRO, E. 112/254/6, 7, and 21 with those in E. 159/475, Hil. 11 Chas. I, rot. 65, estreat of St. Ch. fines for Braydon riots, Trin. 1635.

53. No Exchequer bills or answers survive in this case but the defendants are named in the final decree, PRO, E. 125/7, ff. 75-84, June 23, 1629. The names of the rioters are to be found in S.P. 16/232/43 and S.P. 16/362/103, two lists of fines taxed in St. Ch., Mich. 1632.

suspected rioters. At the Dean Forest eyre of 1634 one hundred and twenty freeholders and copyholders submitted claims to common rights, but only four of them, all yeomen, were among the known or suspected rioters.[54]

The occasional appearance of yeomen involved in the Exchequer cases among the fined rioters is not to be explained by a mass movement of a stratum of society deprived of essential parts of its income and reacting to the disruption of traditional patterns of life. Such riotous yeomen had simply calculated that more profit was to be made from open forest than the enclosed compensatory allotments were worth. The case of John Wolridge was characteristic. A yeoman and bailiff of Gillingham Manor at the time of the disafforestation, Wolridge was fined £200 for his part in the riots. His motive was no doubt the loss of the perquisites due to him out of the Bailiff's Walk by virtue of his office, such as the right to all dead trees and windfalls.[55]

There were of course other people in the forests, namely, poor cottagers; it is from them that the bulk of the riotous opponents to disafforestation were probably recruited. It could in fact be argued that there were two types of forest inhabitants, those with land who went to law to protect their rights, and those with little or no land who rioted to defend their interests. The bitter irony of disafforestation was that those people most dependent on the forest as open waste either had no legal title to the rights of common they exercised and thus no valid claim to compensation, or the tenements for which they had a valid claim to common were so small that the compensation received was miniscule. As the records of the disafforestations make clear, the inhabitants of new-erected cottages, whether built on the manorial or forest waste or on other men's tenements and sublet, had absolutely no legal right to common and thus none to compensation.[56]

54. PRO, E. 112/179/28, Winter et al. vs. A-G, Hil. 1626/7; C. 99/10/1-120, claims to common submitted at the Dean Forest eyre, July 10, 1634; names of rioters and suspects are to be found in a variety of sources: see above, pp. 129-30.

55. PRO, E. 134/3 Chas. I/Eas. 17, Wolridge's depositions in A-G vs. tenants of Gillingham; JRL, Nicholas MS 65, ff. 10-12, customs of Gillingham Forest *temp.* Eliz. I.

56. Gillingham, PRO, E. 178/3732, privy-seal letter to the Ld. Treasurer et al., Dec. 7, 1625; E. 134/3 Chas. I/Eas. 17, depositions in A-G vs. tenants of Gillingham; E. 125/3, ff. 250-1, decree in the case, May 28, 1627; E. 178/3732, commission to make adjustments in the allotments, June 13, 1627. Braydon, E. 178/2470, commission to disafforest, July 26, 1627; E. 126/3, f. 380, decree in A-G vs. inhabitants of Braydon, June 10, 1630. Feckenham, E. 125/8, ff. 296-99, order in A-G vs. inhabitants of Feckenham, June 16, 1630.

On occasion, even tenants of ancient copyhold cottages were treated as if they had no right or title to common.

One of the misconceptions integral to the orthodox interpretation of disafforestation is that all inhabitants in and around the forests had legal rights of common that they lost as a result of the Crown's arbitrary actions. This view simply ignores the cottagers and assumes that forests were inhabited only by freeholders and substantial copyholders. The cottagers, though they may be ignored by historians, were not ignored by the Crown, which did what it could to provide compensation for these cottagers who had no legal claim to it. This action on the part of the Crown further weakens the concept of disafforestations as examples of arbitrary enclosures. It does not involve replacing the Whig view of an arbitrary and despotic Stuart monarch riding roughshod over the rights of Englishmen with the idea (appealing to some historians) of a paternalistic king solicitous for the welfare of his poorer subjects, but it is a fact that the government appreciated the importance of the unenclosed forest to the cottagers and realized that disafforestation would be a grievous blow to their way of life. As the following passage indicates, the compensation made to the cottagers was intended to soften the blow as much as possible without depriving the Crown of desperately needed income.

And his Majestie being very tender of the wellfare of the inhabitants and borderers about the said forest and that the poorer sort of them who had noe right of common at all but yet had used to common might not bee left destitute but might in some reasonable measure bee provided for mearely out of his Majesties compassion and grace.[57]

Although the foregoing refers specifically to Braydon, similar sentiments were expressed concerning the poor of Gillingham and Feckenham.[58]

The provision made for the poor was a recognition of the pressing social problem that was the ultimate cause of the riots. The total sum seems quite generous, but the amount disbursed to each cottager was a mere pittance. With one hand the Crown deprived the large and

57. PRO E. 126/3, f. 380, decree in A-G vs. inhabitants of Braydon, June 10, 1630.
58. PRO, E. 112/173/3, information in A-G vs. tenants of Gillingham, Trin. 1626; E. 134/3 Chas. I/Eas. 17, depositions in the case; E. 125/7, ff. 75-84, decree in A-G vs. inhabitants of Feckenham, June 22, 1629.

growing population of poor cottagers in each forest of an essential part of their income—free access to thousands of acres of waste ground—and with the other offered to them the crumbs left over from the feast consumed by the King, his farmers, and the substantial landholders in the forests.

In examining the compensation given to the poor it is occasionally impossible to distinguish the provision for tenants of ancient cottages from that set aside for tenants of those new-erected or to discover if the Crown really believed the tenants of ancient copyhold cottages had, as copyholders, a legal right to common and compensation for loss. Another way in which the cottagers were categorized was as laboring poor and impotent poor. Often it is difficult to differentiate the compensation for one type of poor from the other, since the commissioners who had to survey and allot the land were themselves uncertain which group it was intended to benefit.

At the disafforestation of Gillingham the total compensation provided for the poor was 250 acres, and of this amount the exact disposition of 220 acres can be discovered.[59] Included among the poor with no legal right to common in the forest were tenants of ancient copyhold cottages.[60] The allotment made to each cottager was one acre to be enclosed at the King's expense. For thirty cottagers in the village of Motcombe, within Gillingham Manor, a total of thirty acres was alloted. Another seven acres were provided for seven new-erected cottages. Sixty acres went to the cottagers in the township of Gillingham outside the perambulation of the forest, and fifty to new-erected cottages in Gillingham Manor.[61] Little provision was made for the cottagers of Mere: instead of receiving one-acre allotments, they were to share in the hundred-acre common set out for the tenants of the manor. Despite a recommendation made in the 1630s that some compensation be provided for the poor of Mere, it was not until 1652 that eighty acres were set aside for them. This was after the massive riots of the 1640s, during which complaints about this matter were loudly voiced.[62] Some cottagers received nothing, including tenants of

59. PRO, E. 112/173/3.
60. PRO, E. 134/3 Chas. I/Eas. 17.
61. Hutchins, vol. III, p. 649, abstract of the proceedings in the disafforestation of Gillingham.
62. JRL, Nicholas MS 71/2, allegations of the inhabitants of Mere delivered to the House of Lords, Feb., 1646/7; T. H. Barker, pp. 308-9, prints two documents that are relevant to this business.

cottages erected since 1623 and all subtenants; the latter, from the evidence of surveys and rentals of Gillingham and Mere, numbered at least sixty.[63] For the impotent poor dependent on charity to survive, three grants were made: fifteen acres to the poor of Motcombe, to which another acre was later added, eight acres to the poor of Burton, to which two more were added, and fifty acres to the poor of Gillingham.[64] The exact disposition of the land cannot be discovered, but by analogy with other disafforestations it was probably granted to feoffees who sublet and used the income from rents to help support the poor.

At the disafforestation of Braydon 100 acres were set aside for the poor of the villages of Chelworth and Cricklade, along with two parcels of 25 acres each for the poor of the two villages of Purton Stoke and Leigh.[65] It is unclear which of the poor these grants were intended to support; certainly they could not have supported all the poor within these villages.[66] Even the commissioners, who set out the allotments, and the inhabitants of the forest were confused on this question.

Steps had to be taken to settle the matter. In 1634 a new commission was appointed to determine the use to which the income from the hundred acres for the poor of Chelworth and Cricklade should be put.[67] The commissioners decided that the bailiff of Cricklade borough, with the constables, overseers of the poor, and churchwardens of the parishes of St. Sampson's and St. Mary's, should jointly manage the income from the land. One-half of the income was to go every year to eight different poor men or women who were industrious but incapable at present of fully supporting themselves by their labor, to enable them to work independently in a trade and to be no further charge on the parish. One-quarter of the income was to be employed annually in binding out three poor children as apprentices and in helping apprentices who had served out their time set

---

63. PRO, E. 178/3732, special commission of June 13, 1627, with articles of instruction and report on execution, Aug. 20-25, 1627.

64. Hutchins, vol. III, p. 649; PRO, E. 178/3732, commission of June 13, 1627.

65. PRO, E. 126/3, ff. 378-85, decree in A-G vs. inhabitants of Braydon, June 10, 1630.

66. PRO, E. 178/2470, commission to John Bridgman et al., July 26, 1626, and commission to Earl of Berks et al., June 25, 1629.

67. PRO, E. 125/13, f. 386, order authorizing the commission, Feb. 13, 1633/4.

themselves up in trade. The other quarter was to be distributed annually as alms.[68]

A commission was appointed in 1637 to settle whether the income of the twenty-five acres allotted to the poor of Leigh should go to poor commoners or to the impotent poor relieved by alms.[69] They found the intention behind the grant to be that the land should help provide only for the poorer sort of commoners. In accordance with these findings the court of Exchequer ordered that the two nearest justices, two constables, and the churchwardens should be entrusted with distributing the income from the land annually to twenty-nine named poor commoners, with power to add new poor in the event that death or some other cause removed any of the original twenty-nine from the list.[70]

These two settlements quite possibly reflect a struggle between the inhabitants of substance and the poorer commoners for control over the disposition of the compensation for the poor. This was at least the case in a settlement at Gillingham in 1652. To put an end to the riots that had erupted repeatedly at Gillingham in the 1640s, John Kirke (holder of one-third of the forest) in January of 1652 conveyed eighty acres of ground in perpetuity, on behalf of himself and the Earl of Elgin (possessor of the other two-thirds) to thirteen trustees drawn from among the best people of the township of Mere. The income from the land was to be used to support the poor of Mere who had received no compensation at the time of disafforestation; they had therefore been at the forefront of the disorders during the Civil War. When this parcel was enclosed the fences were destroyed by the people of Mere, who wanted the eighty acres set out as a common for the use of the poor.

The rioters, presumably including these whom the grant would benefit, did not want the land enclosed and managed by trustees in the interests of the poor. Instead, they viewed the land as an integral part of their livelihood, to be exploited as a common much as the open forest had been. The argument in favor of enclosure made by the

68. PRO, E. 178/2470, commission to William Calley et al., Feb. 12, 1633/4, with return of proceedings, April 15, 1634; E. 125/15, ff. 103-4, order confirming its proceedings, June 12, 1634.

69. PRO, E. 178/2470, order authorizing the commission, June 15, 1637.

70. PRO, E. 178/2470, commission to Egidio Fettiplace et al., June 19, 1637, with report of proceedings, Oct. 14, 1637; E. 125/21, ff. 240-42, order confirming proceedings of the commission, Oct. 27, 1637.

"better sort"—who were the trustees and therefore managed the income from the 80 acres—was that by using the money "the growth of poverty (so much threatened) will be prevented and the poore so well provided for, that the burthen will be eased, and the poore people in farre better condicion." The better sort obviously regarded the land as a charity. The larger argument against a common was the standard one for the period: "increase of comons doe increase, not lessen poore."[71] In this case, as in the two Braydon settlements for the relief of the poor, the propertied inhabitants, as trustees, gained control of the land's disposition. In this way they could exercise some effective power over the poor, such as deciding who among them were eligible to be relieved. In consequence the propertied could prevent the influx of poor seeking to obtain a subsistence from abundant commons.

The surviving records of the disafforestation of Leicester are insufficiently precise to permit an accurate estimate of the total amount of compensation granted to the large population of cottagers in the forest's manors and townships. What can be discovered is that the tenant of each ancient cottage received one-and-a-half or two acres and the tenant of each new-erected cottage received one or one-and-a-half acres out of the lands provided for compensation of all those claiming common. Such parcels were to be enclosed at the expense of the recipient. In addition, the sum of £15 was allocated to raise stock for the poor of the township of Enderby and £20 to the same purpose for the poor of Defford. To help support the poor of Leicester forty acres of land were entrusted to the magistrates of the borough.[72]

Upon the disafforestation of Feckenham sixty acres were divided in severalty among the poor cottagers of Feckenham Parish. The poor cottagers of Hanbury Parish received a total of eighty acres to be held in severalty, with an additional twenty acres the income of which the churchwardens were to distribute to the poorest cottagers. The size of the individual grants cannot be discovered, but it was probably one-and-a-half acres to each cottage; it was certainly no more than two acres. In Bradley Parish no separate provision was made for cottagers, but each tenant of an ancient cottage was to receive one-and-a-half acres, and of a new-erected cottage, one acre, all out of the hundred

---

71. Barker, pp. 307-9; SRO, Alford and Kirke MS (DD/HLM) Box 2, Chancery Decree of 1653 (the source of the quotations). See also below, pp. 235-39.

72. PRO, E. 112/195/10, A-G vs. Hastings et al., commoners of Leicester Forest, Eas., 1627; E. 126/3, ff. 209-21, decree in same case, Feb. 7, 1627/8.

and forty acres provided to compensate those with claims to common. Eleemosynary provisions included 20 nobles (£6.13s.4d.) annually out of the income of the King's soil in the forest to support a free school in Feckenham, if one existed, 20 nobles annually for support of the poor of Hanbury or a free school, and a lump sum of £40 from the same source to the churchwardens and overseers of the poor of Feckenham for relief and maintenance of the poor.[73]

From Leicester and Feckenham, where the provision for the poor was relatively more abundant than in other forests, comes the clearest evidence of dissatisfaction with the cottagers' share. A petition from the inhabitants of Leicester Forest claimed that as a result of the disafforestation the inhabitants of one hundred ancient cottages had been deprived of their livelihood and would become a charge on their parishes. It was also asserted that the same would happen to the inhabitants of innumerable new-erected cottages.[74] After the issue of the Exchequer decree confirming the disafforestation of Feckenham, a number of inhabitants of the forest submitted an answer to the court, not in response to a bill but to express dissatisfaction with the proceedings. It was discovered, after the Attorney-General put in an information against them, that only about 30 of the 184 defendants were entitled to claim common and thus to be compensated for its loss. The rest were poor tenants of assart lands (encroachments on the waste land) and new-erected cottages and subtenants of cottages on other men's lands, all of whom had no legal right to common. Though they were allowed no more than a share in the allotments provided for the poor out of the King's grace and bounty, they insisted that the forest remain open and refused the allotments. Their opposition was in vain, however, as the court in June of 1630 confirmed the original decree.[75] The most glaring example of the inadequacy of the compensation to the poor can be found in Purton in Braydon Forest. Here in 1625 there were at least sixty new-erected cottages in one manor within the parish, but the disafforestation commissioners

73. PRO, E. 125/7, ff. 75-84, decree in A-G vs. inhabitants of Feckenham, June 23, 1629; E. 125/9, ff. 392-94, order for a commission to set out allotments, Nov. 29, 1630.

74. H. of L.R.O., Main Papers, petition with list of grievances from the inhabitants of Leicester Forest to the House of Lords, June 23, 1628.

75. PRO, E. 125/8, ff. 296-99, confirmation of Feckenham disafforestation decree, June 16, 1630; E. 125/7, f. 98, an order of the court in this case, Oct. 23, 1629, also provides important information.

allotted only twenty-five acres to the support of all the poor in the village of Purton.[76] Also from Braydon comes some evidence for the identification of the rioters with the poor. Three of the inhabitants of Leigh fined in Star Chamber for their part in the riot—a husbandman, a carpenter, and a laborer—were among the twenty-nine commoners named to receive the benefit of the twenty-five acres allotted to the poor of that township.[77]

The best evidence for the identification of the rioters with poor cottagers comes from Gillingham Forest; this evidence also allows for the substantial identification of artisans with cottagers. In the manors to be dealt with, the typical cottage—ancient as well as new-erected, copyhold as well as *ad placitum* (at the will of the lord)—had no land attached to it beyond a garden, orchard, or backside. At most, the land was an acre or two of meadow and pasture; very rarely was it arable. In effect, the designation *cottager* came very close to meaning one who was propertyless.

The existence of a number of rentals and surveys of the two forest manors of Gillingham and Mere, along with the relatively small size of the population, makes it possible to identify a number of rioters with the tenants listed in such records, a situation unique to Gillingham Forest. Both Gillingham and Mere were royal demesne manors, which means that the manorial records had a better chance of survival than in forests like Braydon and Dean where nearly all the manors were held by private individuals. Moreover, the much larger populations in and around Braydon and Dean mean that there are many recorded instances, especially in Dean, of two or more individuals with exactly the same name, thereby precluding reliable identification of rioters with manorial tenants. Even the evidence of Gillingham and Mere manors poses problems that in some cases makes identification impossible. It is perhaps best first to present the evidence and then to discuss those problems.

---

76. WRO, Q.S. Gt. Roll, Eas. 1626, no. 136, petition to JPs by the parishioners of Purton; Q.S. minute book (order book), Hil. 19 Jas. I-Hil. 2 Chas. I, order for the JPs of the division to meet and consider the rate to be levied on the lord of the manor of Blunterden St. Andrew, Eas. 1626.

77. They were George Burgh, husbandman, John Williams, senior, carpenter, and John Brookes, laborer. PRO, E. 125/21, ff. 240-42, order of the court of Exchequer, names the twenty-nine poor commoners who were to receive the benefit of the twenty-five acres allotted to the poor of Leigh. All three were fined £20 by Star Chamber, E. 159/475, Hil. 11 Chas. I, rot. 65, estreat of St. Ch. fines for Braydon riots, Trin. 1635.

Sixteen of the forty-five artisans fined for participation in the Gillingham Forest riots can, with a certainty ranging from absolute to reasonable, be identified with individuals named on manorial records as copyholders. Fourteen of the sixteen were cottagers. Seven of them held cottages with only a garden orchard or backside attached. Typical of such cottagers was John Phillips, a tanner fined £200 in 1630 and leader of the riots in the 1640s, who held a cottage with a small garden and tanning house for an annual rent of 3d. Among the other seven were one with a cottage and one-half acre of pasture; three with cottages and between one and two acres of meadow or pasture; one with a cottage and two acres of meadow; one with a cottage and seven acres of pasture. The last of the fourteen definitely held a cottage and one acre of arable land, and perhaps a further five and one-half acres of arable land, although this was quite possibly held by his father. The other two artisans identifiable with individuals on manorial records were butchers who each held over twenty acres of meadow and pasture. Undoubtedly they should not be included among the artisans, since the existence of butchers who were graziers in a big way, fattening cattle for slaughter, was a well-attested phenomenon in this part of the country.

The main problem raised by the evidence is that of explaining why it is impossible to find the other twenty-nine artisan rioters in the manorial records. This problem also arises in trying to discover the holdings of the rioters who are not artisans. The one mercer, Christopher Smart, is probably to be identified with a cottager of that name, but only one out of the four with no given status, three out of the five yeomen, and four out of the sixteen husbandmen can be discovered in the manorial records. Thus only twenty-five of the seventy-four rioters can be identified with reasonable certainty.

A number of possible explanations suggest themselves. Only one of the four extant manorial surveys and rentals, a rental of Gillingham Manor made in 1624, is close enough in date to be completely relevant to this study.[78] The others are either too early—a survey of Gillingham made in 1608 and a survey of the manor of Mere dating probably from the first decade of James I's reign—or too late—a parliamentary survey of Mere dated 1651.[79] In many instances, then,

78. JRL, Nicholas MS 66, ff. 1-6, rental of Gillingham Manor, Oct. 28, 1624.
79. PRO, L.R. 2/214, ff. 1-77, survey of Gillingham Manor, Sept. 26, 1608; L.R. 2/207, ff. 21-24, undated survey of manor of Mere, *temp.* Jas. I; E. 317/Wilts, no. 40, parliamentary survey of the manor of Mere, 1651.

the tenants named are either the fathers and uncles or the children and nephews of the rioters. This explanation does not, however, provide a full answer, since only seventeen of the forty-six rioters named as inhabitants of Gillingham can be identified even on the Gillingham rental of 1624. The most probable explanation is that for a number of reasons many of the inhabitants of Gillingham and Mere would never be included in even the fullest record of the manorial tenants. Some rioters might have been sons of recorded tenants, still living at home. This is borne out by the fact that nearly all of the surnames of the rioters are to be found in the manorial records, although only one rioter (Nicholas Reekes, fined £40, a son of Thomas Reekes, yeoman) can be identified. What little can be discovered about the ages of rioters from Exchequer depositions and the parliamentary survey of Mere shows no discernible pattern, unlike the Oxfordshire Rising of 1596, where the ringleaders were all identified as young single men.

More to the point is the general failure of rentals and surveys to name subtenants. The only exception, the Gillingham survey of 1608, names the holders of fifty-eight subtenancies that include eleven cottages with less than four acres, sixteen small tenements or cottages with four to ten acres, nineteen tenements between ten and twenty-five acres, and twelve tenements larger than twenty-six acres.[80] Nine of the subtenants held copyhold lands in the manor and are thus named elsewhere in the survey. The other forty-nine are named only as subtenants. The Gillingham rental of 1624, on the other hand, lists no subtenants, although it is reasonable to assume that at least as many subtenants existed then as in 1608. Even the survey of 1608 does not identify all subtenants. At that time there were at least thirty-one cottages with less than four acres, thirteen of them with less than one, held by unnamed subtenants. In 1624 this number had risen to at least thirty-seven. In addition, the feoffees of the parish lands of Gillingham held twelve small cottages, ten of them only with gardens and two with three acres of pasture each, whose tenants were not named.[81] This means that in 1624, in addition to the 202 copyhold tenants in Gillingham Manor, there were something like 100 unrecorded subtenants, two-thirds of whom were inhabiting cottages with less than four acres attached.

Although neither of the Mere manorial surveys names subtenants,

80. PRO, L.R. 2/214, ff. 1-77.
81. It is clear from the rent paid that the holdings of the feoffees were the same in 1624 as in 1608.

the existence of at least twelve, each of whom held a cottage with less than one acre of land, can be inferred. There can be little doubt that a considerably larger number of subtenants actually existed. For example, William Wilson, a miller of Mere fined £40 for his part in the riots, although nowhere to be found in the manorial records, in fact held two corn mills in Mere as subtenant of Stephen Doddington, a gentleman who was the copyhold tenant named in the survey.[82] If the subtenants in both manors could be identified it is probable that many otherwise unidentifiable rioters would be found among them.

There is one further weakness in surveys and rentals; they do not generally bother with tenants of cottages new-erected on manorial waste who were holding *ad placitum*. The one exception is the Mere parliamentary survey of 1651, which indicates a growing number of such tenants. In the survey of James I's reign there were sixty-one tenants in the manor; in 1651 there were ninety-eight.[83] The main reason for the increase is that in 1651 twenty-six tenants-at-will were added: twenty-two held cottages on the waste, of whom twenty had only gardens and two had less than one acre of land; four held pieces of enclosed waste ranging from one-half acre to four acres. Although such tenants of new-erected cottages are not to be found recorded in Gillingham manorial records, the existence of at least fifty in this forest manor with abundant waste is revealed in a number of the records connected with the disafforestation.[84]

The final omission from manorial surveys and rentals is the obvious one; they exclude lands outside the manorial structure, including ecclesiastical lands. The only surviving terrier is one made in 1640 of the church lands of Mere.[85] Not surprisingly, because of its late date, only three of the twenty-eight rioters from Mere can be identified on it. A fourth, Christopher Phillips, a baker, appears here and in the parliamentary survey of Mere, in each holding one-half of the George Inn. It is worth noting that of the twenty-three tenancies eighteen were cottages with only gardens or orchards and three others were cottages with land of four acres or less.

---

82. PRO, E. 134/4 Chas. I/Eas. 13, Wilson's deposition in Doddington vs. Alford et al.
83. PRO, L.R. 2/207, ff. 21-4; E. 317/Wilts, no. 40.
84. Hutchins, vol. III, p. 649, abstract of the proceedings in the disafforestation of Gillingham.
85. Barker, pp. 274-76.

To what conclusions does the evidence so far presented lead? Undeniably, the disafforestations were not arbitrary enclosures but in effect enclosures by agreement; equally certainly, the rioters were men of low status and not persons of substance. As Thomas Yerworth, yeoman, said of the Dean rioters: "All the persons that ever he could heare of that were in the said accion were very beggerly and naughty people and such as he never saw or tooke notice of."[86] The conclusion that the rioters were men of little standing is supported by examining the disafforestation proceedings. No doubt some yeomen and substantial husbandmen were angered enough, by the loss of their rights to common and what they conceived to be paltry compensation, to join in the riots. Yet the allotments they received were more generous than those granted to the cottagers, and if they lost some profit from the forest it was only a fraction of their total income. For the poor the loss of income came out of their flesh. The compensation for the poor cottagers was woefully inadequate; in place of what amounted to common without stint, each cottager who received any allotment at all obtained an enclosed parcel of ground normally one acre in extent, exceptionally as much as two acres.

To what degree does the case study of Gillingham illuminate the Western Rising as a whole? The Gillingham riots can be characterized as an artisan rising in which those participants identifiable on the manorial records were invariably cottagers. The applicability of this conclusion to the other riots which constitute the Rising is no doubt problematic; want of evidence for forests other than Gillingham makes the possibility of identifying the social and occupational status of more than a handful of individual rioters remote. Nonetheless, a general conclusion that the Western Rising was an expression of the social and economic grievances of virtually landless artisans and cottagers fits the larger economic and social development of forested and industrial areas in the seventeenth century.

86. PRO, S.P. 16/195/5, examination of Thomas Yarwood (Yerworth), June 24, 1631.

Chapter VI

Artisans, Cottagers, and Rural Distress

The standard treatment accorded to those who engaged in non-agricultural occupations in the countryside provides an interesting demonstration of the dominant role agriculture has come to play in the minds of those who study the social history of rural England in the sixteenth and seventeenth centuries.[1] The equation of rural with agrarian in a predominantly agrarian society comes easily to the historian; inevitably, perhaps, in work devoted largely to agrarian history rural life has been viewed exclusively from the point of view of agriculture. It has become commonplace to regard rural industries mainly as a means of providing important supplements to the basically agricultural sources of support for farming families in wood-pasture districts. Rural crafts are frequently referred to as by-employments, integral but supplemental sources of income for an agrarian population. In this view the rural artisan was a hybrid: he was a peasant/craftsman who toiled part of the time as a farmer and the rest at a craft, or he was the head of a household, spending most of his time working at a trade while the other members of his family tended the farm.[2]

So dominant is this approach that the best study by far of cottagers is marred by the author's too-ready identification of landless or near-

1. The work which seems best to embody this dominance is J. Thirsk, ed., *Agrarian History of England and Wales 1500-1640*, 1967.
2. Joan Thirsk's own contribution to *Agrarian History of England and Wales 1500-1640*, "The Farming Regions of England," pp. 1-112, is the most comprehensive statement of this

landless cottagers with farm laborers.[3] Professor Alan Everitt provides much valuable information on the nature and extent of chronic rural poverty, working from a survey of 43 manors in which 651 of the holdings were cottages with no more than five acres, too small to support their tenants by the grain they grew or cattle they pastured. Forty-one percent of the cottages had no land beyond a garden or backside, while a further twenty-six percent had only one acre; only seven percent had as much as four or five acres. For these poor cottagers, common rights such as grazing for cattle and the taking of wood for fires and building materials were more important as a means of support than were their individual holdings.

Clearly, cottager families could not support themselves from such small holdings alone, but it is difficult to accept Professor Everitt's assumption that all cottagers supplemented their income as farm laborers and that all cottages can be called farm-laborers' holdings. Even where there is clear evidence that cottagers were engaged in woodland and forest crafts and in the spinning and weaving of wool and flax, these are represented by Professor Everitt as the part-time by-employments of farm laborers. He seems to believe, in fact, that artisans who lived by their craft alone and could therefore be identified socially and economically by it were mainly urban.

This results in a serious misunderstanding of the Western Rising. Professor Everitt contends that this was a laborers' rising, although in Gillingham forty-five out of the seventy-four rioters convicted in Star Chamber were artisans and only two were laborers. He circumvents this evidence by describing the Gillingham rioters as "urban tradesmen and weavers," even though there was nothing remotely resembling an urban unit near the forest, except perhaps the market town of Shaftesbury. At any rate, contemporary records identify the rioters as inhabitants of the forest townships of Gillingham, Motcombe, and Mere.

One implication of Professor Everitt's argument is probably correct: it was far easier for an unskilled laborer to exercise a trade than the existence of the Statute of Artificers would lead one to

---

view; see also her "Industries in the Countryside," in *Essays in the Economic and Social History of Tudor and Stuart England*, 1961, and "Seventeenth-Century Agriculture and Social Change," in *Land, Church and People*, 1970.

3. A. Everitt, "Farm Labourers," in J. Thirsk, ed., *Agrarian History of England and Wales 1500-1640*, pp. 396-465.

suppose. This is certainly indicated by the normally haphazard enforcement of the statute and by demands in times of declining employment opportunities for its strict enforcement against journeymen who had not served proper apprenticeships and against those who had too many apprentices.[4] It would also be erroneous to draw a sharp distinction between the quality of life and social position of artisans and that of laborers. Professor Everitt's very valuable discussions of the wealth and position of laborers within the manorial structure of agricultural areas of England could be applied with little or no alteration to workers in the western broadcloth areas and the new-drapery, to Dean Forest miners, and to the artisans in the variety of trades to be found generally in English forests.

One crucial distinction must be emphasized. The authors of the *Agrarian History of England and Wales, 1500-1640* view work in a trade as a by-employment for the agricultural population, but the evidence indicates that in most of the important industrial and forested areas of seventeenth-century England the cottagers' main source of support was wage work in skilled or unskilled occupations. The fortunate cottager who had an acre or two of ground or access to the wastes of a forest received supplements to his income, but these were subordinate in importance to his wages. In effect, the cottagers had ceased to be peasants and had become members of a rural proletariat.

The Statute of 1589, which specified that no new cottage was to be erected with less than four acres of ground attached, expressed a pious hope unrealizable in the social and economic reality of Tudor and Stuart England.[5] Another of the Elizabethan statutory measures designed to cope with a crisis, it followed the depression and scarcity years of 1586 and 1587, and demonstrates how the needs of economic self-sufficiency and public order coincided. It aimed to encourage food production by preventing the division of tenements into units of agricultural production too small to be viable, and was also intended to prevent proliferation of propertyless cottagers dependent on non-agricultural occupations, especially in the cloth industry.

4. See Davies, *Enforcement*, passim, Supple, pp. 26-27, *HMC Various*, vol. I, pp. 74-75, and above, pp. 76-78.

5. *Statutes of the Realm*, 31 Eliz. c. 7. It ought to be noted that cottages erected for the habitation of workers in any mineral works, coal mines, or quarries were excluded from the operation of the Statute.

As with most Elizabethan social legislation, systematic enforcement lagged far behind ambition. Licenses issued by justices of the peace and judges of assize to permit cottages of less than four acres to be erected with the consent of manorial lords were common throughout the late sixteenth century and well into the seventeenth; moreover, unlicensed cottages were erected in large numbers, particularly in forests.

As early as the mid-fifteenth century certain manors in Gloucestershire and Wiltshire (already important centers of the cloth industry) witnessed a development that was to become characteristic of western clothmaking areas over the next two centuries, namely, the growth of a class of landless journeymen clothworkers. In the manor of Castle Combe in northwest Wiltshire, held by Sir John Fastolf, there were fifty such landless artisans in 1435-1440, sixty in 1440-1445, and seventy in 1450. As there were also fifty-five tenants holding directly of the lord, this more than doubled the number of inhabitants in the manor. To accommodate these artisans and their families, at least fifty new cottages were erected between 1409 and 1454.[6]

By the late Elizabethan-early Stuart period there existed a large, and growing, group of propertyless cottagers within the main western clothmaking areas. Gillingham Forest seems to have been the southernmost extension of the important clothmaking area that ran the length of western Wiltshire and eastern Somerset. The existence of at least three fulling mills, the fact that twelve of the rioters convicted in the Star Chamber were employed in the cloth industry (nine of them as weavers), and the relatively frequent occurrence of clothworkers as deponents in Exchequer suits relating to Gillingham and Mere all lead to the conclusion that the cloth industry provided an important source of employment for the inhabitants of the area.

In addition to the population of cottagers in the forest, there was an increasing number within the bounds of the manors. Within Gillingham Manor in 1624 there were 202 copyhold tenants. Ninety-nine of them were cottagers holding less than four acres, and at least half of those held cottages with less than one acre. Combined with the evidence of subtenants (over 60 out of a total of 100 were cottagers) and the evidence of 50 new-erected cottages, this means that somewhere between one-half and two-thirds of the manor's tenants

---

6. E. M. Carus-Wilson, "Evidence for Industrial Development on some Fifteenth Century Manors," in *Essays in Economic History*, vol. 2, pp. 151-67.

were cottagers holding less than four acres; the majority of these had no holdings at all.[7] The number of cottagers in the manor continued to grow during the 1620s; in 1627 Exchequer special commissioners found that the already large number of "poor" was increasing as a consequence of the continued erecting of new cottages and the taking of inmates or lodgers into existing cottages.[8]

The same situation existed in the manor of Mere, where over half of the ninety-eight tenants held cottages with less than one acre.[9] Here, also, the number of cottagers continued to grow. Early in the seventeenth century a surveyor complained about the common practice of splitting tenements into small cottages which were then sublet.[10] In 1628 a number of tenants of Mere deposed in an Exchequer case that the population of both township and manor had greatly increased as a result of erecting new cottages and dividing and subletting existing tenements.[11]

There is no direct evidence linking these cottagers of Gillingham Forest with the cloth industry—although in at least one source they are described as poor artificers[12]—but there can be little doubt that the presence of a large number of cottagers who could not possibly support themselves from agricultural occupations, in an area with an important cloth industry, was more than coincidental. The intimate and necessary connection between propertyless cottagers and the cloth industry becomes obvious when the heartland of the English broadcloth industry, the forested areas of eastern Somerset and western Wiltshire, is examined. It is impossible to document actual numbers, but the general impression left by the evidence is of a large population of marginally poor artisans living in cottages and totally dependent on wages earned in the cloth industry.

The town of Frome in Somerset and neighboring Frome Selwood Forest in Somerset and Wiltshire had an especially large population of poor clothworkers. Local landowners profited from this situation by

7. PRO, L.R. 2/214, ff. 1-77; JRL, Nicholas MS 66, ff. 1-6; Hutchins, vol. III, p. 649, abstract of proceedings at the disafforestation of Gillingham.

8. PRO, E. 178/3732, commission of June 13, 1627, executed Aug. 20-25, 1627.

9. PRO, L.R. 2/207, ff. 21-24; E. 317/Wilts, no. 40.

10. PRO, L.R. 2/207, f. 22.

11. PRO, E. 134/4 Chas. I/Eas. 13, depositions by commission in Doddington vs. Alford, taken April 22, 1628.

12. PRO, E. 134/3 Chas. I/Eas. 17, depositions in A-G vs. tenants of Gillingham.

erecting on their manorial wastes new cottages with little or no land attached and renting them out to the poor. For example, in 1624 Edmund Leversedge, Esq., and Sir Thomas Thynne, of Longleat, Wiltshire (the latter a Wiltshire and Somerset justice of the peace in 1625 and sheriff of Somerset in 1629) were prosecuted in the court of Exchequer by the Attorney-General for erecting sixty new cottages in the forest and letting them to poor people who despoiled the King's woods.[13]

Perhaps the most graphic evidence for the social conditions in the clothmaking district of eastern Somerset comes from the two periods of depression and grain scarcity, 1622-1623 and 1629-1631. In August of 1622 the vicar and inhabitants of Frome Parish petitioned the judges of assize that they were overburdened with 500 poor, too large a number to be relieved by the parish's own resources. According to the petitioners, the cloth industry in the parish had attracted large numbers of people who came to live and work in cottages erected in the forest. Many families supported only by their incomes from weaving, fulling, and spinning were in great want because of the stoppage in the broadcloth industry. To provide aid for the unemployed, the justices ordered that £80 per year be provided by the treasurer of the hospital for the eastern division.[14] In May of 1623 the justices reported that grain was scarce and expensive around Frome, which relied on western Somerset and Wiltshire for its supply. The price had been driven up by the demands of the great number of poor clothworkers living in new-erected cottages dependent on the market in Frome for their food.[15]

Similar conditions were reported during 1631. In February the justices found that the town of Frome and the nearby forest were overcrowded with the cottages of poor who worked in the cloth industry and the other trades that supported most of the town's 6,570

---

13. PRO, E. 112/131/282, information and answers in A-G *ex rel.* Treswell vs. Sir Edward Seymour et al. for despoliation of Frome Selwood, Mich. 1624. Other evidence for the recent erection of cottages in Frome Selwood is to be found in STAC. 8/88/18, Coles vs. Leversage et al., May 21, 1603; STAC. 8/76/5, Sir Charles Berkeley vs. Tynnye et al., Feb. 4, 1624/5; and E. 134/7 Chas. I/Mich. 20, depositions by commission in Pointing vs. Hartgill, taken Oct. 11, 1631.

14. SRO, session roll 43 ii, f. 166, petition of the vicar and inhabitants of Frome Selwood to judges of assize, Aug. 13, 1622, endorsed that the JPs ordered the treasurer of the hospital of the eastern division to provide £80, Jan. 15, 1622/3.

15. PRO, S.P. 14/144/24 XII, certificate of the JPs of the eastern division, April 16, 1623.

inhabitants.[16] In December the justices again explained the continuing high price and scarcity of grain in Frome by its status as a clothmaking center in which the clothworkers were buyers, not producers, of corn, relying on supplies transported from Wiltshire and other parts of Somerset.[17]

One of the most powerful statements of the economic and social condition of the Somerset clothworkers is to be found in a letter of May, 1622, written by the sheriff:

There are such a multytude of poore cottages builte uppon the high waies and odd corners in every countrie parishe within this countye and soe stufte with poore people that in many of those parishes there are three or fower hundred poore of men, women and children that did gett most of their lyvinge by spinnying carding and such imploymentes aboute wooll and cloath: And the deadnesse of that trade and want of money is such that they are for the most parte without worke and knowe not how to live. This is a greate grievance amongest us and tendeth much to mutynye.[18]

The Wiltshire broadclothmaking centers located in Selwood, Chippenham, and Blackmore forests possessed the same social characteristics as Frome Selwood. Erecting new cottages with less than four acres attached, in defiance of the statute of 1589, was a particularly common offense in Chippenham and Blackmore. Widespread building of new cottages and the consequent destruction of woods and surcharging of pastures with cattle by the cottagers were the main reasons given for railing off parts of both forests in 1612 to the sole use of the royal farmer of the herbage and pannage.[19]

Behind this decision lay the findings of an Exchequer special commission set up to determine the cause of the destruction of the woods. The commission's findings contain a quite comprehensive record of cottages new-erected on the lands of private individuals up to 1610.[20] There were 137 new-erected cottages bordering on

16. PRO, S.P. 16/185/40, JPs of Somerset to PC, Feb. 20, 1630/1.
17. PRO, S.P. 16/204/112, JPs of Somerset to PC, Dec., 1631.
18. PRO, S.P. 14/130/73, sheriff of Somerset to PC, May 14, 1622.
19. PRO, E. 112/131/226, information and answer in A-G vs. Fane et al., Hil. 1611/12; no. 232, bill and answer in Nicholson vs. Baynton et al., 1612; no. 237, information only in A-G vs. Francis, Earl of Rutland, et al., 1612.
20. PRO, E. 178/4577, mm. 23-25, special commission and return, June 27, 1610. All statements made on the basis of this commission's findings must be approximate, because the document is in such bad condition that very little of it is legible to the naked eye; even with the use of ultraviolet light some parts remain illegible.

Blackmore Forest and 76 bordering on Chippenham. The dates of construction ranged from within the previous six months to sixty years earlier, but the vast majority had been erected within twenty-five years or less. A number of the tenements were of considerable size and were cottages in name only. Five had thirty-one or more acres attached, five more had between twenty-one and thirty acres, and another nine had between eleven and twenty acres. Of the rest, three had seven to ten acres, eleven had four to six acres, eighteen had one to three acres, while the remaining hundred and sixty-two had no land at all attached.

Approximately 41 of the 162 landless cottages were held rent-free, no doubt an indication of the poverty of the inhabitants. All were subdivisions of existing tenements made by a number of important landowners to augment their income. For example, Sir Francis Fane received annual rents totaling £21.13s.10d. from nine cottages and unrecorded rents from another three; the tenants of twelve cottages on his land paid no rent. This substantial total of 213 cottages, 162 with no land attached, does not include cottages erected on the royal demesne in both forests, nor does the total go beyond the year 1610. As early as 1600 it was found that within the previous fifteen years there had been numerous new cottages built on royal demesne in Blackmore. In 1606 Sir Henry Baynton, Deputy Justice of Chippenham Forest, was accused in the court of Exchequer of permitting the unlawful erection of twenty new cottages in the forest's wastes with consequent despoliation of the woods by their inhabitants.[21]

There are also indications in the records of the disafforestation of Chippenham and Blackmore in 1619 that considerable numbers of cottages had been recently erected on the demesne wastes.[22] In one instance three poor men, who had built cottages in Chippenham Forest for their own use, were proceeded against in Exchequer for despoliation of the King's woods and pastures; they were under the mistaken impression that they had a lawful right to common. Ultimately, the cottages were allowed to stand and at disafforestation the three men agreed to pay a small rent to the King.[23]

21. PRO, E. 178/2453, mm. 3-5, special commission on Blackmore Forest and return, dated Feb. 14, 1599/1600; STAC. 8/47/19, bill and answers in Richard Batten, deputy warden of Pewsham Forest, vs. Baynton et al., Jan. 24, 1605/6.
22. PRO, E. 178/4577, mm. 32-61, special commission and return for disafforestation of Chippenham and Blackmore, Mar. 23, 1618/19.
23. PRO, E. 112/131/254, information in A-G vs. Monday et al., undated but sometime in

One final western example is that of Kingswood, a detached Wiltshire parish neighboring on Wotton-under-Edge, Gloucestershire. In June of 1597 some propertied inhabitants, including the well-known Wiltshire clothier Benedict Webb, petitioned the Privy Council for help in defraying the high poor rate imposed on them by the general poverty of the parish. Of the 170 households in Kingswood, 100 consisted only of cottages with gardens, inhabited by poor people who were utterly dependent for their support on the spinning and weaving work put out by the clothiers.[24]

In addition to this evidence of the existence of large numbers of cottagers in the western clothmaking areas, there are of course reports of want and destitution received from the justices of the peace during periods of depression and scarcity. These demonstrate clearly the poverty and propertylessness of the clothworkers.[25] The complaints of wage-cutting from Warminster in 1595 and Devizes in 1623 and the frequent petitions for relief in the years 1620-1622 from the unemployed weavers of Bromham, Chippenham, Calne, and Rowde (all clothmaking centers located in the forested areas of western Wiltshire) point to the conclusion that the workers were entirely dependent on wages, had no farming income or homegrown foods to sustain them, and had to enter the market to buy their foodstuffs.[26]

1616. This is an omnibus bill charging a whole range of intrusions into the royal demesne. The three poor men were Henry, James, and Richard Cullis, and their answer is Eas. 1617; they indicate here a willingness to pay a small rent to the King and are so charged at the time of disafforestation.

24. *APC 1597*, pp. 221-22, PC to William Peryam and Matthew Ewens, judges of assize on the Oxford circuit, asking them to deal with the petition, June 19, 1597. (This Kingswood should not be confused with the Gloucestershire Chase of the same name, which was an important coal-mining area close to Bristol: see below, pp. 188-90.

25. See above, pp. 58-60.

26. *APC 1595-96*, pp. 43-44, PC to JPs of Wilts on wage-cutting at Warminster, Nov. 1, 1595; PRO, S.P. 14/138/54, mayor of Devizes to PC on wage-cutting, Feb. 20, 1622/3; WRO, Q.S. Gt. Roll, Eas. 1623, no. 243, petition of weavers and others for an increase in wage assessments. See also *HMC Various*, vol. I, p. 94; S.P. 14/115/58, petition of the weavers of Bromham, Chippenham, and Calne to PC, 1620; Q.S. Gt. Roll, Eas. 1622, no. 249, petition from spinners and weavers of Rowde to JPs; no. 250, petition on behalf of 800 clothmakers in Bromham Parish to JPs. For more on these matters, see above, pp. 58-60; further evidence on the wage dependence of Wiltshire clothworkers is to be found in two orders made by the justices in 1603 and 1604 to deal with the distress caused in the clothmaking areas through the disruption of the trade by an outbreak of plague, order made at Mich. Q.S., 1603, in *HMC Various*, vol. I, p. 74, and order at Hil. Sessions, 1603/4, in "Extracts from the Records of the Wiltshire Quarter Sessions," *W.A.M.* XXII (1885): 12-13.

This conclusion is also confirmed by the fairly frequent outbreaks of food riots involving the clothworkers of places such as Bromham, Warminster, and Westbury in western Wiltshire and their neighbors in eastern Somerset.[27]

Landless wage earners were not unique to the western forests. They also lived in the clothmaking areas of Essex and Suffolk, in those places that produced broadcloths as well as the new draperies. The most striking evidence for the wage dependence of the East Anglian clothworkers also dates from periods of scarcity and depression. During the severe grain shortage of the 1590s it was noted that in Dedham, Essex, an area in which "Suffolk" broadcloth was produced, there were 200 households, none with sufficient food; at least 120 of this total were inhabited by poor people dependent on work put out by the clothiers, and these were completely lacking in grain and victuals.[28] During the same period grain had to be shipped into Colchester, a center of the Essex new-drapery industry, to keep its large population of poor clothworkers from starvation.[29] As in the case of the western broadclothmaking areas, the depression years of 1622 and 1629-1631 in the clothmaking areas of Suffolk and Essex witnessed numerous reports of distress from the justices, petitions for work, increased wage assessments, or relief and food riots, all of which demonstrate the clothworkers' lack of property and total dependence on wages.[30] For example, during the depression of 1629 the clothiers of Essex petitioned the King requesting that action be taken to revive the trade in new draperies. Their petition provided a grim picture of the workers' chronic poverty even in full employment:

27. *APC 1595-96*, pp. 43-44, PC to JPs of Wilts, Nov. 1, 1595; Ramsay, *The Wiltshire Woollen Industry*, pp. 72-73; *APC 1613-14*, pp. 457-58, PC to JPs of Wilts, June 7, 1614; pp. 652-53, PC to JPs of Wilts, Dec. 6, 1614; PRO, S.P. 14/129/79, JPs of Wilts to PC, April 30, 1622; Birch, *Court and Times of James I*, vol. 2, pp. 291-92; *Diary of Walter Yonge*, p. 52; *APC 1621-23*, p. 217, PC to sheriff of Somerset, May 12, 1622; S.P. 14/130/73, sheriff of Somerset to PC, May 14, 1622; no. 99, sheriff of Somerset to PC, May 20, 1622; SRO, session roll 64 ii, nos. 200-205, examinations of riot suspects, Nov. 17 and 18, 1630.

28. *APC 1597-98*, p. 69, PC to JPs of Norfolk to permit the inhabitants of Dedham to buy grain, Oct. 30, 1597; pp. 89-90, PC to JPs of Essex, Nov. 3, 1597.

29. *HMC Salisbury*, vol. VIII, p. 526, bailiffs of Colchester to Robert Cecil, Dec. 8, 1597; *APC 1597-98*, pp. 230-31, PC to JPs of Norfolk, to allow grain to be bought in Norfolk and transported to Colchester, Jan. 8, 1597/8.

30. See above, pp. 72-78.

not beeinge able to subsist unlesse they bee continually sett on worke and weekly paied and many of them cannot support themselves and their miserable families unlesse they receive theire wages everie night.[31]

As part of the investigation into this depression in 1629, a survey was made of the main clothmaking centers of Essex: Bocking, Braintree, Coggeshall, Colchester, Dedham, and Witham. The account of each was basically the same, an unrelieved tale of chronic poverty deepened by idle looms and unsold cloth, with the unemployed and hungry wage-earners on the verge of violence. It ends with a general summary of the distress faced by the workers:

And lamentable is the being of all this multitude of people which live by these manufacturers; few or none that can subsist unlesse they bee paied their wages once a weeke; and many of them canot live, unlesse they bee paied everynight; many hundreds of them havinge noe bedds to lye in, nor foode, but from hand to mouth to mainteyne themselves, their wives and children.[32]

Late in 1629, Essex justices investigating complaints about wage-cutting in the new-drapery industry found that the weavers were paid such low wages that the magistrates did not know how they could maintain their families: "The trueth is they are made now soe poore they are neither able to paie rent nor buy any wood but are forced to breake hedges, lopp trees and some tymes fell them by the grounde and to doe many other unlawfull thinges."[33]

The instances of poverty and wage dependence among cloth-workers could be multiplied by drawing on evidence from other locations in Gloucestershire, Oxfordshire, Berkshire, Hampshire, and Norfolk.[34] Enough detail has already been cited to more than substantiate Professor B. E. Supple's conclusion based on the distress suffered by clothworkers in time of trade stoppage:

Cloth production was sufficiently far advanced to have ceased, in the main, to be a by-employment for a predominantly agrarian population. Hence, for the

31. Bod. Lib., Firth MS c.4, p. 487, petition of the clothiers and workmasters of Essex to the King, undated, but probably April-May, 1629.
32. Bod. Lib., Firth MS c.4, pp. 488-91, "A briefe declaration concerninge the state of the manufacture of Woolls in the Countie of Essex." Printed copies are to be found in *Essex Review* XVII (1908): 203-6, and Thirsk and Cooper, pp. 224-26.
33. Bod. Lib., Firth MS c.4, p. 511, JPs of Essex to the judges of assize, Dec. 2, 1629.
34. See above, pp. 59-60, 63-65.

government and for the community at large the existence of the textile industry meant the perennial threat of an outbreak of distress and disorder amongst a landless, and even propertyless, class.[35]

In addition to being a home for broadcloth production, forests harbored other industries that provided sources of support for the cottagers. Four of the rioters convicted of participation in the Gillingham Forest riots were employed in the making of linen, and there is evidence among the deponents in Exchequer suits that a number of other inhabitants in the forest were so employed. In the forest of Dean, for example, mining and the ironworks were important sources of employment, and the existence of a very large population of cottagers there is well-documented. The forests also sheltered large numbers of artisans earning a living in trades that used wood, bark, hides, and animal fat. Among the Gillingham rioters was a concentration of twelve artisans in trades that relied on the forest for raw materials. The presence of substantial numbers of such artisans in any forest seems obvious; evidence of their existence can usually be found among the deponents in Exchequer cases. Dean Forest, in particular, seems to have been inhabited by large numbers of woodworking artisans who lived by despoiling the underwoods and timber.

No doubt every inhabitant of the forests to some degree despoiled the woods and overburdened the wastes with cattle. For the poor cottagers this was often crucial to their survival. Even if the cottagers had other employment—in the cloth industry, mining, or wood-working trades—the forest supplied important supplements to income: pasturage for a few cattle, pannage for swine, game to be poached, and wood which could be used for building materials and fuel. In a petition against the disafforestation of Leicester Forest it was claimed that the borough of Leicester "consisteinge principally of manuall trades wherein are six parishes verie populous and many poore," depended on the forest to supply fuel at no cost to its many poor inhabitants.[36] In the townships bordering on Leicester Forest there were also poor men who owned horse teams with which they

---

35. Supple, p. 6.
36. H. Stocks, ed., *Records of the Borough of Leicester, 1603-1688*, p. 240, petition to the King from the inhabitants of the borough, ca. 1628.

earned a living supplying the borough with coal and wood; they relied on the forest waste for their support.[37]

There were also many inhabitants of forests with no regular employment at all beyond casual labor. Their despoliations are often indistinguishable in the records from those of artisans, since almost all were blamed on poor cottagers. It has already been noted that the main reason given for the enclosure of parts of Blackmore and Chippenham to the exclusive use of the farmer of the herbage and pannage was overexploitation of the woods and pastures by the poor. Such action did not prevent further activities of this kind. For example, thirty individuals were presented for despoliation of the woods in Chippenham Forest in the period between Michaelmas of 1615 and Michaelmas of 1616; twenty-two were laborers, two were weavers, two were tailors, two were butchers, one was a shoemaker (the status of the other was not given).[38] The forest supplied many of the necessities of life for such laborers. In those forests where there were no important industries, most of the poor cottagers must have lived almost entirely off the spoil of the woods and pastures.

This was true of Rockingham Forest in Northamptonshire, subject of an important recent work that provides an interesting case study of Brigstock Village. The main characteristic of Brigstock was a large and growing population of cottagers. In 1596 only 40 percent of all householders had land to farm. There were 110 cottages with no land; the tenants of at least 13 of them took in additional families as lodgers. During the seventeenth century the cottager population continued to increase. In 1627 the lessees of Brigstock Little Park complained that the poor rate had become burdensome because "of the multitude of poor people which have and do increase daily by reason of the continual erecting of new cottages and taking in of new inmates, being at least four score families more in the town of Brigstock in these few years than in any ancient time."[39] In 1637 it was

37. H. of L.R.O., Main Papers, petition, with list of grievances attached, from the inhabitants of Leicester to the House of Lords, June 23, 1628.

38. PRO, E. 178/4577, presentments of the preservators of the woods in Pewsham Forest, Mich. 1615-Mich. 1616.

39. P.A.J. Pettit, *The Royal Forests of Northamptonshire 1558-1714*, pp. 170-71. Source of the quotation is a Chancery bill of 1623, C.3/332/42. See also the similar conditions existing in the forest of Inglewood in Cumberland during the sixteenth century: A. B. Appleby, "Common Land and Peasant Unrest in Sixteenth Century England," *Peasant Studies Newsletter* IV (1975): 21-22.

recorded that 40 new houses, nearly all cottages, had been built in Brigstock since 1600.[40] There was no important industry in Rockingham to support this population of cottagers. There was some weaving, but Brigstock was not an important clothmaking center. Only those industries particularly associated with forests (e.g., tanning) provided some employment. As a result, most cottagers had to depend on the despoliation of the forest for their livelihoods: "There being little work to set them on, but [they] by flocks go moving up and down in the forest parks and inclosed grounds near unto them to the great hinderance of all who have cattle and woods."[41]

Feckenham, Leicester, and Braydon all followed the Rockingham pattern; with no important industries to absorb them, their large cottager populations supported themselves on the woods and wastes. Inhabitants of new-erected cottages and subtenants with no rights of common, who made extravagant claims to compensation, were reported to be the main stumbling-block to the quick and orderly settlement of the Feckenham disafforestation.[42] It has proven impossible to get any figures on the precise number of cottagers in Feckenham, but one witness deposed in 1630 that there was a multitude supported entirely by commoning in the forest, an assertion confirmed by the amount of land set aside as compensation for cottagers at disafforestation.[43]

It was claimed by those who opposed the disafforestation of Leicester that the inhabiants of 100 ancient cottages would lose their main means of support if the forest were improved: "they shall have nothingé left unto them, but only a howse of habitacion and soe shal be exposed to the maintenance of their parishes." There was also in Leicester Forest "a greate and manyfold confluence of poore people" living in new-erected cottages and supported by commoning in the forest.[44] While it is impossible to determine exactly how many

---

40. Pettit, p. 174.
41. Pettit, p. 171; source of quotation is a 1623 Chancery bill, C.3/332/42.
42. PRO, E. 125/7, f. 98, order in A-G vs. inhabitants of Feckenham, Oct. 23, 1629; E. 125/8, ff. 296-99, order in same case, June 16, 1630.
43. PRO, E. 134/6 Chas. I/Hil. 18, deposition of John Baylies, yeoman; E. 125/7, ff. 75-84, decree in A-G vs. inhabitants of Feckenham Forest.
44. H. of L.R.O., Main Papers, petition with list of grievances from the inhabitants of Leicester Forest to the House of Lords, June 23, 1628.

cottages existed in Leicester Forest, this estimate of 100 ancient cottages plus an equal number of new-erected ones conforms to the general impression conveyed by the surviving records of the disafforestation proceedings.[45]

Lacking important industries, beyond some weaving and typical forest crafts, to support them, the cottagers of Braydon Forest had to make do with day labor and the sustenance provided by the forest. In 1611 it was reported that most despoliation of the woods was committed either by the keepers or by the poor.[46] The pressure of a growing population of poor cottagers is particularly well-illustrated by an example from Braydon. In 1625 within the manor of Blunterden St. Andrew in the parish of Purton there were sixty or more recently erected cottages inhabited by poor people who were regarded by the parishioners as an intolerable charge on the poor rate.[47] During the next decade, continued growth in the population of poor cottagers forced the community to resort to a unique expedient to obtain new sources of income. The disafforested lands of Braydon, when granted to the lessees, were to be held quit of all tithes and free of any parochial ties, but the inhabitants of Purton obtained an order from the petty sessions that the former Duchy woods should be rated toward the parish's contribution to ship money.[48] This was part of a larger campaign to draw the Duchy land into the parish and rate it toward relief of the poor by "obtruding and erecting poore cottages upon the borders of the said lands and the said cottagers Christining and burying in the said parrish doe raise pretence for layeing a parochial clayme to the said Dutchie lands."[49] On at least one occasion the court of Exchequer had to confirm the quiet possession of the lessees and enjoin the inhabitants of Purton from attempting to rate the disafforested lands toward the relief of the poor.[50]

45. PRO, E. 112/195/10, A-G vs. Hastings et al., commoners of Leicester Forest, Eas. 1627; E. 126/3, ff. 209-21, decree in the same case, Feb. 7, 1627/8.

46. Manley, "Disafforesting of Braden," *W.A.M.* XLV (1930-32): 555, quoting a Duchy of Lancaster commission of 1611.

47. WRO, Q.S. Gt. Roll, Eas. 1626, no. 136, petition to JPs by parishioners of Purton; Q.S. minute book (order book), Hil. 19 Jas. I-Hil. 2 Chas. I, order for JPs of division to meet to consider the rate to be levied on the lord of the manor, Eas. 1626.

48. PRO, E. 317/Wilts, no. 23 and no. 38, parliamentary surveys of disafforested lands in Braydon, 1651, both of which contain memoranda on this subject omitted in the printed versions of F. H. Manley, ed., "Parliamentary Surveys of the Crown Lands in Braden Forest," *W.A.M.* XLVI (1933): 176-84.

49. PRO, E. 317/Wilts, nos. 23 and 38, 1651.

50. PRO, E. 125/20, f. 191, May 31, 1636.

No doubt at Braydon and elsewhere a substantial number of the cottagers holding a few acres were described not as laborers but as husbandmen. The poor husbandman was, in terms of standard of life, little different from the laborer. He was equally dependent on forest wastes, and at the time of disafforestation his interests lay with those who violently opposed the enclosure—doubtless the participants in the Braydon and Gillingham riots fined in Star Chamber and described as husbandmen were marginally poor small-holders.

Another common source of support for the poorer inhabitants of forests was game. Surviving Star Chamber prosecutions for illegal hunting in royal forests and private chases are numerous. Where the status of the defendants can be discovered, it is clear that poaching was a pastime indulged in by all strata of society, from knights all the way down to artisans and laborers.[51] Some hunted for the exhilaration of the chase, but poachers from the lower strata of society hunted out of economic necessity—to feed themselves and their families or to obtain income from selling their bag. Two examples should suffice to illustrate this point.

In 1603 in Brigstock Park of Rockingham Forest projected improvements caused a riot. The big and little parks totaling over 2,200 acres were well-stocked with deer and heavily hunted by the poor. In December of 1602 both were granted by Queen Elizabeth to Robert Cecil—a grant, confirmed by James I. Cecil, intended to improve both parks by selling off the woods on 900 acres and reducing the number of deer from 1,000 to 600 in order that suitable pastures would be available for cattle. The consequence of these changes was a riot by "the base sort," who tried to stop the cutting of the wood and to prevent the removal of deer from the parks to other areas of the forest. It was only after Cecil made a judicious distribution of alms to the poor that the disorders were ended.[52]

In 1639 a man who had been fined £30 for poaching in New Forest, Hampshire, and imprisoned because of his inability to pay petitioned for his release, claiming he was

a miserable pooreman in lamentable distresse, hath poore wife and vii small children, had great losse by fire, one of his children is a creeple, hath a blind

51. The number of Star Chamber prosecutions for illegal hunting in the royal forests that are the concern of this work are too numerous to list.
52. Pettit, pp. 171-73.

man to his father that wholly lyeth upon him, hath been twice imprisoned for this one fault, and in his present durance is ready to starve for want of food and so are his children at home, at this present £30 in debt, and hath no meanes in the world to releive himself his blind father wife and vii childrene but his painfull labour and never did or will, as God shall help him, commit any fault or offense against his Majesties game but onely one.[53]

The universal presence of poor cottagers in royal forests and the destructions they caused to the detriment of the Crown's revenue were often discussed in early seventeenth-century official proposals for increasing the government's income. During Salisbury's tenure of the Lord Treasureship a special commission found that in the New Forest 250 households together consumed 1,500 loads of wood annually and spoiled many good timber trees. Most of these households were located in new-erected cottages, and the commissioners proposed that they should be excluded absolutely from taking wood.[54] A report of 1609 on the general state of royal forests clearly reveals the official view of cottagers and the problems they created:

At this tyme the waste soyle in all forrests is moste extreamly pesterred and surcharged with all manner of beastes and cattell as well with sheepe goates and swyne beinge beastes not commonable within a forrest by lawe as also with keyne horse mares and colts and other beasts that are commonable by reason of the daylie increase of new erections of tenements cottages dwellinge houses as well uppon the kinges waste soyle as also uppon mens owne inclosed landes which new erections have noe right of common at all within the forest nor little or noe land to keepe any cattell uppon. And those new erections are also inhabited with lewd poore people such as doe live upon the spoyle and destruction of the kinges woodes and deere.[55]

It was a commonplace among officials and private individuals alike that an overabundance of open waste ground and common attracted the vagrant and encouraged idleness, drunkenness, and disorder. In 1618 the Cecil family hoped to establish the cloth industry in Enfield Chase, Middlesex, to give employment to the large number of poor who, drawn there by the abundance of common, lived in idleness,

53. J. C. Cox, *The Royal Forests of England*, p. 309.

54. Bod. Lib., Ashmolean MS 1148, ff. 255-56, undated, report of the proceedings of a special commission to the Lord Treasurer.

55. PRO, L.R. 2/194, ff. 276-77, "a collection of certain great abbuses and wronges done unto his Majestie in his forests," April 27, 1609; see also BL, Cotton MS, Titus B. IV, ff. 332-33, undated, memorandum on the causes of the spoils of woods observed by the surveyors.

despoiled the woods, and overburdened the poor rates.[56] When the Berkeleys came to consider enclosure at Slymbridge in Gloucestershire in 1639, the main argument in favor of it was that the open common drew people from other places who lived in beggarly cottages, erected alehouses, and led lives of idleness and petty crime. Division into severalty would support honest husbandmen who could pay rents, instead of useless beggars and other such lazy and idle people. In proposing this the Berkeleys looked to the contemporary disafforestation of Dean as a model for promoting both private profit and the good of the commonwealth.[57]

In the case of the compensatory allotment set out for the poor of Mere in 1652, and in similar instances at Leigh and Purton after the disafforestation of Braydon, the land was put in the hands of trustees drawn from the "better sort" in order that they could manage the land in the interests of the deserving poor. Their management consisted of enclosing the land and leasing it out to husbandmen who would, by their rents, provide an income to support the poor. Certainly at Mere, and probably at Braydon, this was done to eliminate the alternative of an open common which, it was believed, would attract too many poor people.[58]

The status of the vast majority of rural and small-town artisans suggests that propertylessness was at the root of their involvement in disorders. The wages earned in manual trades virtually their sole support, in standard of life little removed from laborers, artisans (especially those in the cloth industry) were squeezed by depression, unemployment, declining wages, and sharp rises in the price of food in the market. This accounts for the dominant roles they played in attempted insurrections and in food riots. It also helps to account for the increase in the number of vagrants and the prevalence of certain kinds of crime during hard times. Those artisans, and poor cottagers generally, who relied on the forests for their principal or supplementary income found this source of support disappearing with disafforestation.

56. *HMC Salisbury*, vol. XXII, pp. 80-81, a project for setting to work the poor of Enfield Chase, ca. 1618.
57. Thirsk and Cooper, pp. 122-23, reasons in favor of enclosure at Slimbridge, Gloucestershire, 1639.
58. See above, pp. 148-49.

The outbreak of the Western Rising is to be seen as the result of economic pressure put on the poor cottagers. Disafforestation and enclosure threatened them at least with the loss of income supplements, and in some cases with the loss of their livelihood. This combined with a number of other factors which were more or less important depending on local circumstances: the long-term decline in the broadcloth industry, the trade stoppage of 1629-1631 further reducing employment opportunities in the cloth industry, the 1630 harvest failure that drove up the prices of food in places which were not important grain-growing areas, and, finally, a general depression resulting from harvest failure coming in the midst of ongoing difficulties in the cloth trade.[59]

59. There was one other element in the background: a growing population of marginal poor in the forests pressing on the means of subsistence. This seems to have resulted from two factors: natural population increase within the forest communities, and large-scale immigration into the forests from outside. In Gillingham a number of the cottagers were undoubtedly the younger sons of fairly long-established families within Mere and Gillingham manors, as is revealed by the frequent occurrence of a limited number of surnames. For example, among adult male rioters and suspects, there were four Alfords, seven Butts, seven Caves, and six Phillipses. There is also evidence that substantial numbers of the cottagers in Frome Selwood, Braydon, Dean, and the Northamptonshire forests were newcomers to the area, poor men attracted by opportunities for employment or by the natural bounty of the forest. (Frome Selwood, SRO session roll 43 ii, f. 166; Braydon, WRO, Q.S. Gt. Roll, Eas. 1625, no. 136; for Dean see below, pp. 182-83; for Northants see Pettit, p. 171.)

Chapter VII

The Dean Forest Community and the Policies of James I

The Dean Forest disorders of 1631 and 1632 have always been considered an integral part of the Western Rising, and rightly so, for the riots were broadly similar in aim and immediate cause to those that occurred in the other western forests: they followed enclosures within the forest, and they were an outgrowth of the same kind of social conditions that prevailed elsewhere. Many cottagers who were economically dependent on the forest in varying degrees came into conflict with the Crown's fiscal needs and its consequent revivification of legal rights that threatened their livelihood.

Dean deserves separate treatment for two major reasons: first, as a good example of an area in which much employment was provided by the other main industries of the Tudor-Stuart period—mining and metallurgy—and, second, as a case study of a particularly bitter clash between longstanding custom and a unique forest community on the one side and the economic necessity and legal rights of the Crown on the other. Unlike the other western forests, there was no sudden catastrophic disafforestation at Dean to mark the reassertion of the Crown's rights. Instead, the events of the early part of Charles I's reign must be set in the context of a slow revival of royal demesne rights beginning early in the reign of James I. The riots of 1631 and 1632 were not the end of the story; they were only one especially violent episode in a long struggle between the Crown and some segments of the forest population that continued in one form or another up to and beyond the Civil War.

The Forest Community

The uniqueness of the Dean Forest situation was centered in the wealth of the forest, actual and potential. It contained within its boundaries rich deposits of coal and iron ore which could be reached by the digging of shallow pits. In addition, there were large stands of oak suitable for construction. Yet at the beginning of James I's reign, except for selling cordwood to smelt the locally mined ore, the Crown received little profit from the forest. The royal forest administration had been allowed to fall into desuetude and the local inhabitants permitted to exploit the forest at will. "Dean was one of the forests which long ago had been abandoned to their inhabitants. For many generations no hunt had braved its mines and quarries, bogs and hills; only local use saved all its timber from rotting where it had grown; no forest eyre had visited it for 300 years."[1]

Many of the inhabitants earned their livings by direct exploitation of the forest's mineral resources. Since veins of ore were close to the surface, workable pits could be dug by as few as two or three men, with virtually no capital outlay. The miners were members of a close-knit community that had its own court for the settlement of all mining disputes and claimed unrestricted rights to mine coal and iron ore in all lands within the forest bounds, no matter where legal title to the land lay. Like the common claimed by cottagers in other forests, the privileges of the "free miners" had no basis in municipal law. They were founded on custom and long usage.

The extent of the privileges claimed by the miners was a measure at once of the neglect by the Crown of its demesne rights in the forest and of the miners' well-entrenched position, successfully maintained against repeated encroachments by the governments of James I and Charles I. The "rights and privileges" of the Dean miners were of indeterminate antiquity and doubtful legality. They are preserved in three separate seventeenth-century transcripts of an inquisition taken

1. G. Hammersley, "The Revival of the Forest Laws under Charles I," *History* XLV (1960): 89. This article provides the best modern account of the proceedings of the Dean Forest eyre and of the larger political significance of the revival of the forest laws.

before the mine law court at an unknown date, in which a jury of forty-eight miners confirmed the "law of the mine."[2] There also survive at least three different contemporary opinions on the origins of the miners' rights. One was that the existence of the miners' privileges was proved by a deed of the reign of Edward II, though there was no record as to who actually made this grant.[3] Another was that John, Duke of Bedford, granted a charter of privileges to the miners in recognition of their military service in France.[4] (Presumably this was John of Lancaster, brother of Henry V and Regent of France from 1422 to 1435; the only fact that can be determined with certainty, however, is that Dean Forest miners served as sappers in the Hundred Years' War.)[5] The third opinion, which was probably closest to the truth, was that in 1317 the regarders of Dean held an inquest at the justice seat and found that certain payments in money and iron ore were settled on the miners by the Crown to encourage them in their trade. Presumably on this foundation the miners later built their much more elaborate claims.[6] Understandably, this was one explanation not put forth by the miners.

Whatever the origin of their "rights and privileges," the miners were never able to produce an authentic grant from the King or any other palatine lord to prove their right to mine in the royal demesne. Neither could they provide the circumstantial evidence which might have convinced a court that such a grant had once been made. It is most probable that by the seventeenth century the origin of the miners' privileges had been long forgotten; thus, when the Crown began to press for large-scale exploitation of the iron ore, for their own protection the miners wove the few scraps of evidence remaining

2. Printed in full in C. E. Hart, *The Free Miners of the Royal Forest of Dean*, pp. 37-45, where in Chapter 2 there is a full discussion of the various manuscripts. The historian interested in Dean is fortunate indeed in having available the work of C. E. Hart: *Free Miners, Commoners of Dean Forest*, and *Royal Forest*. These studies, along with some smaller ones, provide remarkable testimony to Mr. Hart's love and knowledge of the forest. Not only are they deeply researched and remarkably accurate in the transcripts of documents included, but they provide a sense of place and a knowledge of topography which can come only in the best kind of local history, that based on firsthand acquaintance with the subject.

3. PRO, E. 134/22 Jas. I/Eas. 8, deposition by Christopher Tucker, deputy gaveller of the mine law court.

4. PRO, E. 134/13 Chas. I/Mich. 42, deposition by William Morgan.

5. Hart, *Free Miners*, chap. 1.

6. GRO, D. 421/19/22, abstract of records concerning the claims of the miners of Dean Forest.

in the form of inquisitions remembered or extant into the larger tapestry called the "rights and privileges of the mine."[7] It must be reiterated that the miners had no legal right to their privileges and that the Crown was well within its own rights to encroach on them. The Crown may have acted unwisely and in the larger sense inequitably, but it did not act illegally, as some historians seem to believe.[8]

In another sense the question of legality was irrelevant, for the mine law existed as a fact in the seventeenth century. It is clear from depositions in a number of Exchequer cases that it was operative in regulating the working life of the miners. It was no mere claim to rights; it was a practical code supervising all aspects of the mining of coal and iron ore.

The most contested parts of the mine law were those relating to the claim that the "Myners may myne in any place that they will."[9] The miners assumed an absolute right to enter the soil of any lord, whether the King or a mesne lord, "without the withsaying of any man," and to take coal and iron ore for their own profit.[10] If any freeholder denied them admittance to his land, then the gaveller, an official of the mine law court, was to "deliver the soyle to the Miners" in the King's name.[11] Refusal of permission to enter royal demesne was not anticipated, since it was assumed that the miners had an absolute right to mine in the King's soil. The lord of the soil where the pit was dug was admitted to a full partner's share in the mine without payment of the traditional dues to the gaveller.[12]

The two gavellers were royal officials appointed by letters patent whose duties, exercised in the seventeenth century by deputy, were to collect all payments due to the King out of the mines and to represent his interests in the mine law court.[13] When a pit was sunk and iron ore found, it had to be "galled" before it could be worked—that is, the

---

7. This is certainly the implication of GRO, D. 421/19/22, which can be read to mean that the miners elaborated the mine law in the early seventeenth century to protect themselves against the intrusion of large-scale enterprise.

8. This contention of illegality runs through Hart's various works on the forest.

9. "Miners' Laws and Privileges," sec. 4, in Hart, *Free Miners of the Royal Forest of Dean*.

10. "Miners' Laws and Privileges," sec. 12.

11. "Miners' Laws and Privileges," sec. 13.

12. "Miners' Laws and Privileges," sec. 14.

13. Hart in chapter 3 gathers together much of the evidence relating to this office.

gaveller formally recognized the partnership, admitted the representative of the lord of the soil to the partnership, and received a penny for the King from every partner in the mine. Thereafter the King received a penny a week from each miner whose profits amounted to ninepence or three seams in measure. Once every quarter the gaveller collected the King's law ore: threepence or one seam of iron ore or coal.[14]

The gaveller may originally have been intended to regulate mining in accordance with the rights of the King in his own demesne, by assigning to the miners those parts of the waste in which they could sink pits and by taking the profits from the minerals for the King's use. The earliest evidence for the office's existence comes from the beginning of the fifteenth century. By the seventeenth century, however, lack of concern with the forest on the part of the Crown had led to almost complete assertion of control by the miners themselves over all aspects of mining. The miners still recognized that the King had an interest in the forest; at one point they called themselves the King's miners and paid the already discussed dues and all amercements in the mine law court to the King.

The mine law court enforced the law for settlement of all disputes relating to mines and mining within the forest. Its principal task was "to hear and trye the right of our Soveraigne Lord the King and of Miners and party if any bee."[15] According to the mine law a miner could not be impleaded in any other court for matters concerned with the mines. If this occurred, "then the Constable by the strength of the King shall require and bring the plaint into the Mine Lawe and there hit shall be tryed by the Constable and the Miners."[16] This claim had no legal force, and as time went on it lost all practical importance.

Most of the information on the miners' claims to privileges comes from suits against them in the court of Exchequer by the Attorney-General or the farmer of the ironworks. By the middle of the seventeenth century miners were suing each other in the court of Exchequer over mining matters, in clear violation of their own mine law. One item which continued to be enforced in the mine law court

---

14. "Miners' Laws and Privileges," secs. 15 and 16, further amplified by PRO, E. 134/22 Jas. I/Eas. 8, and E. 134/13 Chas. I/Mich. 42.

15. "Miners' Laws and Privileges," sec. 20; see also PRO, E. 134/13 Chas. I/Mich. 42.

16. "Miners' Laws and Privileges," sec. 21.

was the testamentary disposition of a mine share. A miner could will his share "as his own cattle." If he died intestate the share descended to his heir. To prove a legacy nothing more was needed than to bring the testament before the court with two witnesses to testify to the miner's will.[17]

In spite of the "laws and privileges" that gave them virtual control of the coal and iron ore in the forest, the miners were far from prosperous. The little that can be discovered about their economic position indicates that it was much the same as that of artisans in other seventeenth-century forests and industrial areas: on the margin of poverty, lacking landed property, and living entirely by their labor. In 1613, when James I had begun to reassert royal rights to the iron ore, the Attorney-General began an Exchequer suit against miners who continued to dig ore in violation of a grant made to William Herbert, Earl of Pembroke. It was found

that they were poore labouring men and were wholy susteined with their wives and families with digging and carrying of such myne, ore and synders, acknowledging as well by their answere to the said information as by the counsell at the barre the soile to bee His Majesty's, and that they had no interest therein, humbly preying that they might bee permitted to continue their digging and carrying the said myne, ore and synders as they had been accustomed having no meanes to relieve their poor estates.[18]

This acknowledgment of the miners' poverty is far from unique. Similar views were expressed in the course of other Exchequer suits relating to the mines during the reign of James I.[19] In 1637 it was deposed that about one hundred families in the forest were supported solely by mining.[20] In the same year Thomas Witson, a miner, claimed that as a result of enclosures made at Mailescott Woods by Lady Villiers, widow of Sir Edward Villiers and sister-in-law to the Duke of Buckingham, many poor families born and raised in St. Briavels hundred could no longer work at mining as they had formerly done and were thus in a miserable state, close to starvation.[21] The amount

17. "Miners' Laws and Privileges," secs. 24 and 25.
18. PRO, E. 126/1, f. 270, decree in A-G vs. Monjoye et al., Jan. 28, 1612/13; a transcript is to be found in Hart, pp. 166-68.
19. PRO, E. 112/83/411, answer in Earl of Pembroke vs. Hall et al., Jan., 1613/14; E. 124/27, ff. 54-55, order in A-G vs. Keare et al., June 15, 1618.
20. PRO, E. 134/13 Chas. I/Mich. 42, deposition of Thomas Browne.
21. PRO, E. 134/13-14 Chas. I/Hil. 16.

of profit expected from a share in a mine also points to the fact that
the miners made a poor living. Ninepence a week seems to have been
the normal clear profit of each miner in 1637.[22] In 1656 Joan Parry, a
widow, received a weekly compensation for her late husband's share
from his partners consisting of 1s.6d. and a seam of coal (worth 3d. in
the 1620s).[23] Like the inhabitants of other forests, miners supplemented the income from their labor by exploiting the forest; they
took timber for their pit workings and pastured cattle in the wastes.

Although the miners comprised the most homogeneous community
in the forest, there were also large numbers of other artisans—poor
cottagers and cabiners who lived in the forest and despoiled it for raw
materials, fuel, and building materials. Among them were some poor
men who lived by quarrying grindstones and millstones, called
variously grindstone-hewers, millstone-hewers, or masons.[24] Woodworking and ironworking probably engaged a much larger proportion
of the forest's poor. A report of 1611 emphasized that lack of proper
supervision by the forest officers had bred "a multitude of poor
creatures," who lived on the spoil of the woods.[25] In 1615 there were
found to be 79 cabins and cottages recently erected within the coppices
enclosed for timber. They were inhabited by 340 men, women, and
children who subsisted in the forest as trenchermakers, coopers, and
other kinds of woodworkers.[26]

Sometime in the reign of Charles I a petition complaining of such
people was sent to the Council, probably by some of the substantial
freeholders of the forest:

there are a great number of unnecessarye cabbins and cottages built in the
said forest by straungers whoe are people of very lewd lifes and conversations
leavinge their owne and other countryes and takinge this place for a shelter
as a cloake to there villanies. By which unruly crue your Majesties woods and
Tymber Trees ar cutt downe and imbezeled and your Majesties game of deere
much disquieted and distroyed. And if soe be they continue three yeres in the

22. PRO, E. 134/13 Chas. I/Mich. 42, deposition of Christopher Worgan.
23. GCL, L.F. 1.1, pp. 29-33, proceedings of the mine law court, May 20, 1656.
24. PRO, E. 112/82/296, Morgan vs. Callowe et al., Hil. 1611/12; E. 112/83/351, A-G vs.
Young et al., Trin. 1619; E. 134/19 Jas. I/Eas. 23, depositions by commission in the same case; E.
126/2, ff. 228-29, order dismissing the case, Nov. 22, 1621; E. 112/179/13, A-G vs. Smart et al.,
Eas. 1627; E. 112/181/109, Jenkins vs. Catchmay et al., Mich. 1634.
25. BL, Lans, MS 166, f. 334, reasons to move His Majesty to make use and profit of Dean's
woods, undated; f. 370 is a summary dated Mar. 11, 1610/11.
26. PRO, E. 178/3837, inquisition taken by commission at Mitchell Dean, Feb. 6, 1615/16.

forest then they will looke for maintenance of the Countrey or els they will run away and leave their children upon the countrey.[27]

Although the growth in the number of poor can be explained in part by the possibilities for livelihood that a forest lying waste could offer, it can best be understood as a direct consequence of the Crown's attempt to increase its income from the forest. There is abundant evidence from the reign of James I and early in the reign of Charles that the sawyers and carpenters employed by the farmers of the ironworks cut timber trees reserved for the Crown's own use and, with the connivance of the royal forest officers, converted them to planks, barrel staves, and so forth. These materials were then sold to cardboardmakers, coopers, trenchermakers, tanners, charcoal-burners, and the like, many of whom were attracted to life in the forest by the availability of cheap raw materials.[28] Some artisans using wood and bark continued to cut their own materials, but the employees of the ironworks made raw material available to others on a scale never before possible.[29] People drawn to the forest by this abundance of raw material either built their own dwellings or moved into cabins and other buildings abandoned by the ironworkers.[30]

The grants made to Crown lessees to erect new ironworks in the forest or to operate and expand the existing works normally included permission to erect cabins and cottages in which to house the workers.[31] It has been impossible to discover how many workmen the royal farmers brought into the forest and how many more were attracted to the forest in the hope of obtaining some sort of employment connected with the ironworks. It is clear, however, that a considerable number of strangers permanently entered the forest,

27. PRO, S.P. 16/44/45, petition to King from inhabitants of Dean, undated but probably 1626-1631.

28. PRO, E. 178/3837, commission to George Marshall et al., Jan. 19, 1613/14, with articles of instruction and depositions taken Jan. 25, 1613/14; commission to William Cooke et al., Oct. 15, 1617, with articles of instruction and depositions; E. 134/25 Jas. I/Mich. 24, depositions in A-G vs. Chaloner and Harris; BL, Harleian MS 738, ff. 306-8, proceedings at the justice eyre, 1634.

29. Estreats of fines for waste and spoil of wood in Dean presented at the speech court dealing with minor offenses for some years of James I and Charles I are in PRO, E. 137/13/4 and E. 146/1/34.

30. PRO, E. 178/3837, commission to William Guise et al. to inquire into disposal of woods, Nov. 18, 1615, with articles of instruction and depositions taken Feb. 6, 1615/16.

31. See, e.g., the grants to the 3rd Earl of Pembroke, PRO, C. 99/34, Feb. 17, 1611/12, and C. 99/21, July 7, 1629.

swelling the ranks of the propertyless cottagers. It was reported that when the lease of the ironworks was granted to the Earl of Pembroke in 1612, men came from as far away as Sussex to work as fellers, corders, charcoal-burners, miners, smelters, and forge-workers.[32] In the 1630s Sir John Winter brought in Welshmen to work in the ironworks and Staffordshire miners to work mines on his land.[33] This inevitably led to use of the King's timber to build cottages and cabins. One of the charges against the royal farmers of the ironworks at the justice eyre of 1634 was that "they had brought in a multitude of cottagers and cabbiners who all made their cottages and cabins of the king's wood, and lived upon spoil of the wood."[34]

Even in the best of times the ironworkers' dependence on the forest was great, for they were poor and complained of being underpaid. In 1637 a commission was appointed to investigate abuses connected with the payment of wages to employees of the royal ironworks. The fragments of its proceedings that survive point to the typical and usually justified complaints against the truck system. A corder and two woodcutters stated that the workers were forced to accept a large part of their wages in kind, at rates up to 50 percent beyond those prevailing in the market. Refusal to accept this sytem of payment was met by immediate dismissal from employment.[35]

The importance of the forest as a means of support for such people was enhanced by the fact that on four occasions between 1611 and 1628 the leases of the ironworks were withdrawn before running their alloted timespan.[36] Every time a lease was surrendered it meant that the ironworks ceased to function. On one occasion this lasted for three years, from 1618 to 1621. Although there is no evidence of what the workers did at such times, it can be assumed that they were reduced to living off the forest. It is also probable that each new lease meant a new group of workers brought into the forest, with the result that a permanent pool of unemployed was created. The complaints about large numbers of poor cottagers living solely on despoliation of the forest indicate that there were many more people in the forest than

---

32. PRO, E. 178/3837, depositions taken by commission at Coleford, Jan. 25, 1613/14.
33. PRO, E. 112/179/37, A-G vs. Brooke, Winter, et al., Trin. 1630; E. 134/13 Chas. I/Mich. 42, depositions in A-G vs. Winter et al.
34. BL, Harleian MS 738, ff. 306-8.
35. PRO, E. 178/5304, Sept. 16, 1637.
36. Hart, *Royal Forest*, p. 105.

could be absorbed by available employment. Moreover, in 1630 Sir Basil Brooke and Sir John Winter were accused of bringing in Welshmen "of a very poore and meane condition" to work in the ironworks, instead of employing local inhabitants.[37]

Throughout the seventeenth century the poor cottagers remained a permanent part of Dean Forest society and a constant source of annoyance and anxiety to the Crown. As landless inhabitants of new-erected cottages, they had no rights to common; this did not, of course, stop their use of pastures, underwoods, and timber. Furthermore, they were viewed as a disorderly people who ran alehouses that were the haunts of criminals of various sorts, including some who robbed travellers in the forest.[38]

Assessment of the importance of nonagrarian occupations in Dean Forest and of the proportion of cottagers among the forest's inhabitants is made possible by the survival of two unique sources: a survey of all able-bodied men in Gloucestershire fit for military service, compiled in 1608 by John Smith of North Nibley, barrister and steward to Henry, Lord Berkeley, Lord Lieutenant of the county; and the records of the 1634 justice eyre of Dean Forest. Smith's compilation is particularly useful because it is subdivided by location (manor or borough) and includes status where known.[39] From this source only the data on the localities within the hundred of St. Briavels has been evaluated. St. Briavels, centrally located within the forest, is the only location where the inhabitants claimed the right to mine coal and iron ore as a birthright. (Smith's survey cannot be used as a definitive source, however, since it predates the greatly increased exploitation of the forest's iron ore that began only after 1612. Thus, for example, that part of Smith's survey which deals with Sir Edward Winter's lands in Bledisloe hundred on the fringes of the forest bears little trace of the family's heavy involvement in ironmaking and coal-mining, which came later in the century.)

The occupational structure of St. Briavels hundred is shown in the table below. No doubt the most striking aspect of this evidence is the large proportion of the population employed as artisans and laborers.

37. PRO, E. 112/179/37, A-G vs. Brooke, Winter, et al., Trin. 1630.

38. PRO, E. 178/3837, inquisition at Mitchell Dean taken by commission, Feb. 6, 1615/16.

39. John Smith, *The Names and Surnames of All the Able and Sufficient Men in Body Fit for His Majesty's Service in the Wars, within the County of Gloucester, 1608* . . .; pp. 31-46 cover St. Briavels hundred and pp. 53-58 cover Bledisloe.

Occupational Structure of St. Briavels Hundred
Based on the Survey of 1608

Landed and agricultural population, including lords of manors		Merchants, retailers, and professionals	
Peer	1	Mercer	4
Knight	1	Clothier	3
Esquire	8	Surgeon	1
Gentleman	37	Toothdrawer	1
Yeoman	29	Innkeeper	4
Husbandman	83	Victualer	1
TOTAL	159	Fishmonger	1
		Chapman	4
		TOTAL	19

Mining, metalwork, and other minerals		Wood and animal products	
Miner	30	Carpenter	21
Collier	4	Joiner	5
Oresmith	28	Turner	3
Apprentice	2	Cooper	9
Nailer	30	Trenchermaker	4
Cutler	4	Shovelmaker	3
Pinner	2	Cardboardmaker	1
Ironworker	1	Sievger	3
Metalman	1	Tanner	14
Brazier	1	Chandler	1
Furnacekeeper	1	Currier	2
Grindstone-hewer		Shoemaker	21
Millstone-hewer	13	Glover	11
Mason		TOTAL	98
TOTAL	117		

Occupational Structure of St. Briavels Hundred
Based on the Survey of 1608 (Cont.)

Cloth, related trades, and food production		Miscellaneous	
Broadweaver	17	Tankardmaker	2
Weaver	28	Basketmaker	1
Apprentice	1	Tinker	1
Fuller/tucker	9	Tiler	10
Dyer	1	Plasterer	1
Coverlet weaver	4	Thatcher	1
Tailor	20	Limeburner	5
Bonelacemaker	1	Waterman	4
Hatter	1	Sailor	16
Miller	6	Cosier	1
Baker	2	Dishcarrier	1
Maltmaker	1	Raddlecarrier	1
Butcher	21	TOTAL	44
TOTAL	112		

Servants and laborers		No status given	
Servant of gentleman	54	No status given	71
Servant of yeoman	14	Son (status of	
Servant of husbandman	2	father not given)	27
Servant of artisan	38	TOTAL	98
Servant of professional or retailer	9		
Servant, unidentified	14		
Total servants	131		
Laborers	151		
TOTAL	282		

Of the 831 individuals whose status is reported in the survey, 44.6 percent were artisans and 18.2 percent were laborers. Moreover, a good part of the 15.8 percent of the population classified as servants should be included among the laborers, especially the servants of yeomen, husbandmen, and artisans. The large percentage of artisans and laborers confirms the impression left by the evidence already discussed: much of Dean's population depended on nonagricultural occupations. Some interesting questions are, however, raised by Smith's survey, and they require elucidation.

Some of the occupations to be found in St. Briavels in 1608 had a bleak future. This is particularly true of the cloth industry, which appears with surprising frequency—fifty weavers, including one apprentice, nine tuckers or fullers, one dyer, and three clothiers. With the decline of the broadcloth industry during the next three decades this source of employment must have dried up considerably. The number of oresmiths in St. Briavels, who worked the iron in small forges, no doubt declined in the face of competition from the blast furnaces and large forges erected in considerable numbers after 1612. The fact that the calculated exploitation of Dean's mineral and wood resources did not really begin in earnest until 1612 explains why certain types of artisans are relatively rare or nonexistent in Smith's compilation. For example, an accounting taken later in the century would certainly include more than thirty miners. Woodworking artisans, including coopers, trenchermakers, shovelmakers, and cardboardmakers are also surprisingly scarce, especially given later complaints of their despoliation of the woods. Trades associated directly with the ironworks, such as fellers, corders, and workers in blast furnaces and forges, are virtually nonexistent. No doubt too as the economic life of the forest quickened more inhabitants of St. Briavels took advantage of their claimed birthright to become miners.

Certainly the growth in iron production accompanied by the destruction of woods and timber brought in its wake an increased population of ironworkers and woodworking artisans. In addition, a good number of miners and woodworking artisans may have been concealed among the 151 laborers. There are a number of examples in Exchequer and other legal records of a Dean Forest inhabitant being called a laborer on one occasion and a miner or woodworking artisan on another. In Dean, as in other forests, there was no clear dividing-line between artisans and laborers. Smith's compilation may also seriously underestimate the size of the laboring population in the forest. Each manor within the hundred of St. Briavels is surveyed but there seems to be no mention of lands outside the manorial structure. In 1608 there were approximately 20,000 acres of royal demesne waste in Dean Forest, and presumably even at that date a considerable number of poor cottagers lived there. These inhabitants seem to have been entirely missed, or perhaps Smith avoided them because of their known fondness for drink and disorder.

The size of the population of laborers in Dean is a particularly striking aspect of the records of the 1634 forest eyre.[40] The most notorious offenders punished at the eyre were a handful of iron-masters who had either erected ironworks without license or de-spoiled Dean's woods on a really massive scale, but the vast majority of offenses punished were minor, and most had been committed by men of low status. Leaving aside the activities of the ironmasters, the offenses can be divided into two categories; destruction of wood and timber, and encroachments. A total of 309 people were fined for the former. Of the 256 whose status can be discovered, 114 (44.5 percent) were laborers. Artisans, mostly miners, woodworkers, and leather-workers, totaled 68 (26.5 percent). The other 29 percent was made up largely of gentry, yeomen, and husbandmen.

Nearly all the encroachments punished were for the erection of cottages, either on the King's demesne or on the soil of a mesne lord. Here the predominance of laborers is even more marked. Out of a total of 237 individuals fined for the erection of cottages, the status of 183 is recorded. Of these 125 (68 percent) were laborers. Artisans accounted for 44 (24 percent), most of them colliers and wood-workers. The other 8 percent were mainly gentry, yeomen, and husbandmen. Probably included among the laborers was a consider-able number of miners, woodworkers, and ironworkers. There are a number of examples in the records of the eyre in which an individual accused of more than one offense is variously described as a laborer and as an artisan. Many of the laborers were concentrated in a limited number of locations known to have been the sites of ironworks.

This sort of social pattern, where the majority of inhabitants were propertyless and of low status, can be found in other areas with important mining industries. One striking example is Kingswood Chase, a wooded area in Gloucestershire near Bristol. Kingswood possessed rich deposits of coal which were increasingly exploited by neighboring manorial lords during the first half of the seventeenth century. Its value as an economic asset led to a long and unsuccessful

40. The fullest accounts of the eyre are to be found in Bod. Lib., Gough MS Gloucs. 1 and BL, Harleian MS 4850, ff. 24-59; for other examples of the unlawful erection of cottages on the royal demesne see E. 112/180/55, information in A-G vs. Yate et al., Mich. 1631.

series of lawsuits by the Crown to establish that Kingswood was a royal forest and most of its soil royal demesne. The landowners in and around the chase maintained the contrary, that the disputed lands were part of their manorial waste. According to a survey made in 1615, the claims of the manorial lords "doe swallowe up the whole forest, not allowinge his Majestie the bredth of a foote. The timber, wood, bushes, soyle, coale mines, and all other profittes altogether carryed from his Majestie by unknowne righte."[41] Litigation began in 1602 and was still continuing in 1631, when it inexplicably vanishes from the surviving records of the court of Exchequer.[42] When, in 1652, those appointed by the trustees for the disposal of Crown properties surveyed Kingswood, they found it divided among the neighboring landowners; although these individuals could produce no legal title to the chase, they had effectively deprived the Crown of any practical benefit from it.[43]

The survey of 1615 claimed that there were many cottagers who destroyed the woods and the game in Kingswood. In 1629 there were 46 new-erected cottages whose inhabitants paid rent to neighboring manorial lords.[44] By the time the chase was surveyed in 1652, parliamentary surveyors found that there were 152 cottages erected on waste believed to have been Crown property. Out of the 152, 118 had no land attached beyond a garden; each of the rest had a small close of pasture one-quarter to one-half acre in extent. The tenants of 135 of the cottages paid rents to neighboring manorial lords who had encroached on the King's soil; the other 17 were built on the side of the Bath road and paid no rent to any landlord.[45] As in Dean, a large proportion of the population was engaged in nonagricultural occupations. According to Smith's survey of 1608, 42 percent of the male inhabitants of the manor of Bytten and Hanam bordering on Kingswood were artisans, well over half of them colliers. Another 18 percent were laborers or servants. In the nearby manor of Estor, 55

41. PRO, S.P. 14/84/46, survey of Kingswood Chase in Gloucestershire, 1615.

42. It would take up too much space to list all the entries in the Exchequer order and decree books dealing with this litigation. Other materials are to be found in PRO, E. 134/8 Jas. I/Eas. 33a; E. 134/5 Chas. I/Mich. 19; E. 112/83/160, A-G vs. Chester et al., 1622; E. 112/179/10, A-G vs. Chester et al., 1628.

43. E. 317/Gloucs., no. 12, survey of Kingswood Chase, May 26, 1652.

44. PRO, E. 134/5 Chas. I/Mich. 19.

45. E. 317/Gloucs., no. 12, survey of Kingswood Chase, May 26, 1652.

percent of the population were artisans, with just under one-half of them colliers.[46]

There was one other social group in the Dean Forest community, that of landowners—freeholders and copyholders claiming rights of common in the forest. According to Smith's survey of 1608, gentry, yeomen, and husbandmen made up 17.9 percent of the adult male population of St. Briavels hundred. Like commoners in other forests, they claimed wide and almost unlimited rights to common of estovers and pasture appurtenant to their tenements. Such claims were not, of course, exclusive to landowners; every householder in the forest maintained them. Common of estovers traditionally included dead-wood for fuel and enough wood to build fences and to repair each commoner's house, outbuildings, and farm equipment. In Dean this was regulated by the speech court, through which the forest officers tried to prevent the destruction of timber trees or at least to impose fines for such destruction. Common of pasture included grazing in the forest at all times of the year for commonable cattle, pannage for hogs, and pasture for sheep in unwooded wastes. In return for this, certain yearly sums were paid to the Crown.[47] To these common rights ought to be added the miners' claim to timber necessary for their pit workings and the fact that some of them owned cattle that they pastured in the forest.[48] At the beginning of James I's reign these were all prescriptive rights based on long usage and custom. No court had ruled on their legal validity.

The Crown and Dean Forest in the Reign of James I

Early in the reign of James I the Crown, compelled by financial necessity, began to revive its demesne rights in Dean. It concentrated on exploitation of the iron ore: royal farmers received grants of the right to the iron ore, and authority to erect ironworks and to cut cordwood to be made into charcoal for smelting. In making such grants, the Crown came into immediate conflict with the congeries of

46. Smith, pp. 206-9, pp. 234-36. See also the similar social conditions which existed in the coal-mining area of Broseley, Shropshire: PRO, STAC. 8/86/118 and 8/195/8.

47. PRO, E. 125/4, ff. 269-74, decree in Winter et al. vs. A-G, Feb. 11, 1627/8, gives the fullest statement of common rights.

48. "Miners' Laws and Privileges," secs. 26-28. Evidence for miners depasturing cattle is to be found in records connected with a suit by the A-G against them, e.g., PRO, E. 125/10, ff. 22-23, Feb. 7, 1630/1.

customary rights claimed by Dean's inhabitants. From the Crown's point of view, these customs were longstanding abuses which neglect of demesne rights had permitted to flourish. From the point of view of the people of the forest, the Crown's activities constituted a threat to their long-established way of life. The stage was thus set for a long, at times bitter, and ultimately successful struggle by some of the inhabitants of Dean to defend their customary rights against encroachment.

The opening of the conflict came in 1612 when, after competitive bidding, William, Earl of Pembroke, won the right to erect ironworks in Dean. He obtained authority to build the four blast furnaces and three forges known thereafter as the King's ironworks; for fuel he was granted 12,000 cords of wood annually at four shillings a cord for twenty-one years. As part of the grant Pembroke was given a monopoly on the iron ore; no one was to mine the ore or ship it out of the forest without his permission.[49]

Opposition to the grant took a variety of forms. On August 5, 1612, a group of fifteen men set fire to the wood cut and corded for the Earl of Pembroke's use. The Council ordered the arrest of these "Robin Hoods," but it was found to be difficult to carry out the order. They were "favoured" and protected by the inhabitants, a problem which recurred on a much larger scale during the riots of 1631-1632.[50] This kind of disorder was a common occurrence in Dean whenever an outsider or well-to-do forest inhabitant attempted to profit from the forest's resources. In the summer of 1594, local inhabitants threatened with violence the workmen sent to fell timber trees marked for the Crown's use. The forest dwellers vowed that the trees would never leave Dean; in carrying out this threat they cut fifteen tons of timber into pieces too small to be of any practical use.[51] There was also a riot in December of 1605: about twenty-five people assaulted a group of

49. PRO, C. 99/34, Feb. 17, 1611/12, fully discussed in Hart, *Royal Forest*, pp. 89-91. The competition for the lease of the ironworks can be followed in BL Lans. MS 166, f. 374, the state of the bargains made in the forest of Dean, June 11, 1613; ff. 376-77, copy of a warrant from the Earl of Salisbury and Sir Julius Caesar to the S-G for drawing up a grant to Pembroke; the Sussex cord, still the standard, consisted of 128 cubic feet of wood, while the Dean cord was 151 cubic feet.

50. PRO, S.P. 14/70/49, Earl of Northampton to Secretary Rochester, Aug. 14, 1612; no. 55 I, Northampton to Rochester, Aug. 20, 1612; S.P. 14/66/24, petition of Christopher Bond and Thomas Worgan to Ld. Tr. Salisbury, undated.

51. BL, Lans. MS 76, no. 47, notes on the timber in Dean Forest, Aug. 12, 1594.

Sir Edward Winter's workmen engaged in converting trees into charcoal for use in his ironworks. The rioters claimed that Winter and his servants exceeded his rights of common in exploiting the forest for this purpose and thereby deprived the other inhabitants of their rights to common of estovers.[52]

The miners' opposition to Pembroke's lease took the form of continued mining in the traditional way with complete disregard for his monopoly. To protect Pembroke's interest the Attorney-General in May of 1612 brought an action of intrusion in the court of Exchequer against the miners. His information asserted that the miners "to the preiudice of his Majesties said fermor . . . doe daily digge and carry awaye out of the said Forest the myne and oare there gotten." The miners answered that they were poor laboring men completely dependent on their mining of coal and iron ore. While admitting that the soil of the forest was the King's and that they had no legal interest in it, they appealed for permission to continue to mine and, if need be, to transport the ore out of the forest in search of a market.

The court's decision—in this case agreed to by the Attorney-General—suggests that while the Crown desired to obtain recognition of its legal rights in the forest, it did not intend to deprive the miners of all their claimed privileges. This was no doubt partially due to a desire to avoid further disorder; more to the point, however, the miners were needed to supply ore to the ironworks. The decree emphasized that the forest was royal demesne in which the miners had no legal rights; they were enjoined from taking ore out of the forest. Nonetheless, because of the miners' poverty and the needs of the ironworks, it was ordered that out "of charity and grace and not of right" they could continue to mine in the forest, but only to supply ore to the royal ironworks.

The miners ignored the injunction and continued to sell ore to other ironworks around Dean and to ship it beyond the forest. As a result, process was issued by the court in October of 1612 for the attachment of a number of miners. When the miners appeared to hear the court's determination of the matter in January of 1613, all contempts of the previous injunction were pardoned and the former decree was renewed with an added proviso in favor of the miners. If

52. PRO, STAC. 8/303/7, Winter vs. Catchmay et al., May 10, 1606.

the King's ironworks did not buy all their ore, then they could sell it to other works in and near the forest.[53]

The miners were not disposed to accept even this compromise. In 1613 the Earl of Pembroke began a fresh suit in Exchequer complaining that the miners refused to sell ore to the Earl's agents and, without his license, continued to ship ore to other ironworks in the forest and to places as distant as Ireland. In answer to Pembroke's bill, the miners admitted that the forest was the King's demesne, that Pembroke's grant was valid, and that they had no right or title in the forest lands. Nevertheless, they prayed that the court would recognize the liberties, franchises, and privileges which had belonged to them time out of mind to mine ore and coal in all soil within the forest, to sell wherever they wished, and to regulate mining matters through the mine law court. The crux of the miners' argument was that the injunction, which prohibited the transportation of ore from the forest under pain of a fine of £100 for each offense, deprived them of part of their privileges and would if enforced compel them to break contracts made on the basis of those privileges: William Cheinall, a London merchant with a monopoly on the export of iron ore to Ireland, had contracted for the miners to deliver ore to the river Wye, on the forest boundary, where he and his fellow merchants collected it for transport to Ireland.[54]

No further proceedings in this case have as yet come to light; it certainly did not come to judgment, for there is no decree to be found.[55] The suit was probably dropped because Pembroke had no further interest in the matter. By the end of 1613 his lease had been revoked due to the discovery that his agents were cutting timber trees reserved for the King's use.

The court of Exchequer's 1613 decision prohibiting transport of ore out of the forest but allowing the miners to sell their surplus production within the forest seems to have remained in force for the rest of James I's reign. In the only other Exchequer case during this

---

53. PRO, E. 126/1, ff. 270-71, decree in A-G vs. Monjoye et al., Jan. 28, 1612/13. This seems to be the only extant record of these proceedings.

54. PRO, E. 112/83/411, Earl of Pembroke vs. Hall et al., undated but from E. 124/16, f. 241, it can be dated Eas. 1613.

55. Neither this writer, nor Hart in *Free Miners*, p. 173, nor the compiler of GRO, D. 421/19/22, abstract of records concerning the claims of the miners to 1752, could find a decree or informative order in this case.

period that concerns mining privileges, the injunction was renewed to prevent a number of miners from selling ore out of the forest; nonetheless, "the said mynors whose educacion had bene onely in labour of this kind might be permitted to utter their overplus or remayne of their said oare or myne to the relief of their wives and children to any others who will buye the same."[56] No further attempt was made to limit these privileges during the reign of James I. The Crown was satisfied with a decree to the effect that the miners had no basis in law for their claim to mine anywhere in the forest; their usefulness as suppliers of iron ore to the ironworks insured that they would be left alone to continue their operations.

A parallel to this situation existed in the Crown's dealings with the grindstone-hewers; again, the caution with which the government of James I moved to revive royal demesne rights in the forest is particularly striking. In 1619 the Attorney-General, on behalf of the farmer of the manor and hundred of St. Briavels, Sir Richard Catchmay, sued a number of Dean inhabitants who claimed the right to quarry grindstones in the forest within the hundred of St. Briavels.[57] In its judgment the court recognized that the grindstone-hewers had no title to their claims. Because of their poverty, however, Catchmay was advised not to oppress them in such a trifling matter, especially since the stone was worth no more than the labor involved in quarrying it. In addition, the hewers already paid him an annual rent of 3s.4d. each in recognition of his rights in the matter.[58] In this case, as in those connected with mining, neither grindstone-hewers nor miners were able to prove any right to their privileges. They were only allowed them on sufferance. At any future date, the Crown remained free to exercise fully its rights over the minerals in the soil.

Pembroke lost the lease of the ironworks in 1613 due to opposition to the grant by those people in Dean who claimed the right to common of estovers. The commoners feared that the grant of cordwood and construction timber might be the first step in a campaign to deprive them of their customary privileges. In 1612 they petitioned the Lord Treasurer, maintaining that the grant would

56. PRO, E. 124/27, ff. 54-55, order in A-G vs. Keare et al., June, 15, 1618.
57. PRO, E. 112/83/351, A-G vs. Young et al., Trin. 1619; depositions by commission in this case are in E. 134/19 Jas. I/Eas. 23.
58. PRO E. 126/2, ff. 228-29, decree in A-G vs. Young, Nov. 22, 1621; despite this, Catchmay continued to harass the grindstone-hewers: see E. 112/179/13 and E. 112/181/109.

ultimately result in the despoliation of the whole forest and requesting that a commission be set up to investigate the charge that Pembroke's agents were illegally felling timber trees reserved for the navy.[59] Although the petition was submitted by "poor inhabitants and commoners," the Earl of Salisbury was of the opinion that influential landowners were behind it: "For me to say that these peticioners have incouragement were but to shewe howe the Sunne shineth."[60] Want of evidence makes it difficult to decide if there was any substance to this belief, or if it was simply another expression of the official view that behind every popular disorder stood men of influence. It is certain, however, that in this instance resistance to the reduction of waste available for commoning was as much in the interest of the wealthier landholders as of the poorer inhabitants.

In reply to the petition, Salisbury urged the commoners to submit their claims to the court of Exchequer for judgment. In accordance with this advice they submitted a bill late in 1612 complaining that Pembroke's grant would result in the destruction of the forest and the loss of the commoners' rights to pannage and estovers. To prevent this the Crown was urged to empower a special commission to inquire into the quantity of wood in the forest in order to establish the acreage that should be reserved uncut for the use of the commoners.[61]

Although the bill was withdrawn, the commoners' complaints had some effect. Sometime in 1613 one George Marshall was sent to Dean to investigate the charge that Pembroke's agents were felling timber reserved for the King. Marshall found the charge to be true, and on November 20, 1613, the Privy Council ordered the felling of all types of trees to cease until the matter could be further investigated.[62] In effect, this prohibition closed down the ironworks; before the end of the year Pembroke's lease was revoked.[63] Meanwhile, an Exchequer special commission was able to document fully the wastes and spoils of the woods. The main offenders were found to be Pembroke's agents and the woodwards (Royal officials charged with protecting the

---

59. PRO, L.R. 2/194, f. 242, petition to Salisbury.

60. PRO, L.R. 2/194, f. 244, Salisbury to Sir Julius Caesar, May 7, 1612.

61. PRO, E. 112/82/300, bill of Sallens vs. the Earl of Pembroke, 1612, endorsed "to be withdrawn."

62. *APC 1613-14*, pp. 278-80, PC to the constable of Dean and George Marshall, Nov. 30, 1613.

63. Hart, *Royal Forest*, p. 95.

King's timber from destruction), who for their own profit sold timber trees to cardboardmakers, trenchermakers, coopers, and other woodworking artisans in the forest.[64]

No legal action was taken against Pembroke and his agents beyond the revocation of the lease, but this illegal felling of timber had considerable consequences for future government policy with regard to the forest. Henceforth until the death of James I, the government's attention was directed primarily toward preventing despoliation of the forest by the farmers and their agents, in collusion with forest officials, and by poor woodworking artisans living in new-erected cottages. In the course of the next ten to fifteen years, as each new lease of the ironworks and cordwood was made, the lessees' activities came under close scrutiny by Exchequer special commissions, and the lease was withdrawn whenever illegal felling of timber was discovered. At the same time, the woodwards and other forest officers were constantly instructed, to little or no avail, to limit the number of woodworking artisans in the forest and to prevent the building of new cottages.

In May of 1615 the royal ironworks were again let, this time to Sir Basil Brooke and Robert Chaldecott, a London merchant, for a term of fifteen years. The lessees were to purchase local iron ore at prices to be arranged with the miners; they were also allowed an annual total of 12,000 cords of wood at 6s.8d. the cord.[65] As with the previous grant of cordwood, a commission was simultaneously issued to forest officials, headed by Robert Treswell, surveyor of the royal forests south of the Trent. The commissioners were instructed to insure that the farmers and their agents complied with the provisions of the agreement.[66] This set of instructions marks the beginning of stronger efforts by the government to prevent despoliation of the woods. It contained an important new article ordering the commissioners to halt the erection of new cottages in areas where the cordwood was cut,

---

64. PRO, E. 178/3837, commission to George Marshall et al., Jan. 19, 1613/14, with depositions taken at Coleford, Jan. 25, 1613/14; the commission with articles of instruction to surveyor and woodwards to supervise the felling of cordwood for the ironworks is E. 178/3837, April 3, 1612.

65. BL, Lans. MS 166, ff. 387-88, comparison of the bargains made for the ironworks, Feb. 23, 1618/19; Hart, *Royal Forest*, p. 95.

66. PRO, E. 178/3837, commission to Robert Treswell, George Castle, and William Callowe, April 3, 1612; E. 134/Misc. 2538, articles of instruction; E. 178/3837, commission with articles of instruction, June 8, 1615.

and to prevent strangers, especially workers in wood or timber, from taking up habitation in deserted cottages or other buildings. If such people were already resident in the area where the felling was to take place, then the commissioners were to take sureties from them to prevent despoliation of the woods and, through injunctions obtained from the court of Exchequer, to compel them to move away.[67]

Another commission was issued late in 1615 to determine the extent to which Treswell and his fellow commissioners were carrying out their instructions.[68] Earlier, in the summer of 1615, the government had received information of illegal cutting of cordwood; the evidence discovered by this new commission confirmed that information.[69] It was found that Treswell's two associates, George Castle and William Callowe, had neglected their duty to be present when the cordwood was cut, with the result that good timber trees were felled and the cords were oversize. They were also lax in enforcing the instructions concerning cottagers; seventy-nine new cottages and cabins inhabited by woodworking artisans and their families had been erected in the felled areas.[70]

Despite this evidence of negligence, the commission to Robert Treswell, George Castle, and William Callowe was renewed in October of 1616, accompanied by the same set of instructions.[71] Practically on the heels of this commission, another was issued to inquire into the activities of Castle and Callowe. The findings of the second commission were much as before, namely, that both men neglected to supervise the cording of the wood for the ironworks. They were also charged with appropriating 460 timber oaks to their own use.[72] In 1617 another commission unearthed more evidence of despoliation of the woods. For their own profit, Castle and Callowe had sold trees and wood to turners, coopers, trenchermakers, and cardboardmakers. Since the ironmasters were obviously in collusion with Castle and Callowe, the King, in March of 1618, suspended the

---

67. PRO, E. 178/3837, articles of instruction, item 9, June 8, 1615.

68. PRO, E. 178/3837, commission to William Guise et al., Nov. 18, 1615.

69. PRO, S.P. 39/5/46, warrant for privy seal to constable of St. Briavels, July 20, 1615.

70. PRO, E. 178/3837, depositions taken by commission at Mitchell Dean, Feb. 6, 1615/16.

71. PRO, E. 178/3837, commission to Robert Treswell et al., Oct. 24, 1616, with articles of instruction.

72. PRO, E. 178/3837, commission to Sir William Cooke et al., Feb. 12, 1616/17, with depositions taken at Mitchell Dean, Mar. 25, 1617.

felling of all trees intended for the supply of the ironworks. The farmers lost the lease and the ironworks reverted to the Crown.[73] The ironworks were not leased again until April 6, 1621, when they were let for seven years to Richard Challoner and Philip Harris. William Rolles and Robert Treswell, junior, were appointed as commissioners to supervise the cutting of the cordwood.[74] Almost immediately information began to come to hand that the new farmers and the commissioners were despoiling the woods. In Easter term of 1623, Attorney-General Coventry brought an action in the court of Exchequer against Challoner and Harris. They were accused of cutting oversized cords and of selling timber to woodworking artisans.[75] In Michaelmas term of 1624 the matter came to trial. Verdict was given for the Crown, but before judgment could be entered against the defendants James I died. At the same time that the death of the King stopped the legal proceedings, it put an end to the planned grant of a pardon for Harris and Challoner, which would have taken effect as soon as judgment was given in favor of the King.[76]

In October of 1627 Attorney-General Heath reopened the case on the information laid by Coventry in 1623. The defendants were ordered to plead to the information or have judgment entered against them. They appeared and pleaded not guilty, and the court ordered the case to be tried the following term. It never came to trial, being postponed for a further term and finally disappearing from the records.[77] Sometime during this period—probably toward the end of 1627— Challoner and Harris surrendered the lease. No doubt this is why the Attorney-General allowed the suit to drop. Once the Crown had its

73. PRO, E. 178/3837, commission to Sir William Cooke et al., Oct. 15, 1617, with articles of instruction and depositions of witnesses; GCL, L.F. 6.3, signet letter to the farmers of the ironworks, Mar. 31, 1618; Hart, *Royal Forest*, p. 97.

74. Hart, *Royal Forest*, p. 98.

75. PRO, E. 125/3, f. 307, order in A-G vs. Harris et al., Oct. 30, 1627, recounting the history of the case; E. 134/22 Jas. I/Mich. 42, depositions taken Sept. 23, 1624; Hart, *Royal Forest*, pp. 98-99.

76. PRO, E. 124/37, f. 127, order in A-G vs. Harris, Jan. 28, 1624/5; E. 125/3, f. 307, Oct. 30, 1627; S.P. 14/184/29, Ld. Tr. to Secretary Conway, Feb. 22, 1624/5; for exposition of the kinds of legal proceedings which were abated on the death of the monarch, see *Report of Sir George Croke (James I)*, ff. 13-14.

77. PRO, E. 125/3, f. 307, order in A-G vs. Harris et al., Oct. 30, 1627; f. 337, notice of appearance and order for trial, Nov. 20, 1627; E. 125/4, f. 333, order postponing trial to the following term, May 14, 1628; see also f. 372, similar order in countersuit, Harris vs. A-G, May 26, 1628.

hands on the ironworks again, there was no great need to pursue the farmers for their violations of the terms of the lease.

As part of this policy of close supervision and conservation of Dean's woods, the government of James I attempted to deal with extensive despoliation by wealthy propertyholders who exercised the right to common of estovers. Suits were begun in Exchequer by the Attorney-General, but only one seems to have come to judgment. Brought in 1613, the judgment was finally given in 1618 against Sir Edward Winter, one of the largest landowners in the forest.[78] This case is of great significance because it is the earliest one which has come to light so far in which a court ruled on the legality of the rights claimed by the commoners. Winter was charged with having since 1592 appropriated to his own use 10,000 timber trees and 20,000 loads of tree limbs from the royal demesne.

In his answer Winter presented a number of defenses. He maintained that the lands on which he had felled timber were his own "proper inheritance and freehold," in fact, assart lands for which he had compounded with the King's officers in the forest. Winter claimed further that as chief warden of the forest (an office he first held in 1595 as deputy under Henry, Earl of Pembroke, and then in his own right since Pembroke's death in 1601) he was lawfully entitled to cut two fee trees annually. He also pleaded a pardon issued to him by James I in 1604 for all trespasses and offenses committed before his accession. The final and most important averment was that Winter had for himself and his tenants, as appurtenant to the three manors and scattered freehold lands which he held in the forest, the right "by all the time whereof the memory of man is not to the contrary" to common of estovers of the woods growing in the King's wastes of the forest. Winter confessed that, acting in accordance with this right, he had at various times cut down trees and had taken dead and dry wood.

Since Winter was charged with really massive despoliation of the woods, this last point, the claim of common of estovers, was crucial to his defense. The other three defenses in his answer were really only throwaway pleas: the first, that he cut down timber on his own land, avoided the issue; the second, his claim to fee trees, covered only a very small number; and the third, the pardon, did not cover offenses

---

78. PRO, E. 112/82/310, A-G vs. Winter et al., Hil. 1612/13; no. 342, A-G vs. Hawkins et al., Trin. 1618; no. 343, A-G vs. Throckmorton et al., Trin. 1618; E. 112/83/386, A-G vs. Berrowe et al., Mich. 1623; no. 406, A-G vs. Bridgman et al., 1612.

committed after 1603. The substance of the court's judgment was that in the royal charters conveying the manors to Winter's ancestors there were "no words in the particular purchases of the said mannors to warrant the passing of the commen of estovers claymed." Thus Winter "could not by lawe prescribe nor otherwise bee intitled to the said estovers." As for his claim to estovers belonging to freehold tenements held by him in a variety of townships, the court held the pleading and proof as insufficient because too general, "for that upon such uncertainty the Court cannot judge to which lands estovers doe belonge and to which not." Winter and his tenants and lessees were enjoined from any further taking of estovers. It was also ordered that a commission be appointed to determine the value of the despoliation committed, on the basis of which the court would assess damages.[79]

The court was not asked to decide upon the general question of the legality of the near-universal claim by the inhabitants of Dean to common of estovers. Nonetheless, the judgment for the Crown in this specific instance, and the terms in which the decree was framed, indicate an intention both to maximize the position of the Crown by emphasizing its legal rights to the hilt, and to whittle away at generalized prescriptive rights for which no written proof could be offered. Although the extent to which this judgment was actually enforced against Winter remains unknown, the aim of James I's government (here and in the cases dealing with the miners) was the same: to establish by legal means the King's clear title to the woods, soil, and minerals of Dean Forest. The need for income was the obvious motive behind this policy, but a desire to maintain social peace dictated that the search for money be tempered by prudence. James I's legal rights were never pressed so far that they produced a violent reaction. Furthermore, James I's policy was betrayed by the weakness of the instruments available to the Crown for supervision of the forest. Thus the government was sidetracked into a long, time-consuming, and unsuccessful attempt to bring the activities of cottagers, forest officials, and farmers of the ironworks under control—activities which, ironically, the Crown's own search for money largely fostered. James I did lay the groundwork for the policy of his successor, but although Charles I showed more vigor in asserting the demesne rights of the Crown, it can hardly be argued that he was more successful than his father.

79. PRO, E. 126/2, ff. 140-42, decree in A-G vs. Winter, Feb. 10, 1617/18.

Chapter VIII

The Government of Charles I and Dean Forest to 1641

When Charles I came to the throne, fiscal policy as it applied to royal forests felt the quickening hand of this vigorous young monarch immediately. Disposal of forests and exploitation of Dean's mineral resources had started with James I; during Charles's reign these trends were accelerated. Disafforestation took place on a much greater scale, and the exploitation of the Crown's interest in Dean's iron ore was greatly increased. For the first time, the Crown began to look to the income potential of Dean's coal deposits. This was, of course, only part of a greater whole, as growing political and financial pressures forced a more systematic search for new and increased non-parliamentary sources of revenue.

The vigor of the Crown, which put particular pressure on the means of support relied upon by the miners, woodworkers, and poor cottagers in Dean, was matched by the violence of the forest's inhabitants in defending their claims against encroachment. There were a few innovations in the Crown's dealings with the forest community, such as conciliation of the propertied commoners and revival of the medieval forest eyre as a means of dealing with despoliation. No doubt, too, Charles I made more money out of Dean than his father had done, but the Crown was unable to assert its interests consistently against the forest community. Its failure was demonstrated in 1639 when disafforestation proceedings were commenced.

In 1627, when the lease of the ironworks held by Richard Challoner and Philip Harris was surrendered, there ensued a struggle for its re issue among a number of prominent courtiers and monopolists. The three main protagonists were Sir Sackville Crowe, Sir John Kirle (a Herefordshire ironmaster), and a group connected with the Company of Mineral and Battery Works, including Sir Basil Brooke, George Mynne (a London merchant), and Thomas Hackett. William Herbert, Earl of Pembroke, Lord Steward of the Royal Household and high constable of Dean, conducted the negotiations on behalf of this latter group. After offering payment of £6,600 in advance for a two-year supply of cordwood, Pembroke obtained a twenty-one-year lease of the ironworks and a supply of 10,000 cords a year at 6s.8d. per cord. The Earl then sublet to Brooke, Mynne, and Hackett in return for one shilling on each cord. A year later, in December of 1628, Pembroke was granted a further 2,500 cords annually at the same price.[1] In addition, Sir John Winter got a twenty-one-year grant of an annual supply of 4,000 cords of wood, also at 6s.8d. per cord, to fuel his ironworks in the forest.[2]

Taken as a whole, these grants represented a marked increase over James I's exploitation of the forest, when the annual grant of fuel was 10,000 to 12,000 cords. This increase considerably reduced the open waste available to the inhabitants; after the first grant to Pembroke in 1612, the area in which the felling took place was enclosed after it was cleared of the cordwood. The enclosures, which normally lasted nine years, were intended to keep cattle from destroying the "springs"— the new growth of trees.[3] As a result of these grants by Charles I, 5,000 acres were enclosed and the instructions to the commission appointed to supervise the felling and cording contained the standard prohibitions against the erection of cottages in the fellets and against the settlement of strangers, especially woodworkers, near the area where the cutting was scheduled to take place.

On top of this reduction in the amount of available open waste, the Crown's fiscal policies limited the miners' claimed privileges. There were two significant additions to the commission's instructions. The miners were not to be allowed to take timber for their pit workings,

1. Hart, *Royal Forest*, pp. 102-3; PRO, S.P. 16/122/39, Dec. 12, 1628. Both grants were confirmed on July 7, 1629: see C. 99/21.

2. PRO, C. 99/23, grant under the Great Seal to Sir John Winter, Mar. 17, 1626/7. See also Hammersley, "Revival of Forest Laws," pp. 91-92, for a fuller account.

3. PRO, E. 407/78/4, commission to William Rowse and Robert Treswell, Feb. 12, 1627/8; Hart, *Royal Forest*, p. 107.

which they claimed as of right, unless this was allowed by the deputy constable in the speech court. The commissioners were also to insure that the miners did not carry the King's minerals out of the forest or otherwise dispose of them except by sale to the royal ironworks.[4] These two items reiterated the expressed attitude of the Jacobean government, but this was the first time that an attempt was made to give the Crown's legal ownership of the minerals real practical effect. This establishment of a means of supervising and regulating some of the miners' activities was part of a larger and more ambitious plan by Charles I's government to increase the production of iron ore in the forest.

In the first few years of the reign a number of grants of royal demesne in Dean, totaling about 3,000 acres, were made to officials and courtiers, including Sir Edward Villiers, half-brother to the Duke of Buckingham, who obtained Mailescott Woods, and John Gibbons, secretary to Lord Treasurer Weston, who received Cannop Chase. They were given power to enclose the land, cut wood for charcoal, and sink pits for the mining of iron ore.[5] In conveying the lands the Crown completely ignored the miners' claimed right to dig anywhere they wished within the forest; the grantees alone were allowed this right within the parcels of land to be enclosed. Although this was the first occasion on which grants on this scale were made—giving substance to the King's title to the minerals in Dean's soil, clearly stated in the legal decisions of the previous reign—there are some indications that the Crown had been moving in this direction before the end of James I's reign. A poorly documented Exchequer case of 1623 reveals that at least one such grant had been made by James I; to give it legal effect an attempt was made to impose limitations on the claim of the miners to sink pits at will.[6] In addition, the grant of Mailescott Woods to Sir

---

4. PRO, E. 407/78/4 I.

5. GRO, D. 421/19/22, abstract of recordings concerning the claims of the miners of Dean; PRO, S.P. 38/13, docquet of a grant to Villiers, May 23, 1625; S.P. 16/257/94, *Cartae de Foresta de Deane*; Hart, *Royal Forest*, pp. 101, 107.

6. The records of this case are to be found in PRO, E. 112/83/375, Throckmorton vs. A-G Coventry, Eas. 1623. The bill is so faded as to be illegible and the answer is missing; all that can be read is the replication, which provides a long exposition of the rights of the miners. Depositions by commission are in E. 134/22 Jas. I/Eas. 8. Unlike most Exchequer cases, it is impossible here to determine the point at issue from the interrogatories. It is doubtful that the case came to judgment; no decree can be found.

Edward Villiers seems to have been first made before James I died and then renewed on Charles's accession.

To allay the fears of the commoners who would be excluded from enclosed areas such as Mailescott Woods and Cannop Chase, and to protect the title of Villiers and the others against claims of common, a collusive action, similar to those in contemporary disafforestation cases, was pursued in Exchequer. Through Exchequer injunctions and a privy seal directed to the local forest officers to make drifts of (round up) cattle pasturing in the forest, the Crown compelled the manorial lords and important freeholders in Dean to justify by bill of complaint in Exchequer the rights to common in the forest they claimed for themselves and their tenants. The resultant decree, early in 1628, is a good example of the outcome of a collusive action. For the first time, the freeholders and tenants in the manors within the bounds of the forest had their claims of common recognized at law. Practically every type of common they had hitherto enjoyed—which even they admitted was by prescription, not by title—was given legal effect in the decree with the approval of the Attorney-General. Common of estovers, common of pasture for all commonable cattle, and pannage for hogs in return for payment of pannage silver were all allowed. The only agreed limitation was that these rights had to be regulated by the speech court.

In return the Crown obtained confirmation of its right to make enclosures in the forest and an agreement that all rights of common should be extinguished in the enclosed areas. In future, as further improvements were decided upon, the extent of the common left for the forest inhabitants was to be worked out in detail between the commoners and representatives of the Crown.[7] This accommodation with the commoners in the interest of the peaceful and orderly advancement of the Crown's exploitation of its rights in the forest marked a reversal of Jacobean pressure on the commoners.

Nowhere was this reversal more evident than in the case concerning the Winter family. In the reign of James I the court of Exchequer had refused to recognize Sir Edward Winter's claim to common of estovers appurtenant to the manors and lands he held in Dean.[8] The

---

7. PRO, E. 125/4, ff. 50-54, decree in Winter et al. vs. A-G, Feb. 11, 1627/8; the bill and answer are in E. 112/179/28, Hil. 1627/8. The conclusive proof of the collusive nature of this action is to be found in the fact that bill, answer, and decree are all dated Hil. 1627/8.

8. See above, pp. 199-200.

leading landowner in the forest, whose rights to estovers were recognized in the decree of 1628, was Sir John Winter, son and heir of Sir Edward. The manors and lands for which the rights were established were those he inherited from his father. In the words of C. E. Hart, "After such a satisfactory Decree from the point of view of both the Crown and the Commoners, one would have expected that a period of quiet enjoyment of the Forest customs would have followed."[9] Instead, massive riots against the enclosures broke out in the spring of 1631. Hart's surprise is rooted in the faulty assumption that propertied commoners in the forest were behind the disorders. Like the Crown, he ignored the miners and poor cottagers in Dean who believed their livelihood depended on the forest as open waste.

With this action the government of Charles I had bought the support of the propertyholders in Dean for its policy of piecemeal enclosure. Thus, when the disorders broke out in 1631 Sir John Winter was in the forefront of those who opposed the activities of "Lady Skimington"—at the risk of his life, he reported. For this service the King later pardoned him the fine imposed at the forest eyre of 1634.[10] The plaintiffs in the Exchequer action were all manorial lords and freeholders, ranging in status from knights to yeomen, who claimed common for themselves and their tenants.[11] In the decree those with genuine claims to common—that is, landholders—were distinguished from those with no claim—the landless. Tenants of new-erected cottages—woodworking artisans and many others of the laboring poor—were excluded from any right to common. No miners were to be found among the plaintiffs, either, and no mention of the miners' rights was made in the decree. But the effect of the Exchequer decree, and no doubt one of its intentions, was to keep the miners out of the enclosed areas, which seem to have been particularly rich in deposits of iron ore. When the riots did erupt, these enclosures, along with the enclosed fellets where the cordwood was cut for the ironworks, were the main targets.

It is possible in the instance of Mailescott Woods to demonstrate a close relationship between the miners' insistence on their right to mine anywhere and the outbreak of the riots. By the end of 1629

9. Hart, *Commoners*, p. 24.

10. PRO, S.P. 16/339/93, petition by Winter to the King, undated; no. 94, notes on Winter's pardon among other matters, undated.

11. PRO, E. 112/178/28, bill of Winter et al., Hil. 1627/8.

Mailescott Woods had been enclosed and most of the trees had been felled preparatory to the sinking of pits.[12] In the autumn of 1630 the Attorney-General on the related information of Lady Barbara Villiers, the widow of Sir Edward, brought suit against a number of inhabitants of the forest who continued to mine and to pasture cattle in the woods, thus, in violation of the Exchequer decree of 1628, disturbing Lady Villiers's quiet possession.[13] All of the defendants, as inhabitants of the hundred of St. Briavels, asserted that they had the right to common of pasture and the right to mine in the wastes of the forest. They stated flatly in their answer to the Attorney-General's information that they would not be bound by an Exchequer decree that recognized the right of the King and his grantees to enclose Mailescott and other lands in Dean. Before the injunction to quiet possession sought by the Attorney-General could be issued, riots took place in which the enclosures of Mailescott, all the other lands covered in the decree, and the fellets were destroyed.[14]

The connection between the loss of mining rights and the eruption of the riots is readily demonstrated: as soon as a compromise was reached with Lady Villiers, large-scale rioting ceased. When, late in April of 1631, the court of Exchequer issued an injunction covering the improvements to permit the enclosures to go forward without further interference, Lady Villiers gave her consent to one concession. The miners were permitted to mine iron ore in Mailescott Woods for the use of the royal ironworks as freely as before the decree of 1628.[15] This concession did not completely pacify the forest, but only minor riots occurred after it was made.

Why did the miners so violently oppose enclosure in the forest? The potential for strenuous opposition from propertied commoners seems self-evident; any enclosure would reduce the open areas in which they could exercise their rights to common of pasture and estovers. The Exchequer decree of 1628 was designed to forestall opposition from that segment of the population. Violence directed

12. PRO, E. 178/5307, commission to Egidio Bridges et al. to survey and enclose Mailescott Woods, June 25, 1629, with return of proceedings, Sept. 28, 1629.

13. PRO, E. 112/179/40, Lady Barbara Villiers vs. A-G Heath, Trin. 1630; no. 45, A-G *ex rel.* Villiers vs. Mouselt et al., Mich. 1630.

14. PRO, E. 125/10, ff. 22-23, order in A-G vs. Mouselt et al., Feb. 7, 1630/1; E. 125/9, ff. 237-38, order in same case, April 27, 1631.

15. PRO, E. 125/9, ff. 237-38, order in A-G vs. Mouselt et al., April 27, 1631; ff. 240-41, injunction against the defendants, April 28, 1631.

against enclosures of the areas in which the cordwood for the ironworks was cut could certainly be expected from woodworking artisans. These enclosures were designed to keep such artisans out of those places where raw materials were readily available. But it seems clear that the miners would be among the main beneficiaries of enclosures. From the time of the first grant of the ironworks to the Earl of Pembroke up through the early years of Charles I, the thrust of Crown policy was to make money from Dean Forest by encouraging increased iron production. The growing demand for iron ore must have meant expanded employment opportunities for miners. As long as their privileges were left intact, they were no doubt willing to enjoy these opportunities, but in order to mine in the enclosed areas it was necessary to become the employee of the recipient of a royal grant.

The trend of Caroline policy was to create, or stimulate the creation of, larger units of production in the mining of iron ore and the making of iron. Independent miners selling ore to the ironworks were to be replaced by workmen in the employ of Crown grantees who held monopoly rights over the minerals in selected parts of the forest. No doubt the local miners refused to cooperate, which explains why Sir John Winter, when he began to exploit intensively the iron ore and coal on his own lands in the forest, brought in Staffordshire miners to work the pits. There were other instances of capitalists importing workers for the ironworks.[16] It is also quite possible that those workmen, employed by Sir Giles Mompesson to mine in Mailescott on behalf of Lady Villiers, who were assaulted by the rioters in 1631 were strangers. The miners' economic independence was bound up with the preservation of the mine law. Even if that independence was somewhat chimerical and their standard of living no better than that of wage-earning miners elsewhere, their tenacious attachment to their way of life compelled them to react with fury to any changes in the forest which threatened their status. In resisting these developments the Dean miners were swimming against a tide that was sweeping away other self-employed mining communities (such as that in the Derbyshire Peaks) and reducing their members to wage-earners.[17]

In the period immediately following the riots of 1631 and 1632 the Crown began to reassess its position with regard to the forest. The regulatory instruments utilized by both James I and Charles I had

16. See above, p. 183.
17. *VCH: Derbyshire*, vol. II, pp. 332, 337.

proven unequal to the task. Exchequer decrees and injunctions, without proper institutions of enforcement behind them, were totally inadequate means for establishing royal rights against the claims of the miners. The same inadequacy was evident in Exchequer special commissions intended to keep down the number of cottagers and cabiners in the forest. The commissions had also failed in their main tasks of preventing despoliation by the agents of the farmers of the ironworks; such depredations continued unabated throughout the early years of Charles I's reign.[18] The fate of royal policy in Dean provides further confirmation for the by now commonplace view of Tudor-Stuart governments: that the framing of policy outstripped the means of enforcement; thus achievement lagged behind ambition.

While the aim of Charles I remained the same as that of his father—to realize the largest possible income from Dean—after the riots his government began casting around for other methods to deal with the problems of the forest. There were two possible alternatives. One was to disafforest, thereby bringing policy in Dean into line with that in other western forests. The advantages of disafforestation were that it would mean a speedily realized and substantial windfall of cash and that it would solve the central problem posed by the weakness of the Crown's administrative machinery. Although riots could be expected to occur, as they eventually did in 1641 when Dean was ultimately disafforested, there was a finality to the wholesale felling of trees and the enclosure of forest land for agriculture or mining. Whatever riots took place would be simply a desperate stand against an irreversible process. Disafforestation had disadvantages, however. Dean had been kept separate from the other western forests because of its value as a capital asset which, if properly managed, would yield an increasing annual income to the Crown. The second alternative had the advantage of increasing revenue from the forest while leaving the future possibility of disafforestation open: this was the revival of the medieval forest laws to be enforced by a forest eyre.

The Exchequer decree of February 11, 1628, was worded in such a way that it could be used as the basis for gradual disafforestation. After

---

18. Evidence for continued destruction of the woods is to be found in PRO, E. 112/179/37, A-G vs. Sir Basil Brooke et al., Trin. 1630; E. 112/180/66, A-G vs. same, Eas. 1632; S.P. 16/236/82, John Broughton to Humphrey Hallwood, April 15, 1633; S.P. 16/250/80, a survey made by Broughton, Nov. 19, 1633.

the riots, this began to receive serious consideration. Toward the end of 1633 two courtiers, acting on the assumption that Dean was to be disafforested, made an offer for 8,000 acres.[19] Their proposal was rejected because the government had decided instead to set up a forest eyre.

During 1632 the eyre was first used, at Windsor Forest.[20] By April, 1634, the decision had been made to extend the eyre to Dean, where it met on July 10, 1634.[21] Use of Exchequer special commissions and frequent regrants of the lease of the ironworks had not stopped illegal felling of timber. Through fines imposed in the forest eyre the despoilers, both the poor cottagers and the wealthy recipients of royal grants, could at least be made to feel the King's displeasure and, it was hoped, could be compelled to pay heavily for their actions. Suits in Exchequer, the usual means of pursuing the farmers of the ironworks, were not suitable for this purpose; they were lengthy and subject to accident (such as the death of James I, which deprived the Crown of a favorable judgment in its case against Challoner and Harris). Furthermore, the aim of Exchequer suits was not to make money through fines but to force the farmers to relinquish their lease. The forest eyre had advantages as a moneymaking proposition. It was very speedy, almost summary, in procedure and had built-in advantages for the Crown. It used a jury of local inhabitants whose manifest dislike of the royal farmers and the owners of other ironworks was advantageous to the Crown. Without the elaborate pleading and evidential requirements of an English bill court such as Exchequer equity side, the forest eyre, lasting only ten days from beginning to end, succeeded in imposing very heavy fines on the farmers and others.

The total amount of the fines imposed was £134,000, although in the end a substantial portion of this was not levied. Four individuals were fined a total of £79,000; three of them, Sir Basil Brooke, George Mynne, and Sir John Winter, were punished for felling quantities of wood far in excess of the amount specified in their contracts with the Crown; the fourth, John Gibbons (secretary to Lord Treasurer Weston), who had received a grant of Cannop Chase, was fined for

19. Hart, *Royal Forest*, p. 110, and *Commoners*, p. 29.
20. Hammersley, "Revival of Forest Laws."
21. PRO, S.O. 1/2, pp. 352-53, signet letter to Sir John Bridgman, Chief Justice of Chester, April 12, 1634.

spoiling wood and for enclosing more land than had been stipulated in his grant. The other fines, £55,000 in all, were spread among a large number of offenders. A total of £17,000 was imposed on the other ironmasters and big landowners for despoiling the woods. The remainder ranged from £100 for destruction of timber to a multitude of small fines for the erection of new cottages and minor offenses against the woods ordinarily punished in the speech court. In spite of the spectacular fines imposed on the wealthy, it was the lowly offenders, those who erected cottages and destroyed the woods— miners, workers in wood, and laborers—who made up the bulk of those fined, about 80 percent of the total of 438 offenders whose status is known.[22]

The purpose of the eyre was therefore as much to impress the "common sort" and reduce them to some sort of compliance with the Crown's will as it was to make money from a handful of big-time offenders. The former intention was also served by the psychological advantage possessed by a forest eyre. In an earlier time the forest law had terrorized those who lived within its jurisdiction; no doubt the government of Charles I hoped its revival would have the same effect on the despoilers of Dean. Like the assizes, it involved imposing the visible panoply and substance of the central government, with its aura of omniscience and omnipotence, on the local community. In this case the Crown was represented by Henry, Earl of Holland, chief justice in eyre of the forests south of the Trent, assisted by three common-law judges assigned as deputies to advise him on the law.[23]

This intention to overawe the unruly natives was particularly important for the rest of the eyre's proceedings, which were in effect a restatement of Caroline policy toward Dean and its inhabitants. The privileges claimed by the miners were rejected as totally without foundation. The scraps of evidence that record this indicate that the miners could not prove they were a legal corporation with a charter from the Crown.[24] To preserve the minerals and the woods from

22. The fullest reports of the eyre's proceedings are to be found in BL, Harleian MS 738, ff. 295-311; Harleian MS 4850, ff. 24-59; and Bod. Lib., Gough MS Gloucs. 1. The best modern account is in Hammersley. There were another 86 offenders whose status was not given.

23. PRO, C. 99/31, m. 1, copies of signet letters to Sir William Jones, JKB, June 16, 1634, Sir Thomas Trevor, Baron of the Exchequer, June 16, 1634, Sir John Bridgman, CJ of Chester, July 5, 1634.

24. GRO, D. 421/19/22, abstract of records concerning the claims of the miners; PRO, S.P. 16/297/45, Sir Sackville Crowe to the Earl of Holland, Sept. 15, 1635; BL, Harleian MS 4850, f. 59.

illegal exploitation, the judges were ordered to transmit a new set of instructions to the forest officers.[25] These took a much tougher line toward the activities of Dean's poorer inhabitants than previous instructions sent by way of Exchequer special commissions had done. One clause specified explicitly that the miners were not to be permitted to carry ore out of the forest or to sell it to any ironworks but the King's.

Most of the instructions were directed at control of cottagers and woodworking artisans. To prevent the movement of cottagers into the forest, all cabins not inhabited by employees of the ironworks were to be demolished. Their occupants were to be expelled from the forest, giving good sureties never to return. Woodworking artisans such as trenchermakers, cardboardmakers, shovelmakers, saddletreemakers, turners, and others who "do apparently supply themselves with timber for their several uses by stealth and destruction of his Majesties timber," were to be prohibited from living in Dean. Great care was to be taken to suppress all unlicensed alehouses in the forest; they were the haunts of lawless and disorderly people and an offense particularly associated with those who came to the forest to live from despoliation of the woods.

The rest of the instructions, while including the customary charge for close supervision of the cutting and cording of wood for the ironworks, also commanded close regulation through the speech court of the commoners' rights to estovers. The commoners, in fact, were the only group in the forest who benefited from the eyre. Here again the Crown continued its apparent policy of conciliating Dean's propertied inhabitants. One hundred and twenty claims to common of pasture and estovers were allowed by the judges, the claimants ranging in status from an Earl and a goodly number of esquires and gentlemen, to lesser landholders, mainly yeomen.[26]

After the eyre the Crown further intensified its exploitation of Dean's resources. The lessees of the ironworks and cordwood, Brooke, Mynne, and Winter, quickly and voluntarily surrendered their leases, no doubt in the hope of having their fines reduced. During 1635 negotiations were opened for a new lease of the concessions in Dean. Furious competitive bidding drove up the price offered for a

25. PRO, C. 99/31, m. 2, instructions for forest officials.
26. PRO, C. 99/10/1-120, claims to common entered at the forest eyre, July 10, 1634.

cord of wood from six shillings to eleven shillings. On July 12, 1636, the ironworks and an annual supply of 12,000 cords of wood were leased for twenty-one years at an annual rent of £6,600 to Sir Baynham Throckmorton, Sir Basil Brooke, and their partners.[27]

In addition, the coal in Dean was for the first time the subject of a royal grant. While leases of the ironworks usually included authority to sink pits or buy ore from the miners, the position of the King's farmers with regard to the mining of coal was unclear. Legally, the right to the coal was the same as the right to the iron ore; it was part of the royal demesne and could be disposed of at will by the Crown—a position confirmed by the forest eyre. Whether or not the right to mine coal was included in the grants made to the farmers of the ironworks was a question which only became important when in 1635 Edward Terringham, a gentleman of the bedchamber, petitioned for a concession of the Dean coal mines. He claimed that such a grant would not infringe on the grants to the royal farmers, since they did not use coal in the ironworks.[28]

Acting on this petition, the Crown's advisers discovered that although the coal belonged directly to the King he was receiving no profit from it. It seems that the Earl of Pembroke, on the basis of his lease of the ironworks in the reign of James I, had tried to assert a right to mine coal, but the Crown's law officers had given an opinion based on the actual wording of the lease—the lessee, while he could take coal from existing iron mines, could not extract coal from any new iron mines sunk by him nor could he sink any coal mines. In 1635 it was discovered that the miners, although unable to prove any right or title to the coal found in their iron mines, had extracted the coal and sold it to their own use, the only profit to the King being the silver paid to the gaveller.[29] On the basis of these findings, Terringham in 1636 received a grant for thirty-one years of all existing coal mines and grindstone quarries in the demesne soil of Dean.

In spite of all this activity on the Crown's behalf, the government was unable to prevent the miners from continuing in their daily work

27. Hart, *Royal Forest*, pp. 116-18. Evidence for the various proposals is scattered throughout the State Papers and the Bankes MSS in the Bodleian and is well summarized in Hart.
28. PRO, S.P. 16/303/61, petition of Terringham to the commissioners of the Treasury, 1635.
29. PRO, S.P. 16/303/61 II, report by the Surveyor General on Terringham's petition, Dec. 25, 1635; S.P. 16/307/8, undated legal opinion; no. 8 I, legal opinion by John Bramston, Jan. 27, 1635/6.

of winning ore and coal from Dean's soil. The miners ignored both the limitations on their disposal of the iron ore and the grant of the coal mines to Terringham. As early as October of 1635 it was reported that iron ore was still being sold to "stranger" ironworks in the neighborhood and being shipped out of the forest as freely as before the eyre was held.[30] In response, the Council, early in 1636, commanded the forest officers to seize all ore being shipped out of Dean and to call the miners before them to receive orders in the King's name to cease this practice. All who refused to obey were to be bound for appearance before the Lord Treasurer and Chancellor of the Exchequer to answer for their contempts.[31] Predictably, these measures had no effect; late in 1637 the farmers of the ironworks petitioned the King for a proclamation to restrain the miners from their continual habit of carrying "infinite" quantities of ore out of the forest.[32] Although a warrant was drafted for this purpose, the proclamation itself has not yet been discovered. Even if it was actually issued, it is highly unlikely that it produced any substantial results.[33]

Meanwhile, the miners, showing even less respect for the grant to Terringham, continued to dig coal as before. Late in 1636, on Terringham's complaint, the Attorney-General took the well-worn path of commencing an Exchequer suit against the miners, this time for infringing upon the lessee's rights by mining 1,000 tons of coal since the grant had been made.[34] The miners' defense rested upon a full statement of the mine law, particularly the claimed right to dig coal and iron ore in all of Dean's soil.[35] Before the case came to

30. PRO, S.P. 16/299/10, observations on Dean by Sir Sackville Crowe, Oct. 3, 1635.

31. PRO, P.C. 2/46, pp. 67-68, warrant to the deputy constable of St. Briavels et al., Mar. 31, 1636.

32. PRO, S.P. 16/323 (an entry book of petitions, May 10, 1636-Nov. 28, 1638) pp. 210-11, petition by the farmers of the ironworks, undated but sometime in 1637.

33. Bod. Lib., Bankes MS 9/45, warrant for a proclamation, Nov. 12, 1637.

34. PRO, E. 112/181/155, information only in A-G vs. Yearsley et al., Mich. 1636. Sir John Winter is also named as a defendant in this information, but his offense was quite separate from that of the other defendants, all miners. Winter was accused of keeping Terringham out of lands at Lidney which he claimed as his demesne and exempt from the lease of the coal mines. The miners were acting on their own, not as Winter's agents. The parties conducted separate defenses and there are separate sets of interrogatories and depositions for each in E. 134/13, Chas. I/Mich. 42 and E. 134/13-14 Chas. I/Hil. 16. The case against the miners came to judgment but that against Winter did not.

35. While the answer of the miners has not survived, the defense is manifest in the interrogatories and depositions in PRO, E. 134/13 Chas. I/Mich. 42, which, incidentally, provides one of the fullest extant statements of the mine law.

judgment, the miners took matters into their own hands. Sometime in the spring of 1637, a group of them, including a number of the defendants named in the Exchequer action, entered an area of the forest where Terringham's agents were engaged in coal-mining, assaulted some of his workmen, and burned the workings.[36] Two of the miners suspected of involvement in this disorder were old hands at the game, having been enjoined in 1631 from entering Mailescott Woods to dig iron ore and pasture their cattle.[37] On receiving a report on the matter, the Council ordered the justices of Gloucestershire to punish the offenders according to the law; for the future they were to maintain the King's peace in the working of the mines.[38]

By mid-1638 the Attorney-General's case against the miners came to judgment. In finding for the Crown, the court based its decree on a decision reached at the Dean Forest eyre of 1634, in which the liberties claimed by the miners were rejected and the King's title to the minerals in his own demesne confirmed. The miners' privileges were found to have no basis in law, Terringham's possession of all existing and future coal mines was established, and the defendants were enjoined from sinking coal pits in the forest.[39] The miners, however, were far from finished. Late in 1638 coal was still being mined in violation of Terringham's grant and the Exchequer injunction. The court responded by ordering the attachment of the culprits. Except in the case of one individual, however, it was found that none of them had been a party to the suit; as they were neither agents nor workmen of the original defendants, the court held that they could not be attached for contempt of the injunction. To stop the miners it was therefore necessary for Terringham or the Attorney-General to bring action against the new defendants. Terringham probably balked at the idea of beginning the whole matter again, with the possibility that it would have to be repeated *ad infinitum* until every miner in the forest was enjoined by name from mining the coal. In May of 1640 he finally admitted defeat and surrendered his lease.[40]

36. PRO, P.C. 2/47, pp. 303-4, PC to JPs of Gloucestershire, April 2, 1637.

37. PRO, E. 125/9, ff. 237-38, April 27, 1631. The two were John White and James Wisham.

38. PRO, P.C. 2/47, pp. 303-4, PC to JPs of Gloucestershire, April 2, 1637.

39. PRO, E. 125/24, ff. 90-91, order for an injunction in A-G vs. Yearsley et al., June 20, 1638.

40. PRO, E. 125/23, ff. 243-44, order for attachment of miners who ignored the injunction, Oct. 13, 1638; E. 125/24, ff. 140-41, Oct. 17, 1638, and f. 168, Oct. 31, 1638, orders in the same case; Hart. *Free Miners*, p. 194.

The Crown's other problems in the forest continued unchecked after the forest eyre. The inhabitants of Dean and the new lessees of the ironworks, like their predecessors, despoiled the woods at will.[41] It is hard to believe, in fact, that the revival of the forest laws was intended as a plausible solution to the Crown's difficulties in Dean. Instead, it should be regarded as one of the many moneymaking expedients seized upon during the personal rule of Charles I and, ultimately, as a demonstration of the inability of the English government in the seventeenth century to devise a regular and functioning instrument of police power to enforce legal and executive decisions.

There was, of course, a larger political significance to the forest eyre that is beyond the scope of the present study. While the Crown attempted to conciliate the propertyholders by confirming claims to common, the enforcement of the forest laws at Dean, with the insistence on punishing all assarts and encroachments within the bounds of the forest as established in the reign of Edward I, represented a manifest threat to what were regarded, through long use, as property rights. Thus the revival of the medieval forest law at Dean and elsewhere involved a grave political miscalculation by the Crown; this expedient was one of the many fiscal initiatives of Charles I's reign that alienated considerable numbers of the Crown's propertied and powerful subjects.[42]

The Crown's manifest inability to control the activities of the inhabitants of Dean, accompanied by its growing financial need, meant that in the late 1630s disafforestation came to be considered as an increasingly attractive alternative.[43] As early as 1635 plans were afoot to issue a commission for this purpose.[44] Over the next three years, while it was debated whether to disafforest all or only a part of

41. Evidence for the continuing failure of forest officials to prevent despoliation is to be found in PRO, P.C. 2/48, pp. 493-94, order concerning ironworks, Dec. 17, 1637; S.O. 1/3, p. 241, signet letter to deputy constables et al. in Dean, Feb. 18, 1638/9; p. 259, signet letter to same, Mar. 12, 1638/9; E. 112/181/159, information in A-G vs. Throckmorton and Crowe, Hil. 1637/8.

42. See Hammersley, "Revival of Forest Laws," for a fuller discussion of this aspect of the topic.

43. PRO, S.P. 16/408/159, reasons for disafforesting Dean, undated. Despoliation of the woods by the neighboring inhabitants and by the large population of cottagers is here given heavy emphasis as a reason for disafforesting.

44. Bod. Lib., Bankes MS 55/50, warrant for a commission to disafforest, Aug. 2, 1635; PRO, S.P. 16/297/45, Sir Sackville Crowe to the Earl of Holland, Sept. 15, 1635.

Dean, the commission was frequently renewed but never met.[45] During this period a number of proposals made by projectors for the disafforestation and lease of specific lands within the forest were given serious attention by the Crown.[46] What finally impelled the government to dispose of the whole forest was a combination of two elements: a highly pessimistic report on the future of Dean as a source of timber, and a large cash offer from Sir John Winter which could not be refused.

By the late 1630s the view that Dean's resources in wood and timber were close to depletion had become axiomatic in government circles. One of the main reasons for preserving the forest—that it was well-supplied with ship and construction timber that could easily be transported down the Wye and Severn rivers—was challenged as erroneous. It was found on survey that much of the timber was unsuitable for these purposes and that the high cost of transportation by water to Bristol discouraged potential buyers.[47] Also, given the lack of a scientific silviculture to provide techniques for systematic plantation or replantation of waste ground, the exhaustion of the woods was only a matter of time. It was estimated that if the ironworks in the forest continued to use wood at the annual rate of 16,000 cords, in twenty years all the suitable cordwood would be consumed.[48]

While this evidence of Dean's bleak future as a source of revenue was accumulating, Charles I's financial difficulties were nearing their climax. At this juncture Sir John Winter came forward with a solution to the problem: the complete disafforestation of Dean. The Crown, desperate for money, speedily accepted Winter's proposal. In fact, the grant of Dean to Winter was ordered to be made ready with all the financial details spelled out in March of 1639, three months before even the preliminary survey work had been done on the forest. On the letters patent passing the Great Seal, Winter was to pay a lump sum of £10,000 and a further £96,000 in annual payments of £16,000 over the next six years. He was also required to negotiate on the Crown's

---

45. Bod. Lib., Bankes MS 55/50, warrant for a commission to disafforest Dean, Aug. 2, 1635; Bankes MS 43/15, warrant for renewal of the commission to compound with the King's subjects on the disafforestation of Dean, May 8, 1636; Bankes MS 43/9, warrant for further renewal of the commission, Feb. 10, 1637/8.

46. Hart, *Royal Forest*, pp. 122-23, summarizes the various proposals.

47. PRO, S.P. 16/408/159; Hart, *Royal Forest*, p. 122.

48. PRO, S.O. 1/3, pp. 266-68, signet letter to the Ld. Treasurer et al., Mar. 26, 1639.

behalf a loan of £20,000 at eight percent. In return for these handsome services and an annual rent of £2,000, Winter received a grant of the royal demesne in the forest. In addition to the soil, he obtained all existing coal and iron mines and all mining rights. The lease of the ironworks with the grant of cordwood was to stand until expiration, when everything would revert in fee to Winter. He also received all the wood and timber except for the trees already marked for the use of the Royal Navy.[49]

The actual disafforestation proceedings followed the standard pattern in all essentials. An Exchequer special commission was issued on May 16, 1639, to compound with those who claimed rights of common and to allot compensation to them. The commission soon came to agreement with the manorial lords, and other property-holders in Dean. Those with legal rights to common were to receive compensation totaling 4,000 acres, while the rest of the forest—just over 18,000 acres—would be reserved for the Crown or its grantee free and clear of all claims to common.[50] The grants totaling 3,000 acres made in the 1620s, which provoked the riots of 1631-1632, were of course excluded from these proceedings. From this point on, the disafforestation moved with remarkable swiftness and smoothness. In a collusive action typical of most disafforestations, the Attorney-General commenced an Exchequer suit during Michaelmas of 1639 to confirm the agreements made between the commissioners and the commoners. Two hundred and twenty-four defendants, all manorial lords and freeholders of substance, including Sir John Winter, gave their consent to the agreements reached with the Exchequer special commissioners. Before Hilary term of 1639/1640 was over the case had been concluded with an order confirming the disafforestation and an injunction to quiet possession in favor of the Crown and Winter.[51]

As in the other disafforestations, not all of the propertied inhabitants were content with the proceedings. Twenty-one of the defen-

---

49. PRO, S.O. 1/3, pp. 266-68, signet letter to the Ld. Treasurer et al.; see also Hart, *Royal Forest*, pp. 124-25.

50. PRO, E. 178/5304; E. 134/Misc. 236; Hart, *Royal Forest*, p. 123.

51. PRO, E. 112/182/196, A-G vs. Winter et al.; E. 125/26, ff. 185-87, order for injunction to quiet possession in the same case, Feb. 17, 1639/40. The collusive nature of this action is proved by the nature of the answers and by the fact that only one term elapsed between the exhibition of the A-G's information and the final judgment, leaving no time for the issue of commissions to take depositions.

dants were still discontented.[52] Their claims to common had been recognized at the justice eyre of 1634, and they were not opposed on principle to disafforestation. They were dissatisfied with the amount of compensation alloted to the commoners; the aim of their opposition was to get more.[53] This ploy accomplished nothing; in July of 1641 the court ruled against them and confirmed the previous injunction to quiet possession.[54]

Winter hardly had a chance to enjoy quiet possession. In the spring and summer of 1641, while this last suit was in progress, the inhabitants of Dean rioted and destroyed almost twelve miles of enclosures erected around Winter's share of the forest.[55] Nothing more can be discovered about the riots or the identity of the rioters, although on this occasion, as in other disafforestations, the main perpetrators were almost certainly the poorer inhabitants. It has so far been impossible to discover what part, if any, of the 4,000 acres set aside as allotments to the commoners was intended as compensation for the poor. No matter what the poor received, it could in no way compensate for their loss of the open forest. The grant to Winter had effectively deprived the miners of all their mining rights. Those poor who depended on the forest for raw materials in their trades and as a supplement to other income in the shape of pasture, firewood, and building materials found their livelihood directly threatened.

Conversely, the disafforestation of Dean can be seen as another in the series of conciliatory gestures toward propertied inhabitants that marked the policy of Charles I's government. At each important step taken by the Crown, the property-owners' interests were given every consideration, no doubt to insure social stability and good order. When the first enclosures were made early in Charles's reign, the rights to common claimed by the property-owners were given legal recognition in the Exchequer decree of 1628 so that the recipients of the enclosed

52. The opponents of disafforestation are named in PRO, E. 112/182/196, and in a petition to the House of Lords, H. of L.R.O. Main Papers, June 1, 1641.
53. PRO, E. 134/16 Chas. I/Mich. 36 and E. 134/16 and 17 Chas. I/Hil. 1, depositions by commission in A-G vs. Adeane et al.
54. PRO, E. 125/27, ff. 423-24, order for an injunction in A-G vs. Adeane et al., July 12, 1641.
55. *LJ*, IV, p. 219, order of H. of L. that the King and Winter might enjoy quiet possession of Dean, April 16, 1641; PRO, E. 207/43/1 no. 3, affidavit of Henry Gansford and Richard Adam before the Barons of Exchequer, July 12, 1641; E. 125/27, ff. 423-24, order for an injunction against inhabitants of Dean to prevent them from disturbing the Crown's quiet possession, July 12, 1641.

parcels could enjoy quiet possession. During the forest eyre of 1634, the commoners were further conciliated when 120 claims to common were allowed by the judges. Therefore, when disafforestation was implemented, there was no need for the commoners to prove their rights, for these had already been established. All that had to be worked out was the amount of compensation they were to receive. The speed with which agreement was reached between the special commissioners and the inhabitants and the collusive nature of the Exchequer action which confirmed the agreement strongly suggest that the majority of the property-owners in Dean were satisfied with the terms of the disafforestation.

Despite this willingness to mollify the landowners, the course of Crown policy in Dean was far from smooth. This was simply because the government could not possibly conciliate the miners and cottagers in the forest. They stood athwart the path leading to an increased income from Dean's natural resources. Conflict between the Crown's financial necessity and the economic needs of the miners and other poor inhabitants of the forest was inevitable. The most striking aspect of this conflict was the ability of the poorer sort to frustrate the government's plans at almost every turn. The Crown could do nothing to stop the miners from exercising their privileges or to prevent the poor from despoiling the woods. Disafforestation was a significant admission of defeat. The whole problem of controlling the poor was thrown into Winter's lap; to obtain profit he had to succeed where the Crown had failed. The riots of 1641 showed that it was not going to be easy. Exactly how Winter planned to make his possession of the forest more than nominal remains a moot question, because the onset of civil war effectively deprived him of the benefit of his grant.

Chapter IX

A Second Western Rising:
Riot during the Civil War
and Interregnum

Outbreaks similar to the better-known Western Rising of 1626-1632 took place later in the century, particularly during the revolutionary decades of the 1640s and 1650s. It is possible to regard the riots of this latter period, especially those in the 1640s, as a second Western Rising in which violent opposition to enclosure flared up again in forests enclosed earlier in Charles I's reign. The inhabitants of these forests took advantage of political turmoil and the breakdown of regular enforcement of the law to riot with little fear of the consequences. The Earl of Elgin saw this quite clearly when riots broke out anew in Gillingham Forest: "the actors and abettors taking advantage of the tymes have againe brooke downe the mounds, hedges, ditches, gates and stiles of parte of the said forest."[1]

The riots of these two decades were in one sense expressions of the indifference felt by large numbers of common people to the great issues—political, social, and religious—raised by the Civil War and its aftermath. These concerns seemed remote to forest dwellers preoccupied with pressing local problems, including that of enclosure. At the same time, the disorders manifested important affinities with the Western Rising of 1626-1632: continuity of purpose over two to three decades on the part of ordinary folk dwelling in the forests, and the

---

1. JRL, Nicholas MS 74/4, breviat of the Earl of Elgin's case against the rioters in Gillingham, undated, but an earlier draft in 72/3 refers to events of June, 1648.

continued existence of deep-seated social tensions quite unrelated to the Civil War and fundamentally unaffected by the issues involved in that conflict. Finally, the approach taken by those in authority to the problems of managing the forests and dealing with their inhabitants reveals a set of assumptions and methods which in all its essentials was identical to that of the discredited Stuarts.

Discontent with royal forest policy was not confined to the West. In fact, it was in other parts of the country that people first began to take advantage of the troubled times of the late 1630s and 1640s to pay off old scores. For example, the inhabitants of Needwood Forest, Staffordshire, seized on the opportunity of the two Bishops Wars with the Scots to settle grievances over enclosure.

More research is needed on the Needwood disafforestation, but the main outline of events is clear. During Salisbury's tenure of the Lord Treasurership, the forest was surveyed and found to provide no tangible benefits to the Crown. It was of little use for hunting, being too distant from London and having no royal residence nearby. Furthermore, the fees of the forest officers and the widespread destruction of the woods were a drain on royal revenues. Thus it was argued that the only means by which the King could cut his losses was through disafforestation.[2] Like most of the other proposals of this kind made during Salisbury's tenure of office, it came to naught. It was not until the reign of Charles I that disafforestation of one part of the forest, Uttoxeter Ward, actually took place. In 1635 a Duchy of Lancaster special commission was issued to survey the ward to discover its bounds and the existing claims of common upon it. The commission found that all the inhabitants of the manor of Uttoxeter claimed common in the ward, which was about 300 acres in extent.[3]

As in other cases of this sort, a commission was authorized to obtain the commoners' agreement to the improvement and to allot compensation. At the same time the Attorney-General began an action in the court of the Duchy Chamber to confirm the agreement, which gave one-half of the ward to the Crown, free of claims of common, and the other half as compensation to the inhabitants of the manor. In the summer of 1637 this was ratified by a decree of the

2. PRO, L.R. 2/194, f. 25, survey of Needwood Forest.
3. PRO, D.L. 44/1151, commission to Sir Edward Vernon et al., Sept. 28, 1635, with articles of instruction and proceedings, Oct. 7, 1635.

Duchy court which also provided that the compensation should be granted in free and common socage to the commoners of Uttoxeter and their heirs. The King's half was then let to one John Gregory for an annual rent of £40.[4]

Before the issue of the decree, the markers dividing the King's share from that of the commoners were cast down "by divers disorderly persons and idle women."[5] This was the first of a number of riots at Uttoxeter. In the summer of 1639, the enclosures were destroyed by soldiers raised in the area who rioted on their return home from the North.[6] To prevent this from happening again, the Privy Council in 1640 ordered that particular care be taken with the soldiers levied to go on the second northern adventure. But when the 300 men raised for this service from the surrounding hundreds assembled at Uttoxeter on July 1, 1640, a number of them marched out and destroyed the enclosures in the forest. In accordance with the Council's instructions, the constables of Uttoxeter had readied a force of well-armed men to deal with any disorders. Despite these prepara-tions, however, the riots lasted three days; it took all the efforts of the force raised by the constables, supported by the servants of the deputy 'lieutenants, to restore order.[7]

Seventeen of the leading rioters were indicted at a special riot sessions in Uttoxeter later in the month, but their status cannot be discovered.[8] It is an open question if any of them were Uttoxeter men; none of them had held property in the manor in 1630, when a very detailed survey was made. Although the economic and social develop-

4. PRO, D.L. 44/1156, commission to Sir Edward Morley et al., July 9, 1636, with articles of instruction and agreement of the tenants; D.L. 44/1156, commission to the same, Mar. 11, 1636/7, with articles of instruction and agreement of the tenants; D.L. 5/32, ff. 363-66, decree in A-G of the Duchy of Lancaster vs. inhabitants of Uttoxeter, June 28, 1637; f. 449, order of the court, Feb. 19, 1637/8.

5. PRO, D.L. 5/32, f. 310, order for an injunction against the disruption of the King's quiet possession, May 22, 1637; *VCH: Staffordshire*, vol. II, p. 352.

6. PRO, P.C. 2/50, p. 528, PC to JPs of Staffs and PC to judges of assize, July 19, 1639; P.C. 2/51, p. 201, order for the appearance of the constables of Uttoxeter, Dec. 20, 1639; pp. 203-4, PC to JPs of Staffs, Dec. 20, 1639; p. 271, order for release of John Scattergood, constable of Uttoxeter, on a £50 bond, Jan. 31, 1639/40; S.P. 16/444/31, Scattergood's bond, Feb. 4, 1639/40.

7. PRO, P.C. 2/52, p. 569, PC to Ld. Lt. of Staffs, June 21, 1640; S.P. 16/460/8, Dep. Lts. of Staffs to PC, July 15, 1640.

8. PRO, S.P. 16/460/8 II, names of those indicted at private sessions in Uttoxeter, July 14, 1640.

ment of Needwood requires investigation, there was at least one fulling mill at Uttoxeter and a number of new-erected cottages on the waste.[9]

It was as the country was on the downhill slide into civil war that a fairly widespread intention to settle old scores appeared. At Duffield in Derbyshire, a forest with a large population of cottagers and miners, the inhabitants rioted in 1643 and destroyed the enclosures in Chevin Ward, which had been disafforested in 1634.[10] During the years 1642 and 1643 the inhabitants of Windsor Forest, Berkshire, assembled repeatedly in large groups; they then destroyed the enclosures of the parks, killed many of the deer, and plundered the woods. This was the culmination of longstanding complaints against the large number of deer consuming the vert of the forest and depriving cattle of their pasturage.[11]

Similar riots occurred in Waltham Forest, Essex. On numerous occasions between late April of 1642 and February of 1643, large armed crowds gathered and killed as many as 400 of the King's deer. Of the fifty-one suspects whose status can be discovered, there were six gentlemen, thirteen yeomen, seventeen artisans, two retailers, and thirteen laborers, all from neighboring towns such as Barking and Wanstead. During the first series of attacks on the deer, in April, 1642, the rioters were commanded to cease their activities as contrary to the forest laws. In reply, one of them "made answer there was noe Lawe settled at this tyme that hee knewe."[12] Waltham Forest had experienced earlier disorders when on two separate occasions during the depression year of 1629 men transporting grain by Wanstead in the forest were attacked and their shipments seized by "some lewd and ill-disposed people." In the second of the attacks the servants of

9. PRO, D.L. 43/8/111, survey of the manor of Uttoxeter, Mar. 8, 1629/30; there is also an earlier survey of ca. 1609, D.L. 43/21/1. A fulling mill is twice mentioned in the survey of 1630. New-erected buildings are referred to in the findings of the special commission in 1635, D.L. 44/1151.

10. *VCH: Derbyshire*, vol. I, pp. 420-21; J. C. Cox, *Royal Forests*, pp. 202-3.

11. *LJ*, IV, p. 595, order of the House commanding the attendance of the Sheriff of Berks, Feb. 18, 1641/2; other relevant orders and memoranda are in *LJ*, IV, pp. 602, 608; *LJ*, V, pp. 25, 33, 35, 199, 563; LJ, VI, pp. 21, 72; Cox, p. 299.

12. H. of L.R.O., Main Papers, affidavit of John Peacock, underkeeper of Waltham, April 26, 1642; affidavits of forest officers, Feb. 9, 1642/3; orders of the H. of L. and various memoranda are in *LJ*, V, pp. 37, 38, 61, 612, 625.

Sir Richard Salter were assaulted and despoiled of six sacks of rye by a
crowd of sixty men and women armed with pitchforks, muskets,
halberds, and pikes, who said they would first provide for themselves
and then kill the justices of the peace, the constables, and those
employed to buy and sell grain.[13]

The most remarkable measure of the social tensions which persisted throughout the 1640s is to be found in the occurrence of a
second Western Rising, which was allowed to suface by the removal of
traditional social and political controls. The extremely well-documented Gillingham riots of 1642-1648 provide a unique opportunity
to demonstrate the continuities linking the early years of Charles I's
reign with the Civil War period. The riots began in September of
1642, when some of the 700 parliamentary soldiers sent up from
Portsmouth and billeted at Shaftesbury, Dorset, "were put on by some
of the inhabitants of Gillingham and Mere (as the souldyers themselves reported) to cut downe the quickset hedges and lay oppen the
newe inclosed ground of the forest."[14] It is clear, however, that the
soldiers' main concern was not to aid the inhabitants of the forest out
of sympathy with their cause, but rather to use the destruction of
property as a means of extorting money and supplies from propertied
inhabitants like Thomas Brunker, the Earl of Elgin's agent in
Gillingham. The soldiers soon found more lucrative employment in
plundering the houses of local recusants and royalist sympathizers. In
the end it took the officers ten days to get their men under control and
march them off to join the Earl of Essex's army in Worcestershire.

In April of 1643 a number of men of Mere, Wiltshire, issued a
proclamation summoning the inhabitants of the forest to assemble at
White Hill on market day, April 25, and to march from there with
drums and muskets to destroy the enclosures.[15] From this date
through the first half of July, the people of Mere and Gillingham
frequently assembled in groups of up to 300 armed with muskets,
fowling pieces, and other weapons to destroy enclosures and, when

13. PRO, S.P. 16/133/19, Earl of Totnes to Conway, Ld. Pres. of the Council, Jan. 27, 1628/9,
enclosing 19 I, Sir Nicholas Coate to Totnes, Jan. 27, 1628/9; *APC 1628-29*, pp. 309-10, PC to
Dep. Lts. and JPs of Essex, Jan. 30, 1628/9.
14. JRL, Nicholas MS 72/1, report of Thomas Brunker, the Earl of Elgin's agent at
Gillingham.
15. JRL, Nicholas MS 73/4, copy of a proclamation made by the inhabitants of Mere, April
24, 1643.

none were left standing, to demonstrate their contempt for the Earl of Elgin and his agents.[16] In the summer of the following year some further disorders took place, and in May and June of 1645 large-scale riots again erupted, during which most of the re-erected enclosures were destroyed.[17]

The next series of disorders took place in June of 1648 when, with the outbreak of the second Civil War, the inhabitants "taking advantage of the comotions" again destroyed some of the enclosures.[18] These riots were on a much reduced scale, involving only a handful of men. A final flare-up occurred in the spring of 1651, when there were rumors abroad of meetings by the inhabitants to plan more riots; a troop of horse was sent to the forest to maintain order.[19]

Such a brief chronicle cannot convey the intensity of violence exhibited in this series of riots. These were by far the most violent of all the western riots. On a number of occasions during 1643 rioters were shot and wounded either by soldiers or by Thomas Brunker, Elgin's agent, and by his servants. Finally, during May, 1645, a rioter was killed when in a melee Brunker's servants, outnumbered three to one, were forced to fire for their own protection. The rioters in turn gave as good as they got. In the riots of 1643, Elgin's tenants and Brunker's servants were frequently assaulted, and in May of 1645 one of Brunker's servants was beaten and left for dead.[20] For most of this period Thomas Brunker went in fear of his life; at one point he sent to London requesting a brace or two of pistols. They were unobtainable

16. JRL, Nicholas MS 72/2, Brunker to Elgin, April 29, 1643; 73/12, John Dolman to Lady Bruce, May 6, 1643; 73/19, report of Brunker, May, 1643; 73/38, Brunker and Dolman to Elgin, May 20, 1643; 73/24, Brunker to Elgin, June 4, 1643; 74/1, examinations of witnesses before Mathew Davis, JP of Dorset, May 7 and June 9, 1643; 74/29, examinations of witnesses before Davis, July 7 and July 8, 1643, with 74/30, covering letter from Davis to H. of L., July 8, 1643. Another copy of the examinations of June 9 with a covering letter from Davis, June 10, 1643, is to be found in the H. of L.R.O., Main Papers.

17. JRL, Nicholas MS 73/6, Brunker to Thomas Christie, secretary to the Earl of Elgin, June 28, 1645.

18. JRL, Nicholas MS 72/3, state of the case concerning the Earl of Elgin; 74/4 is another copy containing more details; *LJ*, X, p. 351, order for attachment of the rioters; H. of L.R.O., Main Papers, deposition on oath before the H. of L. by Richard Martin, July 28, 1648.

19. PRO, S.P. 25/96, p. 187, Council of State to Major-General Desborough, May 17, 1651.

20. JRL, Nicholas MS 73/19, single leaf of a letter from Brunker, probably to the Earl of Elgin, May 13, 1643; 73/22, Brunker to Elgin, May 20, 1643; 73/24, Brunker to Elgin, June 4, 1643; 74/1, examinations of John Godwin and Richard Ridgley before Mathew Davis, JP of Dorset, June 9, 1643; 73/28, Brunker to Thomas Christie, July 8, 1643; 73/6, Brunker to Christie, June 28, 1645.

in Dorset, he observed, and "wee ryde very naked without them this dangerous time."[21]

The violence on the part of the rioters was part of what seems to have been a well-thought-out plan to deprive the Earl of Elgin of all profit from the forest. By means of threats, followed where necessary with assault, destruction of property, or seizure of cattle for ransom, the rioters succeeded to a considerable degree in compelling the tenants of the enclosed forest grounds to allow the destruction of the enclosures and to stop payment of rent to the Earl.[22] By June, 1643, Brunker was complaining that the tenants of the enclosed grounds "will pay noe more rent untill their pastures be againe inclosed, and they may quietly injoy them."[23] Three years later he informed his master that the forest lands were yielding only about one-half of their usual rents and that it would be years before the enclosures could be fully restored and rents returned to normal.[24] Sir Edward Nicholas, Principal Secretary to Charles I and sharer of his son's exile, held a mortgage on Elgin's share of the forest and also had some land of his own there. In July of 1644 he was notified that his tenants wanted to be quit of their bargains because they were unable to pay their rents, no doubt because of the riots.[25]

The success of the rioters in these years, during which "they carry all before them without any controule," was largely attributable to the inability of those in authority to maintain order.[26] Since this part of Dorset and Wiltshire was under the control of parliamentary forces, and since the Earl of Elgin's sympathies lay with Parliament in its struggle with the King, it was to Parliament that Elgin and his agents turned for the legal authority to suppress the riots and to bring the offenders to trial. In responding to the riots, Parliament, particularly the House of Lords, assumed the role of Privy Council and defunct

21. JRL, Nicholas MS 73/16, John Dolman and Thomas Brunker to Elgin, May 13, 1643. Brunker's request for pistols is added in a postscript in his own hand; his fears are a constant refrain in the letters of these years.

22. JRL, Nicholas MS 73/28, Brunker to Thomas Christie, July 8, 1643; 74/1, examinations of John Godwin, Richard Ridgley, and Nicholas Boune before Mathew Davis, JP of Dorset, June 9, 1643.

23. JRL, Nicholas MS 73/24, Brunker to his son-in-law, June 4, 1643.

24. JRL, Nicholas MS 73/6, Brunker to Christie, June 28, 1645; 72/16, Brunker to Christie, Jan. 20, 1645/6.

25. Donald Nicholas, *Mr. Secretary Nicholas 1593-1669*, p. 196; see also pp. 84, 182, 188.

26. JRL, Nicholas MS 72/2, Brunker to Lady Bruce, April 29, 1643.

Star Chamber, but a time of armed strife, which disrupted the normal processes of local government and law enforcement, added to the usual difficulties connected with the suppression of disorder that were evident during the first Western Rising. This made it well-nigh impossible for any effective action to be taken against the rioters until 1648.

To deal with the riots in the spring of 1643 the Earl of Elgin, who had sat in the House of Lords since his elevation to the English peerage in August of 1641 as Baron Bruce of Whorlton, obtained an order from the House addressed generally to the justices of the peace, deputy lieutenants, and sheriff of Dorset, along with the officers in command of the trained bands. They were instructed to apprehend any rioters disturbing Elgin's quiet possession and to send them before the House.[27] To insure that the rioters could not plead ignorance of this action, the Lords further commanded that the order be read publicly in the parish churches of Mere, Gillingham, and Shaftesbury. This was followed by an ordinance passed by both houses of Parliament on May 3, 1643, instructing the local parliamentary commanders—Sir Walter Earle for Dorset, Sir Edward Hungerford for Wiltshire, and Sir John Horner for Somerset—to use their forces to suppress all disorders and arrest the ringleaders.[28]

Further orders for the punishment of the rioters were speedily issued. On May 11, 1643, two Dorset justices, Mathew Davis, and William Whitaker (who had played an important role on the government's behalf in dealing with the Gillingham riots in the early years of Charles I's reign), were ordered by the Lords to examine witnesses and certify the names of notorious rioters to the gentleman usher of the House and his deputies, who were to bring the suspects back to Westminster for punishment.[29] To aid the gentleman usher, the

27. The Earl of Elgin was created Baron Bruce of Whorlton, Yorks, on July 29, 1641. He was introduced into the House of Lords on August 5, 1641: *LJ*, IV, p. 342a; *LJ*, VI, p. 15b, warrant to draft the order, April 24, 1643. Copies of the order itself are to be found in H. of L.R.O., Main Papers, and JRL, Nicholas MS 73/34.

28. C. H. Firth and R. S. Rait, eds., *Acts and Ordinances of the Interregnum, 1642-1660*, vol. 1, p. 139. Other copies are in *LJ*, VI, p. 30a, and JRL, Nicholas MS 73/33. See also *LJ*, VI, p. 26a, p. 28b, and *CJ*, III, p. 67b. Somerset was included in the ordinance because of disorders in Frome Selwood Forest: see below, pp. 243-44.

29. *LJ*, VI, p. 42a, note that the order was issued, May 11, 1643. A copy of the order itself is to be found in H. of L.R.O., Main Papers; see also the order to the Gentleman Usher, *LJ*, VI, p. 48b, May 16, 1643; copy in JRL, Nicholas MS 74/11.

Lords in July, 1643, ordered Edmund Ludlow, at this time a captain attached to the forces in Wiltshire commanded by Sir Edward Hungerford and acting as governor of Wardour Castle, to apprehend the suspects named in the examinations taken by the Dorset justices.[30]

In the execution of these orders the officials and parliamentary commanders on the scene experienced nearly insurmountable difficulties, not the least of which was the utter contempt for the orders of the House of Lords shown by the rioters. The following was a typical reaction to the reading of the order of April 24, 1643, in the parish churches of Mere and Gillingham: Stephen Frye of Mere, it was deposed, "most contemptuously and in dishonor of the Parliament and their authority said that he cared not for their orders and the Parliament might have kept them and wiped their arses with them."[31] In the earliest efforts to enforce the orders of the House of Lords attempts were made to use the sheriff's *posse*. This proved fruitless. When the able men in three Dorset hundreds bordering on Gillingham were summoned to appear fully armed only twenty men turned up, and they came without weapons. No doubt this reluctance was due to sympathy with the rioters or fears of reprisal. The local constables were equally ineffectual. On May 9, 1643, Thomas Brunker and Elgin's other agent, John Dolman, went with a number of unwilling constables to try to apprehend some rioters. After arresting two suspects, the party was met by about two hundred people who compelled the surrender of the prisoners, the constables being unwilling to prevent this "through theire own timerousenes."[32]

The main reason for the difficulties experienced in executing the orders of Parliament lay in the distractions of the Civil War. With the failure of the *posse*, Thomas Brunker and others on the scene turned to the local parliamentary commanders for help, as they had been authorized to do by the various orders sent down from Westminister. In May of 1643 the parliamentary forces closest to Gillingham were those in Wiltshire commanded by Sir Edward Hungerford and engaged in the siege of Wardour Castle, a few miles north of Mere.

---

30. *LJ*, VI, pp. 118a-b; a copy is in JRL, Nicholas MS 74/2, and a draft in H. of L.R.O., Main Papers.

31. JRL, Nicholas MS 72/9, deposition of John Read, June 8, 1643; other choice opinions on the orders of the H. of L. are reported in the examinations of witnesses in Nicholas MS 74/1.

32. JRL, Nicholas MS 72/2, Brunker to Lady Bruce, April 29, 1643; 73/16, Dolman and Brunker to Elgin, May 13, 1643.

But Hungerford could do nothing about the riots until the siege was over. However, on May 3, Colonel William Strode, on his way from Somerset with a considerable force to join Hungerford at Wardour, happened to be at Shaftesbury and was persuaded by Elgin's agents to stop at Gillingham and help to apprehend some rioters. Strode's men were able to take four prisoners, but in their haste northward they had to take their captives along. The four men later managed to escape in the confusion of the siege.[33]

After the successful capture of Wardour, Sir Edward Hungerford sent a troop of soldiers to aid in arresting the rioters, but most of the soldiers, being from Mere, were reluctant to act against their neighbors. The troop, coming upon a large body of rioters, allowed them to escape until the officers and Elgin's agents intervened; only after much discussion were the soldiers persuaded to capture some suspects. The seven prisoners so taken were imprisoned in Shaftesbury for the night and then shipped to Blandford, where Sir Walter Earle, the parliamentary commander in Dorset, was quartered. Earle committed six to jail, where they spent two nights in irons; the seventh had escaped in Shaftesbury.

Before anything further could be done, the Civil War again intervened. Earle, receiving a report of the approach of the King's forces, released the prisoners on the promise that they would join the parliamentary service.[34] Finally, Captain Edmund Ludlow, the parliamentary governor of Wardour, was ordered on July 3, 1643, to apprehend a number of named rioters, but "by reason of the troubles of these partes, the orders could not be put in execucion."[35] On the basis of these events there seems to be every justification for Thomas Brunker's conclusion that "for the help wee get from the Leiftenants and Collonells, it is so longe ere wee cane procure it and with soe much charge, and the litle effect it takes, by reason that the ryoters taken are soe soone set at libertie which doe rather incourage them then take them of, make our paynes and dilligence for the suppressing of them to little purpose."[36]

33. JRL, Nicholas MS 73/12, John Dolman to Lady Bruce, May 6, 1643; for the siege of Wardour see C. H. Firth, ed., *The Memoirs of Edmund Ludlow*, vol. 1, Appendix II.

34. JRL, Nicholas MS 73/3, Brunker and Dolman to Elgin, May 15, 1643; 73/38, same to Elgin, May 20, 1643.

35. JRL, Nicholas MS 74/22, undated, document on the state of the Gillingham Forest case.

36. JRL, Nicholas MS 73/22, Brunker to Elgin, May 20, 1643.

The failure of parliamentary forces and local officials to effect any really positive action against the rioters meant that Elgin's agents were compelled to rely upon their own devices. These included taking advantage of the fortunes of war. On June 26, 1643, eight troopers of the King's forces came to Thomas Brunker's house to search for arms, but he was able to divert them from their purpose by offering money. As they left the house the troopers met with some rioters and fell upon them, wounding one severely. The rioters, believing that Brunker had purposely brought in royalist troops to restore order, informed the local parliamentary commander of this suspicion. Brunker strenuously denied the accusation but took pleasure in the action as a well-deserved punishment and an object lesson to the others: "that action hath wrought some thinge upon them for since that time they have bene in noe disorders about the forrest business."[37] Finally, with the aid of his own servants, Brunker was able to capture seven or eight rioters. This is a very small number, considering that Brunker named 126 suspects and their abettors in a list sent to Elgin.[38]

Additional difficulties resulted from what seem to have been political divisions among the local magistrates. When on May 7, 1643, the Earl of Elgin's agents and their servants captured seven rioters, they took their prisoners before two Dorset justices, Mathew Davis and William Whitaker, for examination. The available but far from complete evidence seems to indicate that the attitude toward the riots taken by each justice was determined by political outlook and personal connections. Whitaker was all for taking a hard line against the rioters, favoring their imprisonment without bail until they could be brought before the Lords. He had been prominent in the suppression of the earlier riots in Gillingham, providing the Privy Council with important information about the leaders, Henry Hoskins and John Phillips, and acting as counsel for the King in the Gillingham disafforestation case before the court of Exchequer.[39]

There is strong evidence that during this period Whitaker developed a close relationship with Sir James Fullerton and his stepson, Lord Bruce, later Earl of Elgin: in 1625 he had been made steward of

37. JRL, Nicholas MS 73/28, Brunker to Thomas Christie, July 8, 1643.
38. JRL, Nicholas MS 73/35.
39. See above, p. 98-99; he is named as counsel for the King in PRO, E. 125/3, F. 299, Oct. 19, 1967; f. 316, Oct. 27, 1627.

the manor of Mere, probably on Fullerton's recommendation; in the 1630s he acted as steward for some of Elgin's Dorset properties and leased some of the disafforested lands in Gillingham from the Earl.[40] Indeed, during the riots of April, 1643, Whitaker's recently planted orchard was cut down.[41] In the 1640s Whitaker remained closely connected with Elgin. At one point the Earl wrote to Whitaker, in terms that one imagines were reserved for faithful family retainers, to urge him to do all in his power for the speedy suppression of the riots.[42] No doubt as a result of his connection with Elgin, Whitaker was expressly named in the order of the House of Lords of May 11, 1643, as one of the justices who were to examine witnesses and certify the names of the notorious rioters to the gentleman usher of the House.[43] In addition, Whitaker, as a member of the Long Parliament and a long-time personal friend of John Pym, could be counted on to uphold the authority of Parliament in such matters.[44]

Whitaker's colleague, Mathew Davis, was much more lenient. He released three of the rioters outright; the others were bailed on sureties of £20 to be of good behavior and to appear at the next assizes. This drove Elgin's agents to despair; they claimed that such lenient treatment would encourage the rioters rather than suppress them. In fact, the released rioters were soon again at work destroying the enclosures.[45] In the face of criticism, Davis maintained that "hee would baile any of them if they had sewerties for it was not for Feloney."[46]

Was this merely the result of a concern for legal nicety on Davis's part, or does the fact that he bound the rioters over to the next assizes—in a period during which civil war had already prevented the holding of the winter assizes in 1643 and when there was no prospect for a summer assizes—reveal the unwillingness of a royalist justice to

40. Barker, pp. 330-31, warrant appointing Whitaker as steward of Mere, Nov. 24, 1625; M. F. Keeler, *The Long Parliament 1640-1641: A Biographical Study of Its Members*, p. 390.

41. JRL, Nicholas MS 72/8, a note by Brunker on the activities of the rioters, May 6, 1643.

42. JRL, Nicholas MS 73/20, copy of a letter from Elgin to Whitaker, undated, but can be dated to May 12, 1643.

43. JRL, Nicholas MS 73/18, copy of a letter from Elgin to Brunker, May 13, 1643.

44. Keeler, pp. 389-90. Whitaker sat in the Commons for Shaftesbury in the Parliaments of 1624, 1625, 1626, and 1640, and in the Long Parliament until his death in 1646. Beyond his close personal relationship with Pym nothing can be discovered about his political views.

45. JRL, Nicholas MS 73/16, Dolman and Brunker to Elgin, May 13, 1643; 73/38, same, May 20, 1643.

46. JRL, Nicholas MS 73/13, Dolman to Elgin, May 8, 1643.

enforce the orders of Parliament for political reasons? This is a question which cannot be answered with any certainty. The Earl of Elgin was not sure whether his coldness was "occacioned by feare or disaffeccion."[47] Davis's political sympathies were moderately royalist. A Member of the Long Parliament, he began to absent himself in 1642, finally being disabled on March 16, 1643. He then sat in the Oxford Parliament for a while, but in 1646 he compounded for his delinquency. After this he seems to have taken no active part in national political life. In spite of his leniency in May, Davis was praised by Brunker later in 1643 for being "very willinge and forward to helpe us in anything he may possible doe."[48] During the riots of 1645 Brunker was even more fulsome in his praise of Davis's help in the work of maintaining order.[49] The reasons for this change in attitude are unclear, though letters exchanged between Elgin and his agents indicate that Davis had some personal obligations to the Earl.

Thomas Brunker summarized the weakness of those charged with maintaining order in Gillingham when he wrote to his son-in-law that "in respect of the times which they knowe and thereuppon presume, ther is noe way to stay their furry but by strengthe and which way yt should be done, I cannot imagine."[50] In 1643 only one rioter, Richard Butler—one of the men bailed by Davis and then retaken—was brought before the Lords for punishment. He was committed to Newgate, but escaped in June of 1644. As Brunker wrote to his son-in-law, the punishment of the rioters would have to wait upon better times.[51]

From Brunker's point of view the better times were a long time in coming. Parliament's military position in Wiltshire worsened during 1644 and the royalists recaptured Wardour Castle on March 18, which meant that no military forces could be spared to deal with the rioters.[52] By late 1645 the work of suppressing the riots and arresting

47. JRL, Nicholas MS 73/18, Elgin to Brunker, May 13, 1643; Keeler, p. 154.

48. JRL, Nicholas MS 73/24, Brunker to his son-in-law Rainborow, June 4, 1643.

49. JRL, Nicholas MS 73/6, Brunker to Thomas Christie, June 28, 1645.

50. JRL, Nicholas MS 73/24.

51. JRL, Nicholas MS 73/16, Dolman and Brunker to Elgin, May 13, 1643; *LJ*, VI, p. 128b, order committing Butler to Newgate; p. 609b, order for Keeper of Newgate to appear before the House to explain why Butler escaped, June 29, 1644; p. 613a, order for attachment of Keeper of Newgate, July 3, 1644.

52. Firth, vol. 1, Appendix II, p. 455; JRL, Nicholas MS 74/13, a draft of an undated order by the H. of L. which refers to the loss of Wardour Castle as the reason why Ludlow could not execute the previous order directed to him.

the rioters was no further advanced. In September Brunker complained that no justice of the peace could be found to aid him in the
arrest of suspects or the prevention of future riots. As a result, he
requested that orders be issued to whatever troops were in the area to
come to his aid.[53]

In response, both Houses of Parliament issued an order in October
instructing the deputy lieutenants of Dorset, Wiltshire, and Somerset
and the commanders of parliamentary forces in those counties to
suppress all disorders and to take into custody all persons whose
names were certified by Thomas Brunker, including those named in the
order of July 3, 1643.[54] This was followed in November by a similar
order from the Committee of the West to the local officials of
Dorset.[55] These orders were no more effective than their predecessors. The local parliamentary commanders promised that they would
aid Brunker, but there is no indication that they ever did so.[56]

Brunker's problems in these years were further intensified by the
disruption of local government. Sittings of quarter sessions where
rioters might be indicted and tried or bound over, in anticipation of
the restoration of the assize circuits where they could be tried, were
irregular occurrences. When quarter sessions did sit it was to little
purpose; in January of 1646 the meeting was on such short notice that
there was no time to draw up indictments of the rioters or for Brunker
to obtain the advice of counsel.[57]

For the next two years the Gillingham matter disappears from the
record. This may mean that all was quiet in the forest, or the silence
may be illusory, the result of the loss of the kind of very full reports
sent to Elgin by Thomas Brunker and John Dolman, which provide so
much detail on the period 1643-1646. Since there is no mention of
Gillingham in the records of the House of Lords for this period, it is
probable that the end of the first Civil War brought sufficient
restoration of the normal processes of government and law to make
the rioters reluctant to act. In any case, it was not until the middle of
1648 that some effective action was finally taken. Early in June of that

53. JRL, Nicholas MS 72/17, Brunker to Christie, Sept. 13, 1645.
54. JRL, Nicholas MS 74/14, draft order by both Houses of Parliament, Oct., 1645.
55. PRO, P.R.O. 30/24/32/6, ff. 7-8, Committee of the West to the Standing Committee,
Dep. Lts. and JPs of Dorset, Nov. 5, 1645; another copy in JRL, Nicholas MS 78/25.
56. JRL, Nicholas MS 72/16, Brunker to Christie, Jan. 20, 1645/6.
57. JRL, Nicholas MS 72/16, Brunker to Christie, Jan. 20, 1645/6.

year, a number of inhabitants of Gillingham, taking advantage of the renewal of civil war, again destroyed the enclosures. The House of Lords, on a sworn affidavit that the rioters had acted in contempt of its earlier orders of 1643, ordered their attachment.[58] On July 8, five rioters were apprehended; on July 28 they were brought before the House to answer for their acts.[59]

At last, after five frustrating years, the Earl of Elgin had his day in court. What an anticlimax it was! As argued by his counsel before the Lords, Elgin's case was simple and straightforward. In 1643 the enclosures of the forest had been cast down, "and by an order of the 24 of Aprill 1643 they [House of Lords] did forbid from that tyme forth all ryotts in breakeing downe hedges, ditches, gates and pales and any other way tending to disquiett the possession of the Earle of Elgin without due processe of lawe." During June of 1648 the defendants, in contempt of this order, destroyed the enclosures. They acted two at a time to avoid prosecution for riot, which at law required the concerted action of three or more persons; in consequence they disturbed "the possession of the said Earle without due processe of lawe." Witnesses were produced to prove these matters and to attest to the reading of the order of April 24, 1643, in the parish churches, in case the defendants pleaded ignorance of the order. Elgin's counsel moved for what can only be called a Star Chamber judgment: that the defendants should be fined, give bond for their further good behavior, and pay the Earl £5,000 in costs and damages.[60]

The actual judgment against the rioters was remarkably lenient, especially in view of the fact that the riots were once described as "an

58. JRL, Nicholas MS 72/3, breviat of Earl of Elgin's case delivered to the Lords concerning the riots of June, 1648; *LJ*, X, p. 351a, order of H. of L. for the attachment of suspected rioters, June 29, 1648.

59. H. of L.R.O., Main Papers, petition of John Phillips et al to the Lords, Aug. 4, 1648; *LJ*, X, p. 401, order of H. of L., July 28, 1648.

60. JRL, Nicholas MS 74/6, breviat of the Earl of Elgin's case, undated; other undated copies are 74/4 and 74/5. There is one earlier draft of this in 72/3, on the dorse of which is the reference that this deals with riots at Gillingham in June, 1648. Nicholas MS 74/6 and other undated copies can also be dated by the references to the affidavit of Mr. Willes and the order for attachment of June 29, for which see *LJ*, X, p. 351a, June 29, 1648. There is a copy of 72/3 in the H. of L. Main Papers which is misplaced and therefore wrongly calendared, as of 1644 in *HMC 6th Rep.*, "H. of L. MSS 1643-1647," p. 40a. [Incidentally, this seems to be one of the few occasions in the seventeenth century when the words "due process" were used in an English legal context and with the same ostensible meaning as the more common American usage: see T. G. Barnes, "Due Process and Slow Process in the Late Elizabethan-Early Stuart Star Chamber," *American Journal of Legal History* 6 (1962): 221-49, 315-46.]

open Rebellion and resistance of all officers and government."[61] On August 4, 1648, the rioters were ordered released from imprisonment, their only punishment being "an admonition to give better obedience to the orders of this House and to carry themselves peacably and quietly." The House of Lords, like its predecessor in these matters, the court of Star Chamber, refused to deal with questions of title to land, in this case the right of the defendants to common in Gillingham Forest. The rioters were left free to engage in "trial of their right in a legal and just way."[62] This admonition, administered to the five rioters at the bar of the House on August 7, represents the sum total of punishments imposed for participation in the Gillingham riots. The difficulties of maintaining good order and punishing lawbreakers during a period of civil strife had in the end made it virtually impossible for those in authority to work their will.

Like any other seventeenth-century pursuer of "justice," the Earl of Elgin had more than one string to his bow. His active consideration of two additional remedies demonstrates once again the seriousness of the riots and the difficulties faced in suppressing them. One of these remedies, the Statute of Westminster II cap. 46 (1285), has already been encountered in use during the Dean Forest riots of the 1630s. The Earl of Elgin undoubtedly wanted to see the rioters punished, but he also desired financial recompense for the damages incurred. Westminster II seemed to provide the means to obtain it. By this statute, if the sheriff made inquiry by means of a jury to discover the names of rioters who destroyed enclosures and returned a finding to King's Bench that the riot was committed by persons unknown, the aggrieved party could then obtain process of distraint, which would compel the neighboring communities to pay damages. In deciding whether to proceed on the statute, Elgin was able to draw upon some of the best legal counsel available, including John Maynard, later serjeant-at-law, and a prominent Presbyterian leader in the Long Parliament.[63] There exists a much-corrected and incomplete draft of a

61. *LJ*, VI, p. 48b, order of the H. of L., May 16, 1643.

62. *LJ*, X, p. 418b, order of the H. of L., Aug. 4, 1648; p. 412b, noted that the rioters were brought before the bar of the House and received their admonition on Aug. 7, 1648.

63. There are a number of legal opinions and precedents scattered throughout JRL, Nicholas MS. They include 74/24, Maynard's advice upon proceeding on Westminster, II, Cap. 46; 74/9, 27, two opinions on the statute, counsel unidentified; 73/30, 74/28, two copies of Judge Rolle's precedents on the statute; 74/7, 8, 25, 26, transcripts from K.B. *Coram Rege* rolls of previous cases on the statute as precedents. These are all undated and at present can be dated no closer than 1643 to 1646.

writ of *inquiras* directed to the sheriff of Dorset, which would have started the proceedings upon the statute. The surviving evidence indicates, however, that this legal remedy was never carried beyond the stage of discussion.

The Statute of Westminster II provided the complainant with a means of obtaining damages when on an occasion of severe rural unrest the local upholders of law and order were able to make little headway and were therefore unable to identify and arrest the rioters. One of the precedents made available to Elgin by Henry Rolle, judge (later chief justice) of the King's Bench, was the case of John Gibbons, whose enclosures at Cannop Chase were destroyed in the Dean Forest riots of 1631; this fitted the provisions of Westminster II cap. 46 precisely.[64] There was one crucial difference in Elgin's case: the names of the rioters were known by means of examinations made before Dorset justices and by depositions on oath made before the Lords.[65] No doubt the question raised by Maynard and other counsel—whether a statute designed to cover cases where the rioters were unknown was operative when they were known but could not be apprehended—was the determining factor in the Earl's apparent failure to move against his opponents by this means.[66]

When it was discovered that twelve of the actors and abettors in the riots of 1643 and 1644 had been fined in Star Chamber for participation in riots in the late 1620s, John Maynard recommended exploring another legal remedy, the levying of the old fines.[67] Elgin, as heir to Sir James Fullerton, had inherited the right to the fines, which Fullerton had agreed not to levy so long as the inhabitants of Gillingham behaved themselves. In a case already discussed, Elgin had levied the fine when, during the 1630s, John Wolridge continued in active opposition to the enclosure.[68] Thus in the 1640s there existed a direct precedent, and in 1646 one of the rioters, John Phillips, was

64. JRL, Nicholas MS 73/30, 74/28, two copies of Judge Rolle's precedents on the statute; for Gibbons's case see above, p. 116.

65. Copies of the examinations and depositions are in JRL, Nicholas MS 74/1, 29, 30, 74/12, 72/9, 10, 15 and H. of L.R.O., Main Papers, June 9, 1643.

66. This question is raised in JRL, Nicholas MS 74/24 and 27.

67. JRL, Nicholas MS 74/24, "the course intended to be prosecuted in the Gillingham riott by Mr. Maynard's advice"; 74/21, the names of those fined in Star Chamber who participated in the riots of 1643 and 1644.

68. See above, pp. 110-12.

ordered brought before the Barons of Exchequer to answer for his fine.[69] Although it is doubtful that Phillips actually paid the fine, this procedure does provide an interesting illustration of the way in which a means of law enforcement connected with a discredited and thus abolished instrument of the old regime could be put to the same use by a "revolutionary government" and its supporters.

The Earl of Elgin, seeking both punishment of the rioters and pecuniary damages with at best indifferent results, was also interested in achieving some kind of compromise with the rioters that would result in the establishment of peace and the resumption of the orderly flow of rents into his hands. The compromise finally worked out reveals the entrenched position the rioters had achieved by the late 1640s. The rioters' ultimate aim was no doubt to restore the forest to its open condition. While this may seem unrealistic, they had another, more limited, and hence more realizable aim: an allotment of forest ground for the poor of Mere who had been overlooked at the disafforestation. The lack of such provision was a powerful irritant to the inhabitants of Mere; it was the men of Mere who initiated the riots in April, 1643, by publishing a call to the people of Gillingham to assemble and destroy the enclosures.[70] By concentrating on satisfying this demand, Elgin was able to achieve a settlement that finally brought a measure of peace to the forest.

The evolution of this compromise is difficult to elucidate because the evidence is incomplete; what follows is therefore somewhat tentative. In 1645 an agreement was made between Elgin and the "ablest and best quality" people of Mere that 200 acres of the forest should be set out open and unenclosed as a common for a period of six months, to be enjoyed by the inhabitants of the township while they attempted to prove their legal right to compensation on disafforestation.[71] The 200 acres of common were laid out in the one-third of the forest that had been granted in 1631 to George Kirke by the Earl of Elgin in satisfaction of Sir James Fullerton's debts. The reason for choosing this location is not readily apparent, although it may simply

69. PRO, E. 159/486, Mich. 22 Chas. I, rot. 34.
70. JRL, Nicholas MS 74/4, copy of a letter sent from the men of Mere to the inhabitants of Gillingham, April 24, 1643.
71. JRL, Nicholas MS 73/6, Brunker to Christie, June 28, 1645; SRO, Alford and Kirke MS (DD/HLM) Box 2, Chancery decree in Elgin and Kirke vs. Awbrey et al., tenants of Mere, Mich. 1653.

be that Kirke's share of the forest was on the Mere side. One thing is certain: Kirke, a royalist, had as much interest as Elgin in bringing the riots to an end. The reports of Brunker and Dolman to the Earl indicate that the rioters made no distinction between the shares of the forest held by the two men.

The inhabitants of Mere failed to make their claim good. In what court they tried to pursue this matter remains unknown; possibly it was in Parliament, although Parliament had consistently refused to countenance suits relating to right and title.[72] The 200 acres were ultimately taken back into the hands of John Kirke, George's son, and re-enclosed, although this did not take place until a few years later. In December, 1646, George Kirke compounded for his delinquency; among his estates was the fee farm interest in Gillingham, which he conveyed to John Kirke in July, 1650. The freehold interest in this one-third of the forest was still in the Crown; Elgin had obtained a grant of the other two-thirds in fee simple in January of 1632. Thus the Crown's freehold interest in Kirke's one-third of the forest was among the estates included in the Act for the sale of Crown lands on July 16, 1649. The land was then surveyed by the parliamentary surveyors, who finished their work on November 26, 1650. Sometime following this, John Kirke bought the fee-simple interest from the trustees appointed to sell the late King's estates.[73] It is unclear when Kirke re-enclosed the 200 acres, although it was probably in the spring of 1651, for in November, 1650, when the land was surveyed, it was still lying open. When the new enclosures were erected they were immediately destroyed; these were probably the tumultuous proceedings in Gillingham referred to by the Council of State in May, 1651.[74]

After the inhabitants of Mere attempted unsuccessfully to establish their right to the 200 acres before the committee for removing

72. JRL, Nicholas MS 73/6, Brunker's letter of June 28, 1645, mentions a bill (of complaint?) put into Parliament by the inhabitants of Mere. See also Nicholas MS 71/11, an undated reply by Elgin to a petition of the inhabitants of Gillingham submitted to Parliament. A copy of this petition is probably 71/2 delivered to Elgin in February, 1645/6.

73. The evidence for this is to be found in PRO, E. 317/Dorset, no. 6, parliamentary survey of Mr. Kirke's farm of one-third of Gillingham Forest, Nov. 26, 1650; *Calendar of the Proceedings of the Committee for Compounding*, vol. 2, pp. 1469-70; SRO, Alford and Kirke MS (DD/HLM) Box 2, Chancery decree, Mich. 1653, and a conveyance of 80 acres of Gillingham Forest by John Kirke to trustees for the use of the poor of Mere, Dec. 2, 1656.

74. PRO, E. 317/Dorset, no. 6, pp. 2-5; S.P. 25/96, p. 187, Council of the State to Major-General Desborough, May 17, 1651.

obstructions to the sale of Crown lands, a treaty was reached between John Kirke and the Earl of Elgin on one side and some inhabitants of Mere on the other. In January of 1652 it was agreed that 80 of the 200 acres should be conveyed in perpetuity by Kirke to thirteen trustees, chosen from among the "ablest" people, and their assignees, who were to use the profits for the support of the poor. In turn, the inhabitants of Mere agreed that Elgin and Kirke should enjoy all the other lands of the former forest quietly and free of all claims to common.[75] Elgin had already agreed to compensate Kirke with a grant of 53 acres, his share of the 80 acres as owner of two-thirds of the forest.[76]

Opposition to this agreement soon appeared, however, and the enclosures of the 80 acres were destroyed. The opponents wanted the 80 acres as a common, like the 100 acres set out at disafforestation as compensation for the use of the tenants. Despite this violence, the agreement was confirmed by a decree in the court of Chancery in Michaelmas, 1653, as a result of a collusive action brought by Elgin and Kirke against the trustees.[77] As a result of this treaty, Gillingham Forest seems finally to have had a measure of quiet restored to it.[78]

The Gillingham and Mere inhabitants' persistent opposition to enclosure and disafforestation can by itself be taken as an indication of the continuance of deep-rooted and unaltered social problems for which an open forest was the only means of amelioration. This continuity with the disorders of the 1620s is even more marked when the social status and identity of the rioters is examined. While many

75. PRO, E. 317/Dorset, no. 6, pp. 4-5; SRO, Alford and Kirke MS (DD/HLM) Box 2, Chancery decree of Mich. 1653; Barker, pp. 307-8.

76. SRO, Alford and Kirke MS (DD/HLM) Box 2, Agreement between John Kirke and the Earl of Elgin, Nov. 25, 1651.

77. Barker, pp. 308-9, Richard Greene to Richard Major, Mar. 23, 1651/2; SRO, Alford and Kirke MS (DD/HLM) Box 2, Chancery decree of Mich. 1653; see above, pp. 148-49.

78. There is one other interesting item connected with this business which ought to be noted here. In SRO, Alford and Kirke MS (DD/HLM) Box 2, there is a copy of a grant by John Kirke to the trustees for the poor of Mere of the residue of the term of 41 years and 3 months left on his fee-farm interest in the 80 acres; Kirke also agreed to pay the annual rent. In the same place, dated Mar. 20, 1656/7 is a lease of 53 acres of land in the forest by Elgin to Kirke in return for a peppercorn rent. This seems to be a somewhat inexplicable duplication of the treaty already negotiated, although it could be conjectured that Kirke, anticipating that at some future date his freehold interest purchased from the confiscated estate of the late King would be successfully challenged and his grant in perpetuity to the trustees nullified, based this second grant on the earlier and unchallengeable grant in fee-farm.

suspects were named in various reports sent to the Earl of Elgin, only occasionally were their occupations given. The names of 186 people suspected of involvement in the riots of 1643-1645 are known. Only in the case of the township of Gillingham can the status of a reasonable number be discovered, but even here the proportion is quite small— thirteen out of sixty-four suspects; eleven were artisans, one was a husbandman, and one was a gentleman.[79] The gentleman was only suspected of being an abettor and, as the evidence from the first Western Rising demonstrates, to be accused of participation in riot, especially for a gentleman, was far from proof.

The most striking demonstration of continuity is to be found in the identities of a number of the rioters and in the nature of the leadership. Twelve of the participants in the riots of 1643-1645 had been fined in Star Chamber for their part in the disorders of the 1620s; eight were artisans, one was a mercer, two were husbandmen, and one was of undetermined status.[80] Four of them were noted as notorious offenders in the 1640s, including a fuller who acted as drummer and John Phillips, tanner, who took over leadership of the riots in 1644 from Richard Butler, a poor linenweaver. It is clear from the examinations of witnesses that Butler had been the leader of the riots in 1643 until he was apprehended and brought before the Lords. His opinions, as reported by a number of witnesses, show considerable contempt for Parliament and for Elgin's agent, Thomas Brunker. At the beginning of the disorders in 1643 he went into a shop to buy gunpowder. When told it cost 1s.6d. per pound, "hee sayd his monie would not hold out to have soe much, but desired her to lett him have 2 pennyworth and sayd it would be enough to serve Tome Brunker and for his proclamation [Parliamentary Ordinance] I care not a fart of mine arse."[81]

Butler was one of the seven rioters captured by Brunker and his servants on May 7, 1643, and then bailed by Mathew Davis. As soon as

79. Lists of riot suspects compiled by Brunker are JRL, Nicholas MS 73/35 and 72/15. These can be supplemented by 72/12, a list compiled by the bailiff of George Kirke, and by examinations of witnesses in 74/1 and depositions in 72/5, 72/9, and 72/10. The figures for the village of Motcombe are forty-five suspects, of which one was an artisan and one a butcher; for Mere, seventy-seven suspects—four artisans, one husbandman, one mercer, and two gentlemen abettors.

80. JRL, Nicholas MS 74/21, list of rioters 1643-1645 fined in Star Chamber.

81. JRL, Nicholas MS 72/8, note of the names and offenses of rioters in Gillingham sent by Brunker, May 6, 1643.

he was released under bond to keep the peace and to appear at the next assizes, he was again back at work against the enclosures. A few days later Butler, described by Brunker as "a little short man" and a "notorious and cuninge knave," had been recaptured and was shipped to London.[82] In the interest of security he was soon moved from the New Prison in Clerkenwell to Newgate, where he remained for about a year. It was hoped that confinement would make Butler, a poor man, willing in return for his freedom to reveal the names of the men of quality who were thought to be behind the riots.[83] In this as in almost everything else connected with the riots, the Earl of Elgin and the Lords were to be disappointed; there were no men of standing manipulating the riots from behind the scenes. Sometime in June of 1644 Butler escaped and returned to Gillingham, where he was reported to be raising new riots.[84]

At this point Butler fades from view and his place is taken by John Phillips, tanner, holder of a small cottage and tanning house in Gillingham Manor, fined £200 in 1630 for his part in the earlier riots, and later imprisoned for continued opposition to the enclosures. Phillips was active in the riots of 1643, and by 1644 he had emerged as the leader. By this time an old man of sixty-six, he was an example of fanatical dedication to reversing the disafforestation.[85] In January of 1644 he urged the men of Mere to beat down the re-erected enclosures, insisting he would do it alone if they did not join him. In July, Phillips went into the area of the forest where the enclosed allotments for the tenants of the manor of Gillingham had been set out in compensation for their loss of right to common in the forest. These enclosures had been partially destroyed by the rioters in 1643; Phillips rode a horse in and out of the gaps in the fence of one close, telling its tenant "that if he made up his hedges any more he would come and

---

82. JRL, Nicholas MS 73/16, Brunker and Dolman to Elgin, May 13, 1643; 74/16, notes on the case against Butler.

83. H. of L.R.O., Main Papers, application for the removal of Butler from the New Prison in Clerkenwell to Newgate, July 12, 1643; *LJ*, VI, p. 128, order for committal to Newgate, July 12, 1643; JRL, Nicholas MS 73/5, notes drawn up by Mr. Maynard on the course to be taken with Butler, Dec., 1643, another copy in H. of L.R.O. Main Papers; other proposals are to be found in Nicholas MS 72/18, 73/9, 74/15, 16, 18.

84. *LJ*, VI, p. 609, order for appearance of Keeper of Newgate before the H. of L., June 29, 1644; 613, similar order, July 3, 1644.

85. John Phillips was 60 in 1638 when sworn and examined as a witness in Wolridge's case against the Earl of Elgin: PRO, E. 134/14 Chas. I/Eas. 24.

bringe some others with him and pull it downe againe before his face." At another time, Phillips rode through all the closes, saying, "I ryde in and I ryde out of these groundes at my pleasur, and I take and will keepe the possession of them."[86]

In June of 1645 Phillips was again active against the enclosures, but from this point until 1648 his activities are shouded in considerable obscurity.[87] Sometime in 1646 he was put in jail by the sheriff of Dorset. In November of that year he was ordered brought before the Barons of the Exchequer to answer for the Star Chamber fine that had been imposed in 1630.[88] Whether or not Phillips paid the fine, he remained undaunted. At seventy, he was one of five men attached for the destruction of the enclosures in June, 1648. Although discharged with an admonition by the House of Lords, Phillips and his compatriots were still petitioning for their release from prison sometime after August 7, 1648. The reason for their continued restraint was that they could not afford the £170 in fees owed to the Clerk of the House of Lords and his deputy, the gentleman usher and his deputies, the messengers, and the jailers.[89]

The abundance of material available on the riots at Gillingham contrasts markedly with the few scraps of evidence so far discovered on the renewal of opposition to the enclosures in the other forests of the first Western Rising. It has already been noted that in the spring and summer of 1641 Sir John Winter's enclosures in Dean Forest were destroyed in a series of riots.[90] Little else is known of the opposition to the disafforestation, but in 1642 Winter effectively lost his title because of his recusancy and what were thought to be fraudulent dealings in obtaining the grant in the first place. As a result the forest returned to its unenclosed state for a number of years, satisfying the complaints of the inhabitants.

The enclosures in Braydon Forest were destroyed sometime after the outbreak of the Civil War "by the poore of the neighboring

---

86. JRL, Nicholas MS 74/10, accusations against John Phillips.
87. JRL, Nicholas MS 74/19, Morgan Horder's accusation against Phillips.
88. PRO, E. 159/486, Mich. 22 Chas, I, rot. 34.
89. *LJ*, X, p. 421, order for release of John Phillips and others, Aug. 7, 1648; petitions of Phillips and his friends are in H. of L.R.O., Main Papers, Aug. 4 and Aug. 7, 1648. There is another petition, undated but clearly datable to after the order for release. It is mis-calendared as of August 7, 1645 in *HMC 6th Report*, "H. of L. MSS 1643-1647," p. 73b.
90. See above, p. 218.

parishes,"[91] and opposition to the enclosure of Leicester Forest also surfaced again. A petition was submitted to the House of Lords on June 25, 1641, on behalf of the corporation of Leicester, that the enclosure be declared illegal. Nothing seems to have come of this, but in 1649 six men met to plan a riot, "hearinge there was leave granted by the parliament for the throweinge downe of the forest of Leicester."[92] One final echo of the first Western Rising occurred at Slymbridge, Gloucestershire, where in 1631 some soldiers reported to be lieutenants of "Skymington" from Dean Forest had offered to cast down the enclosures. During the first Civil War the inhabitants finally rioted and destroyed the enclosure of 300 acres of ground new-gained from changes in the course of the river Severn.[93]

During the 1640s and 1650s riots also took place in two other western forests, Neroche and Frome Selwood in Somerset, which had been peacefully disafforested earlier in the reign of Charles I. Frome Selwood lay just north of Mere and extended along the eastern boundary of Somerset. It was the location of an important segment of the western broadcloth industry and the scene of food rioting in 1622 and 1629-1631. Although comparatively uneventful, the disafforestation of Frome Selwood was a lengthy process, commencing in 1627 with the issue of the first commission and not completed until 1640, when the last agreements with neighboring landowners were confirmed in the court of Exchequer.[94] In 1642 and 1643, after the outbreak of the Civil War, most of the enclosures were destroyed, and for years thereafter riots aimed at the remaining enclosures in the forest continued to break out.[95] In only a few instances can more than a bare notice of their occurrence be discovered.

91. PRO, E. 317/Wilts, no. 23, survey of Braydon great lodge, 1651; no. 38, survey of Langshopshill and Hatton lodges, 1651; E. 125/37, ff. 314-16, decree in a case concerned with the resurvey of the 150 acres allotted in Braydon to the inhabitants of Chelworth at the time of disafforestation, April 25, 1657.

92. H. of L.R.O., Main Papers, petition to the H. of L., received June 25, 1641; see also Stocks, *Records of the Borough of Leicester, 1603-1688*, pp. 302, 307.

93. *LJ*, VIII, p. 200, order for Lord Berkeley's quiet possession of the enclosed newly gained ground at Slymbridge, Mar. 5, 1645/6; p. 201, petition of Ld. Berkeley, Mar. 5, 1645/6; p. 611, renewal of order of Mar. 5, Dec. 14, 1646.

94. Barnes, *Somerset 1625-1640*, pp. 157-59.

95. PRO, S.P. 18/97/36 I, deposition of Peter Daniel before John Ashe and John Cary, JPs, May 4, 1655, mentions that in 1643 most of the enclosures in the forest were destroyed. It was no doubt because of these disturbances that Frome Selwood was included in the ordinance of May 3, 1643, ordering the parliamentary commanders in Wilts, Dorset, and Somerset to suppress disorders: see above, p. 227 and n. 28.

One series of riots was aimed against the enclosure of Kilmington Heath, only three miles west of Mere. At the time of disafforestation this 636 acres of waste was claimed by John Hartgill as parcel of his manor of Kilmington. Under the disafforestation agreement confirmed by an Exchequer decree of November 28, 1635, the heath was divided into equal thirds among the King, the lord of the manor, and those with valid claims to common. In 1636 Sir Charles Berkeley of Bruton, Somerset, bought Kilmington Manor and the two-thirds of the heath belonging to Hartgill and the King. He then proceeded to erect enclosures and make other improvements at a cost of £318. In 1642 a number of the neighboring inhabitants who claimed common on the whole heath took advantage of the wars, as Berkeley claimed, and destroyed the enclosures. For the next ten years the lands lay open to the benefit of the people in the vicinity. Like that of the Gillingham rioters, this success was due to the Civil War's breakdown of the normal institutions of law enforcement. When in April, 1652, Kilmington Heath was once more enclosed, there was another riot.[96] Berkeley's enclosures of land at Bernard's Combe, which he obtained on the disafforestation of Frome Selwood, were also destroyed early in the Civil War and lay open until at least October of 1649. When re-erected they were again destroyed, in 1652 or early in 1653.[97]

In June, 1653, Berkeley and other holders of disafforested lands in Frome Selwood whose enclosures had been destroyed petitioned the Council of State for action to prevent further outbreaks. In response the Council ordered the justices of Somerset to keep the county quiet, authorizing them to call on the troops quartered nearby to provide necessary assistance.[98] Also destroyed in this period were Lord Broghill's enclosures of former forest land in which the inhabitants of Maiden Bradley in Wiltshire and Yarnfield in Somerset claimed common. At the disafforestation of Frome Selwood this land had been claimed as waste appurtenant to Sir John Hippisley's manor of Marston Bigot. Hippisley received a one-third share; he proceeded to enclose and to lease it in parcels to some of the inhabitants of Maiden Bradley. In 1641 the manor and the enclosed lands were sold to Lord Broghill (son of the Earl of Cork and a distinguished

96. PRO, E. 112/331/74, bill and answers in Berkeley vs. Madox et al., Trin. 1652.
97. *Calendar of the Committee for Compounding*, vol. 2, p. 1339.
98. PRO, S.P. 18/37/109, copy of a letter from the Council of State to the JPs of Somerset, June 17, 1653.

Parliamentarian), who enjoyed quiet possession until 1643 when, during his absence in Ireland, the enclosures were destroyed. From then until 1654 the inhabitants of Yarnfield and Maiden Bradley enjoyed the land as an unenclosed common.[99]

In August of 1654 Lord Broghill petitioned the Council of State—in terms much like those of Sir Charles Berkeley's petition of the previous year—requesting protection for his recently re-erected enclosures. In response, the Council instructed the justices of Somerset to maintain the peace of the county, by the use of soldiers if necessary.[100] In spite of this, the new enclosures were destroyed in another riot in April of 1655. The Council of State then administered a severe rebuke to the justices in a style reminiscent of the Stuart Privy Council.[101] Stung by accusations of negligence, the justices called before them the inhabitants of Maiden Bradley and Yarnfield, who promised to cease rioting and to content themselves with Broghill's offer of a trial at law to determine their rights in the enclosed lands.[102]

The course of events at Neroche Forest in Somerset followed the pattern set by Frome Selwood: a lengthy but relatively peaceful disafforestation in the 1630s, followed by rioting in the 1640s and 1650s. Although the first commission for the disafforestation of Neroche was issued simultaneously with that for Frome Selwood in 1627, the commissioners were still at work in 1640. The division of the forest also conformed to the same pattern: one-third for the King, which was sold to neighboring landowners, one-third for the manorial lords and freeholders, and one-third for those tenants who could prove rights to common, as compensation for loss of their rights in the rest of the forest.[103]

A minority of the inhabitants, who could not prove right to common and received no compensation, opposed disafforestation from the first. For a good number of years their opposition was confined to raising legal objections to the enclosure, but in October of 1641 many of the enclosures in the forest were riotously destroyed by

99. PRO, S.P. 18/97/36 I, deposition of Peter Daniel of Marston Bigot before John Ashe and John Cary, JPs, May 4, 1655.

100. PRO, S.P. 25/75, pp. 537-38, Council of State to JPs of Somerset, Aug. 28, 1654.

101. PRO, S.P. 25/76, p. 35, order by the Council of State on petition of Lord Broghill for a letter to be sent to the JPs of Somerset, April 18, 1655; the letter itself is on p. 36.

102. PRO, S.P. 18/97/36, John Ashe and John Carey to Henry Lawrence, President of the Council, May 12, 1655, enclosing 36 I, deposition of Peter Daniel, May 4, 1655.

103. Barnes, *Somerset 1625-1640*, pp. 156-59.

a crowd estimated at one hundred. Following this disorder, the court of Exchequer issued an injunction to quiet possession in favor of the holders of enclosed lands. As a result of other riots during the Civil War, most of the forest was still lying open when it was surveyed in 1652.[104] The kind of opposition enclosure faced is well demonstrated by one example from Neroche. In December of 1647 Thomas Samwaies, a sergeweaver of Widney, dug up part of the enclosures of 194 acres of forest land set out for the lord of the manor of Broadway. In February, 1648, Samwaies was served with an Exchequer injunction renewing that of May, 1642; he ignored this new injunction, saying that he would pull the enclosures down because "hee could but lye in the goale for it." In March of the same year Samwaies was again discovered tearing down enclosures; the court of Exchequer thereupon ordered his attachment for this contempt of its injunction.[105]

Opposition to the enclosures continued. In 1656 Attorney-General Prideaux, in a desperate move, filed an information in Exchequer against over two hundred defendants, including William Seymour, Marquis of Hertford, who held lands in and around Neroche. It was hoped that the defendants could be compelled to identify those who continued to destroy the enclosures in the forest. Most of the defendants claimed ignorance; only a handful of names were gathered.[106] This judicial activity produced only two results: the renewal in 1658 of the injunction to quiet possession, and an order for the attachment of one of the rioters. The case was still in progress late in 1659 when Prideaux died and proceedings temporarily stopped.[107]

Depression in the cloth trade and food scarcity, coming on top of chronic social problems untouched by the outbreak of Civil War, produced new food riots in western Wiltshire. During 1647 there were numerous petitions about unemployment from the weavers in

104. PRO, E. 125/9, ff. 409-15, order concerning those who continued to claim common in Neroche, June 29, 1631; E. 125/29, ff. 184-87, injunction to quiet possession which summarizes the affidavits made before the court giving evidence on the riots, May 21, 1642; E. 317/Somerset 36A, survey of Neroche Forest, Sept. 4, 1652.

105. PRO, E. 125/31, f. 299, order for attachment of Thomas Samwaies summarizing affidavits on his activities, June 14, 1648.

106. PRO, E. 112/331/140, information and answers in A-G vs. Marquis of Hertford et al., Eas. 1656.

107. PRO, E. 125/38, ff. 95-96, renewal of injunction, Feb. 3, 1657/8; f. 171, order for attachment of William Standerwick, May 15, 1658; f. 339, order stopping proceedings because of the A-G's death, Nov. 12, 1659.

many of the broadclothmaking centers in the county; one symptomatic complaint was that many young men had taken advantage of the
disordered times to set themselves up in trade without having served
out their apprenticeships.[108] Next, the harvest failure of 1647 resulted,
in 1648, in reports of scarcity from the clothmaking areas of
Wiltshire. Food rioting occurred around Devizes, with an increase in
crimes such as the stealing of grain and of sheep; in consequence the
justices, at the direction of the judges of assize, instituted emergency
measures, based on the Book of Orders, to regulate the markets and to
supply the poor with grain at less than the prevailing price.[109]

The second Western Rising demonstrates the indifference of many
ordinary people in the West to the issues involved in the Civil War.
Battles were being fought close by—for example, the long struggle for
Wardour Castle took place only a few miles away from Mere—but
much more pressing problems were faced by the poor in the forested
areas. At best, the Civil War, with its weakening of the traditional
institutions of social and political control, provided an occasion to
strike with near-impunity at the objects of popular animosity. At
worst, it was an intolerable and distracting nuisance subjecting
ordinary folk to pillage by both sides. The presence of soldiers,
furthermore, might prevent them from casting down enclosures. It
was no accident that the Clubmen appeared in the neighborhood of
Frome Selwood, Mere, and Gillingham in 1645. As Professor Underdown puts it: "By June the most intense centre of 'club' activity was
the region where the three counties of Somerset, Dorset and Wiltshire
came together. It was an area long affected by food shortage and
depression, and with a history of riots against enclosure and disafforestation."[110] The Clubmen were a form of organized neutrality:
countrymen joined companies formed by parish as a kind of home
guard to protect themselves against plunder by both sides. Although
in some parts of Wiltshire and Dorset the Clubmen were tinged with
royalism, and in central and northeastern Somerset with parliamen-

108. *HMC Various*, vol. I, "Records of Wilts," pp. 114-15, petitions to the Q.S. by the weavers
of Westbury and by the weavers of Chippenham, Calne, and Seend, 1647; Cunnington, pp. 189-
90, petitions of the weavers of Westbury and Devizes, 1647.
109. PRO, Assizes 24/21, ff. 104-6, order made at Salisbury assizes, Mar. 6, 1647/8;
Hoskins, "Harvest Fluctuations and English Economic History, 1620-1759," p. 29; *HMC
Various*, vol. I, pp. 115-17; Cunnington, pp. 180-83, p. 200.
110. D. Underdown, *Somerset in the Civil War and Interregnum*, p. 98.

tarianism, those of Frome Selwood, Gillingham, and Mere seem to have been genuinely neutral.[111]

The main purpose of the Clubmen of Mere and Gillingham seems quite clear: to organize in such a way that they could keep the soldiers out and allow themselves a free hand against the enclosures. The riots at Gillingham in 1645 began on May 28, when "there was a generall meetinge of the Clubbemen upon the downes near Shasbury at which time Gillingham and Motcombe men being gathered together in Troopps as they went to their randenoves did teare up the hedges and made manye gapps in the forrest mounds." On their return the Clubmen destroyed more enclosures. When some of Thomas Brunker's servants tried to intervene, they were severely beaten. In his report on these disorders Brunker clearly saw the advantage that the club organization gave to the rioters: "The Clubbe armie which I feared would put boldnes into them conserneing our forrest busines, hathe brought them to this insolencie, before they stode in some awe of comanders and souldiers, nowe they respect no man nor will give any obedience to any but conteme all supperiors whatsoever and doe what they please."[112]

The Clubmen were regarded by the commanders of the New Model Army, at this time in the West, as a royalist fifth column. On August 4, 1645, Oliver Cromwell with 500 dragoons, acting on the orders of General Fairfax, the commander of the New Model, broke up a meeting near Shaftesbury, killing twelve Clubmen.[113] As Brunker noted in his next report on conditions at Gillingham, "our Clubbmen have bene quiet ever since Coll. Cromwell met with them."[114]

In an area where riots were aimed at the property of a parliamentarian like the Earl of Elgin, it is understandable that the suspicion would naturally arise that the rioters were moved by royalist sympathies. The ordinance of May 3, 1643, urging suppression of the riots, was motivated by the fear that "upon such occasions persons ill

111. Underdown, pp. 98-99, 105-6, 111-12; Bod. Lib., Tanner MS 60, ff. 163-64, articles of association of the Clubmen of Dorset made at Gorehedge Corner, May 28, 1645, with additions made at Sturminster Newton, June 24, 1645; f. 182, examination of Christopher Dale of Salisbury, July 2, 1645. There is a good recent discussion of the Clubmen in J. S. Morrill, *The Revolt of the Provinces: Conservatives and Radicals in the English Civil War, 1630-1650*, pp. 98-111.

112. JRL, Nicholas MS 73/6, Brunker to Christie, June 28, 1645.

113. Underdown, pp. 112-13.

114. JRL, Nicholas MS 72/17, Brunker to Christie, Sept. 13, 1645.

affected to the state may meet together and grow into a Body and so break out into open warre and hostility." There is no evidence to bear out this suspicion. Richard Butler, linenweaver, who until his capture led the riots of 1643, sought to remove this fear of royalist sympathies from the minds of the Lords by indicating "that he is willing to serve the parliament for Religion, liberty, etc."[115]

The hallmark of the riots in the 1640s, indifference to the Civil War, can best be explained in terms of the continuity of the issues involved. The same condition that triggered the first Western Rising—a large population of near-propertyless cottagers dependent on wages in nonagricultural occupations for their basic livelihood and on open forest wastes for important supplements—was still there in the 1640s.

Hostility to the Crown's policy of disafforestation between 1626 and 1632 did not politicize the ordinary forest dwellers and drive them into the hands of Parliament in its struggle with the King. When Civil War came, the inhabitants of forests rioted against those who held and profited from the enclosed lands. It did not matter that the Earl of Elgin was a parliamentarian, that George Kirke and Sir John Winter were royalists, or that Lord Broghill was a royalist turned parliamentarian: political alignments were incidental to the hated reality of enclosure. This kind of attitude toward men of property and power is best exemplified in a minor popular rising that took place in Kent during June of 1643. During the plundering of a gentleman's house by a group of twenty men led by two blacksmiths, the following conversation, between one of the smiths and another of his band, was overheard:

Parry the smith said: "We have sped well heare. Let us go to Hadlow and
   Peckham and plunder there, for they are rich rogues, and so we will go
   away into the woods."
Smale replied: "But we must plunder none but Roundheads."
Parry the smith replied with a great oath: "We will make every man a Round-
   head that hath anything to lose. This is the time we look for."[116]

An attempt has been made to argue that at least the Wiltshire

---

115. JRL, Nicholas MS 74/18, notes on a petition submitted by Butler praying for his release from prison.
116. "Papers relating to Proceedings in the County of Kent, 1642-1646," *Camden Miscellany*, vol. III, p. 31, a true relation of the insurrection at Sevenoak, July 18, 1643.

segment of the Western Rising was a prelude to the Civil War, insofar as hostility to the Crown's policy of disafforestation was symptomatic of the kinds of discontents which would create potential parliamentarians.[117] The argument falls down, however, because it is based upon two erroneous assumptions. One is that because prominent gentlemen who held land around Braydon Forest, such as Sir Edward Baynton and Sir Neville Poole, were parliamentarians in 1642 they must have been hostile to the disafforestation of 1631. There is no proof of this; indeed, both men were amply compensated at the time of disafforestation. The second, and related, assumption is that important gentry manipulated the riots from behind the scenes for their own purposes. This has already been examined and found groundless.[118]

In fact, it can be argued that the division in the forests in the 1630s was not between the Crown and its projectors as proto-royalists and the gentry as proto-parliamentarians, but between the propertied and powerful, whether future royalists or parliamentarians, and the poor and powerless. Landowners agreed on the necessity for a paternalistic social policy to prevent clothworkers and other artisans from engaging in riot or other socially destabilizing activities, but paternalism had its limits. Whenever the financial and property rights of the Crown and its powerful subjects came into conflict with the needs of these same artisans and other poor cottagers, the interests of the poor were largely ignored.

Whatever may have been the issues, great and small, which brought on the Civil War and over which it was fought, enclosure of the royal forests was definitely not among them. In the 1620s and 1630s future parliamentarians like John Pym and William Whitaker were heavily involved in enforcing Crown policy and, at least in Whitaker's case, profiting from it. This was also true of the Earl of Elgin: given the source of his titles and his forest lands, he owed the Crown a debt of gratitude, yet he turned out to be a staunch parliamentarian. In his attitude toward enclosure, however, Elgin was no different from George Kirke, his partner in Gillingham, or Sir John Winter in Dean, both of whom became royalists.

Continuity also marked official policy toward forest riots. The parliamentary government of the 1640s was as committed to maintaining good order, social stability, and property rights as the government of Charles I's personal rule. During the 1650s, when the government of the Protectorate began to cast around for means of raising revenue, it fastened upon the forests which had not yet been disafforested. By two acts, in 1653 and 1654, the disafforestation and sale of practically all remaining royal forests was authorized.[119] The attitudes in the 1650s toward royal forests were exactly as they had been in the reigns of James I and Charles I. They were regarded as potentially profitable but undeveloped resources that bred "idle, vagrant, pilfering and pernicious persons," who lived by robbing travellers or by despoiling the woods and pasturing cattle in the waste. Improvement of the forests would have the advantage of employing these idle people in the construction of enclosures, as well as financially benefiting both the Commonwealth and those who leased the land for agricultural purposes.[120]

The Protectorate, by adopting the forest policy of the Stuarts, not only inherited popular hostility to the longstanding enclosures in forests such as Gillingham, Frome Selwood, and Neroche, but created new antagonisms of its own. Two examples come from Needwood Forest in Staffordshire and Dean Forest. Following the disafforestation of Uttoxeter Ward, there had been intermittent riots in Needwood between 1637 and 1640; it was one of the forests included in the Act of 1654.[121] The procedure followed in the disafforestation and sale of the whole forest was in essence that utilized in similar cases under Charles I: in 1657 a commission was appointed by Parliament to survey the forest and award compensation to the commoners.[122] Strong opposition to enclosure had already appeared in 1655 when the terms of the act for disafforestation became known. Many of the inhabitants petitioned the Protector requesting that the forest be left unenclosed. They pleaded that large numbers of cottagers had no clear proof to right of common, but sustained themselves and their families by living off the forest. If they

119. Firth and Rait, vol. 2, pp. 783-812, act for disafforestation and sale of royal forests, Nov. 22, 1653; 993-99, act for sale of forests reserved as security for soldiers' pay, Aug. 30, 1654.

120. Thirsk and Cooper, pp. 135-40, proposals for the improvement of waste ground submitted to the Committee for the Advancement of Trade, 1653.

121. See above, pp. 221-22.

122. Firth and Rait, vol. 2, pp. 1116-22, an act of instruction for commissioners appointed to disafforest Needwood and other forests, June 19, 1657.

lost this means of sustenance, an intolerable burden of poor relief would be imposed on the communities around Needwood.[123] This opinion was endorsed by the justices, who wrote to the Protector that enclosure would result in great misery for "thousands of indigent persons," far more than could be sustained by poor relief.[124]

The effect of this activity on the course of events is unclear; it did not stop the disafforestation, but it may have helped produce the rather generous compensation for the commoners. After considerable bargaining, it was agreed in 1658 that 4,610 acres should go to the government and 4,610 to satisfy the inhabitants of the twenty-two townships claiming common. It was believed that this agreement gave the great landowners more than ample satisfaction, the substantial middling sort their full rights, and the poor more than they could claim in strict legality. Despite this, the inhabitants were not satisfied; as early as May of 1657 it was reported by the surveyors of the forest that a troop of horse would be needed to protect the improved lands from the depredations of the inhabitants. Late in 1658, when the enclosure began, troops were needed to suppress the riots that took place. Rioting seems to have continued sporadically until March of 1659.[125] At the Restoration the plans for enclosure were dropped; Needwood was not finally disafforested until 1801.

Predictably, the treatment accorded to Dean Forest during the 1640s and 1650s was unique. In March, 1642, the House of Commons voted that the grant of the forest to Sir John Winter should be voided because of his recusancy, his failure to fulfill his end of the bargain with the Crown, and the fact that the grant "was prejudicial to the Commonwealth." Winter's offer to surrender his patent to the commissioners of the Treasury was accepted; however, as a result of the outbreak of the Civil War this was not actually done. Therefore, at the Restoration Winter was able to revive his claim to the forest.[126] The immediate practical effect of the Common's vote and Winter's

123. PRO, S.P. 18/94/56, petition to the Ld. Protector from the inhabitants adjoining Needwood, undated, but noted that it was referred to the Council for advice, Feb. 5, 1654/5.
124. PRO, S.P. 18/94/57, undated, letters of JPs of Staffs to the Ld. Protector.
125. PRO, S.P. 18/155/18, commissioners surveying Needwood to the Ld. Protector, May 9, 1657; *VCH Staffordshire*, vol. II, pp. 352-53.
126. PRO, S.P. 16/489/35, copy of the votes of the Committee of the Forest, Feb. 14, 1641/2; S.P. 16/491/50, Commissioners of the Treasury to James Kirle, deputy constable of Dean, July 1, 1642; no. 86, (?) to Winter, July 22, 1642; GRO, D. 421/E5, copy of an undated post-Restoration petition of the inhabitants of Dean.

later sequestration as a royalist was that the forest reverted to its unenclosed state.

In 1645 the ironworks and the right to cordwood, which had been leased in 1636 to Sir Baynham Throckmorton and two Bristol merchants, were leased anew to Colonel Edward Massey by authority of a parliamentary ordinance.[127] From this point until 1659, the pre-disafforestation policy of the Stuarts—the exploitation of the forest as a source of timber, cordwood, and iron ore—was reintroduced. With this inheritance went all the problems in the forest that Stuart governments had to face. Despoliation of the woods by the lessees of the ironworks and the inhabitants of the forest, rich and poor, continued.[128] Complaints about the activities of the poor grew more frequent during this period and pushed all other causes of despoliation into the background. In 1646 it was reported that good timber was being used as firewood by 300 cabiners.[129] The following year the lament was taken up by the forest officers:

There is still great spoyle done in the forrest in cutting downe very many of the best oake and beech trees by the Cabbiners and others poore and beggerly persons wee are not able to suppresse them; they resist us and have often beaten and abused most of us ... if there be not some speedy course taken for the pulling downe of the cabbins and for the punishing of theise beggerly persons that are common spoylers of the timber there wilbe every day more and more spoyles made and committed.[130]

A commission reported in 1649 that hundreds of cabiners, "chiefly poor vagabonds and strangers who had crept into the Forest," still made a living "by cutting, cording, burning, and carrying for the ironmasters" with no regard to the type of trees, the requirements on size of cords, or the locations where they should be cut. Makers of cardboard, shovels, trenchers, and barrel staves also continued to despoil the woods. By 1653 there were estimated to be about 400

127. *LJ*, VII, p. 662-3, ordinance relating to Dean Forest, Oct. 27, 1645.
128. There are many surviving Exchequer cases connected with despoliation of woods and timber in Dean during this period: see, e.g., the series of informations against multiple defendants by the S-G, Oliver St. John, all Hil. 1646/7, in PRO, E. 112/183/230-240. There is also a series of similar informations by A-G Prideaux dating between Mich. 1650 and Hil. 1652/3, in E. 112/300/5, 7, 26-32. See also Hart, *Royal Forest*, pp. 132-51.
129. Hart, *Royal Forest*, p. 133.
130. PRO, E. 101/141/6, report of George Oldfeilde and other forest officers, Mar. 11, 1646/7.

cottages and cabins in the forest whose inhabitants lived off the forest's woods and pastures.[131]

Plagued, like its predecessors, by widespread despoliation in Dean, the Protectorate resorted to the Stuart remedy, enclosure. In June of 1657, one-third of the forest was enclosed for the preservation of future timber growth. The other two-thirds were left to the inhabitants, who were given legal rights of common so wide as to amount to complete license: rights to every kind of wood and timber, and the right to assart, enclose, and hunt at their pleasure.[132]

Despite this generosity, some inhabitants rioted, not merely against the then enclosure of one-third but also out of fear that over time the rest of the forest would be divided into small enclosed parcels. Throughout April and May of 1659 fences around coppices enclosed to preserve young timber were destroyed and cattle driven in.[133] At this point the situation at Dean was much complicated by the appearance on the scene of royalist conspirators like Edward Massey, a former parliamentary officer turned royalist plotter, who intended to raise Gloucestershire for the exiled Charles II. Massey and his fellow conspirators seem to have held a number of meetings with the inhabitants of Dean, hoping to turn their discontent over enclosure into an armed and effective royalism. It was reported that at one of these meetings some people of Dean professed that their hard usage at the hands of Parliament would force them to turn Cavalier.[134] On the whole, however, the royalists found the inhabitants of Dean much more interested in their forest privileges than in the restoration of the King.[135] It is not at all certain that any of Dean's inhabitants actually took part in Massey's rising, a total failure which had fizzled out by July 31.[136]

131. Hart, Royal Forest, pp. 137-38, and Free Miners, p. 207.

132. Firth and Rait, vol. 2, pp. 1114-15, an act for mitigating the forest laws in Dean and for the preservation of the timber, June 9, 1657.

133. PRO, S.P. 18/202/70, John Wade to the commissioners of the Admiralty, April 8, 1659; S.P. 18/203/29, Daniell Furzer to the commissioners of the Admiralty, May 30, 1659; CJ, VII, p. 648a, H. of C. order for suppression of reported riots at Dean, May 11, 1659; p. 798b, H. of C. referred to Council of State to preserve order in Dean, July 9, 1659.

134. Bod. Lib., Clarendon MS 63, f. 4, Alan Broderick to Sir Edward Hyde, July 22, 1659.

135. HMC Bath, vol. II, pp. 132-33, Thomas Ross to Gervase Holles, June 4, 1659.

136. D. Underdown, Royalist Conspiracy in England 1649-1660, pp. 260-65. This was not the only time that ordinary folk in the West got swept up with royalist conspiracy. In W. W. Ravenhill, ed., "Records of the Rising in the West, 1655," W.A.M. XIII (1872): 139-42, there is a list of 136 prisoners captured during Penruddock's rising in 1655. The social status of 128 of

The post-Restoration history of Dean is beyond the scope of this work, but we should note that it was one of the few forests in which disafforestation was permanently reversed. Although Sir John Winter successfully revived the grant Charles I had made to him, in 1668 Dean was reafforested by Act of Parliament and the forest administration was restored. This meant returning the forest to an open common to be exploited by the inhabitants. While the rights claimed by the miners were no longer challenged, their importance declined in 1672, when to protect Dean's woods the King's ironworks were permanently closed. During the next 150 years, however, the inhabitants frequently rioted against attempts to erect enclosures or to impose regulations on their right to common.[137]

To the time of the Restoration, then, the issue of disafforestation and enclosure was very much alive, and the underlying social problems that had produced food riots and the Western Rising of 1626-1632 continued to cause disorders. Elizabethan and Stuart governments instituted paternalistic measures to meet the needs of the hungry and unemployed in times of depression and scarcity, but they had no second thoughts about disafforestation: income was a necessity, and the forests were an important and undeveloped resource available to the state. Although the development of the forests as a source of revenue was the main consideration, no government proceeded in a totally high-handed and arbitrary fashion; respect for legally protected property rights was too deeply ingrained. Disafforestation was conducted with scrupulous regard for property rights and in such a fashion that "due process" was guaranteed and the propertied inhabitants were generally satisfied. If there had been no other forest inhabitants, no doubt matters would have gone quite smoothly. Forces beyond the control of officialdom—population growth and economic development—had, however, produced a large population of artisans and other poor who relied on the waste of the western forests for

---

them is noted and—not surprising for a rising organized and led by royalist gentlemen—there are listed 2 esquires, 27 gents., and 11 servants of gents. The surprise is that the rest of the prisoners included only 20 husbandmen, 6 yeomen, and 1 laborer, while there were 57 men employed in nonagricultural occupations. About 40 of them were artisans from a wide variety of trades. Surely it was not royalism which prompted these people to join Penruddock but, rather, the opportunity to vent social and economic grievances.

137. See C. E. Hart's various works on the forest for more detail on the post-1660 period.

important—at times essential—income supplements. This population, to a large degree outside the conventional social arrangements in the countryside, lacked the property rights and consequently the legal protection afforded to other inhabitants of the forests. The riots that resulted persisted through several political regimes and taxed the police powers of the state. In retrospect, the attempt to stand against enclosure seems doomed to failure, but one must admire the dogged resistance of the poor in the forests.

Chapter X

Conclusion

The people who engaged most intensely in the popular disorders characteristic of Elizabethan and early Stuart times—the forest riots, food riots, and related insurrections—were artisans, skilled men in rural areas or small towns working in nonagricultural employments. I have used the word "artisan" loosely to cover a wide range of skilled workers, from weavers to miners. Nonetheless all skilled men shared certain common social and economic characteristics, which might lead the adventurous historian into thinking in terms of a class.

In addition to the possession of manual skills which differentiated them from laborers and husbandmen alike, artisans in major manufacturing areas of pre-industrial England—the clothmaking locations of the West, the South, and East Anglia, and the mining and ironmaking areas of the West—depended largely on wages provided by capitalist employers. The miners of Dean Forest were not technically wage-earners, and they clung tenaciously to their independence as enshrined in the mine law, but they were heavily dependent on the farmers of royal ironworks and private ironmasters who bought iron ore by the load. Despite their independence, the self-employed Dean miners did not enjoy a standard of life markedly different from that of wage-earning miners or artisans in others parts of the West. A similar marginal independence was also the hallmark of the (presumably) self-employed artisans who earned their livings by exploiting the raw materials available in the wood/pasture regions of the forested West. Another characteristic common to artisans and miners that intensified their wage dependence—or, perhaps more accurately, their skill dependence—was their status as landless or virtually landless cottagers. Even if a cottager held one or two acres, the land was most likely meadow or pasture; rarely was it arable, so artisans were forced to rely on the market for the staples of their diet.

The combination of these common and closely related characteristics accounts for the high degree of artisan participation in popular disorders during the late sixteenth and early seventeenth centuries. The wage or skill dependence of clothworkers and other artisans is reflected in their recorded involvement in food riots and attempted insurrections during times of cloth-trade depression or harvest failure. Even when no evidence for the status of rioters has survived, the heavy concentration of riots in clothmaking areas suffering from unemployment convincingly links riot with a wage-dependent population of cottager/artisans. Clothworkers and other artisans of the forested West supplemented their incomes by exploiting the relatively abundant commons available in the unenclosed wastes of the royal forests. The forest policies of Charles I's government, which threatened these supplements and the livelihood of miners, workers in wood, hide, and animal fats, and laborers living in the forests, caused the riots known collectively as the Western Rising. Artisans provided much of the leadership, and laborers living in cottages on manorial or forest waste (who comprised a considerable proportion of the marginal poor in Tudor-Stuart England) undoubtedly supplied a large share of the rank-and-file in the riots against disafforestation and enclosure. Although some of the poor cottagers holding ten acres or less were probably classified by contemporaries as poor husbandmen, their interests at disafforestation no doubt lay with the artisans and laborers, not with substantial husbandmen and yeomen.

It seems obvious, almost a commonplace, that the bulk of Elizabethan social legislation, and Stuart conciliar implementation thereof, must be explained in terms of the existence of a sizable rural-industrial proletariat. The Statute of Artificers (1563), the Statute on Cottages (1589), the Poor Laws, the Vagrancy Statutes, and the Book of Orders are only comprehensible as a series of attempts to deal with a crucial social problem—a large and growing class of unruly and marginal poor liable to erupt into violent action in an era of recurrent depressions and harvest failures. Such paternalistic statutory measures were agreeable alike to Crown and country gentlemen—the latter, as members of Parliament and local magistrates, playing active roles in the passage and enforcement of legislation; the objectives were maintenance of the public peace and the social order. In the disafforestation proceedings social stability took second place to the pressures of financial necessity. Throughout the proceedings, however, the attempt was made to forestall destabilizing disorder through a consistent policy of respecting the property rights of substantial landholders and thereby confining riot to the marginal poor. Only, perhaps, in the case of the revival of the forest laws at Dean and elsewhere was insufficient care taken to mollify the propertied; the threat posed to property rights by the revival of this medieval institution—dating from a time when the will of the prince was law—meant that when the day of reckoning came the oppressions of the forest law would be a substantial item in the bill of complaint against the policies of the personal rule.

Our claim that artisans' wage-dependence and their resultant status as propertyless cottagers accounts for their active role as leaders and participants in riots of the Tudor-Stuart period rejects universal applicability to the orthodox model of rural England. In this model the working population is regarded as fundamentally peasant; the main source of livelihood is in agriculture, either in husbandry or through labor in other men's fields, supplemented by rights of common. Work in rural industries is taken to be an important but secondary means of supplementing agricultural earnings. As a consequence, it has become standard to refer to rural crafts as the by-employments of the agrarian population. The impression left by this model of rural employment is that the hybrid peasant/craftsman was a typical and universal figure in the English countryside before the Industrial Revolution.

It must be insisted to the contrary: the by-employment model of rural crafts, found in certain parts of the country, is rarely to be met with in the main rural locations of manufacturing in the Tudor-Stuart period. Peasant or yeomen/craftsmen in this period undoubtedly existed; for example, they are well documented in a recent study of the parish of Myddle in Shropshire.[1] But, as the author of the study notes, "the local crafts were never developed into an industry."[2] This was

1. D. G. Hey, *An English Rural Community: Myddle under the Tudors and Stuarts*, pp. 143-62.
2. Hey, p. 7.

largely an agricultural community and most of the crafts evolved to meet the needs of the agrarian population; the craft population, as recorded in the parish registers, never rose above 14 percent of the total.[3] Moreover, the peasant/craftsmen holding land at Myddle seem to have been a wealthy minority among the artisans; they were substantial enough to have inventories made of their possessions. The impression left by such people at Myddle, especially those called tailor/yeomen, is that they were not in fact artisans who worked in a trade, but entrepreneurs with investments in land and raw materials which were put out to be worked on by others. Even in such an agricultural community there were considerable numbers of poor artisans who depended on wages supplemented by commoning for their livelihood. As Dr. Hey notes, the quality of life of such artisans was little different from that of laborers: "Many of them could hardly be distinguished from laborers except that they worked for a large part of their time at a distinctive craft."[4]

Whatever the state of artisans in those parts of England where agriculture provided the main source of the livelihood (and even here, as Dr. Hey's study demonstrates, a considerable proportion of the artisans producing for the local market were landless), there can be no doubt that in the industrial areas of Tudor-Stuart England—the broadcloth centers in the South and forested West, the East Anglian new-drapery, and mining and metallurgical locations such as Dean and Kingswood—the skilled as well as unskilled work force was overwhelmingly propertyless and dependent on wages. Although these artisans obtained important supplements to their wages through grazing a few beasts on an acre or two of pasture (if they were lucky enough to own cattle and hold such land) or through commoning in forests and other wastes, they had ceased to be peasants.[5]

Food riots and related disorders during times of cloth-trade depression and food scarcity were unquestionably the work of the common

3. Hey, p. 53.   4. Hey, p. 165.

5. What I mean by ceasing to be peasants can be illustrated by a contemporary example. In the bucolic surroundings of Santa Cruz, California, two of my colleagues raise pigs on an acre of ground owned by one of them. One purpose of this is to supplement their salaries, but by no stretch of the imagination are they peasants or even hybrid peasants/professors of literature. The care of a few animals is a spare-time affair, taking up so little time that it is not worthy of the term "occupation"; furthermore, its practitioners can hardly be described as rooted to the soil.

people; forest riots may need more careful examination. Certainly there survive a number of contemporary opinions, or rather fears, emanating from the Privy Council that men of standing were behind the Western Rising. At best, these opinions were simply that, opinions which in fact never had any substance, but they do provide evidence of the official attitude toward popular disorder: the multitude were by nature untrustworthy and inclined to disorder and, at the same time, too brutish to organize themselves into a coherent and well-directed movement; for this the manipulative and natural leadership capacity of disaffected aristocrats was required.[6]

The disorders were genuine expressions of popular discontents, the consequence of the effects of unemployment, rising food prices, or enclosure on the livelihood of virtually landless wage-earners. In such situations the "common sort" were quite capable of producing their own leaders, usually artisans, who organized and directed the riots. There is no evidence to indicate that men of standing—gentlemen or above in the social scale—provided leadership or connived at the riots from behind-the-scenes for their own purposes.

In dealing generally with popular disorders in the early modern period, historians have too uncritically accepted the fears expressed by officials as genuine evidence for the central leadership or behind-the-scenes role played by men of social standing.[7] This is particularly true in the rather skimpy historiography of the Western Rising; the inevitable influence of the Civil War has tempted historians to regard the forest riots as a warm-up match for the main event, with progressive gentry allied to a popular anti-enclosure cause against the antiquated and politically unwise fiscalism of the Crown.[8]

Most modern historians of popular disorders seem to start from the assumption that, in a hierarchical society within which deference was

6. For examples of the official attitude see Francis Bacon, *On Sedition*; A. Fletcher, *Tudor Rebellions*, especially chaps. 1, 2, and 9; Hill, "Many-Headed Monster"; Walter and Wrightson, "Dearth and the Social Order."

7. This is certainly true of Roland Mousnier's *Peasant Uprisings in the Seventeenth Century: France, Russia, and China*, and C. S. L. Davies's attempt to apply his ideas to early modern England, "Peasant Revolts in France and England." See also the criticisms of Mousnier on this very point in M. O. Gately et al., "Seventeenth Century Peasant 'Furies': Some Problems of Comparative History," *Past and Present* 51 (1971): 74-75.

8. This is to be found in Kerridge, "Revolts in Wiltshire," pp. 64-75, and in Hill, "Many-Headed Monster," pp. 297-98, 316.

inbred and virtually automatic, disenchanted aristocrats, noble or gentle—in effect, those endowed with the capacity for leadership— must have been behind all serious disorders, unless it has been proved to the contrary. The fears and rumors that gentry were behind the forest riots and the instances of gentlemen accused of participating in the riots have been taken to confirm this assumption. The fact that only one gentleman was convicted and fined for participating in the Western Rising can then be taken as confirmation of the further assumption that the manipulators were so successful in concealing evidence of their role that the government could not obtain convictions. In this light, it could also be argued that in the aftermath of the Western Rising the hostility of the forest communities, including the gentry and magistrates, shielded offenders of high social status from the long arm of the Privy Council, Star Chamber, and commissions of oyer and terminer.

It is true that the best conspiracies are those that have left no trace behind, but the historian, like the law, needs evidence to prove a conspiracy. As soon as a rumor of the gentry's participation in the forest riots was received, the Stuart Privy Council was as quick as any modern historian to leap to the conclusion that a conspiracy was afoot, but after due investigation, the Council could never discover any involvement by the gentry. The historian is therefore left with a body of evidence against conspiracy, evidence indicating that popular causes were generated by popular grievances and that the ordinary forest dwellers provided their own leadership. It is certainly true, as this study has amply demonstrated, that the police and military powers available to the Crown were woefully inadequate to the task of suppressing riots and bringing rioters to justice before assizes, commissions of oyer and terminer, or the court of Star Chamber. This inadequacy, allied on occasion with paralyzing fear, explains the difficulties local officials experienced in the face of massive riots much better than does an assumption of officials sympathizing with the rioters.

This very inadequacy of available police power—whether in the shape of constables, *posse comitatus*, or militia—combined with officialdom's assumption that the common sort were incapable of organizing and leading major insurrections by themselves, makes the strongest case for the genuinely popular character of the Western Rising. On the belief that men of standing had to be behind all serious disorders, and acknowledging that they could not apprehend all suspects, the Crown and its officers always went after the big fish, letting the small fry slip through the net. Their failure to land big fish is a most striking aspect of the Western Rising. The court of Star Chamber operated under a set of assumptions which would lead it to strike hard at offenders of high status; it was the Crown's responsibility, as font of justice, to punish the intimidating practices engaged in by overly enthusiastic litigants who attempted to use their high social status and large following of clients to engage in peace-disturbing self-help or to intimidate juries and otherwise corrupt the processes of the law. From its inception the court was designed to seek out the men of standing behind the most seemingly trivial crimes or disorders. Not only were such men a political and social danger, they could also be made to pay heavily for their infractions. Given this, plus the rewards available for information against aristocratic malcontents, and the visibility of gentlemen participating in disorders, the historian is drawn to the inescapable conclusion that gentlemen escaped punishment after the Western Rising only because they were not involved in it.

The Crown's apprehensions about the reaction of the men of standing to its policies probably accounts for its conciliatory actions during all of the disafforestation proceedings. Enclosure by agreement, often achieved by collusive actions in the court of Exchequer, satisfied the interests of substantial freeholders and forestalled potential dangers. Only, perhaps, in the case of the revival of the forest laws and the consequent trial and punishment of offenders at Dean and elsewhere by the judgment of a forest eyre did the Crown's financial needs compel it to encroach (to its ultimate peril) on what were felt to be the property rights of freeholding subjects. Even here, however, the Crown tried to conciliate by recognizing claims to common and later by pursuing a collusive action in the court of Exchequer leading to a disafforestation and enclosure by agreement, but by that time the political damage had been done.

The most striking confirmation of the popular nature of the forest riots which comprise the Western Rising is their recurrence during periods of heightened political tension—from the Bishops' Wars through the Civil War and after. At least for the West, there is no evidence at all for the assertion that the riots were directed at royalist landlords because they were royalists, or manipulated on behalf of

Parliament in its struggle with the King.[9] If the Civil War is regarded
as essentially the consequence of a crisis within the elite governing
England, then it provided forest inhabitants with a golden opportunity to settle old grievances. With the attention of their social
betters and "natural leaders" drawn off by conflict over issues of
national import, ordinary people in the forested and industrial areas
of England were left free to engage in their own form of direct action.
In at least one case, that of Gillingham, the rioters were led by the
same popular leaders who had been in the forefront of riots almost
twenty years before. In such activities the political sympathies of the
local object of animosity were irrelevant.

The disorders that have been the subject of this work fit within a
long tradition of anti-aristocratic and anti-gentry popular rebellion in
England; this type of disorder was the result of social and economic
grievances of such intensity that they took expression in violent
outbreaks of what can only be called class hatred for the wealthy.
Traditionally, such outbursts took place in times of economic or social
dislocation severe enough to free discontents from deferential controls. This tradition can be traced back to the Peasants' Revolt of 1381,
but a more recent precursor was in the events of 1549.[10] Then, under
the impact of a series of jarring religious and economic developments,
popular risings were bruited or occurred in a variety of locations

9. There is little solid evidence that the widespread outbreaks of popular disorder in 1641 and
1642 were in any real sense motivated by pro-Parliament political sympathies or viewed with
anything but suspicion by prominent parliamentarians. The evidence gathered from literary and
printed sources by B. Manning in his recent work, *The English People and the English
Revolution 1640-1649*, especially chaps. 6 and 7, does not seem to me to demonstrate widespread
popular support for Parliament. It indicates, rather, on the part of the poorer sort—many of
whom were artisans, by Manning's own reckoning—a deep-felt hostility to men of property,
status, and wealth, especially landlords. The fact that many of the people toward whose persons
and properties the populace directed their animosities happened to be royalist was quite
incidental. Certainly the riots which broke out in the new-drapery areas of Suffolk and Essex in
1642 owed much more to the chronic problems of poverty and underemployment among the
workers than they did to any deep-rooted political sympathies for Parliament. Furthermore, the
local parliamentary gentry were horrified at this potentially dangerous manifestation of real
social conflict: on this see C. Holmes, *The Eastern Association in the English Civil War*, chap. 3,
passim but especially pp. 43-45.

10. Neither the Revolt of 1831 nor Ket's Rebellion was exclusively a peasant rebellion. In
each case there was sizable artisan participation. Furthermore, as the most recent historian of
1381 has noted, the seedbed of the revolt was in the southeast, where there were large numbers
of propertyless artisans; this was the "most industrialized and commercialized part of the
country." See R. Hilton, *Bond Men Made Free: Medieval Peasant Movements and the English
Rising of 1381*, especially pp. 165-85, and Bindoff, *Ket's Rebellion, 1549*, p. 20.

across the country—the most memorable and threatening being the Western Rebellion and Ket's Rebellion in Norfolk. The rebels expressed intense hatred of the gentry, who were blamed for the prevailing economic and social conditions; as the most recent historian of Tudor rebellions has noted, only in the case of the disorders of 1549 "was class hostility a major element in sixteenth-century popular disorder."[11] Similar economic and social dislocations were to occur in the years 1594-1597, 1622-1623, and 1626-1632; in their prevailing economic distress and intense social tension the periods 1594-1597 and 1626-1632 probably came closest to equaling 1549. It is therefore no surprise that in the disorders of these years the same hatred of men of property can be discovered; these outbursts were the expression of genuinely popular discontents stemming from economic influences such as inflation, unemployment, food scarcity, and enclosure.[12]

Many rebellions in the sixteenth century were of course led or connived at by the nobility or gentry, with the common people as the rank-and-file.[13] Generally, although not exclusively, these rebellions were conservative or reactionary in nature and were provoked by monarchical attacks on traditional religious practice or on aristocratic power monopolies. Included among them were the Pilgrimage of Grace in 1536 and the Northern Rising of 1569. Related to this type of aristocratic rebellion, but bridging the gap between it and the popular rising, was the revolt with aristocratic direction and leadership, but where the aims and motives of the rank-and-file were not those of the leaders.

Two different processes occurred in establishing the aristocratic leadership of this kind of disorder. In one case, the disaffected common people would compel reluctant gentry to take leadership and thus give organization and a measure of legitimization to the

11. Fletcher, *Tudor Rebellions*, p. 9.

12. The Midland Rising of 1607 and the violent opposition to drainage of the Fens probably ought to be included in this category, but they have not yet been subject to thorough and systematic study.

13. The most comprehensive account of sixteenth-century rebellions is that of Fletcher. It should be supplemented by the following excellent accounts of particular risings: C. S. L. Davies, "The Pilgrimage of Grace Reconsidered," *Past and Present* 41 (1968): 54-76; M. E. James, "Obedience and Dissent in Henrician England: The Lincolnshire Rising, 1536," *Past and Present* 48 (1970): 3-78; M. E. James, "The Concept of Order and the Northern Rising, 1569," *Past and Present* 60 (1973): 49-83.

movement. This was characteristic of taxpayers' revolts such as that in Cornwall (1497) and Suffolk (1525); it was also true to some degree of the Western Rebellion of 1549. In the other case, the leader's ability to attract a large following was merely fortuitous, that is, the discontents of the common people needed only a leader or an issue to set off a rebellion. The leaders, acting as igniters, often attracted a following out of all proportion to the cause they represented. It may be surmised, then, that the rank-and-file projected their cause onto the leader. This seems to have been at least partly true of the Pilgrimage of Grace. It was probably true of Wyatt's Rebellion during Mary's reign, when the ability of Sir Thomas Wyatt to attract large numbers of Kentish artisans to his cause must certainly be related to significant social or economic developments.[14]

This phenomenon is also to be met with a century later, during the Civil War, in royalist rebellions such as Penruddock's in 1655 and the attempt to recruit the inhabitants of Dean Forest for the King's cause in 1659. The final seventeenth-century example of this type of quasi-popular disorder was the Duke of Monmouth's Rebellion in 1685. The Restoration of Charles II did not eliminate the social problems which have been the concern of this study; rather, western artisans vented their discontents in other ways during the late seventeenth century. The culminating expression was in Monmouth's Rebellion, when in 1685 hundreds of clothworkers and other artisans of western England flocked to the standard of this bastard son of Charles II. Their reward came at the slaughter on Sedgmoor, on the gibbets of the "Bloody Assizes," or as indentured convicts in the West Indies.

The tradition of artisan radicalism did not, of course, die in 1685. On the contrary, during the next 150 years English artisans became steadily more politically conscious and more articulate in the expression of sophisticated democratic political ideas. In the early decades of the nineteenth century it was through the medium of artisan leadership that a popular democratic political heritage—embodied in the ideas of Thomas Paine and his seventeenth-century precursors, the Levellers—was transmitted to the new industrial working class.

14. For Wyatt's Rebellion, see Fletcher, *Tudor Rebellions*, pp. 78-90, and D. M. Loades, *Two Tudor Conspiracies*.

Bibliography

Manuscripts

Bodleian Library, Oxford

Ashmolean MSS

    1148. Report of proceedings of a special commission on the New Forest, Hants, undated, ca. 1608 x 1612 (ff. 255-56).

Bankes MSS (manuscripts of Attorney-General Bankes)

    Bundle 9. Warrant for a proclamation to prohibit the miners of Dean from taking iron ore out of the forest, Nov. 12, 1637 (no. 45).

    Bundle 43. Warrant to renew the commission appointed to disafforest Dean, Feb. 10, 1637/8 (no. 9); warrant to renew the commission to disafforest Dean, May 8, 1636 (no. 15).

    Bundle 45. Bond of £2,000 by John Williams *alias* Skimington for his good behavior, Aug. 12, 1637 (no. 72).

    Bundle 55. Warrant to appoint a commission to disafforest Dean, Aug. 2, 1635 (no. 50).

    Bundle 56. Petition by John Williams *alias* Skimington to the King, received May 6, 1637 (no. 6).

Clarendon MSS

    63. Alan Broderick to Sir Edward Hyde, July 22, 1659 (f. 4).

Firth MSS

    c. 4. A letter book containing correspondence of the Dep. Lts., JPs, and other officials of Essex, 1608 to 1639.

Gough MSS

    Gloucs. 1. Proceedings of the Dean Forest eyre, July 10 to July 18, 1634.

Rawlinson MSS

B 443. Survey of Pewsham and Melksham forests, Wiltshire, Mar. 23, 1618/19.

D 119. Proceedings of the Dean Forest eyre, July 10 to July 18, 1634.

Tanner MSS

60. Articles of association of the Clubmen of Dorset, May 28, 1645, with further additions June 24, 1645 (ff. 163-64); examination of Christopher Dale of Salisbury, Clubman, July 2, 1645 (f. 182).

British Library, London

Additional Charters

40105. Star Chamber Commission of Rebellion to the sheriff, JPs, and Dep. Lts. of Wiltshire to apprehend suspected Braydon Forest rioters, July 7, 1631.

Additional MSS

32092. Lord Chief Justice Popham to the JPs of Wiltshire to insure that the markets are well supplied with grain, Jan. 12, 1596/7 (f. 145).

39245. A letter book containing correspondence of Suffolk JPs and Dep. Lts., 1608-1640.

Cotton MSS

Vespasian F. IX. Examination of Richard Passinger of Selborne, Hampshire, tailor, before Francis Coffe, JP, June 14, 1586 (ff. 147-48).

Titus B. IV. Memorandum on the causes of the spoils of woods, undated *temp.* James I (ff. 332-33).

Harleian MSS

738. Proceedings of the Dean Forest eyre, July 10 to July 18, 1634 (ff. 295-311).

4850. Proceedings of the Dean Forest eyre, July 10 to July 18, 1634 (ff. 24-59); opinion of the judges of England on certain questions concerning royal forests put to them by the Earl of Northampton, justice in eyre of the forests, and the Earl of Dorset, Lord Treasurer, undated but early in reign of James I, before 1608 (ff. 87-88).

Lansdowne MSS

54. James Ritter to Lord Burghley, Aug. 7, 1587 (no. 60).

66. Henry Cooke, JP of Herts, to Lord Burghley, Jan. 1, 1590/1 (no. 20).

76. Draft of a Privy Council order renewing the Book of Orders, 1594 (no. 40); notes on the timber in Dean Forest, Aug. 12, 1594 (no. 47); Sir Henry Cooke, JP of Herts, to Lord Burghley, Sept. 31, 1594 (no. 58).

78. JPs of Kent to Lord Cobham, Oct. 9, 1595 (no. 61).

166. (Sir Julius Caesar's papers) "Reasons to move his Majesty to make use and profit of Dean's woods" undated (f. 354); a much abbreviated extract of the same, Mar. 11, 1610/11 (f. 370); "the estate of the

bargains made in the Forrest of Dean," June 11, 1613 (f. 374); copy of a warrant from Ld. Tr. Salisbury and Sir Julius Caesar to the S-G authorizing the drafting of a grant to the Earl of Pembroke (ff. 376-77); "Forrest of Dean: the difference of the bargains," Feb. 23, 1618/19 (ff. 387-88).
639. (Cotton's Treatise on Star Chamber) writ grounded on the Statute of Northampton (1328) issued by the court of Star Chamber for the apprehension of rioters at Gillingham and Mere, Mich. 1628 (f. 16).

Dorset Record Office, Dorchester

Miscellaneous deposited documents
Deed 4780. Assignment to Lord Bruce by Sir James Fullerton of his interest in Gillingham Forest, Dec. 28, 1630.

Gloucester City Library

Manuscripts
L.F. 1.1. Transcripts of records relating to Dean Forest, undated.
L.F. 6.3. Signet letter to the farmers of the royal ironworks in Dean Forest, Mar. 31, 1618.

Gloucestershire Record Office, Gloucester

Winter family papers
D. 421/19/22. Abstract of records concerning the claims of the miners of Dean Forest, undated, mid-18th century.
D. 421/E5. Copy of a petition of the inhabitants of Dean to Parliament, undated, ca. 1660.

Harvard Law School Library, Cambridge, Massachusetts

L.MS 1128. Report of cases in Star Chamber, Hil. 1626 to Mich. 1640. A transcript of this document made by Prof. Thomas G. Barnes was used for this work.

Henry E. Huntington Library, San Marino, California

Ellesmere MSS
485. A number of aphorisms collected by Lord Chancellor Ellesmere.
2770. A Star Chamber cause list for the reign of Charles I. Transcripts of both documents made by Prof. Thomas G. Barnes were used for this work.

House of Lords Record Office, London

Main Papers 1628-1648.

John Rylands Library, Manchester

Nicholas MSS (Papers of the Nicholas family)
  65. Customs of Gillingham Forest, undated *temp.* Eliz. I (ff. 10-12).
  66. Rental of Gillingham Manor, Oct. 28, 1624 (ff. 1-6).
  69. Orders in Gillingham Manor Court, 1611-1637 (ff. 2-11).
  Bundle 71. State of the forest of Gillingham, undated ca. 1643-1645 (no. 1); some allegations of the inhabitants of Mere concerning their claims of common in Gillingham Forest, Feb. 1646/7 (no. 2).
  Bundles 72-74. Three bundles of documents relating to the Gillingham riots of 1643-1648, including a number of reports from Thomas Brunker —the Earl of Elgin's agent in Gillingham—lists of suspects, examinations of suspects and depositions of witnesses, drafts of orders of the House of Lords, and a number of legal opinions on how best to handle the punishment of the rioters.
  Bundle 78. Mr. Pierpont's exceptions to the orders drawn up in October, 1645, for suppressing the Gillingham riots (no. 24); copy of a letter sent by the committee of the West to the Dep. Lts. and others in Wilts, Somerset, and Dorset to suppress Gillingham riots, Nov. 5, 1645 (no. 25).

Lincoln's Inn, London
  A manuscript in press C. 4 which includes reports of Star Chamber cases 1629-1635. A transcript of this document made by Prof. Thomas G. Barnes was used for this work.

Public Record Office, London
Assizes
  Assizes 24/20-21. Western Circuit order books, 1629-1640 and 1640-1652.
Chancery
  C. 66. Patent rolls.
  C. 99. Forest proceedings.
  C. 231. Crown Office docket books.
Duchy of Lancaster
  D.L. 4. Depositions and examinations.
  D.L. 5. Order and decree books of the Court of the Duchy Chamber of Lancaster.
  D.L. 39. Forest proceedings.
  D.L. 43. Rentals and surveys.
  D.L. 44. Special commissions.
Exchequer
  E. 101. King's Remembrancer, Accounts Various.
  E. 112. KR, Bills, answers, etc.
  E. 123. KR, Order and decree books of the Court of Exchequer, series I,

1 Elizabeth 1-3 James I.

E. 124. KR, Order and decree books of the Court of Exchequer, series II, 1 James I-1 Charles I.

E. 125. KR, Order and decree books of the Court of Exchequer, series III, 1 Charles I-13 Charles II.

E. 126. KR, Decree books of the Court of Exchequer, series IV, 2 James I to 1841.

E. 133. KR, Depositions taken before the Barons of the Exchequer.

E. 134. KR, Depositions taken by commission.

E. 137. KR, Estreats.

E. 146. KR, Forest proceedings.

E. 159. KR, Memoranda rolls.

E. 178. KR, Special commissions of inquiry.

E. 207. KR, bille.

E. 317. Augmentations office, parliamentary surveys, Commonwealth.

E. 407/78. Exchequer of Receipt, miscellanea, forest proceedings.

King's Bench

K.B. 8. (Crown side) *baga de secretis.*

K.B. 9. (Crown side) ancient indictments.

K.B. 27. (Crown side) *Coram Rege* rolls.

K.B. 29. (Crown side) controlment rolls.

Land Revenue

L.R. 2. Miscellaneous books.

Privy Council

P.C. 2. Privy Council registers.

Public Record Office, gifts and deposits

P.R.O. 30/24/32. Miscellaneous forest documents.

P.R.O. 30/38/21-23. Star Chamber process books, 1626-1631.

Signet Office

S.O. 1/1-3. Irish letter books, 1626/7-1642.

State Paper Office

S.P. 12. State Papers Domestic, Elizabeth I.

S.P. 14. State Papers Domestic, James I.

S.P. 15. State Papers Domestic, Addenda, Elizabeth I and James I.

S.P. 16. State Papers Domestic, Charles I.

S.P. 18. State Papers Interregnum, 1649-1660.

S.P. 25. Council of State, etc., 1649-1660.

S.P. 38. Docquets for the Great Seal.

S.P. 39. Sign manual warrants.

Star Chamber

STAC. 8. Star Chamber proceedings, James I.

Somerset Record Office, Taunton

Deposited documents
  Alford and Kirke MSS (DD/HLM)
    Box 2. Papers relating to Gillingham Forest, 1651-1684.
  Phelips MSS (DD/PH)
    212. Account of the proceedings to enforce the Book of Orders in the division of Sir Robert Phelips and Sir Edward Hext, Feb. 28, 1622/3 (no. 56).
    222. Resolution of the Somerset JPs for the execution of the Book of Orders, Jan. 14, 1622/3 (no. 91); PC to Sir Robert Phelips, April 30, 1629 (no. 92).
Indictment rolls, 1622-1631
Sessions rolls, 1622-1631

Wiltshire Record Office, Trowbridge

Miscellaneous deposited documents
  130/486/5. Star Chamber commission of rebellion to the sheriff, JPs, and Dep. Lts. of Wiltshire to apprehend those suspected of riot in the forests of Chippenham and Blackmore, July 21, 1631.
Quarter Sessions minute books (order books), 2 vols. 1623-1630.
Session rolls, 1622-1631.

Printed Primary Sources

Acts of the Privy Council of England 1586-1631. 33 vols. London, 1897-1964.

Baildon, W. P., ed. *Les Reportes del Cases in Camera Stellata 1593 to 1609 of John Hawarde.* London, 1894.

Barnes, T. G., ed. *Somerset Assize Orders, 1629-1640.* Somerset Rec. Soc., vol. LXV *(1959).*

Birch, T., ed. *Court and Times of James I.* Vol. 2. London, 1849.

———. *Court and Times of Charles I.* 2 vols. London, 1849.

Bland, A. E., P. A. Brown, and R. H. Tawney, eds. *English Economic History: Select Documents.* 2nd ed. London, 1915.

Calendar of Essex Quarter Sessions Records 1595-1631. (A typescript in the possession of the Essex Record Office, Chelmsford. A microfilm of this typescript in the General Library, University of California at Berkeley, was used for this work.)

Calendar of the Proceedings of the Committee for Compounding. Vol. 2. London, 1890.

Calendar of the State Papers, Domestic, Elizabeth, 1581-1603. 5 vols. London, 1865-70.

Calendar of the State Papers, Domestic, James I, 1603-1625. 4 vols. London, 1857-59.

Calendar of the State Papers, Domestic Addenda, Elizabeth I and James I, 1580-1625. London, 1872.

Calendar of the State Papers, Domestic, Charles I, 1625-1649. 23 vols. London, 1858-97.

Clark, A., ed. "Essex Woollen Manufactures 1629," *Essex Review* XVII (1908).

Croke, George. *Reports (James I).* London, 1657.

————. *Reports (Charles I).* London, 1657.

Cunnington, B. H., ed. *Annals of the Borough of Devizes.* Devizes, Wilts, 1925.

————, ed. *Records of the County of Wiltshire.* Devizes, Wilts, 1932.

Edwards, A. C., ed. *English History from Essex Sources 1550-1750.* Chelmsford, Essex, 1952.

"Extracts from the Records of the Wiltshire Quarter Sessions," *W.A.M.* XXII (1885).

Firth, C. H., ed. *The Memoirs of Edmund Ludlow.* 2 vols. Oxford, 1894.

Firth, C. H., and R. S. Rait, eds. *Acts and Ordinances of the Interregnum, 1642-1660.* 3 vols. London, 1911.

Foedera, Conventiones, Literae. Vols. XVII-XX. London, 1726-35.

Gardiner, S. R., ed. *Reports of Cases in the Courts of Star Chamber and High Commission.* Camden Society, London, 1886.

Guilding, J. M., ed. *Reading Records.* 4 vols. London, 1892.

Historical Manuscripts Commission, Calendar of Bath Manuscripts. Vols. II-IV. London, 1907-1968.

Historical Manuscripts Commission, Calendar of Salisbury Manuscripts. Vols. II-XXII. London, 1888-1971.

Historical Manuscripts Commission, Fourth Report. App., "House of Lords Manuscripts." London, 1874.

Historical Manuscripts Commission, Fifth Report. App., "House of Lords Manuscripts." London, 1875.

Historical Manuscripts Commission, Sixth Report. App., "House of Lords Manuscripts." London, 1877.

Historical Manuscripts Commission, Seventh Report. App., "House of Lords Manuscripts." London, 1879.

Historical Manuscripts Commission, Eleventh Report. App. I, "Skrine Manuscripts." London, 1887.

Historical Manuscripts Commission, Twelfth Report. App. I and II, "Cowper Manuscripts." London, 1890.

Historical Manuscripts Commission, Fifteenth Report. App. VII, "Somerset Manuscripts." London, 1903.

Historical Manuscripts Commission, Various Collections. Vol. I. London, 1901.

Horrocks, J. W., ed. *The Assembly Books of Southampton 1602-16.* 4 vols. Southampton Rec. Soc. (1917-25).

Hughes, P. L., and J. F. Larkin, eds. *Tudor Royal Proclamations.* Vols. 2 and 3. New Haven, 1969.

Jones, William. *Les Reportes (James I-Charles I).* London, 1675.

Journal of the House of Commons. Vol. III. N.p., n.d.

Journal of the House of Lords. Vols. III-X. N.p., n.d.

Manley, F. H., ed. "Parliamentary Surveys of the Crown Lands in Braden Forest (1651)," *W.A.M.* XLVI (1933-34).

"Papers relating to Proceedings in the County of Kent, 1642-1646," *Camden Miscellany.* Vol. III. London, 1854.

Peck, F., ed. *Desiderata Curiosa.* Vol. I. London, 1779.

Ramsay, G. D., ed. "The Report of the Royal Commission on the Clothing Industry, 1640," *E.H.R.* LVII (1942).

Ravenhill, W. W., ed. "Records of the Rising in the West, 1655," *W.A.M.* XIII-XV (1872-1875).

Roberts, G., ed. *Diary of Walter Yonge esq. J.P. & M.P. for Honiton co. Devon 1604-1628.* Camden Society. London, 1848.

Rushworth, J., ed. *Historical Collections.* Vol. III. London, 1722.

Sasche, W. L., ed. *Minutes of the Norwich Court of Mayoralty, 1630-1631.* Norfolk Rec. Soc. (1942).

Smith, J. *The Names and Surnames of All the Able and Sufficient Men in Body Fit for his Majesty's Service in the Wars, within the County of Gloucester, 1608 . . . .* London, 1902.

Statutes of the Realm. 9 vols. London, 1810-1822.

Steele, R. R., ed. *A Bibliography of Royal Proclamations of the Tudor and Stuart Sovereigns, 1485-1714.* Vol. I. Oxford, 1910.

Stocks, H., ed. *Records of the Borough of Leicester, 1603-1688.* Cambridge, 1923.

Tawney, R. H., and E. Power, eds. *Tudor Economic Documents.* 3 vols. London, 1924.

Thirsk, J. and J. P. Cooper, eds. *Seventeenth Century Economic Documents.* Oxford, 1972.

Williams, N. J., ed. *Tradesmen in Early-Stuart Wiltshire.* Wilts. Arch. & Nat. Hist. Soc. Records Branch. Vol. XV (1960).

Secondary Sources

Allan, D. G. C. "The Rising in the West, 1628-1631," *Econ. H.R.*, 2nd series, V (1952).

Appleby, A. B. "Common Land and Peasant Unrest in Sixteenth Century England," *Peasant Studies Newsletter* IV (1975).

———. "Disease or Famine? Mortality in Cumberland and Westmorland, 1580-1640," *Econ. H.R.*, 2nd series, XXVI (1973).

Aylmer, G. *The King's Servants: The Civil Service of Charles I, 1625-1642.* New York, 1961.

Barford, K. E. "The West of England Cloth Industry: A Seventeenth Century Experiment in State Control," *W.A.M.* XLII (1924).

Barker, T. H. "Notes on the History of Mere," *W.A.M.* XXIX (1897).

Barnes, T. G. *Somerset 1625-1640: A County's Government during the "Personal Rule."* Cambridge, Mass., 1961.

Beier, A. L. "Vagrants and the Social Order in Elizabethan England," *Past and Present* 64 (1974).

Beveridge, W. H. "A Statistical Crime of the Seventeenth Century," *Journal of Econ. and Bus. Hist.* I (1928-29).

Beveridge, W. H., et al. *Prices and Wages in England from the Twelfth to the Nineteenth Century.* Vol. I. London, 1939.

Bindoff, S. T. *Ket's Rebellion, 1549* (Historical Association Pamphlet no. 12). London, 1949.

———. "The Making of the Statute of Artificers," *Elizabethan Government and Society: Essays Presented to Sir John Neale.* S. T. Bindoff et al., eds. London, 1961.

Birrell, J. "The Peasant Craftsmen in the Medieval Forest," *Ag. H.R.* XVII (1969).

Bowden, P. J. *The Wool Trade in Tudor and Stuart England.* London, 1962.

Carus-Wilson, E. M. "Evidence for Industrial Development on Some Fifteenth Century Manors," in *Essays in Economic History.* Vol. 2. E. M. Carus-Wilson, ed. London, 1962.

Chalkin, C. W. *Seventeenth Century Kent: A Social and Economic History.* London, 1965.

Cheyney, E. P. *History of England from the Defeat of the Armada to the Death of Elizabeth.* Vol. II. New York, 1926.

Clark, A. "A Lieutenancy Book for Essex, 1608-1631 and 1637-1639," *Essex Review* XVII (1908).

Clark, P. "Popular Protest and Disturbance in Kent, 1558-1640," *Econ. H.R.*, 2nd series, XXIX (1976).

Coleman, D. C. "Labour in the English Economy of the Seventeenth Century," *Econ. H.R.*, 2nd series, VIII (1955-56).

Cox, J. C. *The Royal Forests of England.* London, 1905.

Davies, C. S. L. "Peasant Revolts in France and England: A Comparison," *Ag. H.R.* 21 (1973).

———. "The Pilgrimage of Grace Reconsidered," *Past and Present* 41 (1968).

Davies, M. G. *The Enforcement of English Apprenticeship 1563-1642.* Cambridge, Mass., 1956.

Fisher, F. J. "Commercial Trends and Policy in Sixteenth Century England," *Econ. H. R.*, 1st series, X (1940).

———. "London's Export Trade in the Early Seventeenth Century," *Econ. H.R.*, 2nd series, III (1950-51).

Fletcher, A. *A County Community in Peace and War: Sussex 1600-1660.* London, 1975.

———. *Tudor Rebellions.* London, 1968.

Fox, L., and P. Russell. *Leicester Forest.* Leicester Arch. Soc. (1948).

Gately, M. O., A. L. Moore, and J. E. Wills. "Seventeenth Century Peasant 'Furies': Some Problems of Comparative History," *Past and Present* 51 (1971).

Gay, E. F. "The Midland Revolt and the Inquisitions of Depopulation of 1607," *T.R.H.S.* XVIII (1904).

Gould, J. D. "The Crisis in the Export Trade 1586-7", *E.H.R.* LXXI (1956).

———. "The Trade Depression of the Early 1620's" *Econ. H.R.*, 2nd series, VII (1954-55).

Gras, N.S.B. *The Evolution of the English Corn Market.* Cambridge, Mass., 1915.

Green, E. "On the Poor and Some Attempts to Lower the Price of Corn in Somerset 1548-1638," *Proc. Bath Nat. Hist. & Antiq. Field Club* IV (1881).

Hammersley, G. "The Charcoal Iron Industry and Its Fuel, 1540-1750," *Econ. H.R.*, 2nd series, XXVI (1973).

———. "The Crown Woods and Their Exploitation in the Sixteenth and Seventeenth Centuries," *B.I.H.R.* XXX (1957).

———. "The Revival of the Forest Laws under Charles I," *History* XLV (1960).

Harrison, C. J. "Grain Price Analysis and Harvest Qualities, 1465-1634," *Ag. H.R.* XIX (1971).

Hart, C. E. *The Commoners of Dean Forest.* Gloucester, 1951.

———. *The Free Miners of the Royal Forest of Dean.* Gloucester, 1953.

———. *Royal Forest.* Oxford, 1966.

Hey, D. G. *An English Rural Community: Myddle under the Tudors and Stuarts.* Leicester, 1974.

Hill, C. "The Many-Headed Monster in Late Tudor and Early Stuart Political Thinking," in *From the Renaissance to the Counter-Reformation: Essays in Honor of Garrett Mattingly.* C. H. Carter, ed. New York, 1966.

Hilton, R. H. *Bond Men Made Free: Medieval Peasant Movements and the English Rising of 1381.* New York, 1973.

Holdsworth, W. S. *A History of English Law.* Vol. III. London, 1909.

Holmes, C. *The Eastern Association in the English Civil War.* Cambridge, 1974.

Hoskins, W. G. "Harvest Fluctuations and English Economic History, 1480-1619," *Ag. H.R.* XII (1964).

———. "Harvest Fluctuations and English Economic History, 1620-1759," *Ag. H.R.* XVI (1968).

Hutchins, John. *History of Dorset.* 3rd ed. Vol. III. London, 1868.

Jackson, J. E. "Chippenham Notes," *W.A.M.* XII (1870).

———. "On the History of Chippenham," *W.A.M.* III (1856).

———. "Selwood Forest," *W.A.M.* XXIII (1887).

James, M. E. "The Concept of Order and the Northern Rising, 1569," *Past and Present* 60 (1973).

———. "Obedience and Dissent in Henrician England: The Lincolnshire Rising, 1536," *Past and Present* 48 (1970).

Keeler, M. F. *The Long Parliament 1640-1641: A Biographical Study of Its Members.* Philadelphia, 1954.

Kelsall, R. K. "Wage Regulation and the Statute of Artificers," in *Wage Regulation in Pre-Industrial England.* W. E. Minchinton, ed. New York, 1972.

Kerridge, E. "The Revolts in Wiltshire against Charles I," *W.A.M.* LVII (1958).

Leonard, E. M. *The Early History of English Poor Relief.* Cambridge, Mass., 1900.

Loades, D. M. *Two Tudor Conspiracies.* Cambridge, 1965.

Manley, F. H. "Customs of the Manor of Purton," *W.A.M.* XL (1917-19).

———. "The Disafforesting of Braden," *W.A.M.* XLV (1930-32).

Manning, B. *The English People and the English Revolution 1640-1649.* London, 1976.

Morrill, J. S. *The Revolt of the Provinces: Conservatives and Radicals in the English Civil War, 1630-1650.* New York, 1976.

Mousnier, R. *Peasant Uprisings in the Seventeenth Century: France, Russia, and China.* New York, 1971.

Nicholas, D. *Mr. Secretary Nicholas 1593-1669.* London, 1955.

Nichols, J. *History and Antiquities of the County of Leicester.* Vol. IV. London, 1811.

Perry, R. "Gloucestershire Woollen Industry 1100-1690," *Trans. of the Bristol & Gloucs. Arch. Soc.* LXVI (1945).

Pettit, P. A. J. *The Royal Forests of Northamptonshire 1558-1714.* Northants Rec. Soc. Vol. 23 (1968).

Phelps-Brown, E. H., and S. V. Hopkins. "Seven Centuries of the Prices of Consumables Compared with Builders' Wage-Rates," *Economica* XXII (1955).

Pilgrim, J. E. "The Rise of the New Draperies in Essex," *Univ. of Birmingham Hist. Journ.* VII (1959-60).

Plucknett, T. F. T. *The Legislation of Edward I.* Oxford, 1949.

Ponko, V. "N.S.B. Gras and Elizabethan Corn Policy: A Re-examination of the Problem," *Econ. H.R.*, 2nd series, XVII (1964).

———. "The Privy Council and the Spirit of Elizabethan Economic Management 1558-1603," *Trans. Amer. Phil. Soc.* LVIII (1968).

Pound, J. *Poverty and Vagrancy in Tudor England.* London, 1971.

Ramsay, G. D. *The Wiltshire Woollen Industry in the Sixteenth and Seventeenth Centuries.* 2nd ed. London, 1965.

Rogers, J. E. T. *A History of Agriculture and Prices in England.* Vols. V & VI. Oxford, 1887.

Samaha, J. *Law and Order in Historical Perspective: The Case of Elizabethan Essex.* New York, 1974.

Spufford, M. *Contrasting Communities: English Villagers in the Sixteenth and Seventeenth Centuries.* Cambridge, 1974.

Strype, John. *Annals of the Reformation and Establishment of Religion . . . during Queen Elizabeth's Reign . . . .* Vols. III & IV. Oxford, 1824.

Supple, B. E. *Commercial Crisis and Change in England, 1600-1642.* Cambridge, 1959.

Tawney, A. J., and R. H. Tawney. "An Occupational Census of the Seventeenth Century," *Econ. H.R.*, 1st series, V (1934).

Tawney, R. H. "The Assessment of Wages in England by the Justices of the Peace," in *Wage Regulation in Pre-Industrial England.* W. E. Minchinton, ed. New York, 1972.

———. *Business and Politics under James I: Lionel Cranfield as Merchant and Minister.* Cambridge, 1958.

Thirsk, Joan, ed. *Agrarian History of England and Wales 1500-1640.* Cambridge, 1967.

———. "Industries in the Countryside," in *Essays in the Economic and Social History of Tudor and Stuart England in Honour of R. H. Tawney.* F. J. Fisher, ed. Cambridge, 1961.

———. "Seventeenth-Century Agriculture and Social Change," in *Land, Church and People: Essays Presented to H.P.R. Finberg.* Reading, Berks, 1970.

Thompson, E. P. "The Moral Economy of the English Crowd in the Eighteenth Century," *Past and Present* 50 (1971).

Thomson, T. R. *Bradon Forest.* Cricklade, Wilts., Hist. Soc. [1952?].

Underdown, D. *Royalist Conspiracy in England 1649-1660.* New Haven, Conn., 1960.

———. *Somerset in the Civil War and Interregnum.* Newton Abbot, Devon, 1973.

Victoria History of the Counties of England: Derbyshire. Vols. I & II. London, 1905 & 1907.

Victoria History of the Counties of England: Dorset. Vol. II. London, 1908.

Victoria History of the Counties of England: Gloucester. Vol. II. London, 1907.

Victoria History of the Counties of England: Hampshire. Vol. V. London, 1912.

Victoria History of the Counties of England: Leicester. Vol. II. London, 1954.

Victoria History of the Counties of England: Oxfordshire. Vol. VI. London, 1956.

Victoria History of the Counties of England: Staffordshire. Vol. II. London, 1967.

Victoria History of the Counties of England: Wiltshire. Vol. IV. London, 1959.

Walter, J., and K. Wrightson. "Dearth and the Social Order in Early Modern England," *Past and Present* 71 (1976).

White, H. T. "A Hampshire Plot," *Hants. Field Club & Arch. Soc.* XII (1934).

Index

281

Compositor:	U.C. Press
Printer:	Braun-Brumfield
Binder:	Braun-Brumfield
Text:	CompSet 500 Garamond
Display:	CompSet 500 Andover (Palatino)
Cloth:	Holliston Roxite C 56602 vellum
Paper:	50 lb P&S offset vellum

DATE DUE

DEMCO 38-297